WORDSWORTH AFTER WAR

William Wordsworth's later poetry complicates possibilities of life and art in war's aftermath. This illuminating study provides new perspectives and reveals how his work following the end of the revolutionary and Napoleonic wars reflects a passionate, lifelong engagement with the poetics and politics of peace. Focussing on poetry and prose from between 1814 and 1822, Philip Shaw constructs a unique and compelling account of how Wordsworth, in both his ongoing poetic output and in his revisions to earlier works, sought to modify, refute, and sometimes sustain his early engagement with these issues as both an artist and a political thinker. In an engaging style, Shaw reorients our understanding of the later writings of a major British poet and the post-war literary culture in which his reputation was forged. **This title is part of the Flip it Open Programme and may also be available Open Access. Check our website Cambridge Core for details.**

PHILIP SHAW is Professor of Romantic Studies at the University of Leicester. He has written extensively on Romantic-period literature, specialising in literary and visual responses to the revolutionary and Napoleonic wars. His books include *Romantic Wars* (2000), *Waterloo and the Romantic Imagination* (2002), *The Sublime* (2006/2017), and *Suffering and Sentiment in Romantic Military Art* (2013).

CAMBRIDGE STUDIES IN ROMANTICISM

Founding Editor
Marilyn Butler, University of Oxford

General Editor
James Chandler, University of Chicago

Editorial Board
Claire Connolly, University College Cork
Paul Hamilton, University of London
Claudia Johnson, Princeton University
Essaka Joshua, University of Notre Dame
Nigel Leask, University of Glasgow
Alan Liu, University of California, Santa Barbara
Deidre Lynch, Harvard University
Jerome McGann, University of Virginia
David Simpson, University of California, Davis

This series aims to foster the best new work in one of the most challenging fields within English literary studies. From the early 1780s to the early 1830s, a formidable array of talented men and women took to literary composition, not just in poetry, which some of them famously transformed, but in many modes of writing. The expansion of publishing created new opportunities for writers, and the political stakes of what they wrote were raised again by what Wordsworth called those 'great national events' that were 'almost daily taking place': the French Revolution, the Napoleonic and American wars, urbanization, industrialization, religious revival, an expanded empire abroad, and the reform movement at home. This was an enormous ambition, even when it pretended otherwise. The relations between science, philosophy, religion, and literature were reworked in texts such as *Frankenstein* and *Biographia Literaria*; gender relations in *A Vindication of the Rights of Woman* and *Don Juan*; journalism by Cobbett and Hazlitt; and poetic form, content, and style by the Lake School and the Cockney School. Outside Shakespeare studies, probably no body of writing has produced such a wealth of commentary or done so much to shape the responses of modern criticism. This indeed is the period that saw the emergence of those notions of literature and of literary history, especially national literary history, on which modern scholarship in English has been founded.

The categories produced by Romanticism have also been challenged by recent historicist arguments. The task of the series is to engage both with a challenging corpus of Romantic writings and with the changing field of criticism they have helped to shape. As with other literary series published by Cambridge University Press, this one will represent the work of both younger and more established scholars on either side of the Atlantic and elsewhere.

See the end of the book for a complete list of published titles.

WORDSWORTH AFTER WAR

Recovering Peace in the Later Poetry

PHILIP SHAW
University of Leicester

CAMBRIDGE
UNIVERSITY PRESS

Shaftesbury Road, Cambridge CB2 8EA, United Kingdom

One Liberty Plaza, 20th Floor, New York, NY 10006, USA

477 Williamstown Road, Port Melbourne, VIC 3207, Australia

314–321, 3rd Floor, Plot 3, Splendor Forum, Jasola District Centre, New Delhi – 110025, India

103 Penang Road, #05–06/07, Visioncrest Commercial, Singapore 238467

Cambridge University Press is part of Cambridge University Press & Assessment, a department of the University of Cambridge.

We share the University's mission to contribute to society through the pursuit of education, learning and research at the highest international levels of excellence.

www.cambridge.org
Information on this title: www.cambridge.org/9781009363167

DOI: 10.1017/9781009363150

© Philip Shaw 2023

This work is in copyright. It is subject to statutory exceptions and to the provisions of relevant licensing agreements; with the exception of the Creative Commons version the link for which is provided below, no reproduction of any part of this work may take place without the written permission of Cambridge University Press.

An online version of this work is published at doi.org/10.1017/9781009363150 under a Creative Commons Open Access license CC-BY-NC 4.0 which permits re-use, distribution and reproduction in any medium for non-commercial purposes providing appropriate credit to the original work is given and any changes made are indicated. To view this license, visit https://creativecommons.org/licenses/by-nc/4.0

All versions of this work may contain content reproduced under license from third parties. Permission to reproduce this third-party content must be obtained from these third-parties directly. When citing this work, please include a reference to the DOI 10.1017/9781009363150

First published 2023
First paperback edition 2025

A catalogue record for this publication is available from the British Library

Library of Congress Cataloging-in-Publication data
NAMES: Shaw, Philip, 1965– author.
TITLE: Wordsworth after war : recovering peace in the later poetry / Philip Shaw.
DESCRIPTION: Cambridge ; New York, NY : Cambridge University Press, 2023. | Series: Cambridge studies in Romanticism | Includes bibliographical references and index.
IDENTIFIERS: LCCN 2023005171 | ISBN 9781009363181 (hardback) | ISBN 9781009363150 (ebook)
SUBJECTS: LCSH: Wordsworth, William, 1770–1850 – Criticism and interpretation. | Peace in literature. | English poetry – 19th century – History and criticism.
CLASSIFICATION: LCC PR5892.P43 S53 2023 | DDC 821.7–dc23/eng/2023005171
LC record available at https://lccn.loc.gov/2023005171

ISBN 978-1-009-36318-1 Hardback
ISBN 978-1-009-36316-7 Paperback

Cambridge University Press & Assessment has no responsibility for the persistence or accuracy of URLs for external or third-party internet websites referred to in this publication and does not guarantee that any content on such websites is, or will remain, accurate or appropriate.

Contents

List of Figures	*page* vi
Acknowledgements	vii
List of Abbreviations	x
Introduction	1
1 Conscripting 'The Recluse'	34
2 Peace Out of Time: *The White Doe of Rylstone*	70
3 Thanksgiving after War	94
4 'Returning, Like a Ghost Unlaid': *Peter Bell* and *The Waggoner*	120
5 Violent Waters: *The River Duddon* and *Ecclesiastical Sketches*	145
6 Wordsworth after Byron: *Memorials of a Tour on the Continent, 1820*	174
After Wordsworth	209
Notes	221
Select Bibliography	259
Index	272

Figures

1 *Our English Lakes, Mountains, and Waterfalls, as Seen by William Wordsworth. Photographically Illustrated* (London 1864). Cuttings and title page. *page* 2
2 *Soldiers of the Machine Gun Corps* (c. 1916–1918). 20
3 Joseph Priestley, from *A New Chart of History* (London 1769). 149
4 Friedrich Strass, *Der Strom der Zeiten* (*The Stream of Time*) (1804). 150
5 William Hogarth, *The Gate of Calais, or the Roast Beef of Old England* (1749). 181

Acknowledgements

I considered writing a book about Wordsworth's later poetry many years ago, but these ideas only came into focus thanks to chance conversations with David L. Clark and Jacques Khalip at the 'Late Romanticism: Past and Present' conference at KU Leuven in December 2019. I am grateful to David and Jacques for their encouragement, to Brecht de Groote and Tom Toremans for the opportunity to speak at this conference, and to Tim Fulford and Matt Sangster for their good company. Although not apparent to me at the time, an invitation from Alex Houen and Jan-Melissa Schramm to speak at the 'Sacrifice and Modern War Literature' conference at Pembroke College, Cambridge, in January 2014 contributed significantly to the development of this book. A portion of the chapter that appeared in the volume arising from this conference, *Sacrifice and Modern War Literature*, ed. Alex Houen and Jan-Melissa Schramm (Oxford: Oxford University Press, 2018), is reproduced in Chapter 3, with the permission of Oxford University Press. In 2016, an invitation from Michael Demson and Regina Hewitt to contribute a chapter to their edited collection, *Commemorating Peterloo: Violence, Resilience and Claim-Making during the Romantic Era* (Edinburgh: Edinburgh University Press, 2019), sowed the seeds for my thinking about Wordsworth's River Duddon sonnets in Chapter 5. I am grateful to Edinburgh University Press for permission to adapt some of the material from this chapter. Conversations in the summer of 2015 with Simon Bainbridge, Emma Butcher, Jeff Cox, and the late Richard Gravil, along with many other friends and scholars during numerous Battle of Waterloo bicentenary events, also helped to lay a foundation for this study. The late Marilyn Gaul, a friend of peace, provided support and encouragement at a crucial time. For good cheer and assistance of various kinds, I am especially grateful to the following: Tom Bristow, Julia S. Carlson, Jeff Cowton, Michael Davies, Chris Donaldson, MC Drak, Scott Freer, Tim Fulford (again), Holly Furneaux, Bruce Graver, Martin Halliwell, Ian Haywood, Felicity James, Simon Kövesi, Matthew McCormack, Peter Manning,

Catherine Morley, Julian North, Mark Rawlinson, Nick Roe, Victoria Stewart, Joanna Wilson-Scott, and Claire Wood.

The research for this book was supported by an Arts and Humanities Research Council Leadership Fellow award (AH/S003711/1). I am grateful to colleagues in the University of Leicester Research and Enterprise Division for their assistance both prior to and throughout the period of the award, but I should like to thank, in particular, Alan Ashton-Smith. For help with tracking down manuscripts and securing permissions for images, I am grateful to Jeff Cowton (again) at Dove Cottage and to Erica Persak and Sarah Yukich at the Kerry Stokes Collection. I owe thanks to Bethany Thomas at Cambridge University Press for the invitation to contribute a proposal for the Cambridge Studies in Romanticism series and for her advice and support at every step of the way. I wish also to extend my gratitude to the two anonymous readers of my study for their generosity and expertise. I hope this final version meets with their approval.

During the writing of this book, my teacher, mentor, and colleague Vincent Newey passed away. *Wordsworth After War* is dedicated to his memory and to the memory of my dad, Keith Shaw, who told me stories, taught me to write, and gave me books. As ever, I could not end these notes of gratitude without paying tribute to my wife, Sarah Knight: 'In ours, the Vale of Friendship'. The Knight and Shaw families, *ex toto*, are my rock.

***

I began *Wordsworth After War* in the winter of 2019–2020. Work on the book continued during the COVID-19 pandemic and was brought to completion when Russia invaded Ukraine in February 2022. Months later, like most people, I struggle to comprehend these events and wonder just what can be said, with any exactitude, about their long-term effects. This feeling of bewilderment is perhaps a reminder that there is no such thing as a time 'after war', or if there is, then it is not for us. I hope, nevertheless, that readers will find some comfort in this book, which attempts haltingly and against the odds to make time for peace.

This title is part of the Cambridge University Press *Flip it Open* Open Access Books program and has been "flipped" from a traditional book to an Open Access book through the program.

Flip it Open sells books through regular channels, treating them at the outset in the same way as any other book; they are part of our library collections for Cambridge Core, and sell as hardbacks and ebooks. The one crucial difference is that we make an upfront commitment that when each of these books meets a set revenue threshold we make them available to everyone Open Access via Cambridge Core.

This paperback edition has been released as part of our Open Access commitment and we would like to use this as an opportunity to thank the libraries and other buyers who have helped us flip this and the other titles in the program to Open Access.

To see the full list of libraries that we know have contributed to *Flip it Open*, as well as the other titles in the program please visit www.cambridge.org/fio-acknowledgements

Abbreviations

Poetry is cited by line number(s) (l. 1; ll. 1–2); page numbers are preceded by p. or pp. (pp. 1–2). Unless noted otherwise, quotations from Wordsworth's poetry are from the Cornell Wordsworth Collection, which will be cited in full in each first relevant note. Quotations from the Bible are taken from the King James Version.

CWWH	*The Complete Works of William Hazlitt*. Ed. P. P. Howe. 21 vols. London: J. M. Dent and Sons, 1930–34.
JDW	*The Journals of Dorothy Wordsworth*. Ed. Ernest de Selincourt. 3 vols. London: Macmillan, 1941.
Prose	*The Prose Works of William Wordsworth*. Ed. W. J. B. Owen and Jane Worthington Smyser. 3 vols. Oxford: Clarendon Press, 1974.

Wordsworth letters: *The Letters of William and Dorothy Wordsworth*. 2nd ed. Ernest de Selincourt; rev. Alan Hill, Mary Moorman, and Chester L. Shaver. 8 vols. Oxford: Clarendon Press, 1967–1993. Abbreviations as follows:

EY	*The Letters of William and Dorothy Wordsworth, The Early Years, 1787–1805*. Rev. Chester L. Shaver.
MY I	*The Letters of William and Dorothy Wordsworth, The Middle Years, Part I: 1806–1811*. Rev. Mary Moorman.
MY II	*The Letters of William and Dorothy Wordsworth, The Middle Years, Part II: 1812–1820*. Rev. Mary Moorman and Alan G. Hill.
LY I	*The Letters of William and Dorothy Wordsworth, The Later Years, Part I: 1821–1828*. Rev. Alan G. Hill.

LY II	*The Letters of William and Dorothy Wordsworth, The Later Years, Part II: 1829–1834*. Rev. Alan G. Hill.
SNL	*The Letters of William and Dorothy Wordsworth. A Supplement of New Letters*. Ed. Alan G. Hill.
WTDQ	*The Works of Thomas De Quincey*. Ed. Grevel Lindop et al. 21 vols. London: Pickering and Chatto, 2003.

Introduction

Drunk with the Beauty of This World

The book rests on the chair, a family keepsake bound in gilt tooled green cloth – *Our English Lakes, Mountains, and Waterfalls, as Seen by William Wordsworth. Photographically Illustrated*, published by A. W. Bennett in 1864 with contents arranged by location: Winandermere [*sic*], Esthwaite, Langdale, The Rotha, Rydale, Grasmere, Helvellyn, Derwent-water and Ulleswater, Brougham Castle, Black Comb (Figure 1). From its pages fall cuttings from English newspapers of the early 1900s, along with slips of paper containing handwritten quotations from poems by Elizabeth Barrett Browning, Thomas Moore, and Henry Ward Beecher – copperplate memorials to the 'wealth and happiness of our kind', tales of despair relieved by faith, of steadfastness in the face of death.

Among the newspaper cuttings headlines swim into view: 'Unconscious Worry: Why One's Sleep Is Disturbed and Troubled'; 'Come on Shropshires'; 'Hell amid Flowers'. And the year: 1917, which is visible on a folded corner to the left of the title of 'The Haunted Garden', a descriptive prose piece by Edith Nesbit, author of *The Railway Children* (1906), clipped neatly from *The Daily Mail*:

> Soon […] it will be winter here […] and the rain will fall on the garden like tears that are never dried. Let the winter come! This garden has no more need of summer. In winter we leave it lying lonely and cowering over the hearth, drug ourselves with books; but in the summer we walk in the garden and remember. For then the garden is haunted by the shadows of those who used to laugh and linger here in long golden days and starry evenings, before the war broke up homes and made happiness only a memory.

For those who live on, summer has become unbearable, prompting thoughts of those men, lost in the war, who cannot share its 'insolent triumph':

> But autumn we can bear, because then we remember that spring is eternal and that this world is not all. Autumn lays a quiet hand on the bowed

Figure 1   *Our English Lakes, Mountains, and Waterfalls, as Seen by William Wordsworth. Photographically Illustrated* (London 1864). Cuttings and title page.
Source: Author Photograph

head, and we find amid the fading leaves a place for prayer [...] that some of them may come back again—that we may see them with these eyes that have wept so much; see them coming, with kind, living hands held out to us, along the grassy paths of our garden.

Beside this clipping, a pressed lime tree leaf, a small card, and a sealed envelope, on which are mounted pressed flowers. The inscriptions: 'From Ervillers France June 1917'; 'Picked in Hennecourt Wood France on the March Retreat 1918 = A. H. S.='. In his concluding paragraph, the writer of the newspaper article 'Hell amid Flowers' (dated 25 May 1917) imagines the men of the King's Shropshire Light Infantry surrounded by fields of gold, 'drunk with the beauty of this world of life, so that a field all silvered with daisies means more to them than all the war, as I have heard them say'. And now, long since detached from the corncockles, pinks, and the solitary cornflower gathered in France, the remains of a common daisy slip through my fingers.

I stare at these mementos, fallings and vanishings from a beloved volume, and allow my imagination to pursue paths of association while reason prompts me to observe at a distance, to resist the temptation to fall into an affective tone that might dishonour the volume's stark facticity. A bookplate or signature would help; as it is, the absence of these signs adds to the sense of an inaccessible, private reality, which withdraws from my effort to grasp it. For even if that reality could be accounted for – one can imagine a quantum computer able, in some distant future, to gather all these little bundles of reality together, starting with the book's provenance, its family history, the connection with A. H. S., the link with the Shropshires – still we would find ourselves overwhelmed by a flood of accidental or sensual qualities: instances of grieving, pathos, and nostalgia that swirl within, around, and far beyond the book's real qualities – fragments of a reality beyond calculation.[1]

***

Religion is spilt in the most unusual places, and at this point the book I am writing is unsure of itself. But the sense of that excess of feeling, of lives that even after death haunt the imagination, cannot be ignored. Thus, despite myself, I am drawn to the book's connection with 'old, unhappy, far-off things,/And battles long ago', elements of an affective power irreducible to quanta that speak, diffidently yet compellingly, of the afterlife of war.[2] How that afterlife should be conceived will be explored in the discussion that follows, but I am prepared to accept that no single position will account for the life that emerges in Wordsworth, so strangely and with such force, in the aftermath of Britain's victory in the war against France. At the announcement of peace, prematurely declared in 1814 and then confirmed in 1815, Wordsworth's poetry undergoes a change – these, after all, are the years in which *The Excursion* is published and the 'Thanksgiving Ode' is conceived, works that for many readers mark the end of the poet's 'great period' and the beginning of the long, slow descent into creative sclerosis. But setting aside, for now, the question of artistic accomplishment, the claim that the end of war marks a watershed in Wordsworth's poetic development should be qualified by the acknowledgement that many of the currents emerging in this period can be dated back to earlier phases in his career. Moreover, three of the most important poems that Wordsworth published between 1815 and 1822, the post-war years with which this book is largely concerned, were composed in the late 1790s and early 1800s: *Peter Bell*, *The Waggoner*, and *The White Doe of Rylstone*. To adapt a statement made at the beginning of *The Holiday* (1949), Stevie Smith's brittle and unsettling account of life after the Second World War, in the late 1810s, just as 'it cannot be said that it is war, it cannot be said that it is peace, it can be said that it is post-war' so for much of Wordsworth's poetry it cannot be said that it is late, it cannot be said that it is early, it *can* be said that it is post-dated – its meaning determined by a future with which it has yet to coincide.³

A mood of anxious imprecision – is this peace? is this war? – sits very well with the blurring of distinctions between Fancy and Imagination, early and late, that can be detected in the poems Wordsworth wrote and published between Waterloo and Peterloo, not least when the poet seeks to create an impression of his work as a 'legitimate whole', as the system of classification, introduced in the 1815 *Poems* so that 'the work may more obviously correspond with the course of human life', had attempted to accomplish (*Prose* III. 24). For the remainder of his career, Wordsworth stubbornly adhered to this system, preferring the artificial and, as it frequently turned out, labile arrangement of the poems by 'subject [...] mould or form' over the chronological 'history of the poet's mind' favoured by Charles Lamb and Henry Crabb Robinson.⁴ Yet, as the system advanced into a shifting mosaic of forms, thoughts, and feelings, it enabled readers to forge connections between poems that a more conventional 'history' might have precluded. A particularly resonant example is the surprising yet, as I go on to argue in Chapter 5, wholly appropriate sequential arrangement of the Immortality and Thanksgiving odes in the 1820 three- and four-volume collected *Poems*. More so, I think, than present-day readers, Wordsworth's contemporary audience understood the porosity of these great expressions of peace and war, of how delicate affirmations of recovery could bleed into plangent avowals of national triumph.

The belief, however, that Wordsworth fades into irrelevance after Waterloo maintains a firm hold on our understanding of the poet's history, and in large measure this is due to how our sense of the work that Wordsworth produced in the aftermath of war has been shaped by the reactions of a culturally significant yet statistically unrepresentative group of contemporary readers. The 1816 'Thanksgiving Ode' is usually recalled, if at all, as the poem that set the seal on Wordsworth's reputation among the second-generation poets, providing confirmation that the poet of *The Excursion* (1814) was indubitably of and for the establishment. Following its damning reception, Wordsworth, while maintaining an active interest in domestic politics, engaged very little with matters of international import, preferring instead to issue quietly authoritative pronouncements on the nature of the good life from the perspective of a Cincinnatian recluse. An account of this period in the poet's development might well conclude, on the basis of the complex sequence of reactions and counter-reactions that determined the publication of *Peter Bell* and *The Waggoner* (1819), followed by the wilful embrace of parochialism, dullness, and whimsy that appears to inform the *River Duddon* volume (1820), the *Ecclesiastical Sketches* (1822), and the *Memorials of a Tour on the Continent, 1820* (1822), that Wordsworth at the end of war, having forgone the loftier claims of Imagination in favour of the 'embrace' of History's 'closing deed magnificent', has nothing more to say.[5]

The reasonableness of this conclusion is apparent from the dejected assessment of one of Wordsworth's staunchest allies. Writing to Dorothy Wordsworth in 1826 Crabb Robinson complained that the poet who had written 'heroically and divinely against the tyranny of Napoleon' was 'quite indifferent to all the successive tyrannies which disgraced the succeeding times'.[6] Adopting the voice of 'some future commentator' he announces, with damning sardonicism: '"This great poet survived to the fifth decennary of the Nineteenth Century, but he appears to have died in the year 1814, as far as life consisted in an active sympathy with the temporary welfare of his fellow creatures".'[7] Robinson's judgement is directed against Wordsworth's seeming indifference to the recent Bourbon interventions in Spain, which attempted to restore King Ferdinand VII to the absolute power of which he had been deprived during the Liberal Triennium, but it addresses broader, far-reaching concerns, akin to Coleridge's frequently voiced criticisms about the poet's failure to write the grand 'philosophical Poem, containing views of Man, Nature, and Society',[7] about the worth of Wordsworth's work in the modern age.

Responding to Robinson in the pointedly titled sonnet 'Retirement', Wordsworth defends himself from the Thomist accusation of *recusatio tensionis* by announcing to his 'patriot Friend' (l. 3) that 'Peace in these feverish times is sovereign bliss' (l. 9), a line that manages simultaneously to function as a defence of royal prerogative while linking the transcendence of worldly agitation to the ecstasy of self-governance.[8] But the sense of joyful release afforded by the refusal of the *vita activa* in favour of the *vita contemplativa* is more aptly conveyed in 'Not Love, nor War, nor the tumultuous swell'.[9] Composed in 1821, the sonnet's opening quatrain, with its gathering of six negative comparators, emulates Shakespeare's sonnet 65 in seeking to weigh the charms of ephemeral beauty against the pains of 'civil conflict' and 'the wrecks of change' (l. 2). But while Shakespeare converts dissension and conjecture into a confident closed couplet declaration of artistic endurance ('O none, unless this miracle have might,/That in black ink my love may still shine bright', ll. 13–14),[10] Wordsworth, drawing on the fluid resources of the Petrarchan form, counters negativity though a technique of patient insistence, effacing the not/nor constraints of the conflicted world by linking together images of 'sage content' and 'placid melancholy' (l. 10), by instilling a sense of protracted ease through the use of hendecasyllables and a closing alexandrine, through the repetitive insistence of the verb *to be*, and the lulling effect of the correspondent double rhymes. Thus, the muse watches 'the blue smoke of the elmy grange,/ Skyward ascending from the twilight dell' (ll. 6–7):

> She loves to gaze upon a crystal river,
> Diaphanous, because it travels slowly;
> Soft is the music that would charm for ever;
> The flower of sweetest smell is shy and lowly. (ll. 11–14)

Such poetry might easily be dismissed as a mode of reactionary escapism – Peterloo, after all, had only recently raised the spectre of a return to civil conflict – but the verse is informed by memories of an earlier phase in Wordsworth's development, the period in which, as a young radical, the poet envisaged the triumph of the meek. In this new world of peaceable delight, shared alike by all forms of life, discord through love and war is accepted as the origin of history but is effectively cordoned off from the ensuing state of beatific languor. In the absence of a governing 'I', the sonnet surveys the changing nature of things with unselfconscious equanimity, released from the violent ardour of self-definition.

'Not Love, nor War' is a poem of the Fancy, and in the pages that follow I examine more closely how this aesthetic category, along with its counterpart Imagination, came to be associated in Wordsworth's poetry with the dialectical relation between peace and war, a notion that raises the spectre of Hegel's account of the violent underpinnings of individuation in the *Philosophy of Right* (1821). If, as the sonnet implies, peace consists in self-abnegation, allowing the self to melt into a fanciful dream of unity with the world, then war, as Hegel maintains, can be seen as a form of self-definition, for it is only through the disruption of passivity that individuals may attain self-consciousness, insofar as war confronts the individual with the finitude of his existence.[11] In this, Hegel follows in a tradition of radical enlightenment thought that, even as it seeks to institute peaceful co-existence in the struggle for individuation, ends up granting, and at times even applauding, the necessity of war.[12] In 'The State of War' (c. 1750s), Rousseau, for instance, condemns the effects of state-sanctioned violence ('I see fire and flames, countrysides deserted, and towns sacked [...] I see a scene of murders, ten thousand men slaughtered, the dead piled up in heaps, the dying trampled underfoot by horses, everywhere the image of death and agony') only to admit that conflict is 'the fruit' of those 'peaceful institutions' on which society is founded.[13] The state of nature in which man dwells in peace turns out to be illusory, since to live this way, all men must agree to do so. In other words, the state of nature demands a social contract, which entails the creation of institutions to regulate the relations between 'land, money [and] men' – 'all the spoils that can be appropriated thus become the principal object of mutual hostilities'.[14]

In related manner, Kant, in the *Critique of Judgement* (1789), suggests that war enhances the vitality of civil society, going so far as to declare that 'war has something sublime about it'.[15] War for Kant is sublime because the struggle of a people in the face of danger mimics the way in which reason stands its ground in the encounter with excessive magnitude and power. Elsewhere, Kant avers that war may act as 'an incentive' for the growth of 'culture'. 'Though war', he argues, 'is an intentional human endeavour (incited by our unbridled passions), yet it is also a deeply hidden and perhaps intentional endeavour of the supreme wisdom, if not to establish, then at least to prepare the way for lawfulness.'[16] Since 'a prolonged peace [...] tends to make prevalent a mere commercial spirit, and along with it base selfishness, cowardice, and softness, and to debase the thinking of that people', periodic outbreaks of hostilities with rival nation states are not only historically inevitable but also desirable if a nation is to maintain its integrity.[17] A few years later, however, at a time when Europe had suffered the destabilising impact of France's revolutionary struggle, Kant, in what appears to be a swerve from the militant fatalism of the third *Critique*, turns his attention to 'Perpetual Peace' (1795). But Kant's title, as the opening paragraph declares, is taken from a Dutch inn keeper's sign on which a graveyard is painted.[18] Here, as Peter Melville points out, Kant is attuned to the ironies of perpetual peace, aware of how, as an 'intolerant universal law', perpetual peace must strive to eliminate not only all existing but all possible forms of opposition, including 'its own opposition to opposition as such'.[19] However, the self-defeating logic of perpetual peace conceals a deeper truth: that peace must open itself to its own constitutive violence. By remaining hospitable to opposition, perpetual peace may be refigured as an '"impure" regulatory ideal': a promise that aspires towards (but cannot attain) a state of harmony that, in the Derridean sense, is always to come.[20]

In the letter to the Bishop of Llandaff, written in the spring of 1793, Wordsworth advances remarkably similar arguments for the impossibility of peace, declaring that 'Liberty' 'in order to reign in peace must establish herself by violence' (*Prose* I. 33). A year later he had reversed his opinion, announcing: 'I recoil from the bare idea of a revolution [...] I am a determined enemy to every species of violence [...] I deplore the miserable situation of the French' (*EY* 124). Abandoning the instrumentalist framework that, in the Llandaff letter, provided justification for revolutionary violence, Wordsworth nevertheless identifies as an 'enemy' of violence, thereby replicating the cycle in which pacific ends founded on relations of antagonism perpetuate violence. He goes on to advance similar arguments for the maintenance of enmity as a mode of individual and collective self-preservation, a position that would place him at odds with radical critics of Kant, such as Thomas Beddoes, who despaired of the German philosopher's pessimistic account of the ability of political institutions to furnish lasting peace, as well as later positive peace campaigners, such as William Cobbett, William Roscoe, and Leigh Hunt.[21] Yet, despite the drift towards acceptance of the necessity of war, there remains in Wordsworth's writing a lingering attachment to the dream of irenic fulfilment, typically manifested in poems like 'Not Love, nor War' that, in their Ovidian voluptuousness, query Virgilian ideas of duty, discipline, and self-restraint, the politico-affective qualities most associated with the later poems.

That Wordsworth's later verse does not always conform to our presuppositions concerning the distinctions between sensual and austere, playful and authoritarian, tranquil and combative is deepened further when we attempt to frame this poetry in terms of its relations with contemporary political philosophy.[22] In the search for conceptual affinities in Wordsworth's writings scholars have long been in the habit of negotiating a tricky path between radical and conservative thinkers, finding, for example, in the 1793 Letter to the Bishop of Llandaff Rousseaustic influences and clear affinities with Burke in *The Prelude*. Note has also been made of Coleridge's influence on Wordsworth's political development, which in the 1790s had embraced revolutionary pacifist and pacificist thought before transitioning in the 1800s to pro-war conservatism.[23] In designating the point at which Wordsworth moves from radical enlightenment poet to reactionary Tory bard, critics inspired by one or more of these readings isolate *The Excursion* as the poem in which the poet finally abjures his earlier Jacobin self, in the guise of the Solitary, to embrace the role of a loyal supporter of the conservative establishment.[24] Unsurprisingly, it is in *The Excursion* that Wordsworth presents his most sustained poetic critique of revolutionary pacifism; yet, as I go on to argue in Chapter 1, it is in this poem and more vividly in 'The Recluse' fragments that precede it that Wordsworth delivers some of his most persuasive and touching descriptions of how peace might appear in a post-war world. Not insignificantly, many of these descriptions, such as the radically panpsychist account of the 'active principle alive in all things' that initiates Book IX of *The Excursion*, have their origins in a much earlier phase of Wordsworth's poetic development, suggesting again how stark chronological distinctions obscure how poems have 'properties which spread/Beyond themselves, a power by which they make/Some other being', perhaps a later poet or a later reader, 'conscious of their life'.[25] Later, most concertedly in *The White Doe* and *The Waggoner*, sporadically in the *River Duddon* poems and *Memorials of a Tour on the Continent, 1820*, and even, at times, in the Thanksgiving volume and *Ecclesiastical Sketches*, we find renewed stirrings of this early, radical desire for peaceable existence, a desire not wholly expunged by the poet's shift towards reactionary bellicosity.

Wordsworth After War is, then, not a book about Wordsworth's later poetry; nor, for that matter, is it a book that argues concertedly for a singular view of the late Wordsworth as a poet of war or as a poet of the peace. Barring his friendship with the Quaker Thomas Clarkson, a founding member of the Society for the Promotion of Universal and Perpetual Peace, there is no evidence to suggest that Wordsworth held any sympathy with views that, even after Waterloo, continued to be associated with revolutionary politics.[26] By the same token, setting aside his correspondence with the military theorist Sir Charles William Pasley, it would be reductive to portray late Wordsworth as an ardent supporter of the '*War-faction*'.[27] Rather, as will become clear, my concern is with the persistence in the poetry of attitudes, orientations, and affective states that, from their emergence earlier in his career, marked Wordsworth out as a poet driven towards the complication of what can be expected of life and art in the aftermath of war. Instead of seeing the termination of the war with France as an opportunity to hymn the triumph of legitimacy over tyranny, we see in Wordsworth's poetry a fascination with the failure or incompletion of the revolutionary experiment, a fascination that homes in on thoughts and feelings that cannot be accommodated within the cultural framework of the post-war settlement. In this sense, the poetry Wordsworth writes after war is haunted by revolutionary 'traces', to adopt a word used by Hazlitt to affirm a form of radical nostalgia in his review of *The Excursion*.[28] As I go on to explore, it is precisely as a result of its ghostliness, its recollection of older, revolutionary impulses, of those aspirations to a better life, free from sanguinary competition, as well as the atavistic promptings of warlike counter-currents, that this poetry, so often dismissed as slight, anti-climactic, socially conservative, and artistically constrained, speaks so volubly to the present age, an age that shares with the post-war culture of Regency England a combustible mood of impatience and anxiety, disillusionment and despair.

Where Have All the Flowers Gone?

In concert with those supplementary paper figures, tied to yet detached from *Our English Lakes, Mountains, and Waterfalls*, sibylline predictions of weal and woe drift through Wordsworth's post-war poetry, driven by gusts that create momentary attachments, complicating affinities that might, in less accomplished hands, appear close-minded, anti-climactic, or straightforwardly banal. Work will need to be done to capture the precise forms of strangeness that inhabit this poetry,[29] but we might already see, in the unfinished, contested, and infinitely suggestive form of this mid-Victorian keepsake, an indication of how this work should proceed. Although the focus of this book is on work published in the wake of the defeat of imperial France, from the outset of his career Wordsworth was, in a sense, always writing *after* war – looking ahead, that is, to a possible future when war would be either relinquished or retained as a lamentable but necessary element in the march and progress of human history. Before proceeding to address how these possible futures emerge in Wordsworth's writing and at how this book will develop, I want to look at a set of poems that bear directly on the material evocation of peace with which this discussion began.

Pages 158–68 of *Our English Lakes, Mountains, and Waterfalls*, at the head of a selection of Wordsworth's 'Poems on Flowers': 'To the Daisy' ('In youth from rock to rock I went'), 'To the Same Flower' ('Bright Flower!'). Composed shortly after the announcement of the Treaty of Amiens (25 March 1802–18 May 1803), the brief cessation of Britain's conflict with France seems to have provided Wordsworth too with a breathing space, an interval in which 'the mind should be permitted to recover from its perturbation or astonishment'.[30] If, as Jerome Christensen has argued, the peace offered respite, not only from the socio-economic and moral shocks of war but also from the daily bombardment of cultural astonishment, then we can perhaps begin to see how Wordsworth should find in 'To the Daisy' a means to suspend those 'stately passions' that 'in me burn' (l. 49).[31] Relief from war provides the poet with an opportunity to observe and, as it were, become absorbed by an object of 'less ambitious aim' (l. 29) than those totems of epic insistence – the noble warrior, the besieged castle, the grand clash of arms – that wartime culture demanded.

'To the Daisy' signals its release from stately passions by adopting as epigraph some lines from George Wither's *The Shepherd's Hunting*, 'Eclogue 4', which are addressed to his muse:

> Her divine skill taught me this,
> That from everything I saw
> I could some invention draw,
> And raise pleasure to her height,
> Through the meanest object's sight.
> By the murmur of a spring,
> Or the least bough's rustelling;
> By a Daisy whose leaves spread
> Shut when Titan goes to bed;
> Or a shady bush or tree;
> She could more infuse in me
> Than all Nature's beauties can
> In some other wiser man.[32]

Along with related works by Drayton and Jonson, conveniently extracted in Robert Anderson's *Poets of Great Britain* (1795), a collection that Wordsworth read, devotedly and closely, from 1800, Wither's lines provide a touchstone for the celebration of the bare, innocent life that is represented in 'To the Daisy'. Opening with a recollection of 'youth', a period of self-bafflement when 'from rock to rock I went,/From hill to hill in discontent/Of pleasure high and turbulent,/Most pleased when most uneasy' (ll. 1–4), the poem is not, however, entirely released from worldly concerns. The oxymoronic yoking of 'discontent' and 'pleasure' conveys well the sense of a mind at odds with itself, in striking anticipation of 'the experience of internal disruption' that Jacques Khalip identifies as 'a form of wartime ontology'.[33] Still, for Wordsworth, the hope endures that release from conflict may be found in this time: 'But now', the poet proclaims, 'my own delights I make,—/My thirst at every rill can slake,/And gladly Nature's love partake' (ll. 5–7). To this boast of self-determination, the poem gives way to a serial depiction of the daisy's triumph over time and change. In learning to love *the* daisy, as generic species, Wordsworth sees in the flower's ability to withstand seasonal change, and its indifference to worldly acclaim, the design of a life released from constitutional antagonism.

Thus, reflecting on the daisy's thoughtlessness, the poet loses, albeit briefly, both the sense of terror involved in staying alive and the sense of melancholy that attends the coming of peace.³⁴ As intimated by Kant, the desire for perpetual peace, for a state of being delivered from agonistic competition, belongs to the 'End of All Things' (1794) in which 'reason does not understand either itself or what it wants [...] because people would like at last to have an *eternal tranquillity* in which to rejoice, constituting for them a supposedly blessed end of all things; but really this is a concept in which the understanding is simultaneously exhausted and all thinking itself has an end'.³⁵ Kant's account of post-war melancholy is echoed in the numerous public pronouncements that followed, in print, in parliament, and in pulpit, the declaration of the 1802 peace. Despite declarations of enthusiasm for the peace, uniting loyalists and liberals alike in expressions of relief and patriotic fervour,³⁶ the fear persists that the blessings of peace will replace the manly vigour of wartime competition with carnal indulgences, effeminate languor, and terminal inertia.³⁷ Following the signing of the definitive Treaty of Paris in 1815, images of exhaustion, wastage, and ennui would once again come to the fore, most notably in the self-cancelling despair of Byron's *Manfred* (1817), the valetudinarian lethargy of Austen's 'Sanditon' (1817), and in the burnt-out cases of Keats's 'Hyperion: A Fragment' (1819).

An attempt to imagine post-war restoration not as the sad, slow erasure of individual and corporate vitality but as the occasion for blissful participation in the life of the world is set out in 'To the Daisy'. Taking its cue from a cancelled passage in 'The Ruined Cottage' MS. D, in which the 'impious warfare' of division and 'disconnection' yields to the embrace of the 'one life' in which 'All things shall live in us, and we shall live/In all things that surround us',³⁸ 'To the Daisy' conveys its release from the burden of self-consciousness through anaphoric indeterminacy and an accumulation of abstract qualities detached from the grasp of an overseeing 'I':

> A hundred times, by rock or bower
> Ere thus I have lain couched an hour,
> Have I derived from thy sweet power
>   Some apprehension;
> Some steady love; some brief delight;
> Some memory that had taken flight;
> Some chime of fancy wrong or right;
>   Or stray invention. (ll. 41–8)

Commenting on these lines, Gregory Leadbetter observes: 'The rich dance of thought in this list includes love, delight, memory, fancy, invention—presented as unpredictable forms of grace [...], with an unfixedness that allows for the "stray" and even the "wrong"'.³⁹ Leadbetter is right to call this movement a 'rich dance', but we cannot quite evade the uneasiness encoded in the bluntly stressed tail-rhymes 'apprehension' and 'invention', as if creation itself were, in some way, partnered ineluctably with traces of anxiety and alarm. It might not be easy, still less blissful, to find oneself released from the zeal for self-governance only to become lost in a realm of fleeting fixities. But equally, one might find it impossible to endure those stately passions that prompt the thought of permanence. A 'chance look' (l. 50) at the flower is enough to dissolve that imposing posture, allowing the self to take a 'lowlier pleasure' in 'The homely sympathy that heeds/ The common life our nature breeds' (ll. 52–6). If 'common life' reminds us of the 'one life' there is, as Leadbetter suggests, 'less implication of supernatural metaphysical insight here' (l. 228), but Wordsworth points nonetheless to an order of experience freighted with significance. In the collective 'our nature', and the glad, animal-like audacity of 'breeds', the poet is aligned with forms of life that appear indifferent to the correlation of Being and Thought. Leisure and play are the operative words in the lines that follow, allowing poet and flower to delight in 'kindred gladness' (l. 60) while avoiding the temptation to ground such points of contact in the notion of a universal lifeworld. Reluctant to pin down this experience, the poet embraces a form of cultivated vagueness: 'An instinct call it, a blind sense;/A happy genial influence,/Coming one knows not how, nor whence,/Nor whither going' (ll. 69–72). Here is tranquillity of a different order to the emphasis on peace as the 'silent horizon' of foundational violence.[40] By eschewing definition and participating in collective joy, Wordsworthian peace, at least in this incarnation, departs from the tensile knot in which release from war can only be imagined as life-denying extinction.

First printed in 1807 in *Poems, in Two Volumes*, 'To the Daisy' reappears in 1815 at the head of Poems of the Fancy, as categorised by Wordsworth in the collected *Poems*, a work that appeared in print in the very month that Napoleon returned from exile to dramatically reignite the war against France. In the Preface to this edition Wordsworth remarks that the 'law under which the processes of Fancy are carried on is as capricious as the accidents of things, and the effects are surprising, playful, ludicrous, amusing, tender, or pathetic, as the objects happen to be appositely produced or fortunately combined' (*Prose* III. 36–7). The sense of momentary, otiose enthralment realised in 'rapidity and profusion', and the 'felicity' with which 'thoughts and images' are 'linked together', allows Fancy its brief triumph over 'the indestructible dominion' of Imagination. As Wordsworth memorably concludes: 'Fancy is given to quicken and to beguile the temporal part of our nature, Imagination to incite and to support the eternal'.[41] Inviolate and eternal, the Imagination bears some structural resemblance to the notion of peace as a state of eternal rest. By contrast, Fancy appears to have something in common with notions of process, even of assemblage, in its devotion to rapidity, profusion, and linkage.[42] In the 1800 note to 'the Thorn', Wordsworth delineates the character of those 'Superstitious men' who, 'with a reasonable share of imagination', are yet 'utterly destitute of fancy, the power by which pleasure and surprize are excited by sudden varieties of situation and by accumulated imagery': 'their minds are not loose but adhesive'.[43] As a creative faculty, Fancy shares with Imagination the ability to 'aggregate and to associate, to evoke and to combine' (*Prose* III. 36), but while Imagination abstracts and modifies its materials, affecting changes 'proceeding from, and governed by, a sublime consciousness of the soul in her own mighty and almost divine powers',[44] Fancy dwells among 'the slight, the limited, and evanescent',[45] eschewing consciousness of self for protean delight in the shifting surfaces of the world.

With echoes of the 'wraithlike mutation—whether understood as endless production or endless dissolution—of Self into Other' to be found in John 'Walking' Stewart's *The Revelation of Nature* (1795),[46] Fancy, as it is developed in the 1815 Preface, counters the emphasis on militant individuation that one might assume in Wordsworth's post-war writing. Of relevance here is David Fairer's account of 'Walking' Stewart's 'panbiomorphic universe' in which there is no such thing as 'positive or absolute identity' but living organisations of matter 'emerging through the continual alternation of incremental and excremental dynamics within nature (like the ebb and flow of the tide)'.[47] As a temporary mode of common substance, human identity is no different from a flower, a river, or a drop of rain. To be caught up in those glad animations that 'had no need of a remoter charm/By thought supplied' is thus to reconceptualise individuality as a form of Spinozian *conatus*,[48] or confederate striving, distinct in kind from the Cartesian emphasis on the separation of mind and body, but characterised, above all, by a sense of universal delight in the interanimation of all material things: 'The budding twigs spread out their fan,/To catch the breezy air;/And I must think, do all I can,/That there was pleasure there'.[49]

The peace that may be found in *conatus*, with its emphasis on alternating states of 'motion and rest, speed and slowness', is markedly different from the state of melancholy inertia envisaged by Kant.[50] In Chapters 1, 2, and 4 I will have more to say about how peace, founded in *conatus*, is represented in 'The Recluse', *The White Doe of Rylstone*, and *The Waggoner*, but in advance of this reading I should like to anticipate and respond to concerns regarding the 'politically open-ended and even utopian' aspects of the account of Wordsworthian peace that has been presented so far.[51] It is generally assumed, and with good reason, that political open-endedness and utopianism cannot be found in Wordsworth's post-war poetry – that is, in the poetry Wordsworth wrote and published after Waterloo – but we need not deviate into counter-factual realms to discover lingering traces of that early attachment to the poetics and politics of Fancy. The appearance in the 1815 collection of a second poem entitled 'To the Daisy' ('With little here to do or see'),[52] dating again from the early 1800s, makes explicit the flower's ability to generate associations dissociated from conscious control, to discover in 'Loose types of Things through all degrees' (l. 11) the resources for a reimagining of the world as an inter-animated realm of mutually constitutive motions and affections, a world in which freedom is recognised in and through aesthetic play as the necessity of contingency. To read 'To the Daisy' in 1815 is to allow oneself to participate, however briefly, in a dynamic process of loss and gain, a process in which the dissolution of identity may be attended by feelings of pleasure as well as pain. Assisted by the adoption of Drayton's eight-line *rime couée*, a pattern used to great effect in the mock-epic fairy tale *Nimphidia* and echoed more recently in Burns's modification of standard Habbie, the reader is swiftly absorbed by the poem's incantatory rhyme scheme. Adrift in the 'humour of the game' (l. 15), the reader also becomes entangled in a 'web' of 'similies' (1. 10): 'Nuns demure [...]/Or sprightly Maiden' (ll. 17–18); a bejewelled Queen and a 'Starveling in a scanty vest' (ll. 21–2); a little Cyclops 'Staring to threaten and defy' (l. 25); a fairy shield 'In fight to cover' (l. 30). Carried forward in joyful vigour, the poem dallies with Horace's satirical depiction of woman as the 'most terrible cause of war',[53] tracing a course through three states of female maturation – virginal seclusion, sexual awakening, and sovereign power – to end with mock-heroic images of masculine defiance. But if this immersion in the associative chains of romance implies a departure from the sterner business of sense making, we are reminded too in the comparison between the 'fair' daisy (l. 35) and the 'Self-poised' star (l. 40) of 'She dwelt among the untrodden ways', a poem that forges fanciful similes to simultaneously confront and waylay the stark reality of loss.

'To the Daisy' is no doubt too delicate a creation to sustain such troubling thoughts, but that of course is the point, for whatever 'thought comes next [...] instantly/The freak is over,/The shape will vanish' (ll. 27–9). Thus, as 'To the Same Flower' ('Bright Flower!') enjoins, deliverance from the consciousness of death may be found in the life of 'A thoughtless thing' (l. 10): 'Meek, yielding to the occasion's call/And all things suffering from all' (ll. 20–21). But just as in the Hegelian model of art consciousness is led through its engagement with thoughtlessness to an awareness of its estrangement from nature prior to its arrival in the higher, dialectical stage in which the conflicts and antimonies of philosophical reasoning are at last overcome, so the daisy's absence of thought is surveyed from the perspective of a point beyond the laws of time, change, and contingency: 'Thy function apostolical/In peace fulfilling' (ll. 23–4). Here, then, we return to the notion of peace as the melancholy remainder of war – a condition 'outside being' that, by virtue of its exceptional status, serves at once to confirm and deny the possibility of a messianic suspension of hostilities.[54] Yet when surveyed as an aspect of the 'unassuming Common-place/Of Nature' ('To the Daisy': 'With little here to do or see', ll. 5–6), the daisy, delighting in its protean existence, appears indeed to manifest all the signs of a life delivered from the struggle for individuation. And it is in this sense that the world of justice, of a life redeemed because of its openness to the world and its irreparability, would seem to have been fulfilled.

Still, it might be argued that the conclusion of 'To the Same Flower' suggests a more conventionally eschatological stance: the promise of that 'eternal spring', celebrated by Milton and Cowper, when, at the end of days, the world is 'delivered from the bondage of corruption' (Romans 8. 21).[55] Wordsworth himself appears to have wrestled with the theological implications of his daisy poems. To Isabella Fenwick Wordsworth expressed surprise that some readers should consider '"Thy function apostolical" as being little less than profane. How could it be thought so? The word is adopted with reference to its derivation implying something sent on a mission; &, assuredly, this little flower, especially when the subject of verse, may be regarded, in its humble degree, as administering both to moral & to spiritual purposes'.[56] Like the suffering servant of Isaiah 53, the daisy depicted in 'To the Same Flower' might be read as a prefiguration of Christ: 'For he shall grow up before him as a tender plant, and as a root out of a dry ground: he hath no form nor comeliness; and when we shall see him, there is no beauty that we should desire him' (Isaiah 53. 2). The audacity of reversing the direction of the simile no doubt accounts for the charge of profanity, but the parallels with Isaiah 53 root the poem in Christian orthodoxy, allowing the 'Pilgrim' (l. 2) flower, 'whose home is everywhere' (l. 1), to serve as an emblem of 'hope for times that are unkind' (l. 15). In its function as a missionary, the daisy 'wanderest the wide world about' (l. 17), providing humanity with a lesson in how to withstand the temptations of 'pride' and 'scrupulous doubt' (l. 18), along with the effects of neglect and approbation. Assisted by the inverted syntax and present participle of 'Thy function apostolical/In peace fulfilling', the daisy, as apostle, speaks of a peace that has already arrived.[57]

Something of what it might be like to encounter peace in the world in which we live, rather than at the end of days, is given in 'To the Daisy' ('Sweet Flower! belike one day to have'), a poem written during the period of suspense when, for six weeks, John Wordsworth's body lay unclaimed 'beneath the moving Sea' (l. 36).[58] Composed in late May–July 1805, and added to the 1815 *Poems*, 'Sweet Flower!' cements from the outset the daisy's association with peace, justice, and the life that is to come. Meditating on John's death, Wordsworth perceives in the loss of that silent poet an intimation of his own demise when, no longer subject to the commanding 'Word!' (l. 29), the 'gentle Soul and sweet' will join the flower 'in undisturbed retreat' (l. 48). Drawing on John's description of the sight of daisies 'after sunset [...] like little white stars upon the dark green fields',[59] 'Sweet Flower!' discerns in their 'starry multitude' (l. 28) an image of life released from the struggle for recognition. Peace is often defined as 'the absence of war',[60] impossible to imagine, that is, outside of an ontology founded on and informed by hostility. Yet in 'Sweet Flower' witness is granted to a world in which life is no longer orientated around a perilous core of self-division. Sufficient unto itself and at peace with others, the daisy posits a form of life after death that is at once imminent and transcendent, transient and eternal, suggesting the possibility of a world in which even the injustices suffered by the fallen can be redeemed in the here and now, a point to which I will return, in the context of further reflections on the death of John, in Chapters 3 and 5.

In Wordsworth's daisy poems, then, we gain a glimpse, yet no more than a glimpse, of what peace might look like: a 'happy, genial influence', a 'kindred gladness'; peace as a place of suspension between the human and the non-human; peace as the reign of contingency; peace as absolute hospitality; peace as the establishment of non-juridical Justice. Underlying all these formulations, and indeed encoded in the linking of one formulation to another, an activity akin to the fanciful production of similes, or more appositely to the weaving of a daisy chain, is the idea, formulated by Walter Benjamin, of peace conceived as a means rather than as an end. In 'Toward the Critique of Violence', Benjamin identifies non-violent conflict resolution as neither a means to an end nor an end in itself but rather as a technique that exceeds instrumental or teleological reasoning. For Benjamin, peace is an open-ended, ongoing practice, distinct from the juridical drawing up of contracts that Rousseau and Kant regard as the source of conflict. As technique, therefore, peace is manifested in discussion or, to be more precise, in the 'proper sphere of "coming-to-understanding"' that is 'language as such'.[61] As a manifestation of what Benjamin goes on to describe as 'divine violence',[62] language as such, in its disregard for law-preserving boundaries, evokes a mode of peace that is active in the everyday even as it gestures towards a time of fulfilment that has yet to arrive.

Responding to Benjamin's 'Critique', Giorgio Agamben writes of peace conceived not as *pax* but as *otium*, 'a word whose uncertain correspondences with Indo-European languages (Gr. αὔσιος empty, Gr. αὔτως in vain; Gothic *aupeis*, empty; Isl. *aud*, desert) hover around the semantic field of emptiness and the absence of finality'.[63] Used originally by the Roman military to describe the periods of leisure experienced by soldiers in between bouts of conflict, *otium* offers a playful alternative to the state of posthumous nullity in which peace has been habitually conceived. As the daisy teaches us, peace is not a state in which we dwell but rather one in which we 'sojourn—nocturnal, patient, homeless—in non-recognition'.[64] Displaying none of the symptoms of nostalgia, the malady that in the eighteenth-century came to be associated with the displaced victims of war,[65] there is a sense in which Wordsworth's affirmation of the flower's uprootedness, focussed on the image of an object that is at once homeless but whose home is everywhere, marks a departure from the near-compulsive attention given to the destruction or absence of the home in Wordsworth's early anti-war poetry. Markedly different in tone from 'The Female Vagrant', 'The Discharged Soldier', 'The Old Cumberland Beggar', and 'The Ruined Cottage' – poems in which conflict is responsible for social conditions that force ordinary men, women, and children to wander the earth in fugue-like states, exiled from homes that may or may not exist or that fall into desuetude while their occupants return to the ground – the daisy poems reveal that 'Peace is the perfect empty sky of humanity; it is the display of non-appearance as the only homeland of man'.[66] The idea that the drive to satisfy such a basic want as shelter can be overcome, and that openness to a form of radical homelessness might erase the competition for land and property that leads to conflict, takes Wordsworth in directions that appear untenable; yet, as we shall discover, the poetry that Wordsworth publishes after war raises important questions about the reimagining of hospitality when homes are subject to ruin.[67]

***

How these daisy poems, with their affirmative yet, at times, unsettling visions of life after war, were understood by the early readers of *Our English Lakes, Mountains, and Waterfalls* may not, of course, be determined. Denounced in 1815 as 'trifles' by the *Augustan Review*,[68] and condemned for their 'exuberant sensibility' by the *Quarterly Review*,[69] Wordsworth's poems of Fancy appeared at the close of the First Great War to be woefully out of step with the times, and there is little evidence to suggest that readers in 1915 felt any differently – unless, that is, we consider how closely Wordsworth was taken to heart by ordinary soldiers of the line, as this picture illustrates (Figure 2).

Paul Fussell has described how modernists, such as Herbert Reed, viewed Wordsworth's poetry as 'hopelessly sentimental and archaic', a poetry of 'synthesis' no longer at home in a landscape ravaged by heavy bombardment.[70] Such antipathy may have been provoked by attempts at the beginning of the war to claim Wordsworth as 'the Poet for the Trenches—the Minstrel for the Offensive', singling out the patriotic sonnets and 'Character of the Happy Warrior' as confirmation of the poet's suitability for the part.[71] But other readers, like the men identified as 'We Are Seven', appear to have responded to something other than sentiment or bombast in Wordsworth: a capacity for irony; a refusal of easy consolation; a determination to believe in the continuity of life after death, despite evidence to the contrary, or perhaps more straightforwardly, but no less radically, the sense of a better world. A clue to how Wordsworth's poetry might have been understood by such men is given in Edmund Blunden's 'A House in Festubert', a lyric account of a bombed-out house that, 'with gashes black, itself one wound' (l. 3), provides shelter to those 'who laugh unkilled' (l. 9).[72] Transplanted from 'Tintern Abbey', the hermit who 'might have built a cell/Among those evergreens' (ll. 16–17) is forced into hiding, jeopardised by the 'hum' (l. 21) of 'steel-born bees' (l. 24). In Blunden's conflicted pastoral, the acceptance of impermanence, of rapidly shifting juxtapositions and violent amalgamations, has become a condition of life. Yet still, antique notions of joy in widest commonality spread persist, offering, in ways that surmount the crushing weight of irony, a sense of accord with those creatures who, 'fond of summer' (l. 23), find love amid the ruins.

Might A. H. S., the unknown soldier whose name has fallen from *Our English Lakes, Mountains, and Waterfalls*, have found common cause with the idea that in the daisy 'there abides [...] Some concord with humanity' ('Bright Flower', l. 6)? Perhaps the image of that flower finding 'shelter under every wind' (l. 14) in 'times that are unkind' (l. 15), 'Meek, yielding

Figure 2 *Soldiers of the Machine Gun Corps* (c. 1916–1918).
Source: The Louis and Antoinette Thuillier Collection.
Courtesy of the Kerry Stokes Collection, Perth.

to the occasion's call,/And all things suffering from all', would have struck a chord with a soldier enduring the deprivations of war. The recognition of 'concord' with a flower 'whose home is everywhere' (l. 1) may well have provided the soldier and his family with some degree of comfort, a reminder that, amidst the horrors of war, peace may yet be found. And there is the possibility, too, that through recognition of the flower's vulnerability, at risk of destruction 'from a freak of power,/Or from involuntary act of hand/Or foot unruly with excess of life', a soldier might 'stop/Self-question'd, asking wherefore that was done'.[73] In that concurrence of attitudes, spanning distinctions of space and time, minds and bodies, Wordsworth's daisies announce the possibility of a life regained.

England in 1802

In March 1802 Wordsworth composed 'The Sailor's Mother', a poem that, in its focus on an encounter with a wandering victim of the war, echoes 'Old Man Travelling' and 'The Discharged Soldier'. Beneath her cloak the indigent woman conceals a bird and cage, property of the son who 'many a day/Sail'd on the seas' but now 'is dead' and 'cast away' (ll. 21–2).[74] The woman explains that the 'Singing-bird' (l. 28) accompanied her son on many voyages, but when 'last he sail'd' he left the bird behind, 'As might be, perhaps, from bodings of his mind' (ll. 29–30). Saved, then, from extinction, the bird may 'pipe its song in safety' while serving as a tangible reminder of the son's 'delight' (l. 35) in the life of the world. Holding on to that life, the mother connects with the son, but we might also see in this 'transmutation of wars casualties into song' a means of surmounting personal and collective grief.[75] To carry lyric delight while adrift on the roads of England is to state one's faith in the healing mission of poetry after war. The work that Wordsworth undertook in the productive spring and summer of 1802 – the new edition of *Lyrical Ballads*, 'Resolution and Independence', the 'Immortality Ode', and the outpouring of bird, flower, and butterfly poems – gives some indication of how that mission would be carried forward. But other poems dating from this period display more discomforting thoughts and feelings. And all this at a time when peace had enabled the possibility of a reunion with Annette Vallon and the poet's first meeting with their daughter, Caroline – a meeting that would serve as a settling of accounts prior to the poet's wedding to Mary Hutchinson in the autumn.

To tease out these counter-currents in Wordsworth's post-war poetry, first as they presented themselves in 1802–3 and then as they re-emerged in the wake of Napoleon's first and second defeats, let us attend to two poems, hiding in the shadows of Amiens, that express fears of how the poetics of Fancy might waylay the 'manly strain of nat'ral poesy'.[76] In 'The Barberry-Tree', an air of cultivated uncertainty places the utopian leanings of Fancy in abeyance, subjecting its pacific charms to anaphoric doubt and moral dubiety. Thus, riffing on themes that would emerge, with greater precision, in 'I wandered lonely as a cloud', the poet speculates on whether the breeze that animates the tree feels the same pleasures 'that ev'n now/ In my breast are springing' (ll. 23–4) and whether 'Those golden blossoms dancing high' (l. 27) have 'in themselves of joy a store' (l. 28), only to conclude that 'If living sympathy be theirs' (l. 37), if 'the piping breeze and dancing tree/Are all alive and glad as we' (ll. 39–40), 'I cannot tell, I do not know [...] I do not know, I cannot tell' (ll. 42–4). Still, as if in a trance, the poet stands statue-like, transfixed by the scene, only to be roused from his reverie by the plangent sound of church bells. Unfinished and irresolute, suggestive of pleasures unknown to poets of more sober disposition, pleasures that may, as the puzzling allusion to Peter Grimes suggests ('I to Grimes had pledg'd my word', l. 60), lead to criminality, guilt, and ostracisation, 'The Barberry-Tree' tests the limits of Fancy, granting visions of gleeful release from the antagonistic labour of being that, for all the charm of nature's 'whispering sounds' (l. 72), must, for the sake of the peace, remain in thrall to the call of Anglican authority.

Fancy cannot be trusted to speak so consistently on behalf of the cause of peace, and the accession to gentle dissolution in the shifting motions of the world provides only a partial account of how Wordsworth's poetry responds to the aftermath of war. The Peace of Amiens, while broadly welcomed by a populace eager for relief from the social and economic burdens of the war, was nevertheless viewed by many observers with a mingled sense of apathy and distrust. The general denunciation of sloth, effeminacy, and self-indulgence that emerged in debates around this time concerning the effects of peace on the national character shades no less into the discourse of poetry. Wordsworth's sonnet 'How sweet it is when mother Fancy rocks' grants direct expression to this mood of oneiric distraction, likening Fancy's seductive appeal to a 'bonny Lass' at a country fair, who 'plays her pranks' (l. 6) 'While she stands cresting the Clown's head, and mocks/The crowd beneath her' (ll. 8–9).[77] Though momentarily distracted 'with such gleam/Of all things' (ll. 12–13), the 'wayward brain' (l. 2), overwhelmed by ceaseless novelty, causes the poet to 'shrink' in 'fear' and to 'leap at once from the delicious stream' (ll. 13–14). With its confusing investment in feminine archetypes – Fancy is both a deceiving mother and a coquettish girl, the poet resembles Arethusa fleeing from the river god Alpheus, as depicted by Ovid – the sonnet becomes a performance of the sort of trouble that a work of pure fancy can bring to the world.[78] Unhoused and ungentle, the female figures represented in this poem belie the conception of peace as a welcoming mother, offering comfort and reassurance to her war-ravaged sons; instead, the girl assails the poet like a 'wandering Mountebank' (l. 7), transforming 'the whole world [...] link by link' (l. 11) into an uncanny and ungraspable hyper-object, a ceaselessly proliferating realm of unreality far removed from the state of peace in which gendered identities are stabilised and things are objectively present.[79]

Beneath the peace, a battle rages, infecting even the most seemingly pacific of discourses. For Wordsworth, this other war is evident in poetry, and not least when poetry seeks to overcome its relationship with dissonance and division, offering in plain sight a vision of concord founded in conflict. Given what has been said so far about the warlike undercurrents of the poetry eventually collected in *Poems, in Two Volumes*, readers may not have been surprised to discover, at the head of the volume, the Virgilian motto '*Posterius graviore sono tibi Musa loquetur/Nostra: dabunt cum securos mihi tempora fructus*' ('Hereafter shall our Muse speak to thee in deeper tones, when the seasons yield me their fruits in peace').[80] Notwithstanding that on the surface the motto may be read as an apology for the volume's apparent lightness of tone ('To the Daisy' is the opening verse), the word *securos* (an inflection of *securus*, meaning 'without care') would have resonated with readers for whom questions of national security were a daily concern. As Brian Folker points out, the English translation of *securos* as 'peace' is misleading, since unlike the state of irenic self-containment described by '*pax*', *securos* designates peace as a condition that is 'by implication circumscribed, surrounded by a larger realm of less desirable conditions'.[81] At best, the volume suggests, we may look forward to a time that is secure from anxiety, danger, or pain but not to a time in which such threats have come to an end.

In light of this qualification, it is helpful to think about the 1807 volume's most famous exploration of peaceable life, the 'Immortality' ode. Composed on 27 March 1802, a date coincident with the conclusion of the peace settlement, the opening four stanzas of the ode convey feelings of deflation and defeat, offering echoes of rejuvenation, of a world in 'bliss' (l. 41), only to reduce the thrill of that 'timely utterance' (l. 23) to blank indifference: 'the Pansy at my feet/Doth the same tale repeat' (ll. 54–5).[82] While other flowers bloomed in this uneasy spring, reprising that older, Spinozian faith in festive joy, the jerky enchantments and disenchantments of the ode – a form traditionally offered on a day of national thanksgiving – gave vent to thoughts of private grief at odds with the season of collective renewal. Marjorie Levinson has claimed that the Peace, which privileged the imperial regime, underlining the duplicity of the revolutionary experiment and the errors of its first principles, amplified the gap between Wordsworth's benighted Jacobin 'first affections' and his mid-life identification as a patriot and loyalist.[83] Levinson goes on to read the ode as an attempt to close this gap by folding the opening recollections of lost revolutionary glory – conveyed by the anaphoric insistence and rhyming present participles of lines 35–50 – into a radically conservative narrative of consolation and compromise. Understood as a poem articulating the transition from melancholy to mourning, the ode laments the loss of the instinctive pleasures of youth, the 'simple creed' of 'Delight and liberty' (l. 141), only to discover recompense for their passing in the transition from heedless joy to sober reflection. In 'thoughts that spring/ Out of human suffering' (ll. 186–7), 'Thoughts that do often lie too deep for tears' (l. 206), the pansy's lost glory is recollected, tenderly but without pain, in 'the meanest flower that blows' (l. 205). Reduced to an abstracted, correlationist object, its fullness of being jettisoned to the other side of that 'eternal Silence' (l. 158) that separates Man and God, the pansy ceases to trouble the poet with feelings of rapture; now, having relinquished instinctive 'delight' (l. 193) to live beneath a more 'habitual sway' (l. 194), the poet can repeat, in finer tone, the procedural dreariness that quelled those early recollections of revolutionary bliss, reconfiguring that period's 'noisy years' (l. 157) in the quiet imprecision of that 'peace which passeth all understanding' (Philippians 4.7). Thus, Wordsworth 'will grieve not' (l. 183) for the loss of that profane, effervescent time in which the 'senselessness of joy was sublime';[84] now the holiday is over, and Amiens has shown how 'peace itself is a coded war',[85] the poet will turn to the 'faith that looks through death' (l. 188), projecting into that inaccessible and unrealisable beyond the impression of a life delivered from enmity and strife.

In Chapters 3 and 5 we will consider the ode again, setting its chronicle of ideological continuity within the larger contexts of the 1816 Thanksgiving volume and the 1820 *Miscellaneous Poems*. In these chapters we will see how the complex sequence of emotional, geographical, and legal manoeuvres that Wordsworth undertook during the Peace of Amiens resonated in subsequent post-war writings – most notably in poems published after Waterloo and after Peterloo. Eric C. Walker has written persuasively of how marriage serves in post-war culture as a form of conflict resolution, healing divisions exacerbated by armed struggle, offering the promise of enduring peace.[86] Might those victims of conflict portrayed in the anti-war poetry of the 1790s, wandering souls bereft of husbands, wives, sons, and homes, be exorcised now that war had come to an end? Certainly, the treaty of 1802 provided Wordsworth with the means to resolve at least one, highly personal, case of estrangement: the marriage that did not take place with Annette Vallon and the settlement that was not bestowed on the child of that unsanctioned union. The marriage to Mary Hutchinson that followed in the wake of this meeting would grant to Wordsworth the promise of restitution, enabling through union with a native of Cumberland the healing of those geopolitical and psychological divisions forced by Britain's entry into war. The epigraph to the 'Immortality' ode, taken from Virgil's Fourth Eclogue, is, in this respect, and when considered in light of the volume's opening motto, apposite: *Paulò majora canamus* – a plea for songs of higher import from a poem written in anticipation of a new golden age, heralded by the Peace of Brundisium and affirmed by the wedding of Antonius and Octavia.

Yet, even as Wordsworth's settlement with the past was enacted, traces of that old, revolutionary enthusiasm would return to haunt the poet, requiring further, strenuous, acts of containment. It is in the sonnets that Wordsworth composed during his stay in Calais over the summer that the effort to quell the promptings of the past is most overtly expressed. Precisely dated and, for the most part, prosaically titled, the Calais sonnets document the poet's attempts to overcome a gathering sense of estrangement on revisiting sites that, a decade before, had offered the hope of lasting, communal peace.[87] Adrift in this uncannily familiar setting, the former Jacobin seeks relief from the recollection of those 'festivals of new-born Liberty', long since reduced to a 'hollow word', in the image of a child sheltered 'in Abraham's bosom'.[88] Discovered at the close of a poem that clusters around a snapshot portrayal of a father and daughter walking along the beach at Calais, the divine child, most likely Caroline, the poet's illegitimate daughter, bears a striking resemblance to those blessed children in the 'Immortality' ode who, no longer subject to the transitory gladness of the Revolution, 'sport upon the shore' of an 'immortal sea' (ll. 164–70). But the sonnet's allusion to Luke 16.22, in which the faithful are gathered up into eternal life, signals the trace of that other, more disturbing, Abrahamic story: the account of the child called to sacrifice by the word of God. To dwell in 'that imperial palace' ('Immortality' ode, l. 84) from whence she came, the child must be detached from all that is at enmity with the holy, the calm, and the free.[89] That 'homeless sound of joy' ('To a Friend, Composed near Calais, on the Road Leading to Andres, August 7th, 1802', l. 5), materialised in the festal atmosphere of 1790 and invoked mechanically by the zombie citizens of 1802, must either be housed, expelled, or consigned to a time of 'Fair seasons' in which political 'despair' will be effaced by 'hopes as fair' (ll. 12–14).

Soon after his return to England, in 'Composed in the Valley, *near* Dover, on the Day of landing',[90] Wordsworth discovers the peace that was denied to him in France, finding joy in 'Kent's green vales' (l. 7) as, lulled by the anti-alarum of 'the Smoke that curls' (l. 2) and soothed by the sounds of church bells and 'this little river's gentle roar' (l. 5), white-shirted boys play cricket in the meadow ground. But while the fair hopes of 'To a Friend, Composed near Calais' appear to have been realised in the appreciation of these demilitarised and, crucially, native sights and sounds, the dismissal of the likely return to conflict ('Europe is yet in Bonds; but let that pass', l. 9) is limned, nevertheless, by thoughts of the transience of peace, by concern that 'joy enough' is not enough and that 'perfect bliss' (ll. 11–12) cannot be sustained while discord looms. Despite the poet's best efforts to protect the happy hour from the intrusion of conflicted thoughts, the sonnet foresees that other 'moment' (l. 10) in which the freedom that is to be found in aesthetic play is supplanted by the recognition of violent necessity.

Sadly, then, in the Calais sonnets, the prospect of lasting peace remains elusive, and war continues to serve as the arena in which individual and collective identity is forged. Within a few months, following the collapse of the peace accord, the passage from imagined fears to present anxieties would find direct expression in 'To the Men of Kent. October, 1803', 'Anticipation. October, 1803', and 'October, 1803' ('Six thousand Veterans practis'd in War's game'). In these invasion sonnets, the readiness with which the king's subjects subscribe to the defence of the realm suggests that, for Wordsworth, the breach between individual conscience and collective will, a breach evinced in *The Prelude*'s account of how the young republican sulked when prayers were raised for the victory in the war against France, has at last begun to heal. To commit to war is to commit, then, to the belief in the general equivalence of war, politics, and reality; it is to accept that war is the crucible in which individual and collective identity is forged. Such a belief may well have prompted the poet to volunteer his services to the Grasmere militia – a gesture that prompted Dorothy to declare: 'surely there never was a more determined hater of the French nor one more determined to destroy them if they really do come' (*EY* 403).

Might Wordsworth have found some pleasure in acceding to this thanatoid belief? Published in the *Morning Post* in April 1803, on the facing page of an editorial expressing hope for 'real peace, or actual and vigorous war',[91] 'It is not to be thought of that the flood' is markedly different in tone from the pacifying sentiments of the poet's initial foray into political sonneteering. In 'I griev'd for Buonaparte', 'Books, leisure', and 'the talk/Man holds with week-day man' (ll. 10–11) are prized over success in 'battles' (l. 5),[92] but signs of growing dissatisfaction with England's post-war greed and complacency, evident in 'The world is too much with us' ('Getting and spending, we lay waste our powers', l. 2),[93] as well as 'Written in London. September, 1802' ('No grandeur now in nature or in book/Delights us. Rapine, avarice, expence,/This is idolatry; and these we adore', ll. 8–10),[94] are fully realised in 'It is not to be thought'. Alluding to a passage from Samuel Daniel's *Civil Wars* ('"with pomp of waters, unwithstood"', l. 4),[95] the poet displays some disappointment that the 'freights' of liberty should be born to 'foreign lands' (l. 6), leaving 'this most famous Stream' to 'perish' in 'Bogs and Sands' (ll. 7–8) – a sentiment that chimes with the anti-expansionism of 'England! the time is come when thou shouldst wean/ Thy heart from its emasculating food' (ll. 1–2).[96] To bring freedom home, however, it is necessary that the nation should expose itself to the threat of annihilation and have done, once and for all, with its vitiating obsession with commercial prosperity, a belief echoed by the *Morning Post* in its chary notice of a rally on the stock market as hopes were raised for a renewed settlement with France. Thus, in anticipation of Wordsworth's later engagement with the sacrificial origins of the classical sacred spring tradition, most evident in *The River Duddon* and *Ecclesiastical Sketches*, the poet affirms that 'the Flood/Of British freedom' is 'sprung/Of Earth's first blood' (ll. 13–14), a claim that responds to the recollection of those 'invincible Knights of old' (l. 10) who, rejecting worldly gain for spiritual worth, give up their lives in defence of the realm.

The rousing imperative at the core of 'It is not to be thought', 'We must be free or die' (l. 11), a phrase uttered in the 'tongue/That Shakespeare spake' (ll. 11–12) and enshrined in the 'faith and morals' of Milton (l. 13), is carried forward to the October 1803 invasion sonnets. In 'To the Men of Kent' the poet desires that 'words of invitation' (l. 5) be sent to France so that parleying may cease, and war may commence.[97] In this climate of dialogic collapse, the enemy appears transfixed by the sight of 'glittering' lances (l. 7) as, transformed into emblems of British liberty, the Men of Kent, who once, as boys, played on the meadow-ground, respond with 'one breath' (l. 12) to the ontologically self-cancelling, but sonically harmonious, command: "'tis Victory or Death!' (l. 14). At the end of war, at the limit of expression, only a dactylic 'Shout' (l. 1) remains, heralding in 'Anticipation. October, 1803' the beating of drums and the blowing of trumpets that disturb the sleep of the foreign dead.[98] In this poem's disturbing vision of a successfully defended homeland, with corpses 'lying in the silent sun' (l. 4), the afterlife of war seeps into daily life, witnessed in those 'little Children' who 'stun' their grandmothers with 'pleasure' of their 'noise' (ll. 8–9): a sequence of words that queasily conjoin violence and rapture, sickness and dispute. Only in the mind of God or, mundanely, through the reparative work of metre and rhyme can such sights and such sounds be made agreeable:

> Divine must be
> That triumph, when the very worst, the pain,
> And even the prospect of our Brethren slain,
> Hath something in it which the heart enjoys:—
> In glory will they sleep and endless sanctity. (ll. 10–14)

In what sense *must* 'triumph' be 'Divine' and how, precisely, is the appeal to religion linked with that 'something' in 'the prospect of our Brethren slain' that the 'heart enjoys'? Like 'something evermore about to be', a calculated vagueness ensures that the horrifying likelihood of British losses is sublated, transformed by the assurance of eternal 'glory' into a sublime object of desire.

What does Wordsworth's affirmation of the logic of sacrifice, evident in works published in the aftermath of Amiens, amount to if not a diminution of the ability of Fancy to arouse thoughts of an alternative to the life that exists only to be negated? Fancy has a significant part to play in my discussion of Wordsworth's post-war verse, but its importance should not be over-emphasised. As evidenced by the gloomy necessitarianism of 'The Small Celandine', a poem appearing amid the daisy poems, flowers cannot be relied on to sustain ideas of blithe, pacific joy. 'Stiff in its members, withered, changed of hue' (l. 19), 'an offering to the Blast' (l. 11), the decayed flower elicits a chilling response, 'I smiled that it was grey' (l. 20), on a par with the sociopathic enjoyment in destruction evoked in 'Anticipation'. If the poetry Wordsworth wrote and published in the aftermath of war demonstrates an unexpected yearning for the 'surprising, playful, ludicrous, amusing, tender, or pathetic', caring 'not how unstable or transitory may be her influence', it yet remains in the shadow of Imagination, which the poet maintains 'is a word of higher import, denoting operations of the mind upon [absent external] objects, and processes of creation or composition, governed by certain fixed laws' (*Prose* III. 31).

To track the emergence of a discourse of peace in Wordsworth's poetry is therefore to commit to the pursuit of a phantom figure, unstable and transitory, but nonetheless detectable, and perhaps not least in those poems in which the note of unbridled militancy most stridently resounds. In the chapters that follow we will lose sight of this phantom, to the extent that doubts will set in as to whether it can return; moreover, as the argument proceeds, moving more or less chronologically from the beginnings of Wordsworth's great engagement with the poetics of peace and war, 'The Recluse', before reaching a provisional terminus at the end of a thirty-year period of international and civil conflict with the *Memorials of a Tour of the Continent, 1820*, we will come to believe, at times, that peace has been exorcised from Wordsworth's writing. What will sustain us, however, is the surety that it is the relationship between peace *and* war, rather than the opposition of peace and war, that animates this writing, complicating the appearance of a straightforward binary to reveal thoughts, feelings, and beliefs that migrate between these states.

Ad Utrumque Paratus

Writing to the liberal-minded Francis Wrangham, not long after the announcement of Napoleon's first abdication in the spring of 1814, Wordsworth provocatively declared himself to be a member of the '*War-faction*'. Centring on a reading of 'The Recluse', the 'long poem' with which the poet hoped to advance his reputation (*MY* II. 144), Chapter 1 opens with a consideration of the representation of peace in 'Home at Grasmere' (1800–06), a poem later known as '*Part first Book first*' of '*The Recluse*'.[99] Through close readings of the 1808 'Recluse' fragments that Wordsworth went on to adapt for *The Excursion*, the chapter investigates how remnants of the poet's early interest in radical, pacificist thought, described by Hazlitt as 'traces, which are not to be effaced by Birth-day and Thanksgiving odes, or the chaunting of *Te Deums* in all the churches of Christendom' (*CWWH* XIX. 18), speak against the poem's declared allegiance with the values of Britain's political and religious establishment. Noting how the poem's composition is bisected by the composition of the pamphlet on the Convention of Cintra (1810), and the letter to the military theorist Sir Charles Pasley (1811), writings that explore the links between armed struggle, national independence, and the primacy of the Imagination, the chapter goes on to consider how *The Excursion*, through the character of the Solitary, grants expression to the revolutionary hope for perpetual peace, world citizenship, and delight in Fancy's 'mutable array' (Book III. l. 740).¹⁰⁰ By revealing, in Spinoza's sense, the relationship between hope and uncertainty ('Hope is an inconstant joy, born of the idea of a future [...] whose outcome we to some extent doubt'),¹⁰¹ I argue that the Solitary's abandonment of hope paradoxically paves the way for its return, allowing for the possibility of forms of peaceful co-existence that, while they cannot be foreseen, may yet be conceived.

In Chapter 2 attention turns to *The White Doe of Rylstone*, a poem arising out of familial grief whose engagement with the melancholic afterlife of war was brought into sharp relief following its publication in the year of Waterloo. To contemporary readers, attracted by the 'strong passion and violent excitement' of Walter Scott's epic-romances, *The White Doe*, with its air of 'profound sadness, settled grief, the everlasting calm of melancholy, and the perfect stillness of resignation', seemed out of step with the times.¹⁰² To some readers, however, the poem spoke all too well of the need for a 'gentle' and 'subdued' alternative to Scott's militant poetics.¹⁰³ Framed by descriptions of loss and desolation, *The White Doe* casts the hegemonic ambitions of its protagonists as symptomatic of a degraded Imagination. Mistaking material ambition for spiritual salvation, the home of the Catholic Nortons falls into ruin; but ruin enables a different kind of imaginative flourishing, one that allows for the emergence of strange and unforeseen forms of being. Whether encountered in the love between the human and the non-human, in the slow effacement of Rylstone Hall, or in the merging of the sacred and the profane, *The White Doe* offered a way for post-war readers to imagine peace, not as the 'bootless bene' of history but as a form of aesthetic play that, even as it risks jettisoning actually existing peace to the realm of transcendental inaccessibility, discovers in the comingling of absence and presence, lack and plenitude, finitude and infinitude the preconditions for a life no longer marked by the struggle for self-definition.¹⁰⁴

Focussing on a reading of the 'Thanksgiving Ode', and its accompanying shorter poems, Chapter 3 sets Wordsworth's post-Waterloo compositions within the context of broader, contemporary debates concerning the relations between war, religion, and sacrifice. Poised between gratitude for the decisive victory over France and frank acknowledgement of that victory's human costs, Wordsworth's nomination of 'carnage' as the 'daughter' of God ('Thanksgiving Ode', l. 282) proved a step too far for many of the poet's younger supporters,¹⁰⁵ confirming, in Shelley's words, that the herald of 'Liberty,/Justice and philosophic truth' had 'Fallen on a cold and evil time'.¹⁰⁶ While elsewhere in the Thanksgiving volume attempts are made to cleanse the 'stains' of a 'perturbèd earth' ('Elegiac Verses', ll. 1–4),¹⁰⁷ the 'Thanksgiving Ode' remains dogged in its attention to the recalcitrant remains of 'victory sublime',[108] an attention that, this chapter argues, should be read within the larger context of Wordsworth's struggle to submit the militant striving of Imagination to the superintendent power of the divine. If in one sense, the ode displays vatic indifference to human suffering, figuring in the sacrifice of Imagination to History's 'closing deed magnificent' (l. 167) a gesture akin to the numerous corporeal sacrifices enacted on the field of battle, in another sense the poem is informed by an acute awareness of how ideological abstractions are scored in human flesh. Taking as inspiration Spenser's *Epithalamion*, a poem supposed to be sung before the door of a wedding chamber, the ode steers Wordsworth's earlier, more celebrated experiment with the odal form in directions that are at once glaringly public and obscurely intimate. With memories too of how, in 1802, peace conflated the distinctions between union and disunion, legitimacy and illegitimacy in Wordsworth's sexual relations, the 'Thanksgiving Ode' tacitly acknowledges the recent wedding of the poet's daughter, Caroline Wordsworth-Vallon. Figured as the bearer of conflict *and* as a principle of restitution, Caroline hovers on the margins of the ode, a symbol of peace founded in war. In other poems from this period, most notably in 'Laodamia' and 'Dion', the ability of marriage to heal the traumatic divisions and aberrant liaisons of war comes under increasing strain, to the point where, as the chapter concludes, peace becomes fugitive.

Following consideration of Wordsworth's low reputational and creative stock in the years following the Thanksgiving volume, Chapter 4 opens with a discussion of the composition, publishing, and reception histories of *Peter Bell* and *The Waggoner*, both of which appeared in 1819. Here, my focus turns to the abandoned narrative poems volume that would have paired these poems with *The White Doe of Rylstone*. To imagine this volume is to see again how elements of Wordsworth's purportedly abandoned interest in the poetics of peace resurface in the later work, complicating our understanding of the poet's cultural, artistic, and political development. In a reading of *Peter Bell*, the chapter reflects on the representation of violence and on the poem's attempts to negotiate the terms of a peaceable relationship between the human and the non-human. In the discussion of *The Waggoner*, an account of the poem's reception forms the basis for an examination of the poem's meditation on creative failure, artistic isolation, and the potential for co-operative living in the aftermath of war. Picking up on the conative entanglement of human and non-human entities first addressed in *Peter Bell*, the chapter considers how Benjamin's waggon works like a peaceable commonwealth to realise the potential of its component parts in ways that advance the well-being of the whole.[109] Sadly, this happy assemblage is short-lived, which leaves the poem's depiction of a world committed to the accommodation of ontological diversity an elusive but resonant fancy.

The focus of Chapter 5 is on *The River Duddon*, published in April 1820, just prior to the Wordsworths' visit to Manchester to inspect the site of the Peterloo Massacre. The poems Wordsworth composed in the years just prior to and immediately after Peterloo bear the imprint of the poet's concern for the degraded state of Britain and are marked by his fear of social insurrection. Introduced by a reading of Wordsworth's Autumn poems, 'September, 1819' and 'Upon the Same Occasion', the chapter proceeds to trace the recurrence of patterns of violent imagining in the *Duddon* sonnets, which discover, through their adaptation of the ostensibly pacific but deeply conflicted poetics of the sacred fount tradition, a fitting analogue for the times. Even though, on the surface, the *Duddon* sonnets proffer a vision of peace, predicted on the unity in diversity of its thirty-three component parts, closer inspection reveals a work silted by the material accretions of history. The chapter concludes with an account of how the material contradictions underpinning the fluvial tradition are displayed in the arrangement of the three-volume *Poems* (1820) and four-volume *Miscellaneous Poems* (1820) and in the sequencing of the *Ecclesiastical Sketches* (1822). If the river sequence offers the promise of recuperation, allowing the poet to perceive the accidents of history, whether personal or collective, as divinely ordered stages in a providentially directed narrative, the genre inevitably reveals its origins in bloodshed and ruin. Yet it is from such ruins, as *Ecclesiastical Sketches* go on to suggest, that forms of peaceable life may once again be salvaged. Frequently dismissed as the propagandist remainders of an ossified mind, Wordsworth's account of the rise of the Anglican Church turns out to be surprisingly astute and even at times liberatory in its appreciation of the ordinary, profane life that may be found within 'choirs unroofed by selfish rage'.[110]

Chapter 6 resumes discussion of Wordsworth's experiments with the poetics of riparian nationalism. In *Memorials of a Tour of the Continent, 1820*, the poet follows the course of the Rhine and the Rhône, revisiting scenes that, thirty years earlier, had provided a setting for dreams of radical rebirth. After his visit to Peterloo, Wordsworth's encounter with his own past had begun in Calais, meeting the grown-up daughter whose childhood was glimpsed briefly in 1802 and whose wedding was obliquely acknowledged in the 'Thanksgiving Ode'. A visit to Waterloo yields chastened thoughts of 'horror breathing from the silent ground',[111] while elsewhere peace is recovered in fleeting impressions of sacerdotal calm. Here again, however, the appeal to life-restoring waters is jeopardised by the insistent return of war, by recollections of violent struggle in Europe's long-distant and recent past. But Wordsworth's battle with the past is intensified by another, more pressing, conflict: a spat with Lord Byron, who in Canto 3 of *Childe Harold's Pilgrimage* had forged an impression of post-war Europe heavily indebted to Wordsworth. In *Don Juan* Byron made his distaste for Wordsworth very clear, singling out for disdain both *Peter Bell* and *The Waggoner*. Wordsworth took notice of this attack, and in many respects the *Memorials* can be read as an effort to defend a reputation that, in Wordsworth's eyes, had been traduced by Byron, while attempting at the same time to correct the pro-Napoleonic sentiments that, on account of the popularity of *Childe Harold*, had been allowed to infect the public imagination, casting a pall on the legitimacy of the post-war settlement. The *Memorials* make clear that Wordsworth's efforts to make peace with his own history, a history informed by the conflicted history of Europe, remained unresolved and that by returning to the restorative channels of youth the poet had, in fact, merely reinitiated the repetitive cycle in which peace is coupled with war.

The conclusion to this book offers a perspective on Wordsworth's cultural afterlife, finding in the postscript to Leigh Hunt's pacificist polemic, *Captain Sword and Captain Pen* (1835; revised 1849), and Thomas De Quincey's pro-Crimean essay, 'On War' (1848; revised 1854), the resources for a reading of the politics and poetics of late Romanticism that responds to the contradiction in Wordsworth's poetry revealed in these polarised works: the clash between the hope for perpetual peace and the grim satisfaction of eternal war. Whereas De Quincey, citing the 'Thanksgiving Ode', remains obdurate in his support for the 'dreadful doctrine' that war is 'amongst the evils that are salutary to man',[112] Hunt joins with those later generations of readers who, experiencing war at first hand, found solace in poems celebrating the life of rivers, mountains, and flowers. Though Wordsworth's poems do not flinch from violent imaginings, for such readers it yet remains possible that peace will come.

CHAPTER I

Conscripting 'The Recluse'

It Is Like a Dream

Seven years after the collapse of the Peace of Amiens, an end to the war appears in sight: first, in October 1813, the defeat at Leipzig followed by the retreat to Mainz and the collapse of the northern Italian states; then, at the beginning of 1814, Blücher's crossing of the Rhine followed by three months of fighting in northern and eastern France, the Allied march to Paris, and the announcement, on 6 April, of the emperor's abdication. In Rydal, these events seem barely to merit attention until on 24 April, writing to Catherine Clarkson, Dorothy declares:

> To the last page I am come, and not a word of the Emperor Alexander, the King of France or the fallen Monarch! Surely it might seem that to us, encircled by these mountains, our own little concerns outweigh the mighty joys and sorrows of nations; or I could not have been so long silent. It is not so—every heart has exulted—we have danced for joy! But how strange! It is like a dream—all in a moment—prisoners let loose—Englishmen and Frenchmen like brothers at once!—no treaties—no stipulations. (*MY* II. 142)

In England's dreaming the peace is welcomed by the left and right alike. Even the restoration of the Bourbon king is given a cautious endorsement by opposition figures.[1] Yet, dismayed by Napoleon's ignoble retreat from the battlefield, and perturbed by the liberality of his pension, Dorothy comes to share with commentators as varied in background and opinion as Lord Byron, William Hazlitt, Lewis Goldsmith, and Walter Savage Landor the sense that the scourge of Europe had somehow failed to be himself: better that he should have fought 'to the Death' and then, having 'yielded himself a prisoner', been 'tried for the murders of the Duc d'Enghien, of Pichegru, of Captain Wright—of Palm—of one or all' (*MY* II. 142).[2] The general relief at the announcement of peace yielded, with the arrival of summer, to murmurs of discontent from wartime profiteers, who now found their livelihoods to be in danger, and to declarations of alarm from those members of the political opposition who, having cautiously welcomed the return of Louis XVIII, feared that the menace of 'unlimited and arbitrary power' would injudiciously subvert the constitutional settlement.³

Throughout this period, there is no mention of *The Excursion* – the poem with which Wordsworth has been engaged since 1809 – until, a day after Dorothy's letter, William announces to Francis Wrangham: 'I am busy with the Printer's Devils. A Portion of a long Poem from me will see the light ere long. I hope it will give you pleasure. It is serious, and has been written with great labour' (*MY* II. 144). Adding a degree of portentousness to this mysterious announcement, on 28 April Wordsworth informs Thomas Poole: 'I have at last resolved to send to the Press a portion of a Poem which, if I live to finish it, I hope future times will "not willingly let die"' (*MY* II. 146). Aligning himself with Milton, 'my great Predecessor', while anticipating the judgement of posterity on 'The Recluse', Wordsworth makes plain his wish to claim a place in the English imagination, hoping to restore his dwindling reputation through the publication of a 'portion' of that long, philosophical poem. Amid this dalliance with authority and futurity Wordsworth, signing off to Wrangham, and perhaps wishing to provoke his liberal friend, proclaims: 'I congratulate you on the overthrow of the execrable Despot: and the complete triumph of the *War-faction* of which noble body I had the honour to be active a Member as my abilities and industry would allow' (*MY* II. 144). Wordsworth's allusion to John Stoddart's recent attack in *The Times* on the '*Peace-faction*' who sought a negotiated settlement with France seems unequivocal, and indeed who, having read the patriotic sonnets, the Cintra tract, and the establishment soundings of *The Excursion*'s concluding book, would wish to quibble with this self-assessment?⁴

Published in July 1814 in expensive quarto format, *The Excursion* proclaimed its author's allegiance to the Tory establishment through the inclusion of a dedication to the poet's patron, 'the Right Honorable William, Earl of Lonsdale'.⁵ Although treated with suspicion by liberal readers, and often surveyed as a demonstration of Wordsworth's political apostasy, passages from *The Excursion* were nonetheless cited by these same readers as exempla of those progressive tendencies that the poem, in its bid for establishment approval, had sought to defeat.⁶ The fact that such readers could respond to the poem in this way owes much to its connection with 'The Recluse', the unrealised '*first* and *only* true Phil. [*sic*.] Poem' that would, in accordance with Coleridge's projection, have effected a 'Reconciliation' that would end mankind's 'enmity with Nature', providing, at last, the means to effect the chiastic union of Man, Nature, and Spirit ('true Idealism necessarily perfecting itself in Realism, & Realism refining itself into Idealism').[7] Though it fell short, in some measure, of Coleridge's vision of millenarian fulfilment, *The Excursion* advanced its own vision of how peace might be restored, presenting in the character of the Solitary a case study in how disappointment with the political amelioration of mankind may be assuaged through an awakening to the love of Nature leading, in turn, to the love of God. It would be some time before the poem's rejection of communitarian solutions to the crises of the age and its endorsement of a form of individualised, therapeutic conservatism would find a receptive audience, but in the immediate post-war period it was the survival within the poem of radical political, ecological, and theological sentiments adapted from poetry drafted in the late 1790s and early 1800s that, with their promise of deliverance from the belligerent antimonies of Enlightenment thought, most appealed to Wordsworth's second-generation contemporaries. In these revenant passages, voiced by characters either excluded from or on the margins of the poem's loyalist community, Keats, Hazlitt, Hunt, and Shelley would find the resources for a radical critique of the post-bellum settlement.

Hidden in plain sight within *The Excursion*, therefore, are traces of a poem that spoke in support of the *Peace-faction* rather than the *War-faction*. In the late 1790s, the first drafts composed for 'The Recluse' – 'The Discharged Soldier', 'The Ruined Cottage', 'The Old Cumberland Beggar' – had engaged almost exclusively with the victims of Britain's prosecution of the war against France.[8] These passages were, in turn, complemented by the series of blank verse fragments, mostly written in Germany, that hinted at a vision of life relieved of antagonism – 'There is an active principle alive in all things', 'I would not strike a flower', 'There are who tell us that in recent times'.[9] In the two-book *Prelude* that emerged from these tentative beginnings, echoes of 'bliss ineffable' (l. 449) emanating from the 'one life' (l. 460) offered consolation to those revolutionary fellow travellers who, like Wordsworth, had succumbed in 'these times of fear' to the 'melancholy waste of hopes overthrown' (ll. 478–9).[10] However, by the time the poem evolved into the thirteen-book *Prelude* most of these anti-war sentiments had been dispersed or waylaid, leaving the aspiration to enduring peace, a dream of Fancy, to be weighed in the balance alongside passages addressing Imagination's dark abyss. The harmony between mind and nature that is presented at the close of the 1806 *Prelude* attempts to bring Imagination into alignment with mortal being, but in 'Home at Grasmere' (1800–6), and then in 'The Recluse' fragments of 1808, we find Wordsworth returning to an older, less fraught, but no less ambitious envisaging of how peace might be found in our relations with the world. It is to the recovery of these pacific inclinations, as they emerged in manuscript and as they appeared in print, that this chapter is, for the greater part, directed.

To understand how 'The Recluse' took shape as a debatable response to the end of war, I begin with a reading of 'Home at Grasmere', paying attention to the poem's uncertain engagement with the poetics of peace, conceived at once as an immanent field of joyful, energetic play *and* as a transcendental domain of immutable concord. From here I move to an account of the 1808 poems, with a focus on 'The Tuft of Primroses', looking at how the desire for eternal peace is fractured from within by the recognition of its own interior violence. In a concluding discussion of *The Excursion*, I consider how the Solitary's recollections of the pacific ideals of the French Revolution, together with passages indulging in fanciful portrayals of peaceful co-existence in nature, transplanted, and to some extent reorientated, from the 1808 drafts, may be read as counterpoint to the support for defensive war outlined in the tract on the Convention of Cintra and in Wordsworth's correspondence with the military theorist Sir Charles Pasley. While the Solitary grants expression to the dashing of revolutionary hope, that very act of negation, as Hazlitt's affirmation of the poem's remembrances of that 'glad dawn of the day-star of liberty; that spring-time of the world' suggests, offers in its recitation of the Revolution's ambition to establish universal and perpetual peace a paradoxical hope for its future success (*CWWH* XIX. 18).[11]

Residency and Redundancy in 'Home at Grasmere'

Between the patriotic sonnets that followed the collapse of the Peace of Amiens and the bellicose prose and poetry that came in the wake of the Cintra affair, Wordsworth's poetry returned to sentiments that would have made of 'The Recluse' an extended meditation on the blessings of peace. This new poetry, overtly local and contemplative, joyful and fanciful, would have shifted Wordsworth's poem away from the war-torn beginnings of the long, philosophical poem. But, as these modal verbs and past participles betray, the drive towards the combative separation of 'coarser pleasures' and 'elevated thoughts' seems always to triumph in the end. By keeping sight of these fleeting yet frequent expressions of animal delight, of blissful absorption in everyday life, it should, however, be possible to imagine a world 'Made for itself and happy in itself',[12] a world as yet unharried by thoughts of insufficiency or understood merely as 'the correlate of human thought'.[13] Conceived in 1800, then shaped into a finished work in 1806 during the period of extraordinary creativity that followed in the wake of John's death, 'Home at Grasmere', also known as '*Part first Book first*' of '*The Recluse*',[14] appears to offer just such a vision.

Centred on a schoolboy's memory of 'a golden summer holiday' (l. 4), the poem's opening lines celebrate the 'thought of clouds/That sail on winds':

> of breezes that delight
> To play on water, or in endless chase
> Pursue each other through the liquid depths
> Of grass or corn, over and through and through,
> In billow after billow evermore;
> Of Sunbeams, Shadows, Butterflies, and Birds,
> Angels, and winged Creatures that are Lords
> Without restraint of all which they behold. ('Home
>   at Grasmere'. MS. B. ll. 25–33)

Edenic in conception yet strangely disconcerting, the ascription of 'delight' to 'breezes' suggests that feeling is no longer the sole preserve of the human but is, as it were, everywhere, imbued in lives that strive, in the Spinozian sense, to pursue their existence. The child's love of the limitless variety and endless succession of organic forms, conveyed rhetorically by alliteration, anaphora, and polysyndeton, prompts the speaker to claim a corresponding expression of 'liberty' and 'joy' in chiastic play: 'To flit from field to rock, from rock to field,/From shore to island, and from isle to shore' (ll. 37–8). The poem is titled 'Home at Grasmere', but in these lines at least, the idea of home as a permanent domicile or residency, centred on the notion of a self-contained unit or other 'substantial' dwelling, is challenged by the emphasis on restlessness and change. Here, operating in accordance with the associative pleasures of Fancy, the idea of home as a protective space, shielding inhabitants from violent intrusion, may be taken for granted, for Wordsworth's happy valley overflows with love for all God's creatures and for all that is around them.

Amid the celebrations, however, something does not ring true, as if the repeated claims to gleeful co-existence, in line with Wordsworth's related attempts to rescue post-political joy from the embers of revolution, were in some way *de trop*. Seeking to account for the giddy absurdism of the poem's opening statements, Kenneth Johnston has observed how '[e]verything about it is circular: its arguments tautological, its syntax redundant and repetitious, its imagery full of rounded reflections which reinforce the circling tensions of its structure'.[15] Here, however, Johnston could be accused of missing the point. In his note on 'The Thorn', Wordsworth writes that 'repetition and apparent tautology are frequently beauties of the highest order', with the qualifier 'apparent' indicating that tautological expressions may well communicate something more than the words they repeat.[16] That sense of 'Something' (l. 164) exceeding the grasp of language, of that which, operating under the sign of the beautiful, sanctions the 'blended holiness of earth and sky' (l. 163) so that life in Grasmere is made synonymous with the state of enduring peace, is, nonetheless qualified by the awareness of how that which is perfect in itself, a 'Whole without dependence or defect' (l. 168), serves also as a 'termination' (l. 166). For, even as 'Home at Grasmere' seeks to substantiate its vision of enduring peace, the stress on the 'spirit/Of singleness and unity and peace/[...] In this majestic, self-sufficing world' (ll. 202–4), along with the repeated emphasis on the poet's attempts to claim ownership of this spirit, underscored and undermined by an excessively qualified variation on the 'Tintern Abbey' dialectic of fulfilment, loss, and abundant recompense, shows that the 'promise' (l. 248) of peace resists the drive towards self-possession:

> the unappropriated bliss hath found
> An owner, and that owner I am he.
> The Lord of this enjoyment is on Earth
> And in my breast [...]
>   What I keep have gained,
> Shall gain, must gain, if sound be my belief
> From past and present rightly understood
> That in my day of childhood I was less
> The mind of Nature, less, take all in all,
> Whatever may be lost, than I am now. (ll. 85–96)

Kevis Goodman has written brilliantly of how, in Wordsworth's poetry, 'Tautology may be homesickness by other means'.[17] Underwriting the tautological formulations of 'Home at Grasmere' we may discern the traces of that longing for home that blighted the minds and bodies of so many Enlightenment outsiders, not least those victims of war who, finding themselves removed from their sense of the everyday, fell prey to forms of compulsive behaviour that, in their somatic and semantic insistence, seek to defend the self against the rapid impress of the times. As if to escape the *-algia* of its yearning for home, it is not long before the poem conjures up an image of belonging understood not as an expression of self-predicated singularity but as a mode of inter-animated multiplicity – as when, at the return of Spring, the Grasmere waterfowl 'show their pleasure' (l. 286) in 'wanton repetition' (l. 296), the 'I', though unable to take 'possession of the sky' (l. 288) yet partakes of their 'thoughtless impulse' (l. 289):

> One of a mighty multitude whose way
> And motion is a harmony and dance
> Magnificent. Behind them, how they shape,
> Orb after orb, their course, still round and round [...]
> In wanton repetition, yet therewith—
> With that large circle evermore renewed—
> Hundreds of curves and circlets, high and low,
> Backwards and forwards, progress intricate [...]
> They tempt the sun to sport among their plumes;
> They tempt the water and the gleaming ice
> To show them a far image. (ll. 290–310)

Aptly conveyed through numerical excess, anaphoric insistence, and materialised tautologies, a sense is gained of what it might be like to embrace self-abnegation, to accept that individual life is formed and deformed by interactions with others, and, perhaps, emulating the example of the birds' apparent scorn for 'both resting-place and rest' (l. 314), to concede that peace, as such, will not be found in the home – at least insofar as home is understood as a form of self-possession.

One might imagine that, buoyed along by this insight at an early stage in its development, 'Home at Grasmere' could simply reiterate the sense of pleasure at being alive in the world, in anticipation of John Clare's delight in the ontographic repleteness of things.[18] But, as conveyed in the stumbling syntax, awkward negations, ambiguous determiners, and elided conjunction of lines 316–21, the poem struggles to sustain the faith in that 'active principle alive in all things' that, in the 1802 preface to *Lyrical Ballads*, had moved Wordsworth to celebrate 'the grand elementary principle of pleasure, by which [man] knows, and feels, and lives, and moves' (*Prose* I. 140):

> Not upon me alone hath been bestowed—
> Me, blessed with many onward-looking thoughts—
> The sunshine and mild air. Oh, surely these
> Are grateful; not the happy Quires of love,
> Thine own peculiar family, Sweet Spring,
> That sport among green leaves so blithe a train. (ll. 316–21)

Who or what is grateful: the sunshine and mild air? The poet's thoughts? Is Nature in harmony with, distinct from, or identical with the mind of the poet? Are those signifiers of textual materiality, the 'Quires of love', identical with or distinct from 'Thine own peculiar family'? And here again, whose family: the poet's quires or the Spring's waterfowl? Moreover, does the qualifier 'peculiar' refer to 'strange' or is its meaning informed by the Old English sense of 'particular' or, more remotely, by the Latin *peculiaris* 'of private property' or 'one's own', a meaning that would be aligned with the poem's previous emphases on claims to ownership? In MS. D, the substitution of 'The penetrating bliss' for 'The Sunshine and mild air' and the shift from 'blithe' to the comparative 'blither' do little to help matters. Strained to the point of unreadability by grammatical and semantic ambiguity, the assertion of joyful indifference to category distinctions calls out for the return of oppositional clarity.

Significantly enough, it is through the recognition of an act of violence that the poem starts to break free from the stultifying consequences of its attempts to articulate a purely irenic language. The moment of recovery occurs when the poet registers the absence of 'two, a lonely pair/Of milk-white Swans' (ll. 322–3), symbolic doubles for that tautologous pair, William and Dorothy. The poem conjectures that the swans may have been killed by a Grasmere shepherd, underscoring the sense in which dreams of undifferentiated harmony, dreams whose vacuity is exposed by the overworked allusion to the 'loveliest' and 'Blest pair' of *Paradise Lost* ('They strangers, and we strangers; they a pair,/And we a solitary pair like them', ll. 341–2),[19] pose a threat to the real life of the valley – the life that recognises violence as integral to existence. Fearing that 'by harbouring this thought' he has, in some way, done 'wrong' to 'this favoured Vale' (ll. 358–60), the poet embarks on a sequence of increasingly strained iterations of domestic tranquillity, ending with an attempt to eclipse the contractual dimensions of peaceful co-existence by presenting it as a natural fact:

> Ah! if I wished to follow where the sight
> Of all that is before my eyes, the voice
> Which is a presiding Spirit here
> Would lead me, I should say unto myself,
> They who are dwellers in this holy place
> Must needs themselves be hallowed. They require
> No benediction from the Stranger's lips,
> For they are blessed already. None would give
> The greeting 'peace be with you' unto them,
> For peace they have; it cannot but be theirs. (ll. 362–71)

As if exposing the potentially fatal contingency of the traditional liturgical greeting were not enough (for what would happen if the greeting were not returned?), the effort to present peace as a state of nature rather than as a promissory act falls foul, as the Latinate phrasing of 'peace they have' and needless insistence of 'it cannot but be theirs' betray, not only of the necessity of predication but of the co-implication of the constative and the performative – an impure or contaminated condition that renders all declarations of peace, insofar as they are readable or intelligible, susceptible to contestation.[20]

A few lines on, the illusion of self-referential concord is qualified still further by the poem's uneasy recollection of ethical improprieties among the vale's inhabitants. The home that is sought for in 'Home at Grasmere' turns out to be a fraught domain that, with its accounts of 'double-dealing, strife and wrong' (l. 438), cannot help but reveal the violent trace that nurtures and informs the dream of eternal peace. Those who, through their actions, draw attention to this trace must suffer – like the adulterer who, stung by guilt, becomes 'his own world, without a resting-place', 'Wretched at home' and 'with no peace abroad' (ll. 516–17). Subsequently removed from MS. D, the adulterer's tale has no place in a poem founded on claims to conjugal harmony. Like the undesirable guest, whose presence in the home exposes the hostility that resides in hospitality, 'Home at Grasmere' must be shielded from the knowledge of the opposition on which the claim to peace is founded.

But even as the poem advertises its savviness in rejecting the delusory assurance of 'pastoral fancies' (l. 628; see also ll. 829–30), still the desire persists for 'a music, and a stream of words/That shall be life' (ll. 621–2) – a language purged of predicative violence that somehow, magically, enables existence to be at one with itself. The search for 'such a stream,/Pure and unsullied' (ll. 628–9), cannot help but recall the paradoxical origins of the classical sacred fount: the source of pastoral peace born of blood sacrifice that, as the poem's earlier recollection of 'Hart-leap Well' (ll. 236–56) had implied, underwrites the claim to domestic harmony. Condemned in this world to pollute the stream of life the poet inquires: 'must we seek [peace] where man is not?' (l. 631). Yet, despite repeated attempts to be at peace with the vale's 'animal being' (l. 673), to be at one with those feelings and sensations that would preclude the urge to individuation, the desire for sovereignty persists. Matters come to a head in lines 875–909 when, returning to the question of vocation, the poet rejects the life of oblivion and, embracing 'duty' (l. 879), asserts the existence of an 'internal brightness [...]/That must not die, that must not pass away' (ll. 886–7), and that, while seeking fellowship with others, is 'solely mine/Something within, which yet is shared by none' (ll. 897–8). Having reached the point where claims to ownership, of being at home in the vale, flounder in the face of repeated encounters with loss (a reminder that the home can never be the home), the poet asserts a claim to singularity that yet must be shared with an audience; hence, the repeated conditionals, 'I would impart it; I would spread it wide [...] I would not wholly perish' (ll. 901–3), even as they signal a determination to move beyond self-scrutiny, run the risk of forestalling the projected poem on man, nature, and society, of reducing it, as *The Prelude* had already anticipated, to a declaration of individual fitness that remains without issue.

What, then, would prevent the still-birth of 'The Recluse'? What principle, found within, would enable the poet, now set apart by virtue of his gift from common life, to communicate with the world? In a passage that survives the poem's final transcription, an attempt is made to connect that elusive 'Something which power and effort may impart' (l. 900) with the poet's youthful enthusiasm for tales of martial prowess:

> Yea, to this day I swell with like desire;
> I cannot at this moment read a tale
> Of two brave Vessels matched in deadly flight
> And fighting to the death, but I am pleased
> More than a wise Man ought to be; I wish,
> I burn, I struggle, and in soul am there. (ll. 928–33)

Couched in the present tense, this arresting account of sanguinary childhood reading habits may have been informed by the poet's more recent preoccupation with Nelson's heroic death at Trafalgar. It is likely, too, that mixed feelings of pain and pride over John's self-sacrifice, touched on in 'Character of the Happy Warrior', are latent within these lines.[21] But what is perhaps more significant is the extent to which the violent proclivities of youth insist on the present, urging the mature poet to repeat past imaginative transgressions, in defiance of monitory wisdom. Even as the adult is 'tamed' and made 'calm' (ll. 934–5) by Nature's influence, prompting the poet to abandon his plans to write a quasi-Miltonic epic on some British theme ('Then farewell to the Warrior's deeds, farewell/ All hope, which once and long was mine, to fill/The heroic trumpet with the muse's breath!', ll. 953–5), the wish to write 'On Man, on Nature, and on human Life' (l. 959) retains in the midst of its Spinozian insistence on the continuity between 'the individual mind' and 'being limitless' in the 'one great Life' (ll. 969–71) a sense 'of foes/To wrestle with and victory to complete,/Bounds to be leapt and darkness to explore' (ll. 946–8). When read in this light, the poem's celebrated statement of correlationist intent – 'How exquisitely the individual Mind [...] to the external world/

Is fitted; and how exquisitely too [...] The external world is fitted to the mind' (ll. 1006–11), a denouement that repeats the chiastic self-circling that is the poem's dominant rhetorical mode – appears less pacific than it might at first appear. So long as the human heart is 'enflamed' by 'longing', 'contempt', and the desire for 'undaunted quest' (l. 949–50), however 'changed their office' (l. 951), the 'great consummation' (l. 1004) of Mind and Nature must be conceived as the final act of an epic struggle, which amounts to saying that while human and non-human entities are conceived as dialectical opponents, and insofar as a non-violent language is untenable, paradise will not be regained on this earth and certainly not in this time.

Nevertheless, secreted into the 'Prospectus' is the hope that the poet will be protected from these violent urgings in the 'living home' (l. 991) of the beautiful. At one with the 'green earth' (l. 991), Beauty 'Pitches her tents' (l. 995) as the poet traverses the sublime 'haunt and main region' (l. 990) of his song, presenting an image of shelter that manages, simultaneously, to domesticate the threat of the sublime while raising the prospect of how, like the temporary shelters used by soldiers on a military campaign, the tent provides the mere illusion of protection from the risk of '[ ] vacancy' (l. 986).[22] Subsequently informed in MS. D by the comparative adjective 'blinder' (shades here of the desire to out-trope Milton), the materialised absence of MS. B speaks more profoundly of that violence to opposition that, according to Derrida, results in 'the worst violence': the violence of indifference, of nothingness, of pure non-sense.[23]

'The Ghostliness of Things': Ruin and Revival in the 1808 'Recluse' Poems

Unable to come to terms with its structural dependence on violence, and all too reliant on self-validating proclamations of harmony to protect the purity of its domestic ideal, 'Home at Grasmere' shows how claims to ownership, to self-possession, to being at peace with oneself and the world are open to the threat of home invasion, to the return of those 'passions' that, as Wordsworth suggests in his note on 'The Thorn', trouble the distinction between words, minds, and things.[24] The truth that 'Home at Grasmere' reveals is how tautology, born out of a desire to efface this distinction, exacerbates the disturbance that prevents the mind from finding a place in the world.[25] The idea that for peace to hold sway home should be given to that which violates home, that by acknowledging its structural dependence on war the home should be understood as, in a sense, radically home*less*, is intimated in subsequent work undertaken for 'The Recluse'. Begun in the spring of 1808 the blank verse fragments 'To the Clouds', 'St Paul's', and 'The Tuft of Primroses' resume Wordsworth's study of the relationship between creativity and bellicosity, signalling again the extent to which 'The Recluse' maps the contours of a wartime imagination.

The extended apostrophe 'To the Clouds' opens with an explicit declaration of militant intent: 'Army of clouds, what would ye?' (l. 1).[26] Different in kind from the melding of singularity, sublimity, and abstraction that marks the opening simile of 'I wandered lonely as a cloud', the use of the second-person plural pronoun alerts us from the outset to the poem's fundamental conceptual difficulty: is the archaic address a formal honorific or an indicator of commonality? By extension, is the poet subordinate to the object of his attention, which darts rapidly across the sky, or is he able to engage with the polymorphic entity as an equal or, better still, as a superior? The answer to the latter question is important because it will determine whether the poet can claim command of a phenomenon that threatens, like the unformed matter of 'The Recluse' itself, to exceed his power. The conjectural barrage that follows the opening address, which deserves to be quoted at length, configures the army of clouds as a rich but volatile source of inspiration, pointedly aligned with the transitory creations of Fancy:

> O whither in this eagerness of speed?
> What seek ye? or what shun ye? of the Wind
> Companions, fear ye to be left behind,
> Or racing on your blue aethereal field
> Contend ye with each other? [...]
> Or were Ye rightlier hail'd when first mine eyes
> I lifted, for Ye still are sweeping on
> Like a wide Army in impetuous march,
> Or like a never-ending Flight of Birds
> Aerial, upon due migration bound,
> Embodied Travellers not blindly led
> To milder climes? [...]
> O whence, Ye clouds, this eagerness of speed?
> Sheer o'er the Rock's gigantic brow Ye cut
> Your way, each thirsting to reveal himself, to secure
> Each for himself an unbelated course?
> Ye clouds, the very blood within my veins
> Is quickened to your pace, a thousand thoughts,
> Ten thousand winged Fancies have Ye rais'd,
> And not a Thought which is not fleet as Ye are. (ll. 4–36)

Unable to create a taxonomy that would, in Goethe's sense, place a limit on 'the indefinite, the unstable and the unattainable',[27] the poet observes these 'silent Creatures' (l. 38) descend into 'some unapproachable abyss' (l. 43), only to witness the renewal of the 'long Procession' in 'wild impulse' from 'a fount of life/Invisible' (ll. 53–4). Reminiscent of the economy of life, death, and rebirth in 'Kubla Khan', but with echoes too of the 'blinder vacancy' in 'Home at Grasmere', the poet's recognition of the interchange between the life-giving fount and the deadly abyss proves to be a turning point in the poem, initiating a shift from the heady, apostrophic dependency of the poem's opening salvo to the calm assertion of creative independence that brings the verse to a close. Acting as a reminder that Fancy, by virtue of its protean nature, raises thoughts of war as well as peace, the 'rapid multitude' of forms (ll. 54–5) responds from here on to the call of a higher power, a 'blazing intellectual Deity' (l. 85), who like Apollo, the solar 'God of Verse' (l. 84) and, notably, of victory in battle, 'showers on that unsubstantial Brotherhood/A Vision of beatitude and light' (ll. 87–8), lending shape and significance to forms of life that would otherwise disappear. Those transient thoughts that, driven by the nomadic impulses of Fancy, had threatened at the beginning of the verse to exceed the conscious control of the poet must now succumb to the shaping spirit of Imagination, which makes of the conclusion an exercise in reterritorialisation, analogous, as the allusion in lines 25–6 to far and middle eastern sun-worshippers had teased, to the pacification of a rebellious colony. Confronted with a figure for control that unfortunately evokes its own form of unruly, pagan, and warlike potency, Wordsworth would add, when the poem was revised for publication in 1842, a suitably Christian conclusion, thereby ensuring that the 'transient' forms of 'the god of verse' find a home 'in the bosom of eternal things'.[28]

In 'St Paul's', the Imagination performs a similar service by relieving the poet of 'conflicting thoughts' (l. 1). Designated a 'holy power' (l. 9), Imagination appears before the poet, in an instant, materialised in a 'visionary scene' (l. 15), in which the emphasis on quietness, vacancy, purity, stillness, and, crucially, silence speaks, as it were, of the end of discourse, and thus of the end of war. Peace is found, then, in a world that is 'noiseless and unpeopled' (l. 24), sublime and sequestered. But the fact that the vision appears by 'Gift of Imagination's holy power' (l. 9), an act of self-divinisation worryingly akin to Napoleon's act of self-coronation in 1804, aligns this pacifying gesture once more with the will to extinguish opposition, including the opposition to opposition on which the vision of perpetual peace is raised. As Geoffrey Hartman long ago averred, the

Wordsworthian Imagination is combative in form and nihilistic in intent, forever on the verge of bringing the poetry to an apocalyptic dead stop – materialised in 'St Paul's' as a vacant zone of 'purest white' (l. 18) – with no promise of millennial glory.

The question of how to bring such warlike imagining to book preoccupies Wordsworth throughout the composition of 'The Recluse' poems but finds its most extended treatment in 'The Tuft of Primroses', especially so in those passages that would eventually find their way into *The Excursion*. While 'To the Clouds' and 'St Paul's' speak of a power that blurs the distinction between peace and war, and that threatens, heretically, to make of the self a deity, 'The Tuft of Primroses' attempts to shield itself from the impulse to self-extinction by choosing, as its agent of peace, an object in nature. A hardy perennial, the primrose undergoes death, but is 'reviv'd,/And beautiful as ever, like a Queen/Smiling from her imperishable throne' (ll. 7–9), an image that recalls the 'throne/Of quietness', set 'Upon a primrose bank' on which Emily is seated, 'like a Virgin Queen', at the close of *The White Doe of Rylstone*,[29] a figure of peaceful endurance, rather than enduring peace, to which I return in the next chapter. As an emblem of beauty, embracing transience as a function of permanence, the primrose offers a way for peace to be decoupled from the deathly stasis of the sublime. Described as 'frail' (l. 11), the plant's location in the 'bosom of this barren crag' (l. 6) nonetheless ensures that it can bloom in 'solitary [...] splendour', unmolested by the depredations of time and change. As the verse unfolds, however, this first impression becomes strained. Recalling the effect of the missing swans in 'Home at Grasmere', the loss of the ash, sycamore, and fir trees in Bainriggs, cut down in the interests of improvement, comes as a shock to the poet. The sight of a few, straggling survivors, left to mourn their 'fellows gone' in 'blanc and monumental grief' (ll. 99–100), suggests once again that the idealised peace of nature, expressed through ideas of species survival, is, when individuals are considered, vulnerable to violent alterations. The thought that imbues the trees with personal identity thus results in the return of that consciousness of death that absorption in the life of nature had promised to allay.

In the lines that follow, Wordsworth works hard to mitigate the effects of the shock of mortality through the invocation of Christian consolation, but the Grasmere steeple that oversees the 'changes of this peaceful Vale' (l. 129) is 'naked and forlorn' (l. 126) and is personified as an injured body observing the 'profanation' and 'despoil' of 'fairest things' (ll. 133–4). Here, in a passage echoing the architectural sympathies of 'The Ruined Cottage', the sad decline of the Sympsons and their cottage is described, its roof 'Laid open to the glare of common day' (l. 143). The account of the garden's descent into wilderness unsurprisingly raises thoughts in the poet of those 'works' (l. 203) that, made for pleasure and as a shelter from the ravages of time, sink into disuse and decay, 'self-lost/ In the wild wood, like a neglected image/Or fancy which hath ceased to be recalled' (ll. 218–20). The threat espoused in this lavishly crafted chain of associations is to memory and to the loss of those creations 'Of love and diligence and innocent care' (l. 229) which, 'sullied and disgrac'd', are swallowed by 'a gulf', locked in a 'cave', or blighted by 'perpetual winter' (ll. 230–34). This meta-reflection on the fate of poetry or, more specifically, on the fate of 'The Recluse', juxtaposing images of nurturing and shelter with images of formlessness, obscurity, and unceasing despair, is made all the more acute because of its contrast with the primrose, which remains, unhoused and unnurtured, 'in sacred beauty, without taint/Of injury or decay' (ll. 236–7). Would that all life, animate or inanimate, could maintain such constancy.

This thought compels the poet to long for some form of universal protection, a guardian spirit to preserve the beasts of the field and the greenleaved thicket from harm. Yet no sooner have the human ministers of this spirit entered the frame, vowing to protect to maintain a 'Continual and firm peace, from outrage safe/And all annoyance' (ll. 261–2), than, revealed in their mundane role as gamekeepers, the poem is once more open to violent intrusion, embodied in the figure of that 'sovereign' who 'Urges the Chase with clamorous hound and horn' (ll. 262–4), an image that returns, yet again, to the poet's unwitting alignment with the oppressors of nature depicted in 'Hart-leap Well'. Still, the poem cannot give up on its projection of a life of peace, founded on a mandate to defend those forms of beauty in which 'the blissful pleasures live' (l. 271). A strong wish to shield such life may be read in the mountains' 'looks of awe' (l. 272), while a voice from the streams 'pleads, beseeches, and implores' (l. 274). Such fancies are, however, swiftly dismissed as 'vain' (l. 275), condemned along with all the resting places of the heart to 'unrelenting doom' (l. 279), an image that serves to recall the blank abyss into which cottage gardens, human lives, and works of poetry are destined to fall.

The 'Tuft of Primroses' has been read productively as a discontinuous litany of ruined forms and ravaged enclosures that in their failure to present a unified image of peaceful sequestration point to a fundamental irresolution at the heart of the poem itself.[30] However, the seeming disparity between the ruins of Grasmere Vale and the scenes of imperilled monastic seclusion in fourth-century Anatolia and modern-day France with which the verse concludes overlooks the extent to which the poem is informed by Wordsworth's reading in the history of continental monasticism and its influence on the formation of Christian communities in ancient Britain. As Jessica Fay points out, from his reading of Thomas West's *Antiquities of Furness* (1774) Wordsworth would have been aware of the considerable reach of St Basil's teaching and its formative role in the development of Cistercian Houses in England and Wales.[31] The poet's overwhelming grief at the destruction of the Grasmere Churchyard fir-grove may well have suggested thoughts of the vital role played by the ruins of Furness Abbey in providing a focal point for 'local identity and collective memory'.[32] But further still, by highlighting the transnational history of monasticism, and by indicating the extent to which religious retreat in all places and at all times is jeopardised by war, Wordsworth's poem begins to look more coherent than it might first appear.

Seeking 'confirm'd tranquillity [...] quiet and unchanged [...] consistent in self rule' (ll. 303–7), the poem dwells for a time on the life of the hermit, 'craving peace' (l. 287),

> The central feeling of all happiness,
> Not as a refuge from distress or pain,
> A breathing time, vacation, or truce,
> But for its absolute self, a life of peace,
> Stability without regret or fear,
> That hath been, is, and shall be ever more. (ll. 288–93)

Here, inspired by a reading of William Cave's life of St Basil of Pontus (1716), Wordsworth entertains a vision of perfect calm, a mountain haven protected from violence by castellated natural forms.[33] Surveying an 'enduring paradise' (l. 362) of herbs, trees, and flowers, Basil is removed from history, unconcerned by the blasting or decay of worldly empires, enjoying precisely the 'refuge from distress or pain' that, only a few lines earlier, Wordsworth had dismissed as motivation for the hermit's retreat from society. Significantly, Cave's biography includes among its early examples of the beneficence experienced in Pontus an account of how God, to 'gratifie his Servants with Delicacies', directs a herd of deer to 'voluntarily' offer 'themselves to the Knife'.[34] The problem of inter-species violence is thus happily expunged. In addition to addressing the destructive urgings of 'Hart-leap Well', the story speaks concertedly of how, in a life informed by works of grace, nature is no longer abused by the economics of survival. As willing sacrifices, rather than as natural resources, the deer are given freely, with no price on their head, with no expectation of return, and, miraculously, without aggressivity. Commenting on Wordsworth's representation of the superabundance of Pontus, Simon Jarvis observes that the poem announces the possibility of 'a different life', a world in which 'the central feeling of happiness' is not bound up with the instrumental life of getting and spending but, like 'the fruits that hang/In the primeval woods', is granted 'freely' and 'Ungrudgingly' (ll. 423–7). In recollection of the daisy's apostolic function, the Pontic monks inhabit the time in which 'hope and memory are as one' (l. 305), enabling them to live a life that is 'quiet and unchanged' (l. 306), a life of peace in which the 'present is continually animated by past and future, hope and memory', rather than cynically voided by calculations of economic worth.[35] The claims to ownership that bedevilled the peace of 'Home at Grasmere' thus no longer apply in Pontus. 'Disturb'd by no vicissitudes' of profit and loss, 'unscarred/By civil faction' (ll. 373–4), beatific pleasure transcends the melancholy dirge of modernity, creating a form of unalienated, uncontested 'common life' (l. 464), 'More beautiful than any [...] hitherto [...] conceived', that shines 'through many an age,/In bright remembrance, like a shining cloud' (ll. 466–73).

Were this vision to have entered the public realm, it is tempting to imagine that it might have been taken as a resounding affirmation of the good life, or more specifically of how peace could be attained by rejecting 'the Glory, the Pomps, Plenty, Grandeur, Luxuries and Pleasures' of the world.[36] But it is more likely that the endorsement of dispossession, inspired by Basil's ambition to 'possess nothing', would have been rejected as proof of seditionary intent or, less grandly, as mere whimsy.[37] Perhaps unsurprisingly, therefore, the description of Basil's influence on the world breaks off, and with it the utopianism of a life free from the effects of violent competition. We will see in Chapters 2 and 4 how, in *The White Doe of Rylstone*, *Peter Bell*, and *The Waggoner*, Wordsworth's earlier indications of the peaceable life were presented to and received by a sceptical post-war public, but to conclude this discussion I want to return to the question of how in 'The Tuft of Primroses' the dream of ascetic retirement survives as a ghostly trace in the sacred ruins of the world, made 'glorious in decay' (l. 493).

Surveying the wreckage of Tintern Abbey and Fountains Abbey, some echo of Basil's teaching outlives 'the ravages of time' (l. 495), but the vulnerability of these mortal forms to 'troubled thoughts or vain desire', to 'perishable bliss' and 'fond regrets' (ll. 501–7; *passim*), underscores the extent to which dreams of enduring peace remain open to the vagaries of history. When read in the light of the poem's faint assertions of the survival of peace in ecclesiastical ruin, the abrupt shift in the manuscript to an account of the occupation of the Grande Chartreuse by French revolutionary soldiers in 1792 is not as jarring as it might first seem. As initially recounted in *Descriptive Sketches* (1793), the desecration of the Carthusian monastery is experienced as an all-encompassing disaster, startling the cloister with 'gleam of arms' (l. 60), prompting the angler to swell 'the groaning torrent with his tears' (l. 67), forcing 'screams' from 'the frighted jay' (l. 68) as demons mock with 'hideous laughter' the cross 'by angels planted on the aëreal rock' (ll. 70–1).[38] Even though the French occupation is formally decried, the apocalyptic and millennial imaginings that resound throughout the poem tend to muddy its striving for ideological clarity, confusing irreparably those 'ideas of morality' that the war for peace, as the contemporaneous Llandaff letter makes clear, inadvertently suspends (*Prose* I. 33).

The struggle to maintain a vision of universal peace, an end founded in and advanced by enmity yet somehow uncontaminated by such means, is evident at the close of *Descriptive Sketches* when, in a continuation of the earlier account of a landscape convulsed by apocalyptic presumptions of death and renewal, allusions to Virgil's fourth eclogue, the Gospel of St Peter, and the Book of Revelation coalesce to inform a description of the millennial transformation of the earth following the triumph of 'Liberty' (l. 774) over 'Pride's perverted ire' (l. 780). Signalled by the 'dull undying roar' (l. 779) of a 'lonely cannon' (l. 776), the war that would establish peace engulfs the land in hellish fire, yet from these 'innocuous flames' arises 'another earth' (l. 783). Attempting to salvage some principle of restoration from the collapse of the Revolution into despotism and terror, Wordsworth surveys the global conflict from a divine perspective, seeming to regard its ultimate end, the 'virgin reign' (l. 784) of Love, Truth, and Justice, as an end sufficient to justify the means. The means by which futurity diminishes the horrors of the present is advanced still further by a prayerful appeal: 'Oh give, great God, to Freedom's waves to ride/Sublime o'er Conquest, Avarice, and Pride,/To break, the vales where Death with Famine scowr's,/And dark Oppression builds her thick ribb'd tow'rs' (ll. 792–5). But while these lines look forward to the triumph of eternal peace, the poem's conclusion, with its allusion to the sorrowful end of *Paradise Lost* ('To night, my friend, within this humble cot/Be the dead load of mortal ills forgot,/Renewing, when the rosy summits glow/At morn, our various journey, sad and slow', ll. 810–13), is a reminder that deliverance from poverty, injustice, and war belongs to a time that is yet to come.

That the most compelling passages in *Descriptive Sketches* relate to its portrayals of destruction raises the suspicion that the poet derives more than a little satisfaction from the conflation of pagan and Judeo-Christian imaginings of the apocalypse, enough at least to inflect the vision of millennial concord with recollections of the discord and division it would ideally transcend. Although muted in 'The Tuft of Primroses', the account of the expulsion of the monks from the Grande Chartreuse nonetheless causes a return of the despondency that dogged Wordsworth following the collapse of the French Revolution and that would blight his attempts to reanimate that 'glorious dawn' as a peaceable, poetic revolution. Seeking again for a principle that would halt the wanton destruction of human and non-human life, the poet invokes the voice of Nature who, seated on an 'Alpine throne' (l. 537), in emulation of the lowly Primrose's throne, implores mankind to '"leave in quiet this embodied dream,/This substance by which mortal men hath clothed,/[...] the ghostliness of things,/In silence visible"' (l. 538–41). More so than the endorsement of 'nature's pure religion' (l. 499), the powerfully resonant '"ghostliness of things"', together with the strangely distorted Miltonic allusion '"silence visible"' (the inverse of 'blinder vacancy'), comes close to capturing the sense in which intimations of peace might, at last, be detectable in forms of oxymoronic and synesthetic violence, illogical figures that, in pushing the limits of the sayable, provide a home for the constitutional opposition that is at the heart of life.

Such hope for peace is, however, swiftly dissipated. Looking to correct the approval of revolutionary violence that forms the climactic core of *Descriptive Sketches*, the voice of Nature urges 'new-born liberty' (l. 546) to 'spare/This House' (ll. 551–2) so that 'Heaven-descended truth' (l. 569) may endure. Nevertheless, as the qualifying formulations and fragmented declarations that follow this pronouncement confirm ('I heard, or seem'd to hear'; '"if past and present be the wings"'; 'Such repetition of that [ ]/My thoughts demanded', ll. 544–68; *passim*), perpetual peace exceeds architectural and verbal incarnation alike. Whatever hope for peace on earth was glimpsed in the poem's previous accommodation of oxymoronic violence appears now to have vanished.

'The Tuft of Primroses' does, however, attempt one final time to locate a home for peace: a '[?lowly] Edifice' (l. 585) inhabited by 'female Votaries' (l. 572), set at a remove from the 'Sublime' (l. 580) arches and towers of the Grande Chartreuse. But, like the frail tents of 'Home at Grasmere' that, operating under the sign of the beautiful, provide temporary shelter from that 'gulf' which 'renders nothing back' (ll. 230–1), the coenobitic dwelling, reminiscent of the Symonds's 'happy House' (l. 149) and, by inference, of Dove Cottage, from which the Wordsworths moved in May 1808, not long after composition was resumed on 'The Recluse', can 'screen and hide' (l. 588) but not protect its inhabitants from the threat of dissolution.[39] Condemned to repeat the same, sad story, a melancholy round of peaceable domains blighted by sickness, poverty, environmental damage, and war that, in their ruin, offer wraithlike intimations of eternal peace, the poem stumbles to a desultory halt. Like St Basil, prompted by 'urgent summons' to leave 'the heavenly Mount' to take up 'a station of authority and power' (ll. 459–61), Wordsworth abandons his poem, discovering in the ill-fated Convention of Cintra an instance of an ignoble and iniquitous cessation of hostilities sufficient to call into question the desirability as well as the possibility of seeking to establish the 'life of peace' that 'hath been, is, and shall be ever more'.

Towards a Community of War: *Concerning the Convention of Cintra*

On 21 August 1808, the British army, under the command of General Arthur Wellesley, attained a decisive victory over the French forces, led by Major-General Junot, at Vimiero in Portugal. Whereas in one sense the victory marked a turning point in the war against Napoleon, in another, the terms on which the French retreat was brokered, widely denounced at the time for their leniency, allowed France to continue its campaign in the Peninsula, leading to the evacuation of General Moore's forces at Corunna in January 1809 and the second invasion of Portugal the following year. Published in May 1809, *Concerning the Relations of Great Britain, Spain, and Portugal, to Each Other, and to the Common Enemy, at This Crisis and Specifically as Affected by the Convention of Cintra: The Whole Brought to the Test of Those Principles, by Which Alone the Independence and Freedom of Nations Can Be Preserved or Recovered*, to give Wordsworth's tract its full, unwieldly title, undertakes a point-by-point analysis of the treaty's numerous shortcomings while negotiating a complex dialogue between neo-Burkean conservatism and radical enlightenment republicanism. As Richard Gravil, David Bromwich, Timothy Michael, and other readers of the *Convention of Cintra* have noted, the tract's 'curious blend of exhortations – "at once republican, nationalist, and cosmopolitan"',[40] highlights the extent to which Wordsworth's observations on British mismanagement in the Peninsula War manifested an internal conflict, one that turns, for our purposes, on the efforts of the Imagination, conceived as the nation's 'inward mind', to transform martial passions into 'instruments of nobler use', raising them 'to a conformity with things truly divine' (2662–8), so that war may be pursued in the interests of peace.[41]

That, ultimately, the national imaginary should be willing to act in conformity with the divine, even to the point of extinction, is implicit in Wordsworth's reasoning but is made clear in his denunciation of that 'specious sensibility, which may encourage the hoarding up of life for its own sake, seducing us from those considerations by which we might learn when it ought to be resigned' (1300–2). Recalling Wordsworth's reservations concerning the political and economic expediency of the Peace of Amiens, the identification of 'life for its own sake' with commercial self-interest and self-preservation becomes shorthand for the moral failings of the Convention; in what amounts to a nihilistic advancement on the radical otherworldliness of Pontus, a nation maintaining steadfast adherence to transcendental principles cares not for temporary relief from danger, still less for life conceived as capital accumulation, but will pursue its aims, buoyed by the conviction of heavenly satisfaction, to the very end; indeed, as the actions of the Spanish people display, contempt for national safety may well be a condition of national identity:

> Riddance, mere riddance—safety, mere safety—are objects far too defined, too inert and passive in their own nature, to have ability either to rouze or to sustain. They win not the mind by any attraction of grandeur or sublime delight, either in effort or in endurance: for the mind gains consciousness of its strength to undergo only by exercise among materials which admit the impression of its power,—which grow under it, which bend under it,—which resist,—which change under its influence,— which alter either through its might or in its presence, by it or before it. (2510–18)

Echoing Burke's thoughts on the analogy between the experience of the sublime and the pains of physical labour ('The best remedy for [the evils of languor, melancholy, and despair] is exercise or *labour*; and labour is a surmounting of *difficulties*, an exertion of the contracting power of the muscles'),[42] Wordsworth identifies war with the effort to attain self-completion, conveyed through a series of ringing repetitions that mimic the striving of the body to control and contain external energies. Though redolent of Spinozian *conatus*, and with traces too of Aristotelian *energeia* or 'being-at-work',[43] the drive towards completion is such that it cannot admit of the possibility that mind might itself be a material that is shaped and informed by opposing forces. Moreover, what cannot be entertained in this scenario is the possibility that the nation, as home, might labour to the point where weakness, diffusion, and indifference are embraced, ending forever the exclusionary logic on which identity is predicated.

In addition to its work on the mind–body relationship, Wordsworth's wartime ontology extends to the consideration of time. While, during times of tranquillity, attention focusses on the present and the past, that is, 'to the self which is or has been', in a state of tension 'the vigour of the human soul is from without and from futurity' (2529–30). The mind that attains self-consciousness by acting on the malleable things of the world is, of course, a mind guided by Imagination, that 'word of higher import, denoting operations of the mind upon [external] objects'.[44] Most importantly, through this act of material transformation, the nation is relieved of those fanciful impulses that would 'quicken and beguile the temporal part of our Nature' and is directed instead to those imaginative values that 'incite' and 'support the eternal'.[45]

As the tract's opening paragraphs illustrate, a nation that loses sight of such values becomes mired in a 'conflict of sensations' (9); beset, in the midst of the 'congratulation and joy' (13) that greeted the Cintra declaration, by 'an under-expression which was strange, dark, and mysterious – and, accordingly as different notions prevailed, or the object was looked at in different points of view, we were astonished like men who are overwhelmed without forewarning – fearful like men who feel themselves to be helpless, and indignant and angry like men who are betrayed' (17–22). In Wordsworth's retelling, the Cintra affair becomes the occasion for a tempering of those emotional extremes which become prevalent during wartime, recalling that state of astonishment that, in Burke's consideration 'Of the passion caused by the SUBLIME', so fills the mind with horror that it is unable to reason on that object which overwhelms it.[46] Thus oppressed, the nation veers from 'a sedate and stern melancholy, which had no sunshine and was exhilarated only by the lightnings of indignation' (123–4) to a state of fervour, prompted by 'the rising of the people of the Pyrenean peninsula' (127). But if, 'from that moment', the British attitude to the contest regained its 'dignity', the change must be attributed to the 'revelation' of that 'state of being that admits not of decay or change, to the concerns and interests of our transitory planet, from that moment "this corruptible put on incorruption, and this mortal put on immortality"' (128–33). The closing quotation from 1 Corinthians 15.53 is oriented to the moment when, at the sounding of the last trumpet, 'Death is swallowed up in victory' (15.54) – in other words, to the moment in which a nation, assured of the triumph of life over death, may regain its sense of 'inward liberty and choice' (135).

The status of knowledge, as Timothy Michael points out, is of central importance to the philosophical work of the Cintra tract.[47] Conceding the role of observational knowledge in determining the war's *Realpolitik*, Wordsworth is eager no less to uphold the primacy of that immutable, a priori knowledge that allows the nation to transform the contingent horrors of war into an object of reason. In stark contrast to that exemplar of the military spirit, Napoleon, whose 'domain of knowledge is narrow' (2764), it is the 'spacious range of the disinterested imagination' (3012) that grants access to that 'higher knowledge' (3009) on which lasting peace is secured. Better to fight in the service of this knowledge than to settle for that phony peace in which, motivated by 'calculations of presumptuous Expediency' (3734), the 'discriminating powers of the mind' are reduced to 'a state of almost savage torpor'.[48] If soldiers and statesmen should be guided by experiential knowledge, moving from the observation of things to ideas, their knowledge, in turn, should be subsumed by that eternal knowledge, which the philosopher and poet, unconstrained by material concerns, bear with them as their own.

As the tract progresses, sentence structure imitates the volatile and protracted nature of the campaign in the Peninsular, rendering the management of the nation's emotional engagement with the war a matter of formal, aesthetic control:

> The history of all ages; tumults after tumults; wars, foreign or civil, with short or with no breathing-spaces, from generation to generation; wars—why and wherefore? yet with courage, with perseverance, with self-sacrifice, with enthusiasm—with cruelty driving forward the cruel man from its own terrible nakedness, and attracting the more benign by the accompaniment of some shadow which seems to sanctify it; the senseless weaving and interweaving of factions—vanishing and reviving and piercing each other like the Northern Lights; public commotions, and those in the bosom of the individual; the long calenture to which the Lover is subject; the blast, like the blast of the desert, which sweeps perennially through a frightful solitude of its own making in the mind of the Gamester; the slowly quickening but ever quickening descent of appetite down which the Miser is propelled; the agony and cleaving oppression of grief; the ghost-like hauntings of shame; the incubus of revenge; the life-distemper of ambition;—these inward existences, and the visible and familiar occurrences of daily life in every town and village; the patient curiosity and contagious acclamations of the multitude in the streets of the city and within the walls of the theatre; a procession, or a rural dance; a hunting, or a horse-race; a flood, or a fire; rejoicing and ringing of bells for an unexpected gift of good fortune, or the coming of a foolish heir to his estate; these demonstrate incontestably that the passions of men (I mean, the soul of sensibility in the heart of man)—in all quarrels, in all contests, in all quests, in all delights, in all employments which are either sought by

men or thrust upon them—do immeasurably transcend their objects. The true sorrow of humanity consists in this;—not that the mind of man fails, but that the course and demands of action and of life so rarely correspond with the dignity and intensity of human desires. (4205–30)

Wordsworth's point here is to draw attention to the existence of an 'object of love and of hatred' (4195–6) adequate to the spiritual demands of the Spanish people, an object born out of foreign military 'Oppression' (4193) that, by way of contrast to the flow of everyday private and public, petty and grand, dissatisfactions, itemised in the passage with such intricate and exhaustive relish, testifies to a unique alignment of actions and desires. But, as well as drawing attention to the moral qualities of the Spanish resistance to French imperialism, the passage serves a more general purpose. Here, in a demonstration of how disparate passions, once guided by Imagination, submit to the control of a higher principle, the reader, initially overwhelmed by the accumulation of subordinate clauses and parentheses, 'with short or with no breathing-spaces', can transcend, manage, and contain the rising tide of feeling. Such, according to Wordsworth, is the state of mind, itself immune to change, best suited to control the affective chaos brought on by war.

The martial sublime advanced in the Cintra tract bears the imprint of Wordsworth's desire to establish himself within a bardic tradition. Horace, Virgil, Milton, and Shakespeare are the most frequently quoted precursors in this tradition, but it is Burke who stands as its guiding light, providing silent authority for the tract's concluding assertion: 'There is a spiritual community binding together the living and the dead; the good, the brave, and the wise, of all ages' (4235–7). Crucially, the 'higher mode of being' (4284) that unites a people during wartime, and that enables them to withstand and overmaster the conflict of sensations – melancholy, fear, wrath, grief, and shame – 'does not exclude, but necessarily includes, the lower […] the sentient […] and the animal' (4285–7). All life, that is, becomes the pliant material of Imagination, a weaponised faculty acting in the service of a people 'encouraged to deem themselves an army, embodied under the authority of their country and of human nature' (359–61). Maintaining a balance between the competing claims of 'the civic and military spirit' (375–6) – the former tending to lassitude, the latter to senseless destruction – presents a challenge, however, and while Wordsworth is keen to embolden the British in their attitude to the war, he is concerned, at the same time, not 'to trust too exclusively to the violent passions' (380–1). Such passions may be useful in times of war but, unless governed by 'contemplative reason' (2655), risk corroding the principles of eternal justice and divine love on which a nation should, ideally, be founded. Notably, Wordsworth makes no appeal in this discussion to politics as a means of tempering the violent passions; indeed, as the unlawful actions of the French imperial forces confirm, the unholy alliance of political and military force is precisely what is at issue insofar as it places the French outside that imagined 'community of war' (1378) in which, unfettered by worldly concerns, a nation, undergirded by civic virtue, realises its identity.[49]

Writing in 1811 to Captain (later Sir) Charles Pasley, the friend of Coleridge and author of *The Military Policy and Institutions of the British Empire*, a lengthy essay published the previous year that was greeted with a surprising degree of popular attention, Wordsworth develops this notion further, directing Pasley to a key formulation from the Cintra tract: 'On the moral qualities of a people must its salvation ultimately depend. Something higher than military excellence must be taught *as* higher; something more fundamental, *as* more fundamental' (*MY* I. 479). Concerned by Pasley's support for an aggressive policy of 'conquest permanently established on the Continent' (478), a policy that, as the letter makes clear, would have dire economic, social, and moral consequences for the British people, Wordsworth provides a model for the establishment of national identity that, even as it accepts perpetual enmity, regards the antagonistic other not as a force to be annihilated but as a necessary check on the desire for unlimited territorial expansion:

> Woe be to that country whose military power is irresistible! [...] If a nation have nothing to oppose or to fear without, it cannot escape decay and concussion within. Universal triumph and absolute security soon betray a State into abandonment of that discipline, civil and military, by which its victories were secured. If the time should ever come when this Island shall have no more formidable enemies by land than it has at this moment by sea, the extinction of all that it previously contained of good and great would soon follow. Indefinite progress, undoubtedly, there ought to be somewhere; but let that be in knowledge, in science, in civilization, in the increase of the numbers of the people, and in the augmentation of their virtue and happiness; but progress in conquest cannot be indefinite [...] (*MY* I. 480)

Wordsworth's 'prayer, as a Patriot, is, that we may always have, somewhere or other, enemies capable of resisting us, and keeping us at arm's length' (480). The nation, that is, is prevented from self-destruction precisely as a result of the boundary confirming the existence of its closest opponents.

A telling irony of Wordsworth's letter to Pasley is its treatment of the aesthetic. While the letter begins with some wry criticism of the first part of Pasley's essay, which, by adopting the techniques 'of a Poet or novelist, who deepens the distress in the earlier part of his work, in order that the happy catastrophe which he has prepared for his heroine or hero', works 'to frighten the People into exertion' (474) rather than persuade them by rational means, the check on the martial spirit that Wordsworth proposes at the letter's conclusion turns unashamedly to the creative faculty that Wordsworth would go on to locate as the cornerstone of his poetic practice in the 1815 preface:

> England, as well as the rest of Europe, requires [...] a new course of education, a higher tone of moral feeling, more of the grandeur of the imaginative faculties, and less of the petty processes of the unfeeling and purblind understanding, that would manage the concerns of the nations in the same calculating spirit with which it would set about building a house. (481)

Finally, and with imperious certitude, the letter makes its prioritising of the role of the artistic spirit in guiding and supporting political affairs abundantly clear:

> Now a State ought to be governed (at least in these times)—the labours of the statesman ought to advance—upon calculations and impulses similar to those which give motion to the hand of a great Artist when he is preparing a picture, or of a mighty Poet when he is determining the proportions and march of a Poem. Much is to be done by rule; the great outline is previously to be conceived in distinctness, but the consummation of the work must be trusted to resources that are not tangible, though known to exist. (481–2)

Nations and poems alike draw on the intangible resources of the Imagination, and while the 'power' of a military force 'is a visible thing,/Formal, and circumscribed in time and space', the element on which it draws is as 'indefinite' as the object of religion. Hence, in his enthusiastic defence of the Spanish juntas, Wordsworth sidesteps some of the more unsettling implications of his subsequent lyric defences of guerrilla warfare, by ensuring that the 'military spirit', which, echoing Longinus's exemplar of the natural sublime, spreads 'like the Nile over the whole face of the land', is kept in check through union with a '*civic* spirit' (361–5; emphasis in original).

Still, the potential for spirits to decouple from their material coordinates remains a problem for Wordsworth. So much so that by the end of the tract mere civic power alone cannot be relied on to resist the politicisation of the sublime. As exemplified by the illimitable 'wickedness' of Napoleon (3286–7), 'sublime and disinterested feelings' (4275), once detached from 'the ground-nest in which they were fostered' (4268–9), are apt to soar into chill regions of ideation, ultimately to return as disfigured and destructive versions of their former promise. Turning to a figure of the beautiful to contain the aberrant energies of the sublime, the tract conjectures an 'all-embracing circle of benevolence' (4270), in which web-like filaments bind the 'higher mode of being' with 'the lower' (4284–5) to prevent the flight into abstraction. Neither the politician nor the soldier can be relied on to 'feed and uphold "the bright consummate flower"' of 'National Happiness' (4288–90); that task belongs to the poet, to one who, like Milton, Petrarch, or, indeed, Wordsworth, is 'retired for wider compass of eye-sight, that he might see in just proportions and relations; knowing above all that he, who hath not first made himself master of his own mind, must look beyond it only to be deceived' (4354–7). As Theresa Kelley has pointed out, Wordsworth's endorsement of the poet's wider compass folds imperceptibly into recognition of the necessity of placing a limit on the powers of the visionary imagination.[50] It is to the exploration of the necessity of self-limitation, as well as to the recollection of those selfless impulses on which the radical ideal of lasting, international peace was founded, that Wordsworth turns next.

Losing Hope in *The Excursion*

The corrective to the fanciful yearning for perpetual peace that Wordsworth encounters in the 1808 fragments, and that the Cintra tract and Pasley letter build into a formal critique of Britain's military policy, culminates with *The Excursion*. Published within weeks of the signing of the Treaty of Paris on 30 May 1814, *The Excursion* entered a cultural sphere torn between feelings of relief at the end of hostilities and uncertainty over the terms and conditions of the peace settlement. Hazlitt's essay 'On the Late War', which appeared in *The Champion* on 3 April on the eve of Napoleon's conditional abdication to the Coalition sovereigns, provides a taste of the fractious political climate that greeted the poem. Responding to Stoddart's attack on the '*Peace-Faction*' in *The Times* and his support for a policy of unbridled conquest, Hazlitt announces that as 'the war with [the Pitt-school] was a war of extermination, so the peace, not to fix a lasting stigma on their school and principles, must be a peace of extermination' (*CWWH* VII. 72). In the same month Dorothy writes that the peace, though welcome, 'is like a dream'. Frustrated, like Stoddart, by the lack of a decisive finale to the conflict and the resultant air of unreality she wishes that the allies had put Napoleon to death while her brother declares himself to be a member of the '*War-faction*', as if in response to Hazlitt's gloomy prognosis of the war's conflicted aftermath.

A concern with the establishment of boundaries between dreams and reality, schools and factions, negotiated conclusions and violent termini seems, then, to characterise the climate in which Wordsworth's poem was first received. Once the war is over, and voices in authority have delineated the contours of the real, we find Hazlitt refusing to accept the terms on which these contours have been set. The post-war dream state may be over, seemingly dispelled forever if not through a 'peace of extermination' then through a re-imposition of the *ancien régime*; but for Hazlitt another kind of dream persists, one that 'will never cease, nor be prevented from returning on the wings of imagination to that bright dream of our youth':

> that glad dawn of the day-star of liberty; that spring-time of the world, in which the hopes and expectations of the human race seemed opening in the same gay career with our own; when France called her children to partake her equal blessings beneath her laughing skies; when the stranger was met in all her villages with dance and festive songs, in celebration of a new and golden era; and when, to the retired and contemplative student, the prospects of human happiness and glory were seen ascending like the steps of Jacob's ladder, in bright and never-ending succession. (*CWWH* XIX. 18)

Hazlitt is responding to Wordsworth's portrayal of the Solitary, but he might as well be recalling the poet's first impressions of revolutionary France, as recounted in Book 6 of *The Prelude*. Though the 'season of hope is past', the Revolution has left behind 'traces, which are not to be effaced by Birth-day and Thanksgiving odes, or the chaunting of *Te Deums* in all the churches of Christendom' (*CWWH* XIX. 18). Slightly revised in 1817 to take account of Wordsworth's and Southey's post-Waterloo encomiums, Hazlitt's review of *The Excursion* casts doubts on the poem's ability to discover in Tory paternalism and Anglicanism a salve for the despair brought on by the demise of the Solitary's early, revolutionary hopes. But more to the point, Hazlitt's affirmation of the ineradicable nature of those 'traces', which, as I go on to show, emerge literally in the poem as remnants from earlier work, may be read as a refusal of post-revolutionary despair and therefore as a denial of the need for the programme of conservative rehabilitation enacted in Wordsworth's poem.

A former army chaplain, the Solitary is well versed in the business of war. It is possible that Wordsworth included this detail in the Solitary's biography as a subtle allusion to the work of Adam Ferguson, the social philosopher, diplomatist, and sometime chaplain of the Black Watch Highlander Regiment. Best known for his *Essay on the History of Civil Society* (1767), Ferguson shares with Adam Smith a belief in the division of labour as a foundational principle of economic prosperity. Unlike Smith, however, Ferguson emphasised the importance of maintaining social order to check the disruptive effects of capital accumulation. Unsurprisingly, the military, with its emphasis on duty and self-sacrifice, is highly prized by Ferguson; through engaging periodically in conflict with foreign competitors, the philosopher affirms, the nation places a check on economic individualism, dissolving self-interest in the service of a higher cause. Like Wordsworth, Ferguson comes to value the existence of enemy states, arguing that 'he who has never struggled with his fellow-creatures, is a stranger to half the sentiments of mankind'.[51] As a critic of British interference in America, Ferguson is nonetheless concerned to place a limit on the nation's martial activities and, again like Wordsworth, comes to decry the economic, social, and ideological costs of 'distant wars'[52] – a position that is in accord with *The Excursion*'s concluding vision of imperial benevolence, a global hegemony founded on the dissemination of knowledge, piety, and 'virtuous habits' (IX. l. 362) with no mention of the violent enforcement of colonial law.

Having strayed alike from the disciplinary concord of military and religious life, the task of *The Excursion* is directed towards the re-education of the Solitary. Drawing on the resonances of the Latin *conscribere* (to write down together, to enrol), and with a knowing glance towards the levying of French troops in 1798, *The Excursion* aims to conscript the Solitary into its ideological texture, effectively re-writing and, when this technique fails, silencing those revolutionary traces that would reanimate the movement for liberty, equality, and universal peace. How the poem negotiates the path between the death of the French Revolution and its spectral return can be considered in those passages in Book III in which the Solitary reflects on his early hopes for the amelioration of mankind. At the start of this dialogue, in lines adapted from the St Basil episode in 'The Tuft of Primroses', one of many instances of creative recycling from earlier, rejected drafts, the Solitary expresses sympathy with the Epicurean who, 'curtained round/With world-excluding groves' (ll. 353–4), prefers 'Tranquillity to all things' (l. 369). Foregrounding the indulgences of pagan *ataraxia* to qualify the earlier poem's effusion on the virtues of monastic piety, the Solitary is therefore shown, from the outset, to be mistaken in his desire for the establishment of worldly peace. Longing for the 'life where hope and memory are as one', where 'earth is quiet and unchanged' (ll. 406–7), for the time when, as the original version of these lines recalled, the relations between the past and the future were not governed by mercantile calculations of present worth, the Solitary's discourse becomes rapidly clouded, its advocacy of 'a calm/Without vicissitude' (ll. 431–2) racked by 'fear—doubt—and agony' (l. 468) for 'Mutability is Nature's bane' (l. 465). Amid the peaceful vale, the Wanderer discovers the Solitary's weatherworn copy of *Candide*, cast aside as a children's plaything. Voltaire's satire on Leibniz's theodicy of optimism is condemned by the Wanderer as a work 'framed, to ridicule confiding Faith' (IV, l. 1003), but as Sally Bushell suggests, *The Excursion*, though opposed to Voltaire's position, nonetheless maintains sympathy with the Solitary's disillusionment with the Panglossian mantra: all is for the best in the best of all possible worlds.[53] Despite the Wanderer's blithe assurance that mortal life, 'howe'er sad or disturbed', is superintended by a Being 'Whose everlasting purposes embrace/All accidents, converting them to Good' (IV. ll. 13–17), at no stage does the poem diminish the felt experience of individual suffering. Rather, as the Solitary's shifting moods confirm, the poem is accepting of the idea that personal anguish may well turn out to be doggedly resistant to assuasive abstractions.

Falling, like Candide, into despair when his dream of rural tranquillity is shattered, the Solitary is at first restored by the 'prophetic harps' (l. 731) of the French Revolution, which ring out the assurance that '"War shall cease"' (l. 732). Hence 'reconverted to the world' (l. 742), the Solitary's soul is 'diffused' in 'wide embrace/Of institutions, and the forms of things;/As they exist, in mutable array,/Upon life's surface' (ll. 746–9), echoing the process philosophy entertained in Wordsworth's earlier poems of fancy; thus distracted from the negative connotations of mutability, the Solitary experiences, albeit briefly, a release from the pain of self-consciousness that had assailed his previous attempts to make peace with the world. Before too long, however, adhering to the familiar narrative that ascribes the expunction of Liberty and the ensuing Terror to the machinations of a self-interested few, the Solitary recounts the tragic decline of the Revolution, mapping its descent into civil and international conflict onto his experience of internal 'strife' (l. 796). Hence, disturbed by the 'iron bonds/Of military sway' (ll. 829–30) and unable to recover peace amid Europe's 'fields of carnage' and 'polluted air' (l. 842), the Solitary travels to America but, as a result of his disassociated condition, is unable to make a home there. Like the female vagrant, whose baleful experiences in the new world results in a perpetual fugue state, the Solitary is condemned to an undomesticated existence, his cottage displaying 'a wreck' of 'broken' and 'shattered' tools (II. ll. 686–97) as if in intimation of Dürer's *Melancolia I* which, through its display of discarded creative objects, portrays a state of inertia, depression, and lost inspiration.

Detached from community and the 'visible fabric of the World' (III. l. 970), the Solitary stands, then, as an indicator of the limits of hospitality – a remnant of those 'blasted hopes' (l. 841) that the post-war settlement, in its overweening pursuit of peace, stability and continuity, would seek to unhouse. Like Margaret, whose tale of wartime ruin opens *The Excursion*, the Solitary is presented at this stage in the poem as one who, having relinquished 'all/We have, or hope, of happiness and joy' (IV. l. 133), has become detached alike from the transient pleasures of 'this unstable world' (l. 157) and the assurance of 'that state/Of pure, imperishable, blessedness,/Which Reason promises, and holy Writ/Ensures to all Believers' (ll. 158–61).[54] Seeking to retrieve grounds for hope while acknowledging with a recollection of Margaret's 'torturing hope' (I. 913) how 'overconstant yearning' (IV. l. 176) for 'what is lost' (l. 172) disrupts the passage of time, rooting the afflicted self to an object cast out of history, the Wanderer, 'speaking now from such disorder free,/Nor rapt, nor craving, but in settled peace' (ll. 185–6), endeavours to instil in his despondent friend a sense of how 'limitless desires' (l. 184) must accede to the limits of the flesh. Once self-limitation is accepted, the Wanderer maintains, the one who grieves will find 'Repose and hope among eternal things' (l. 63). As noted above, the Solitary may be moved by such wise counsel, yet remains stubbornly attached to the memory of history's lost causes. Out of melancholic fealty to that most recent lost cause, the French Revolution, the Solitary's hopelessness stands in the poem as a profane riposte to those who, like the Wanderer, would hope for the return of a 'sacred Spirit' (l. 319) to deliver the world from 'Tartarean darkness' (l. 298). Giving up on hope, which, as the Wanderer's discourse betrays, is founded on the opposition between the broken world and the recovered world that is to come, does not mean abandoning hope per se but rather embracing the possibility of negation on which hope is founded. Echoing Spinoza's account of the relationship between hope and uncertainty ('Hope is an inconstant joy, born of the idea of a future [...] whose outcome we to some extent doubt'),[55] while also looking forward to Quentin Meillassoux's understanding of hope as 'a gift of the just made across time',[56] the Solitary's despair for the salvation of the world paradoxically paves the way for its deliverance, allowing for the possibility of new forms of life and new forms of community that, even if they cannot be foreseen, can yet be imagined. Such, at least, is the hopeful despair, as well as the despairing hope that Hazlitt discovers in Wordsworth's poem, a fractured hope arising from and oriented towards the 'wreck' we 'have around us' (II. ll. 686–7).

To reach this point, however, is no easy task; indeed, to all intents and purposes *The Excursion* works to resist such an unorthodox position, as one might expect given the poem's perceived political and religious conservatism. True enough, peace is postulated as the redemptive horizon of the Wanderer's prayer, but the distinction between mortal inadequacy and divine perfection on which this prayer is offered shows that opposition and separation will not be replaced by the awareness of an irreparable belonging anytime soon.[57] The orientation to a realm of deferred tranquillity, from which derives the sense of the world as alienated and incomplete, aligns *The Excursion* with the ontological violence of the Cintra pamphlet and the letter to Pasley, rendering questionable the hope for peace in these times or, indeed, for any conceivable time. For Wordsworth, as the course of the poem makes clear, the wish to revive the pacific aspirations of the Revolution runs up against the surety that 'confidence in social Man' (IV. l. 262) cannot be sustained in a world fundamentally riven by discord and whose only hope of salvation resides in the hope of a better world to come.

That, by the poem's close, the Solitary should remain mute in the face of the Wanderer's impassioned defence of Britain's imperial destiny – 'Now, when destruction is a prime pursuit,/Show to the wretched Nations for what end/The Powers of civil Polity were given' (IX. ll. 415–17) – signals how concertedly Wordsworth intended *The Excursion* to serve as a rejoinder to the mordant prognostications of the peace-faction. The Parson's final words may be read as a direct response to the Solitary's misplaced faith in the Revolution's pacific intent: 'let thy Word prevail [...] to take away/The sting of human nature [...] let every nation hear [...] and every heart obey [...] then, shall persecution cease,/And cruel Wars expire' (IX. ll. 637–50), confirming that 'peaceable dominion' (l. 665) will be attained on earth only when faith, working through love, conquers the 'dire perverseness' (l. 660) of the atheistic experiment. Held up as a victim of this experiment, it is with the Solitary in mind that the poem offers its final, conjectural prayer, the baroque syntax and overfreighted conditionals transforming what seems, at first, to be a confident expression of the Solitary's recovery from historical trauma into a fraught display of epistemological uncertainty:

> To enfeebled Power
> From this communion with uninjured Minds,
> What renovation had been brought; and what
> Degree of healing to a wounded spirit,
> Dejected, and habitually disposed

> To seek, in degradation of the Kind,
> Excuse and solace for her own defects;
> How far these erring notions were reformed;
> And whether aught, of tendency as good
> And pure, from further intercourse ensued;
> This—(if delightful hopes, as heretofore,
> Inspire the serious song, and gentle Hearts
> Cherish, and lofty Minds approve the past)
> My future labours may not leave untold. (IX. ll. 783–95)

As the progression from the past perfect progressive phrasing of 'What renovation had been brought' to the use of the past subjunctive in the Miltonic 'How far these erring notions were reformed' indicates, the extent to which 'communion with uninjured Minds' provides lasting relief to the 'wounded spirit' has yet to be confirmed. Thus, struggling to access the 'central peace, subsisting at the heart/Of endless agitation' (IV. ll. 1140–41), the Solitary appears admonished rather than converted by the exhortations of his interlocuters. However, as silence grants expression to a counter-hegemonic yet ultimately powerless note of scepticism and despair, there is scope no less for the pulsing of an affirmative revolutionary trace, an '*active* principle' that 'subsists/In all things, in all natures', and that has beneficial properties extending beyond itself (IX. ll. 3–20; *passim*). Adapted from the 1798 fragment 'There is an active principle alive in all things', these lines speak to those hopes that 'breathe the sweet air of futurity' (l. 25), to the remembrance of life conceived not as 'An offering, or a sacrifice, a tool/Or implement, a passive Thing employed/As a brute mean' (ll. 116–19), but as a manifestation of that 'Being' who 'moves/In beauty through the world' (ll. 136–7).

While, in his concluding address, the Parson maintains that the Wanderer's affirmation of peace on earth is a 'transitory type' (l. 619) of the 'Imperishable majesty' (l. 630) of 'highest heaven' (l. 621), elsewhere, drawing on an unused passage in 'Home at Grasmere',[58] the Wanderer and the Poet offer visions of an immersive, immanent life, a world in which the antagonistic separation of thought and being, human and non-human, mind and nature has no purchase. In this 'mighty Commonwealth of things' (IV. l. 345) benignity pervades, joining emmets and moles, clouds and flies, rooks and sunbeams in 'social league', united in 'participation of delight/And a strict love of fellowship', discovering in the 'mild assemblage of the starry heavens' and 'the great Sun, earth's universal Lord!' (ll. 429–66; *passim*), the sense of joy in widest commonality spread. Moved by this speech, the Poet responds with a performance of combinative delight, the lines reaching forward, hurried along by a succession of breathless connectives and associative fancies:

> How divine,
> The liberty, for frail, for mortal man
> To roam at large among unpeopled glens
> And mountainous retirements, only trod
> By devious footsteps; regions consecrate
> To oldest time! and, reckless of the storm
> That keeps the raven quiet in her nest,
> Be as a Presence or a Motion—one
> Among the many there; and while the Mists
> Flying, and rainy Vapours, call out Shapes
> And Phantoms from the crags and solid earth
> As fast as a Musician scatters sounds
> Out of an instrument; and while the Streams—
> (As at a first creation and in haste
> To exercise their untried faculties)
> Descending from the regions of the clouds
> And starting from the hollows of the earth
> More multitudinous every moment—rend
> Their way before them, what a joy to roam
> An Equal among mightiest Energies [...] (IV. ll. 513–32)

Read in correspondence with the earlier lines describing the Solitary's disconnection from collective life, and his subsequent inability to recover meaningful relations in a wreck of broken things, the passage portrays a world in which presences and processes, singularities and multitudes, converge and diverge in ceaseless creative flux, a world no longer viewed as disunified or lacking and therefore in need of sovereign control.

Such a vision cannot, of course, be sustained, and the depiction of untrammeled 'multitudinous' life – a passage that appeared originally in an early *Prelude* draft, emphasising how the depiction of vibrant assemblages accords with the poem's palimpsestic form – is checked by the Wanderer who, while seeming to affirm his companion's Shaftesburian 'strain of transport' (l. 539), confirms that such 'noble restlessness' is but an echo of youthful ambition, a congenial recollection of 'the spots which once he gloried in' (l. 546).[59] Thus, whatever vestiges of radical, communitarian thought these speeches conveyed, whether informed by the native British tradition of agrarian republicanism or by Spinozian notions of the ideal commonwealth, is relegated to the past; now, as *The Excursion* draws to its close, the emphasis turns from the celebration of instinctive sociability to a Hobbesian account of the necessity of contractual restraint. Such is the lesson, taught by the *Convention of Cintra*, of how, in the interests of self-preservation, the society of unregulated natural passions must give way to the government of self-control.[60]

***

Writing to Catherine Clarkson in January 1815, Wordsworth, responding to Patty Smith's criticisms of the '*Spinosistic*' passages in *The Excursion*, strenuously denied that he was 'a worshipper of Nature': 'She condemns me for not distinguishing between nature as the work of God and God himself. But where does she find this doctrine inculcated? Where does she gather that the Author of the Excursion looks upon nature and God as the same?' (*MY* II. 188). Wordsworth goes on to declare his belief in God as an immortal and infinite 'spirit', distinguished from mutable 'objects of sense' (189). However, as we have seen, something of those early, pantheistic sentiments persists in *The Excursion*, surpassing the accession to Anglican doctrine that, to the sober-minded poet, marks the limits of the possible. And this may be enough to encourage us to retrieve an impression of the poetry as pacific even when, as we shall discover, the verse speaks most strongly of the brute realities and deviant appeal of destruction. To claim that such feelings persist throughout Wordsworth's career, extending beyond the watershed of 1815, is not to deny that sense of dissociation extending to coldness and insensitivity that is the pervading impression of the later poetry for most readers, but my point here is that Wordsworth's post-war writing is fundamentally contested, capable of holding up to scrutiny a range of mutually contradictory beliefs, thoughts, and feelings. Such a view is borne out by the reactions of contemporary readers to *The Excursion*, the majority of whom, like Hazlitt, responded as much to the poem's radical unorthodoxies as to its alleged conformism. A passage frequently quoted by reviewers is the Wanderer's account of how 'Man's celestial Spirit [...] Sets forth and magnifies herself' by feeding 'A calm, a beautiful, and silent fire,/From the incumbrances of mortal life' (IV. ll. 167–71). Held up by Francis Jeffrey and John Herman Merivale as evidence of its author's 'cabalistic darkness' and 'mysticism',[61] and more charitably, by Charles Lamb as an expression of 'a sort of liberal Quakerism' or 'Natural Methodism',[62] the Wanderer's densely allusive guide to how paradise might be regained in a post-conflict world beset by 'error, disappointment' and 'guilt' (l. 1072) failed to capture the attention of readers drawn, in the long, hot summer of 1814, to the dissolute glamour of Byron's *Lara* and the antique reassurances of Scott's *Waverley*.[63]

Losing Hope in The Excursion

What hope could a poem charting the course of a nation's experience of war, beginning with the despoliation of a war-widow's cottage and ending with the half-hearted rehabilitation of a former revolutionary, offer to a public eager to forget the hardships of the last twenty years? As Lamb intimated, *The Excursion* was just not ready for these times. Writing to Wordsworth in August, Lamb interweaves praise of the poem with passages offering an arresting view of how, in the wake of Napoleon's defeat, Hyde Park had been transformed into a vast outdoor festival, overwhelmed by 'the stench of liquors, *bad* tobacco, dirty people, and provisions'.[64] But while, via a quotation from 'Hart-leap Well', Lamb anticipates the restoration of the park's natural beauty ('At the coming of the *milder* day/These monuments shall all be overgrown'), he delights at the same time in the festival's bacchic deviations, which seem 'like an interval in a campaign, a repose after battle'. Concluding his letter with an appreciation of the 'finer showers of gloomy rain fire that fell sulkily and angrily' from the firework displays in mock imitation of the 'Last Day', Lamb offers the sly assurance that such scenes and such 'triumphs' cannot distract from the 'calm and noble enjoyment' of his friend's poem.[65] For Lamb, the war may be over, but the incumbrances of mortal life continue to feed a zeal for obliteration that makes of the peace a temporary and conflicted affair.

CHAPTER 2

Peace Out of Time
The White Doe of Rylstone

Victories in the World of Spirit

> When it is considered what has already been executed in Poetry, strange that a man cannot perceive, particularly when the present tendencies of society good and bad, are observed, that this is the time when a man of genius may honorably take a station upon different ground. If he is to be a Dramatist, let him crowd his scene with gross and visible action; but if a narrative Poet, if the Poet is to be predominant over the Dramatist,—then let him see if there are no victories in the world of spirit, no changes, no commotions, no revolutions there, no fluxes and refluxes of the thoughts which may be made interesting by modest combination with the stiller actions of the bodily frame, or with the gentler movements and milder appearances of society and social intercourse, or the still more mild and gentle solicitations of irrational and inanimate nature.
>
> Wordsworth to Coleridge, 19 April 1808 (*MY* I. 222–3)

On 28 June 1815, on the day that news of the Allied victory at Waterloo reached Rydal, Dorothy announced to Catherine Clarkson that *The White Doe of Rylstone* had 'arrived at last' together with an edition of the *Champion* containing a niggardly review of the poem by John Scott (*MY* II. 243).[1] Whether drowned out by triumphalist clamour and the attendant mood of indifference towards works of subtle lyricism and high imagination or by the plain fact of its costliness, outside of the family circle Wordsworth's quarto mostly failed to find an appreciative audience. Considering the poem's long and difficult gestation, and the critical reservations of its initial readers, the unsympathetic reception was perhaps inevitable. In May 1808, Coleridge, responding to Wordsworth's defence of 'victories in the world of spirit' over 'gross and visible action', declared that a lack 'of lively interest, namely, curiosity, and the terror or pity from unusual external Events & Scenes—convent dungeons &c &c' would most likely be an 'obstacle' to the poem's 'popularity'.[2] But it is Lamb's wittily concealed approbation that best conveys the sense of perplexity that greeted the poem's entrance into the world: 'No alderman ever longed after a haunch of buck venison more than I for a Spiritual taste of that white Doe you promise.'[3] By conjoining the appetitive and the contemplative, Lamb's comment highlights the poem's failure to satisfy on either count: for readers expecting a stirring description of the failed Rising of the North of 1569 in the manner of Walter Scott, the poem's lack of incident and adventure was a disappointment; for readers drawn in by the opening descriptions of the mysterious, gentle doe, the sudden shift of focus in Canto 2 to the Norton family and their preparations for the uprising was both disappointing and confusing. That, in contrast to *Waverley*, published the year before to dazzling critical and popular acclaim, the action of *The White Doe* focussed on a rebellion that stopped short of an outright clash of arms, and that it managed, at the same time, to evoke painful recollections of the religious and political divisions that threatened even now, in the aftermath of Napoleon's defeat, to unsettle the establishment of national unanimity, added still further to the poem's lack of accord with contemporary taste and opinion.

Yet, in conception, the poem had been designed to demonstrate how outbreaks of civil strife could be tempered by higher wisdom; as Wordsworth informed Scott, who pointed out that the events depicted in the poem were at odds with historical actuality, the action of *The White Doe* was coloured by the imaginations of 'the people' who, unfettered by the standards of the 'studious', had made of the history a tale of pride checked by providence (*MY* I. 237). In a broad sense, the poem highlighted how wars waged in defiance of the established religious and political order could be surveyed from the perspective of the divine. But this was not the kind of message that a people believing themselves to be released from over two decades of wartime anxiety wished to receive. In the summer of 1815, Britain had secured a decisive victory over its chief antagonist; here was a triumph unparalleled in the history of the world, an event that confirmed the supremacy of Church and State over the forces of atheism and republicanism and that instilled among the people, surely, a sense of peace and unity.[4]

A few years later, in the first of his 'Essays on the Lake School of Poetry' for *Blackwood's Edinburgh Magazine*, John Wilson delineated the respective qualities of Scott, Byron, and Wordsworth, describing them as the 'three great master-spirits of our day'.[5] Though written as a defence of Wordsworth's much-derided poem, Wilson's appraisal of Scott's genius offers a shrewd perspective on just why *The White Doe*, with its combination of metaphorical abstraction, mysticism, and historical narrative, appeared to be so out of sync with the times. In Scott's poems, Wilson writes,

> we feel ourselves hurried from this our civilized age, back into the troubled bosom of semi-barbarous life [...] His poems are historical narrations, true in all things to the spirit of history [...] when it is recollected, that the times in which his scenes are laid and his heroes act were distinguished by many of the most energetic virtues that can grace or dignify the character of a free people, and marked by the operation of great passions and important events, everyone must feel that the poetry of Walter Scott is, in the noblest sense of the world, national; that it breathes upon us the bold and heroic spirit of perturbed but magnificent ages, and connects us, in the midst of philosophy, science, and refinement, with our turbulent but high-minded ancestors, of whom we have no cause to be ashamed, whether looked on in the fields of war or in the halls of peace. He is a true knight in all things,—free, courteous, and brave. War, as he describes it, is a noble game, a kingly pastime. He is the greatest of all War-Poets.[6]

Where Scott succeeded in capturing the attention of the public was in his vivid representations of the heroic passions associated with the noble conflicts of the past. By reviving the spirit of 'old times', Scott's poetry 'prevents History from becoming that which, in times of excessive refinement, it is often too apt to become—a dead letter,—and keeps the animating and heroic spectacles of the past moving brightly across our every-day world, and flashing out from them a kindling power over the actions and characters of our own age'.[7] Wilson, however, is no less attentive to the potential dangers of Scott's poetry, particularly in connection with the arousal of those war-like passions that, in times of peace, ought to be kept within bounds. For readers 'imperiously' demanding 'strong passion and violent excitement' Wordsworth's poem, 'with its gentle lineaments [...] sober colouring [...] and chastened composition', offers 'new and gentle beauties' as conveyed, most touchingly, in the account of the relationship between Emily and the elusive white doe.[8] As well as emphasising the virtue of cultivating a connection between human and non-human, for Wilson the poem is valued chiefly for its study of 'profound sadness, settled grief, the everlasting calm of melancholy, and the perfect stillness of resignation'. In contrast to Scott's poetry of 'turbulent' extremes, in Wordsworth's poem 'looks, words, movements, are gentle, feminine, subdued'.[9] Thus, in its avowedly 'feminine' character, *The White Doe* gives voice, softly and almost imperceptibly, to expressions and sentiments that have no place in the popular discourse of post-war triumphalism. In its focus on the disastrous consequences of 'kingly' ambitions, the destruction of the home, and the elision of natural beauty, the poem speaks of fallings and vanishings that 'Victory Sublime!',[10] as Wordsworth subsequently characterised the Battle of Waterloo, refused to acknowledge.

This chapter builds on Wilson's insight into the gendering of peace in Wordsworth's poem to add a further dimension to the uncertain and often-contested character of the poet's representations of historical violence. In an important essay on *The White Doe*, Peter Manning argues that Wordsworth sought to capitalise on the public taste for epic romance, as evidenced by the popularity of Southey's, Byron's, and Scott's productions in this vein.[11] But while noting Wordsworth's wish to secure a place alongside Byron, Scott, and Southey, we must be alert as well to the ways in which this poem gives voice to those 'gentle, feminine, subdued' emotions that the genre of epic romance, in its bid for cultural dominance, sought to overpower. Much of what I have to say about the depiction of feminine feeling in this poem is connected to Wordsworth's attempt to draw a distinction between Scott's 'customary and very natural course of conducting an action, presenting various turns of fortune, to some outstanding point on which the mind might rest as a termination or catastrophe' and the shift in emphasis in *The White Doe* towards action as a prompt for 'moral and spiritual' reflection,[12] subsequently characterised by Christopher Wordsworth, Jr., as 'the subduing of the will, and all inferior passions, to the perfect purifying and spiritualizing of the intellectual nature'. Just as the doe, 'by connection with Emily, is raised as it were from its mere animal nature into something mysterious and saint-like', so the poem works to purge imagination of its masculinist, materialist, and martial characteristics.[13]

Just a few months prior to the poem's publication Wordsworth had explored, in 'Laodamia', the relations between female virtue and military masculinity. Based on a myth retold and refashioned by, amongst many others, Euripides, Propertius, Catullus, Virgil, and Ovid, the poem recounts the loss of Laodamia's husband, Protesilaus, in the fight against Troy, his brief restoration as a spirit, and his widow's attempts to bring him back to life. Pitting Laodamia's desire for fleshly reunion ('Come, blooming Hero, place thee by my side!/Give, on this well-known couch, one nuptial kiss/To me, this day, a second time thy bride!', ll. 62–4) against the spectre's insistence that earthly passions must be annulled in the service of a higher object, the verse echoes sentiments that Wordsworth had first explored in 'Character of the Happy Warrior'. War, the new poem makes clear, frees the warrior from those 'ignoble games and revelry' (l. 112) that distract from 'lofty thought' (l. 137) and which are identified explicitly with the feminine.¹⁴ Read by Jeffrey Cox as a barbed response to Leigh Hunt's endorsement of love over war in *The Descent of Liberty* (1814), Wordsworth's message to those women whose livelihoods and homes had been blasted by the war against France appears unequivocal: dead soldiers may be mourned but the desire for their return must yield to 'self-government' (l. 140). By way of punishment for her excessive mourning, Laodamia must therefore die. However, as Judith Page notes, Wordsworth, though formally inclined towards the ascetic heroism of Protesilaus, is drawn emotionally to the plight of the grieving widow.¹⁵ Thus, while acting 'in reason's spite', Laodamia is 'yet without crime' (l. 123) and, in a 'trance of passion', is 'Delivered from the galling yoke of time/And these frail elements to gather flowers/Of blissful quiet mid unfading bowers' (ll. 159–63). Disturbed by the poem's unstable moral tone, Wordsworth went on to revise these lines, leaving Laodamia condemned 'as for a wilful crime,/By the just Gods, whom no weak pity moved' to 'wander in a grosser clime,/Apart from happy Ghosts'.¹⁶

I will return to consider the revisions to this poem in the next chapter, but here would note that the fate of the widow raises the question of how grieving femininity should live on in a devastated world. In opposition to Laodamia's unseemly devotion to the flesh – a love of sensual life that links her to those other female victims of war, Margaret and the Female Vagrant – Emily is presented in *The White Doe* as virginal and pure, a bodiless cipher for the impossibility of peace on earth. Her act of mourning – for the loss of her family, but specifically for her brother – although interminable and self-destructive, provides a corrective to Laodamia's overweening grief but has wider implications for how life should continue in the aftermath of war. Wandering as a ghost amid the ruins of Rylstone, Emily, indifferent to the world and with her sights sets on heavenly deliverance, is emblematic of the melancholy of peace: a wounded soul longing for release from a life of unending antagonism. For Page, Emily's fate as a woman excluded from the male-dominated public sphere, and her subsequent religious ascension, is coeval with the implication 'that if violence can neither be understood nor justified, at least it can be transcended in a spiritual realm'.¹⁷ But while Emily's descent into oblivion suggests that neither peace nor womanhood has a place in this world, I would suggest that the great virtue of *The White Doe* resides in its willingness to raise questions about the relations between war, identity, and power.

A clue to how the poem might be read as response to the end of war can be found in the 1815 'Essay, Supplementary to the Preface'. Composed at the same time as Wordsworth was making final revisions to *The White*

Doe, the essay seems, at first, to retrench on the poem's gentler, pacific leanings. As the mention of 'Adversaries', 'hostility', 'attacks', and 'enemies' in the opening sentences of the essay makes clear – a blazon of antagonism inspired, no doubt, by recent criticism of *The Excursion* – forms of militancy cannot be expunged from the relationship between reader and poet (*Prose* III. 62); yet insofar as the reader is called upon to join with the poet in the 'exertion of a co-operating *power*', the triumph of art need not be conceived as a form of hostile takeover (82). Thus, as the poet, like 'Hannibal among the Alps', shapes and clears the road before him, so the reader is 'invigorated and inspired by his Leader' (80). Soon after this declaration, however, Wordsworth moves to cleanse his argument of any lingering traces of militancy. As the 'Essay' goes on to assert, in a pregnant attack on the literary pretensions of Lucien Bonaparte, whose Ossianic (code also for Scott-like) poem *Charlemagne; or, the Church Delivered* (1815) Wordsworth had recently appraised, the epic ambitions of would-be conquerors must be distinguished from the efforts of the 'truly original Poet' to introduce 'a new element into the intellectual universe' (82). In *The White Doe*, the union of poet and reader, 'which owes its being to the struggles it makes' while rejecting the drive towards domination (*Prose* III. 67), finds its analogue in the participatory relationship between Emily and the deer. Founded in beauty and love, this relationship stands as a peaceable alternative to Richard Norton's aggressive devotion to the 'unhallowed Banner' (II. l. 505),[18] and his subsequent 'sublime despair',[19] suggesting that wise passivity, when informed by 'corresponding energy' (*Prose* III. 82), may yet find a place in a conflicted world.[20]

Active and passive, militant and meditative, masculine and feminine, sublime and beautiful, human and non-human, secular and sacred, war and peace, the living and the dead: *The White Doe of Rylstone* is built on conceptual distinctions that cross-fade into each other, generating unexpected correspondences and collisions. In the following reading I trace the ways in which the poem sets out to engage with its internal contradictions, its gestures towards concord unsettled by persistent reminders of the strife it would transcend. Memories of conflict, as I argue throughout this book, shadow the poetry Wordsworth composed in the immediate aftermaths of Waterloo and Peterloo, but this is no less true of poems composed in the 1790s and in the 1810s that did not appear in print until after the wars against France. Entering the world in the year of Waterloo, *The White Doe* dramatises tensions inherent to the conceptualisation of peace, a claim that applies also to *Peter Bell* and *The Waggoner*, poems that did not appear in print until 1819. In connection with these related narrative poems a point that should be noted is the virtual existence of a volume comprising 'Peter Bell, The White Doe, and Benjamin the Waggoner' that Wordsworth had 'resolved upon' in April 1814 (*MY* II. 140). It would be interesting to speculate on how the projected volume, conceived in the month of Napoleon's first abdication and announced on the very day that Louis XVIII returned to France, might have been received, not least had it appeared before the publication of *Waverley* in July. I consider the relations between *The White Doe*, *Peter Bell* and *The Waggoner* in more detail in Chapter 4, but for now *The White Doe of Rylstone* stands alone: composed in a time of war, revised during an interlude of peace, readied for publication in a period of unexpected and rapidly escalating tensions, and finally published within a few days of the war's decisive conclusion, *The White Doe* is a poem out of time, exhibiting in its dislocated compositional and publication history the societal fractures it seeks to transcend. To pave the way for the exploration of the poem's contribution to post-war culture, I wish first to look at how the verse nests an experience of personal grief within a story of historical defeat.

Fictions of Distress

Considering what Wilson has to say about the poem's investment in chastisement and sobriety in the wake of the losses occasioned by war, it seems fitting that the poem should be bookended by representations of grief. As is well known, *The White Doe* bears the imprint of personal loss – of William's brother, John, in 1805 and of William and Mary's children, Catherine and Thomas, in 1812. Over the course of the poem's composition, from inception in December 1807 to publication in 1815, *The White Doe* became a register of familial tragedy as well as a demonstration of the consolatory work of imaginative literature. The description of John's character that Wordsworth gave to Beaumont in the wake of his death casts an intriguing light on how the association between grief, consolation, and the idea of the feminine took a hold on the poem: 'my departed Brother [...] walked all his life pure among the impure [...] his modesty was equal to that of the purest Women. In prudence, in meekness, in self-denial, in fortitude, in just desires, and elegant and refined enjoyments, with an entire simplicity of manners, life and habits, he was all that could be wished-for in man' (*EY* 556). The 'sainted' Emily (VI. l. 1692), who also walks among the impure, suggests the possibility of a continuation of personality after death, her triumph over adversity providing a lesson in fortitude to those who struggle with grief.

The idea that personal grief work could be linked to a nation's recovery in the aftermath of war, and that peace should be linked to feminine purity, takes shape in *The White Doe* in the depiction of the contrast between Emily's patient endurance of loss and her father's headstrong and immodest pursuit of power. If, as Geoffrey Hartman has contended, the poem exists to chasten and subdue the 'wanton' excesses of the pagan or Catholic imagination that is the cause of idolatry, fanaticism, and war, it seeks nevertheless to retain a faith in the existence of natural sympathies as 'vital not only to poetry but also to human development'.[21] Hence the importance of the volume's dedicatory poem, which explores the ability of literature to provide consolation while avoiding 'an over-extension of imaginative hopes' beyond the measure that nature can fulfil.[22] Composed as *The White Doe* was going to press, 'In trellis'd shed with clustering roses gay' gives expression to the effects of 'lamentable change' (l. 21),[23] observing how the 'stream of fiction' (l. 25) fails to provide the grieving couple with consolation until a reading of *The Faerie Queene*, with its story of 'female patience winning firm repose' (l. 50), yields a 'timely promise of unlooked-for fruit' (l. 30). From Spenser's late Elizabethan Protestant romance, Wordsworth retrieves a sense of those sympathies that 'Aloft ascending, and descending deep,/Even to the inferior Kinds' (ll. 44–5), connect the material with the spiritual world without losing a sense of their distinction.

Echoing the emphasis on co-creativity that had been imparted to Coleridge and that was expressed emphatically in the 1815 'Essay, Supplementary to the Preface', Kristin Dugas has argued that 'In trellis'd shed', together with the sonnet 'Weak is the will of Man' and the epigraph from Bacon, 'prepares "readers for the action" of *The White Doe*' by showing how 'every symbolic action, whether in the world or as a response to a fictional representation, requires an extended exercise of suspended disbelief'.[24] A product of Wordsworth's fraught attempts to derive consolation from artifice, Dugas goes on to claim that 'In trellis'd shed' is aware of how 'fictions of distress, however soothing, remain fictions'.[25] Yet such awareness need not invalidate the ability of such fictions to provide readers with solace; if readers can respond empathetically to Spenser's stylised representations of recovery from grief then, by implication, they should also be able to respond to the contrivances of *The White Doe*.[26]

A pre-text for *The White Doe*'s delicate balancing of sympathy and self-consciousness that must be considered in this context is 'Hart-leap Well'. Rooted, like *The White Doe*, in traditional British and German balladry, the opening of the poem sets the thrill of a 'remarkable Chace' alongside pre-emptive indicators of frustrated endeavour and melancholy attainment.

Matching 'Joy' (l. 9) with 'doleful silence' (l. 13) and the cheery huntsman's halloo with a 'weary mountain strain' (l. 20), the chase terminates at the site of the hart's ignoble end: a 'trembling' spring (l. 44) united in sympathy with the 'foaming' (l. 40) expirations of the dying beast.[27] Due to the verse's qualifying notes, the huntsman's satisfaction at this 'glorious act' (l. 37) appears uncertain, hollow, a moment of solitary delight undercut by the pathos of the suffering creature, whose blood, like a sacrificial 'lamb' (l. 39), offers consecration, not to the founding of a holy site but to the raising of a 'Pleasure-house' (l. 57), a space of 'merriment' (l. 92) and illicit, carnal delight. Divided into two parts, 'Hart-leap Well', in anticipation of Wordsworth's desire to deflate the pomp of epic romance, sets the would-be tale teller's wish for 'moving accident' (l. 97) against 'a simple song to thinking hearts' (l. 100). In advance of *The White Doe*, the poem discovers grief in the midst of victory as, revisiting the site of the huntsman's triumph many decades later, the narrator is struck by the ruins of the pleasure house: a 'doleful place [...] It seem'd as if the spring-time came not here,/And Nature here were willing to decay' (ll. 114–16). As relayed by a shepherd, the narrator's 'former rhyme' (l. 123) is now rendered overtly depressing and strange, its heroic potential waylaid by rumour and suspicion. While the fall of 'the great Lodge' (l. 130) tells its own sorry tale, the shunning of the fountain by dogs, horses, sheep, and cattle suggests the possibility 'that here a murder has been done' (l. 137) and that 'blood cries out for blood' (l. 138). The potential for satire on gothic credulity, akin to the teasing out of fact and fantasy in 'The Thorn', does not quite take off; rather, by the close of the poem shepherd and narrator appear united in their response to the desolation of the site and to the hubristic folly on which it was founded. Couched as a dead zone, in stark contrast to the analeptic qualities associated with the hart's nascent spring, the ruined arbour, with its 'lifeless Stumps' (l. 125) and sullied waters, provides a vision of environmental collapse, a state of non-being consequent on the war against nature that looks forward to the universal state of 'despoil and desolation' (l. 1586) that is evoked at the close of *The White Doe*. Unwilling to confirm this gloomy prospect, the narrator of 'Hart-leap Well' observes that even as nature commits the site to 'slow decay' (l. 173), a higher 'Being' (l. 165) mourns this loss in 'sympathy divine' (l. 164). Confident that, under the guidance of this Being, 'Nature, in due course of time, once more/Shall here put on her beauty and her bloom' (ll. 171–2), the narrator proposes to the shepherd that they may 'divide' 'One lesson' (l. 177) from these opposing tales: 'Never to blend our pleasure or our pride/With sorrow of the meanest thing that feels' (ll. 179–80). Thus, artfully insisting on 'difference' (l. 162) as a condition of sympathetic accord, the poem accounts for its own unity in division while at the same time affirming the necessity of a divine exception to the 'bloom' (l. 172) and 'waste' (l. 170) of human and non-human life.

Losing cherished offspring and a beloved brother to the reign of contingency, Wordsworth and Mary may well have been tempted to regard their world as a place dead to the restoration of life and beauty. But if the re-reading of Una's patience offered the grieving couple a way to yield to fiction's consolatory power without abandoning critical awareness, it prompted the thought too of a transcendental principle remote from and unaffected by artifice. The theological thinking that forms the basis of this concord is, however, tantalisingly vague. As noted in Chapter 1, in 1815 Wordsworth felt moved to deny that he was 'a worshipper of Nature', confirming his belief in an immortal and infinite 'spirit', distinct from 'objects of sense' (*MY* II. 189). In what amounts to a formal declaration of this faith in the transcendent God, in the 'Preface to *Poems*' (1815) Wordsworth cites as examples of 'the enthusiastic and meditative Imagination' the 'prophetic and lyrical parts of the holy Scriptures, and the works of Milton [...] and Spenser', selecting 'these writers in preference to those of ancient Greece and Rome because the anthropomorphitism of the Pagan religion subjected the minds of the greatest poets in those countries too much to the bondage of definite form; from which the Hebrews were preserved by their abhorrence of idolatry' (*Prose* III. 34–5). Pronouncing Milton 'a Hebrew in soul' for his related abhorrence of idolatry, Wordsworth goes on to praise Spenser for maintaining

> his freedom by aid of his allegorical spirit, at one time inciting him to create persons out of abstractions; and at another, by a superior effort of genius, to give the universality and permanence of abstractions to his human beings, by means of attributes and emblems that belong to the highest moral truths and the purest sensations,—of which his character of Una is a glorious example. (*Prose* III. 35)

Acknowledging the gap between 'persons' and 'abstractions', Spenser's Christian allegory draws attention to its own fictiveness while avoiding the perils of nominalism.

Thus, artifice and faith are sustained in exquisite tension. But if *The White Doe* marks an advance in the humanisation of religion, substituting the interpretative freedom of 'Protestant' allegory for the dogmatic certitude of 'Pagan' and 'Catholic' idolatry, the poem is no less alert to what might be lost as a result of secularisation. In a world in which prayer is presented as 'a bootless bene' – Lady Aäliza's son will never return; Francis Norton fails to avert his family's catastrophe – the onus falls on 'that sacred power, Imagination',[28] to forge bonds of sympathy between the living and the dead. In its efforts to establish itself as a virtual God, the sacred Imagination makes use of similes to convey a sense of what the world might be like were the dead to be restored to the living. As the poem's several nautical similes reveal, the absentee the poem seeks most ardently to recover is the recently drowned John Wordsworth. Most affectingly, the doe lies down beside the grave of a warrior 'Gently as a weary wave/ Sinks, when the summer hath died,/Against an anchored vessel's side' (I. ll. 143–5), while Emily, in her grief, is 'like a Ship at random blown/To distant places and unknown' (VI. ll. 1633–4). The simile, in its foregrounding of the difference between one thing and another – Emily is only *like* 'a Ship at random blown' – humanely reminds the reader that unity with the dead can only be forged through analogy.[29]

But can the Imagination provide lasting and real consolation unless it takes seriously the notion of a sacred power, beyond the human, that is more than merely analogical? In answer to this question, and with a recollection of how 'apparent' tautologies serve 'not only as symbols of the passion, but as <u>things</u>, active and efficient, which are themselves part of the passion',[30] it is worth noting that, for Wordsworth, as for Coleridge, the failure of language to capture the holy Word was an indication not of divine lack but of divine presence, a transcendental plenitude manifested precisely in the *in*ability of signs to deliver spiritual fulfilment. In the 'Essay, Supplementary to the Preface' Wordsworth reflects further on this paradox, providing a rationale for the 'divine origin' of poetry:

> The concerns of religion refer to indefinite objects, and are too weighty for the mind to support them without relieving itself by resting a great part of the burthen upon words and symbols. The commerce between Man and his Maker cannot be carried on but by a process where much is represented in little, and the infinite Being accommodates himself to a finite capacity. In all this may be perceived the affinities between religion and poetry;—between religion—making up the deficiencies of reason by faith, and poetry—passionate for the instruction of reason; between religion—whose element is infinitude, and whose ultimate trust is the supreme of things, submitting itself to circumscription and reconciled to substitutions; and poetry—ethereal and transcendent, yet incapable to sustain her existence without sensuous incarnation. (*Prose* III. 65)

The White Doe makes much of the breach between the 'ethereal and transcendent' and the 'finite capacity' of 'words and symbols', but the concluding reference to 'sensuous incarnation' should give us pause. Writing under the influence of Hartman's account of the poem, critics have perhaps been too quick to read the depiction of the contest between 'pure religion' and Catholicism as an allegory of the triumph of secular self-consciousness over religious credulity.[31] In a January 1816 letter to Francis Wrangham, Wordsworth describes *The White Doe* as starting from a 'high point of imagination [...] to a still higher; nothing less than the Apotheosis of the Animal' (*MY* II. 276); but while elevation to the spiritual undoubtedly takes place in the poem, it might be more accurate to conceive of the doe as the incarnation of the divine. At once natural and spiritual, the doe becomes the embodiment of the affinities between religion and poetry, which strive alike to bridge the divide between the finite and the infinite.

Wordsworth's fierce objections to Catholic Relief are well known; less well known is his preference for the Gospel of St John, which, with its focus on the Incarnation, has been taken by some critics as an indication of the poet's lingering attachment to Catholicism.[32] Much could be made, and has been made, of the poem's secret sympathy with the faith it would abjure, and rather than rehearse these arguments I would prefer to relate Wordsworth's interest in incarnation to the concern expressed in the second 'Essay upon Epitaphs' with the instability of language: 'if words be not the incarnation of the thought, but only a clothing for it, then surely they will prove an ill gift' (*Prose* II. 84–5). As incarnation, words signal the distinction between nature and spirit while yet allowing for their interanimation. A poem founded on such a principle would sustain fictive self-consciousness even as it maintains faith in God; accepting the necessity of artifice in the work of consolation, a poem of this kind would be sincere in its efforts to provide a communicative link between the living and the dead. Still further, a poem in which the infinite submits 'to circumscription and is reconciled to substitutions' (*Prose* III. 65), abjuring the drive towards tautological correspondence that marked, in 'Home at Grasmere', the sad futility of claiming a home for peace, might, after all, provide the groundwork for a peace in which humans and non-humans sojourn in undifferentiated accord. As Wordsworth would go on to claim, in a letter to Walter Savage Landor: while seeking, like religion, to incarnate infinite truths in finite words, poetry is at its most compelling 'in those passages where things are lost in each other, and limits vanish'. In other words, it is in the ruins of symbolic expression, in those moments where peace is unhoused and the infinite shines through, that the 'aspiration' towards a better life is most fully exercised.[33]

In Sacred Ruins

On what basis, then, is the peace of *The White Doe* founded? Set some fifty years after the failed rebellion, the opening verses describe a gathering of worshippers in 'a rural Chapel', protected 'like a little nest' in 'the shattered [...] heart' (I. ll. 25–8) of Bolton Abbey. If the chapel proclaims the restorative hegemony of Protestantism, it stands no less as an image of harmony after duress, a haven to which, significantly, the congregation 'repair' (I. l. 29).³⁴ As the description unfolds, the covert celebration of the decline of Catholic 'magnificence' (l. 117) in the name of Protestant simplicity is overtaken by the poem's fascination with the fecundity of natural forms: the dormitory of this 'pile of State,/Overthrown and desolate!' (ll. 83–4), is home to wild roses, sapling ash, and elder; the alter, 'whence the cross was rent' is now 'rich with mossy ornament' (ll. 121–2); and, strangest of all, 'gliding in serene and slow,/Soft and silent as a dream' (ll. 58–9), is the solitary doe – 'White she is as lily of June,/And beauteous as the silver moon' (ll. 61–2). The allusion here to Dryden's 'milk white *Hind*, immortal and unchang'd',³⁵ brings back into play the possibility of a resurgence of Catholic belief, or perhaps even, in an extension of Dryden's vision, the prospect of an alliance between the Crown and the Anglican and the Catholic churches against the forces of religious and political dissent. But Wordsworth's poem, despite its apparent Protestant leanings, leaves open to question the status of the doe's pagan or Christian origins:

> Whether she be of forest bowers,
> From the bowers of earth below;
> Or a Spirit, for one day given,
> A gift of grace from purest heaven. (I. ll. 77–80)

The parishioners share this uncertainty, differing in opinion as to whether the creature is the material embodiment of Lady Aäliza's grief for her drowned son (ll. 226–44), a rebel Lancastrian spirit resurrecting traumatic memories of the beheading of the Yorkist Earl of Pembroke in the War of the Roses (ll. 245–66), or a benign shapeshifting 'Fairy' (l. 270), tutoring the Baron Henry Clifford, perceived variously as an abrasive Lancastrian warmonger and as a studious 'Shepherd Lord' (l. 271), in the ways of 'humble quietness' (l. 297).³⁶ The friction introduced into the poem by these 'superstitious fancies' (ll. 218) attests to the persistence of a 'tragic history' (l. 202) of dispute and conjecture, 'Which does the gentle Creature wrong' (l. 219). Doubt as to the creature's origins and intent is shown in the poem to be a remnant of the grief and anxiety brought about by the sectarian conflict and its uncertain settlement. The aftershocks of war that work ceaselessly to derange the peace find their counterpart in the poem's struggle to preserve a 'vision so composed and sweet' (l. 314) within a genre fated to expose the gap between individual consciousness and objectified meaning. That, for a moment, 'the people', overcoming their 'doubting' and 'questioning' (ll. 315–16), are afforded an 'undisturbed repose of heart' (l. 320) highlights the poem's paradoxical logic: only a creature divorced from objectivity can undertake the work of healing after war, but divorce from objectivity is precisely the cause and consequence of war. Thus, as the doe moves delicately through the churchyard, filling 'many a damp obscure recess/With lustre of a saintly show' (ll. 102–3), casting 'glory' (l. 93) on the ruins, the ability of lyric to discover a home for 'solitude, and utter peace' (l. 330) is short lived; because conflict is destined to recur in this world, such dreamlike visions must 'vanish' (l. 323).

As Richard Norton prepares his family for the ill-fated uprising, his son Francis counsels restraint. Like the white doe, Francis is symptomatic of the divide between the individual and collective consciousness, his pleas for moderation falling on unsympathetic ears. As the Nortons venture towards a battle that would fulfil the expectations of epic romance, the son is left at home to brood alone, seemingly caught, like a 'phantasm' (II. l. 423), between the realms of the living and of the dead. Locked in a 'trance' (l. 438), Francis becomes representative of the aporia that bedevils the poem throughout as, echoing Wordsworth's own conflicted feelings at the time of the poem's composition – torn on the one hand between adherence to economic, creative, and political independence and on the other bound by loyalty to the demands of his reactionary patrons – he drifts into inertia, unable either to join in with the fray or to sue for a credible peace. That the son can support the father only by widening the breach between thought and action – unable to support the father's 'aims', he will nevertheless join him, 'Unarmed and naked', so that on 'Kind occasions' he may 'See, hear, obstruct, or mitigate' (ll. 511–18; *passim*) – underscores the sense in which conscience, because of its refusal to take up arms, is placed at a remove from the world in which it would intervene. The attempt to recast opposition to war as an act requiring courage akin to that of the warrior remains, as a result, ineffective. Just as the sacralising labour of simile cannot compete with religious conviction, so the claim that Francis and Emily in their 'Forebearance and self-sacrifice' have 'like combatants [...] fared' (ll. 583–4) fails to bridge the divide between analogy and actuality. Understanding as much, the conscientious objector sees in the conflict the source of a deeper and more lasting catastrophe, informing his sister of a 'Time' to 'come that rings the knell/

Of all we loved, and loved so well' (ll. 522–3). Knowing that peace cannot be realised in this time, Francis counsels Emily to 'Hope nothing' (l. 535):

> For we must fall, both we and ours,—
> This mansion and these pleasant bowers;
> Walks, pools, and arbours, homestead, hall,
> Our fate is theirs, will reach them all;
> The young Horse must forsake his manger,
> And learn to glory in a Stranger;
> The Hawk forget his perch,—the Hound
> Be parted from his ancient ground:
> The blast will sweep us all away,
> One desolation, one decay! (II. 550–9)

In this manner Francis prophesises a time when the conflict of individuation recedes, supplanted by a phase of mutual decline: the 'fall' of 'all' into 'desolation' and 'decay'. As persons, objects, and animals descend into oblivion, so too do claims of ownership and obeisance; walks and arbours, homestead and hall, horse, hawk, and hound – in the absence of the social contract, all must succumb to the return of primal violence. But whereas domesticated creatures may learn, in time, to 'glory' in new masters, thereby restoring under the guise of peace the juridical wars that are the origin and end of history, a principle of beauty, distinct from human control, returns to 'her peaceful woods' and 'murmuring floods' (ll. 564–5) and there remains, 'in heart and soul the same […] before she hither came,—/Ere she had learned to love us all' (ll. 564–8). Exempted from human history, the white doe symbolises for Francis a state of peace that is forever divorced from actuality. In related mood, Francis conjectures that Emily 'by force of sorrows high' will be 'Uplifted to the purest sky/Of undisturbed humanity!' (ll. 591–2), further accentuating the sense in which, out of very despair, peace can be conceived only as an unattainable ideal.

As the poem proceeds, a preoccupation with the gulf between earthly despoliation and transcendental preservation becomes ever more apparent. Just as Rylstone Hall is destined to decay, surviving only as a romantic ruin, so Catholicism has fallen into abeyance, persisting only on the margins of society as a self-defeated and ultimately outmoded religious practice. For this reason, the rebels' anti-climactic yielding of 'the unfought field' (III. l. 817) makes perfect sense. Though the bloodless defeat of the Rising of the North frustrates the conventions of epic romance, the absence of battlefield passions works to ensure that latent strains of religious and political extremism are prevented from disturbing the post-war consensus. Unrealisable outside of the virtual future conveyed by a sequence of past modal verbs ('The darksome Altars would have blazed [...] Once more the Rood had been upraised'; [...] 'This Banner' on 'the consecrated breast' of Bolton Priory 'Should [...] have found rest [...] I would myself have hung it high', V. ll. 1276–95), the promise of Catholic 'renovation from the dead' (l. 1279) is drained of any affective force. That the son, out of filial devotion, should commit to honouring the father's wish to place the 'unhallowed banner' on St Mary's shrine, only to fail in this 'high endeavour' (l. 1230), can be read as a further sign of the poem's determination to maintain the distinction between superstitious fancies and sacred imagination. In a world given over to the misrecognition of words and symbols, the son's desire to fulfil the father's wish is interpreted by the enemy as a sign of craven self-interest: 'Behold the Ensign in his hand!/ He did not arm, he walked aloof!/For why?—to save his Father's Land' (VI. ll. 1481–3). Slain as the result of a failure of communication, Francis's death marks, therefore, the end of the father's benighted hopes for 'New life' (IV. l. 1287). And with the loss of the banner comes the end, too, of the defective zeal that would deny the foundational divide in mortal signs, effacing the gap between reference and referent to make palpable the invisible and immaterial Divine.

True to its aim to make of 'Dire overthrow' (VI. l. 1865) a source of spiritual rejuvenation, the poem's conclusion returns once more to its source in familial grief. Emily's encounter with the grave of her beloved brother is described as the 'consummation, the whole ruth/And sorrow of this final truth' (V. l. 1567–8), the end rhymes serving as a poignant reminder of how the supreme height of knowledge contains a mournful core. The sense of uncertainty aroused by the loss of John Wordsworth is sustained in the passage that follows, as the narrator inquires of the poem's tutelary 'Spirit' where Emily has 'fled': 'is a rifted tomb/Within the wilderness her seat?/Some island where the wild waves beat,/Is that the Sufferer's last retreat?' (VI. ll. 1573–9; *passim*). The grieving sister is then discovered, sitting 'alone' and in 'quietness' (ll. 1602–3), her 'fortitude' – the word recalls Wordsworth's evocation of John's qualities in his letter to Beaumont – put 'to proof' (l. 1639) amid the ruins of Rylstone's 'fair domain' (l. 1587). Reminiscent of the blasted landscapes inhabited by the female vagrant and Margaret, the levelling of Rylstone contrasts with the earlier account of 'proud' Norton Tower: an 'Edifice of warlike frame' (IV. l. 1170) that 'fronts all quarters, and looks round [...] Upon a prospect without bound' (ll. 1172–5). Within this toxically altered domain – 'the ravage hath spread wide/Through park and field, a perishing/That mocks the gladness of the Spring' (VI. ll. 1595–7) – Emily maintains a solitary vigil, 'as if the waste/Were under her dominion placed' (ll. 1599–1600). But while Margaret and the female vagrant sink into nullity, Emily maintains composure in grief; likened to 'a Virgin Queen' (l. 1608), negligent of 'outward images of fate,/And carrying inward a serene/And perfect sway' (ll. 1610–12), the sole survivor of the uprising retains her core sense of self, unmoved by outer circumstance.

The allusion to the Protestant Queen Elizabeth recalls the poem's commitment to its historical context; it also evokes the sense in which, *pace* Hartman, the verse seeks to align the triumph of sacred Imagination with the ascendency of Protestantism; but the description of Emily, as it unfolds, is reminiscent too of the Catholic veneration of Our Lady of Sorrows. In lines redolent of the iconography of Mater Dolorosa, Emily is described as having been 'brought/To the subjection of a holy,/Though stern and rigorous, melancholy!' (ll. 1615–16); and while she retains 'the tender gleams/Of gentleness and meek delight', she nonetheless is 'held above' the 'infirmities of mortal love;/Undaunted, lofty, calm, and stable,/And awfully impenetrable' (ll. 1640–6). The point here is not that Wordsworth displays a subterranean sympathy with the old religion but rather that aspects of the defeated faith are shown to migrate into the new regime; as indicated by the lines 'Her soul doth in itself stand fast,/Sustained by memory of the past/And strength of Reason' (ll. 1642–4), as well as by the unostentatiousness of Emily's 'woollen cincture' (l. 1626), echoes of the rationalist, self-reliant, and self-denying precepts of Protestantism are forcefully present in this account, but the portrait of maternal sorrowing that with 'grace/Of awfulness' is displayed in Emily's face (ll. 1616–17) testifies to the persistence of a sacramental, as opposed to instrumental, understanding of the relationship between nature and the divine.

Composed in May–June 1808, just a few weeks after the earliest complete version of *The White Doe*, 'The Tuft of Primroses', as previously observed, returns to the consideration of England's Catholic ruins, depicting through prosodic violence the fall of 'stately Towers', 'crush'd, and buried under weeds and earth' (ll. 479–82). But while the appeal to 'nature's pure religion' supports the transmission of Christian, as opposed to doctrinal, truth in 'line/Uninterrupted' (ll. 499–500; the enjambment is strikingly ironic), the poem, like *The White Doe*, continues to register the grievous shock of the Reformation and to that extent may be read as a sympathetic response to Catholicism. Despite the fact that Wordsworth's political objections to Catholicism were to become increasingly vehement, reaching a crescendo around the time of the 1829 Catholic Relief Bill, in his poetic practice he maintains sympathy for a religion that, 'made glorious in decay' ('The Tuft of Primroses', l. 493), survives as the harried consciousness of the post-Reformation settlement: a mode of supernatural excess at home amidst the ruins.³⁷

Apotheosis of the Animal

As the incarnation of this alienated sublime, Emily, 'from stroke/Of ravage saved' (ll. 1650–1), persists as an image of beauty, foreshadowing 'The Tuft of Primroses', 'like a stately Flower [...] separated from its kind' (ll. 1653–5).³⁸ And it is at this point that the poem enacts its most daring turn, providing a figure for the relationship between earth and heaven that, even as it accepts ontological difference, can accommodate the possibility of intercommunion. From a certain perspective, the reappearance of the doe, in defiance of Francis's prophesy, could be described as a miracle; not only has the preternatural creature survived time and change, but its return from the 'peaceful woods' implies that eternal harmony may, after all, be restored to the world. The passage describing the reunion of Emily and the creature, which Wordsworth revised significantly for the 1815 publication, deserves to be quoted in full:

> Thus checked, a little while it stayed;
> A little thoughtful pause it made;
> And then advanced with stealth-like pace,
> Drew softly near her—and more near,
> Stopped once again;—but, as no trace
> Was found of any thing to fear,
> Even to her feet the Creature came,
> And laid its head upon her knee,
> And looked upon the Lady's face,
> A look of pure benignity,
> And found unclouded memory,
> It is, thought Emily, the same,
> The very Doe of other years!
> The pleading look the Lady viewed,
> And, by her gushing thoughts subdued,
> She melted into tears—
> A flood of tears, that flowed apace
> Upon the happy Creature's face. (VI. ll. 1666–84)

In the draft version, the doe, 'Through fear & through confusion strange', maintains a distance from Emily and is so disheartened as to resign Emily to the care of an 'old Man' as her only comforter.³⁹ In the published version, the encounter is transformed into a scene of mutual recognition and reciprocal delight, suggesting that Wordsworth sought, in the aftermath of war, to convey an impression of how human and non-human, nature and spirit, could be brought together in peaceful co-existence. While 'She melted into tears—/A flood of tears' implies a dissolving of the psychological limits that prevent human beings from overcoming loss, it raises too the prospect of a peaceable alternative to the destructive floods that yield the legend on which *The White Doe* is founded and that, to this point, have flowed through the poem's narrative course.[40] Thus, when at the poem's conclusion Emily is 'Uplifted to the purest sky/Of undisturbed mortality' (l. 1872), the violent waters of Rylstone are transformed into an 'innocent spring' (l. 1876), offering a slender promise of earthly renewal.

The lines that follow the meeting between Emily and the doe add further to the therapeutic dimensions of the encounter as, recalled by the doe's reappearance to memories of past pain and pleasure, Emily is delivered from grief-stricken stasis to joyful recovery:

> Oh, moment ever blest! O Pair!
> Beloved of heaven, heaven's choicest care!
> This was for you a precious greeting,—
> For both a bounteous, fruitful meeting.
> Joined are they, and the sylvan Doe
> Can she depart? can she forego
> The Lady, once her playful Peer,
> And now her sainted Mistress dear?
> And will not Emily receive
> This lovely Chronicler of things
> Long past, delights and sorrowings?
> Long Sufferer! will not she believe
> The promise in that speaking face,
> And take this gift of Heaven with grace? (VI. ll. 1685–98)

In her dual role as a messenger of the eternal and as a 'Chronicler of things/ Long past', the doe moves between realms, a 'gift of Heaven' affording cathartic release for the 'Lone Sufferer', hitherto locked in timeless grief. Alluding to the 'blest pair' of *Paradise Lost* (IV. l. 774), the scene augurs well for the restoration of lost innocence. Intimations of Emily's 'sainted' status have been threaded throughout *The White Doe*, but the description of her meeting with the doe as 'the first of a re-union/Which was to teem with high communion' (ll. 1699–1700) makes the poem's liturgical orientation explicit. Linked to the incarnation of word and thought, the reunion of Emily and the creature evokes the intermingling of flesh and spirit that takes place in the Eucharist. However, in a work that eschews doctrinal clarity, the matter of whether the dialectic of unity and difference that takes place in this 'high communion' should be understood in terms of transubstantiation or consubstantiation is left uncertain.

What is clear is that the doe's reappearance helps Emily to come to terms with all that she has suffered. Key to this process of restoration is the creature's ability to foster a sense of continuity between the recollection of historical trauma and the promise of restoration. If, as Mater Dolorosa, Emily is 'held above/The infirmities of mortal love', the resulting state of equanimity has left her 'separated' and 'Single on the gladsome earth' (ll. 1654–6), unable to participate in those forms of life that would help to restore a connection with the divine. The doe's return brings not only joy but also pain as, following a journey to those familiar spots that document the fall of the Nortons, from the dell where the doe was first encountered to the churchyard where the last of the brothers is buried, Emily is recalled to her connection with the 'trouble-haunted ground' (l. 1720). But it is through this revisitation of the past that Emily is able to re-enter the world 'Of time, and place, and thought, and deed', perceiving in 'her silent Follower's eyes' a record of 'Endless history' (ll. 1734–5). No longer detached from the source of her misfortune, the maid undertakes a 'second, yet nobler birth' (l. 1864) and though set apart from 'human cares' (l. 1878) can sympathise with and participate in the lives of her fellow post-war survivors.[41]

Significantly, however, the poem remains open to the question of how precisely a state of peace is to be realised in a world in which language and history have become synonymous with violence. One possible avenue for peaceable revolution is suggested by the pre-articulate and thus, in Rousseauian mode, pre-societal relationship between Emily and the white doe. Though 'mute', the doe nevertheless has a 'speaking face' (l. 1697), which by means of looks and glances allows Emily to come to terms with the past. The relationship between Emily and the white doe could, of course, be dismissed as a correlationist fantasy, but it is also worth asking what might be gained from the poem by indulging in this fantasy. Following Bruno Latour's defence of anthropomorphism, I would suggest that the beast's ability to communicate and sympathise with her human companion has wider implications for the poem's representation of post-war truth and reconciliation, which aims to heal the breach not only between humans but also between humans and non-humans.[42] Considering the repeated mentions of the doe's expressive face, as well as her ability to comprehend and respond to Emily's facial expressions ('Skilled to approach or to retire,—/From looks conceiving her desire'; ll. 1739–40), it would be reasonable to conclude that, in a Levinasian sense, an ethical relationship has been established. Leaving aside the problematic and potentially scandalous significance of this conclusion (Levinas, for one, would object to the inclusion of the animal in the face-to-face encounter), the doe, as a quasi-speaking subject, opens a space within the poem in which the embodiment of the nudity and defencelessness of all life, including the life conventionally defined as faceless, can articulate a plea not to be killed.[43] Tentatively, then, *The White Doe* advances an image of nature delivered from the silence that separates human and non-human life. As the poem moves to its seraphic conclusion, Emily is 'happy' to receive in 'the mild glance/Beamed from that gracious countenance;—/ Communication, like the ray/Of a new morning' (ll. 1845–50). Seemingly immune to the misrecognition and miscomprehension that bedevils the substitutive play of signs, the rapport between human and non-human appears not only to transcend the primary violence of signification but also to provide an example of how memories of past violence may be recollected without the risk of their traumatic repetition. Though nature is 'wasted' (l. 1773) and 'mournful' (l. 1908), the time of the endless sorrowing of the earth appears to have come to an end. As Emily wanders through the ruins, she comes to regard the recent history of personal and collective loss with a 'Mild, delicious melancholy:/Not sunless gloom or unenlightened,/But by tender fancies brightened' (ll. 1772–9). With eyes set on the 'purest sky/Of undisturbed mortality' (ll. 1870–1), we might say that not only Emily but also nature, as represented by the doe, can cease its lament for the division that language brought to the world.[44]

What Good Is a Bootless Bene?

That Emily's rehabilitation takes place silently in a region set apart from human society should, however, give us pause. As Wilson observes, in *The White Doe* 'looks, words, movements, are gentle, feminine, subdued'; peace, that is, appears to be associated in Wordsworth's poem with a mode of private, apolitical interiority expressly identified as feminine. Should this pre-discursive, pre-societal, and pre-political compound of peace and the feminine be decried or affirmed? Designated by Levinas as 'the other par excellence' femininity, like peace, is in a perpetual state of jeopardy, granted a foundational role in the making of the just society but only on condition that it remains inarticulate, a mode of welcoming that serves as the excluded origin of the world.[45] A distaste for Levinas's theorising of feminine alterity informs Judith Page's criticism of the characterisation of Emily: 'As a woman defined by male culture in terms of weakness, Emily has no voice in the world of power, the public arena of religious and political conflict that causes her loss and isolation. She gains spiritual power only when she accepts the complete loss of everything that would have been hers as a dependent of patriarchy'.[46] However, contrary to this criticism, one could argue that it is precisely on account of her withdrawal from the public arena that Emily is able to suspend the destructive urgings of the masculine world. Indeed, to push this reading further, the equation of feminine alterity – which for Levinas is not relational but absolute – with notions of domestic retreat should prompt us to consider how the drive to self-correspondence and completion is born out of a failure to come to terms with the equivocation that the feminine, as absolute other, introduces into the home.[47] Associated with a series of temporary shelters – an 'island where the wild waves beat' or 'some aspiring rock' (ll. 1578–85), 'a primrose bank' (l. 1601), 'a self-surviving leafless Oak' (l. 1649), 'A Hut, by tufted Trees defended' (l. 1711), a 'thick bower' (l. 1755), 'a rocky cavern' (l. 1758) – Emily highlights the sense in which feminine alterity, associated with the heart of the home while, at the same time, remaining fundamentally unhoused, undoes the zeal for permanence that, perversely, fuels the pursuit of war.

Often overlooked in readings of *The White Doe* that dwell on the associations between peace, withdrawal, and feminine quiescence is the way in which the poem comes, ultimately, to challenge the theological presuppositions on which the dream of lasting peace is founded. Although, as we have seen, Wordsworth sought in the poem to evoke a sense of transcendental plenitude in the disparity between the infinite and its sensual incarnation, in its conclusion the poem steers towards a more sceptical position, or at least one that is able to accommodate an idea of the divine as an effect of artifice:

> When the Bells of Rylstone played
> Their Sabbath music—"God us ayde!"
> That was the sound they seemed to speak;
> Inscriptive legend, which I ween
> May on those holy Bells be seen,
> That legend and her Grandsire's name;
> And oftentimes the Lady meek
> Had in her Childhood read the same,
> Words which she slighted at that day;
> But now, when such sad change was wrought,
> And of that lonely name she thought,
> The Bells of Rylstone seemed to say,
> While she sate listening in the shade,

>   With vocal music, "God us ayde!"
>   And all the Hills were glad to bear
>   Their part in this effectual prayer. (VI. ll. 1780–95)

Affirming the sense in which 'through the sound the soul of the material thing expresses itself' directly to the ear, the passage entertains, albeit briefly, a dream of unmediated contact with the divine.[48] But by drawing attention to the 'Inscriptive legend' on the bells, the lines speak no less of how sonic presence is a mechanical illusion, an effect accentuated by the reproduction of Old English script within the main body of the printed poem. Evoking the power of 'vocal music' while drawing attention to the visual medium in which this power subsists, *The White Doe* blurs the distinction between spirit and artifice while providing a graphic connection to the volume's most despairing pronouncement: 'What is good for a bootless bene?' Pitched between faith and doubt, the poem couches prayer as agonisingly alienated from the promise of restoration; uttered in hope of a face-to-face encounter with God, the 'bootless bene' confirms only that God is always already co-implicated with finitude and, as such, can never transcend the opposition between presence and absence, life and non-life.

***

Peace, God, nature, and the feminine: must the association of these others par excellence with the destruction of the earth be regarded as a diminution of *The White Doe*'s promise of deliverance from the melancholy of a post-war world? Or should the poem's openness to contestation be taken as a marker of its success? Those early readers who struggled to reconcile the poem's epic energies with its drive towards lyrical inertia, and who discovered in its account of a world given over to feminine self-abnegation and protracted grief an unsatisfying model of how life should be imagined in the aftermath of conflict, were no doubt attuned not only to the poem's renegotiation of the heroic but also to its radical undoing of identity. That, in the ravaged land described in the poem, peace remains fugitive, a transient ideal that finds, at best, only a temporary home, speaks of course to the larger sense in which *The White Doe* failed to find a place in the aftermath of Waterloo. Unable to dwell in the busy, self-congratulatory culture that emerged suddenly in the summer of 1815, the poem retreats into silence. The poem's final words may be read as a performance of this retreat, securing victory, of a sort, from its lack of impact in the world. Thus, in the 'twilight of this day' (l. 1891), the doe is encountered one last time, 'Haunting' the spots 'Which her dear Mistress once held dear' (ll. 1898–9). Delighting in homophonic play, the lines postulate a participatory relationship between human and non-human that extends to the relationship between natural 'degree' and 'heaven's grace' (l. 1895). As a 'gliding Ghost' (l. 1902), the white doe mediates between the worlds of the living and the dead, drawing attention amid the ruins of the old religion to something larger and more powerful than the regressive, and painful, longing for home. Amidst 'the mournful waste/Of prostrate altars, shrines defaced' and 'fret-work imagery laid low', the creature 'Paces softly, or makes halt,/By fractured cell, or tomb, or vault', offering mute testimony beside the 'sculpted Forms of Warriors brave' (ll. 1908–16) to a life released from the pursuit of self-completion, the outcome of which is hatred, war, and devastation.

In *Spectres of Marx*, Derrida describes peace as the 'time of learning to live' with 'ghosts', of learning, that is, to accept and accommodate the comingling of absence and presence, lack and plenitude, finitude and infinitude that is the precondition for the emergence of any form of meaning.[49] In such a world, by 'adversities unmoved', 'Calm Spectacle' (ll. 1920–1) resides gently with the ghosts of ruined certitudes in a relationship that comes as close as possible to non-violence. The thematic scope of *The White Doe*, which embraces the subduing of religious and political factionalism, the transition from war to peace, and the recovery from grief, ought, in theory, to have made of the poem a tale for the times. However, as Jeffrey, Wilson, and other commentators hinted, the poem's advocacy of sobriety and restraint placed it at odds with the prevailing mood of triumphalism, and the poem's struggle to come to terms with its own internal contradictions, most notably in its attempt to pitch a weakened, de-cathected Imagination against the dangerous excesses of religious and political dissent, meant that it came uncomfortably close to expressing the underlying melancholy of the post-war settlement. In seeking to secure a sense of transcendental purity, blissfully havened from material objectivity, the *White Doe* merely reconfirmed the divisions between the infinite and the finite, the invisible and the visible, the spiritual and the material, that peace was supposed to heal. Yet in its efforts to show how the 'supreme of things' must submit to 'circumscription' and 'substitutions', the poem provides a way for readers to imagine peace not as the 'bootless bene' of history but as a mode of aesthetic play, unconstrained by the need for certainty and capable of fulfilment in the present.

CHAPTER 3

Thanksgiving after War

England in 1815

Between war's end and war's end the battle goes on. To be followed by: illuminations, exhibitions, songs, poems, bonfires, fireworks, concerts, pantomimes, panoramas, dioramas, thanksgiving sermons, topographical descriptions, expository guides, equestrian displays, celebratory dinners, subscriptions for a national monument, subscriptions for commemorative prints, subscriptions for the wounded, prayers for the dead. After the desperate uncertainty of the hundred days, the war was now truly at an end.

And so, peace at last.

Only, for the residents of Rydal Mount, the sense of an ending left much to be desired. On 15 August, writing to Catherine Clarkson, Dorothy bemoans 'the adulation, the folly, the idle Curiosity' that has attracted sightseers to the Bellerophon before, once again, accusing Napoleon of cowardice for failing to take his own life. In the same letter, lamenting the poor sales of *The White Doe*, Dorothy proclaims: 'I now perceive clearly that till my dear Brother is laid in his grave his writings will not produce any profit' (*MY* II. 244–5), a statement echoed soon after by Wordsworth: 'as to Publishing I shall give it up, as no-body will buy what I send forth' (*MY* II. 334); 'I write chiefly for Posterity' (*MY* II. 292). Thus, thoughts of money, death, and failure of accomplishment circulated wildly in the Wordsworth household, the hope for belated recognition as a great national poet qualified by the adverse reaction to the poet's claims, in the 1815 preface and supplementary essay, to be the worthy successor of Chaucer, Spenser, Shakespeare, and Milton. Over the next eight months, Wordsworth would attempt to make ground on several fronts: attending to the family's financial security by successfully petitioning for a bond to cover his and Dorothy's share of the old Lowther debt; preparing the groundwork for posterity by writing an impassioned defence of the character of Burns; composing poems intended to secure his right to speak on behalf of the nation. In between these activities, slights on the character of the Duke of Wellington, the sanity of Lord Byron (*MY* II. 283 and 304),[1] the moral shortcomings of the radical Whigs (*MY* II. 304), and the literary worth of Hunt's *Defence of Liberty* (*MY* II. 273), as well as the efforts of Hunt's fellow Cockney rebel John Hamilton Reynolds (*MY* II. 345–6), came to the fore. Meanwhile, Caroline Vallon's wedding, and the prospect of a reunion in London, came and went – a meeting that would not take place for another five years. By 11 June 1816, Wordsworth, alarmed by the rise of civil tensions at home and in France, was revisiting his interest in Pasley's plans for the establishment of 'scientific military establishments' (*MY* II. 323) and declaring, just a few weeks later, his disgust with those members of the opposition who, the previous year, had sought to negotiate with Napoleon for peace (*MY* II. 334).

The revenants of peace that haunted *The Excursion* and *The White Doe*, and that drifted through the pages of *Poems by William Wordsworth*, appeared now to have been exorcised. The year's work of piling up resentment against Byron and the Cockney School, whose poetry drew inspiration from the first-generation poet's early radical artistic, political, and erotic leanings, was crisply expressed in Wordsworth's dismissive advice to Reynolds, whose poem 'The Naiad: A Tale' (1816) had clearly touched a raw nerve: 'Your Fancy is too luxuriant, and riots too much upon its own creation' (*MY* II. 346). Though at first Wordsworth remained silent in the months after Waterloo, progress towards the establishment of a body of work that would mark a decisive breach with the poetry of Fancy and that would, whether intentionally or not, sever ties with the rising generation of cultural Napoleonists began to assemble in the late autumn – first with a cluster of Miltonic sonnets published in the *Champion* and the *Examiner* and then with the undertaking of an 'irregular Ode' (*MY* II. 284). With the publication the following May of the slender octavo volume titled *Thanksgiving Ode, January 1816. With Other Short Pieces Chiefly Referring to Recent Public Events*, Wordsworth appeared resolute in his determination to speak on behalf of 'those who were resolved to fight it out with Bonaparte' (*MY* II. 334). Thus, Wordsworth sought to be the voice of the nation, if not as the official poet of state – that title had recently been ceded to Southey – nor as the favoured poet of the public – a role for which Scott and Byron were competing – then as 'The Muses' 'Page of state', a designation applied to 'that gentle bard', Spenser,[2] a poet whose work transcended the 'depression', 'party fury' (*MY* II. 292), and degraded 'appetite' (*MY* II. 334) of a war-torn nation in ways that Wordsworth hoped to emulate.[3]

Despite some recent efforts to rehabilitate the poem, the 'Thanksgiving Ode' has maintained its reputation as an embarrassing anomaly in Wordsworth's canon. Following publication, the poem, despite making very little impression on the poetry-buying public,[4] raised the ire of Shelley, Byron, and Hazlitt, confirming a view, seeded among second-generation readers of *The Excursion*, that Wordsworth had betrayed his early radical promise. As Duncan Wu has pointed out, parodic derivations of the politically inflammatory lines ascribing the 'carnage' of Waterloo to the 'daughter' of God set the seal on Wordsworth's status as a 'lost leader', tarnishing his reputation among progressive poets and thinkers for many years to come.[5] And yet, when regarded in the light of those other poems in which Wordsworth declares a fascination with the destructive power of war, the ode's apparent endorsement of 'carnage' might not seem anomalous; moreover, when considered alongside other competing pro- and anti-war discourses circulating at the time of its composition, and, more controversially, when read through the lens of those biographical circumstances that, at the outbreak of war, prevented Wordsworth from formally acknowledging his daughter and that, in war's aftermath, led to their veiled and somewhat awkward reunion, the lines might well take on a different, more nuanced meaning. Still further, should the lines in which 'Imagination, ne'er before content,/But aye ascending, restless in her pride [...] Stoops before that closing deed magnificent' (ll. 163–6) be taken as a sign of the poet's retreat from the militant artistry of *The Prelude*?[6] And even if this point is conceded, might that retreat be read not so much as 'an apocalypse of the "Imagination"' but as an invitation to resume the peaceful work of Fancy, rediscovering in this transient and gentle faculty a possibility of peace, unfettered by the warlike pursuit of self-definition?[7]

To address these questions this chapter begins with a consideration of newspaper reports and sermons that, in the aftermath of the battle, attempted to justify the shocking toll of victory – an estimated 50,000 dead and wounded – as an act of God.[8] Wordsworth's Waterloo poems, I argue, with their focus on the pleasures and pains of conflict, may be read both as a mode of self-revision and as a contribution to contemporary theological debates about the relations between slaughter, sacrifice, and divine providence. I then move on to read the echoes of Spenser's *Epithalamion* in the 'Thanksgiving Ode' – the former, imitating the ancient Greek extended lyric in praise of a bride and groom to be sung at the door of the wedding chamber; the latter, a 'dramatised ejaculation', 'composed or supposed to be composed on the morning of the thanksgiving, uttering the sentiments of an individual upon that occasion' (*MY* II. 324) – in relation to Wordsworth's long-delayed reunion with Annette and Caroline Vallon. In the concluding section, the chapter looks closely at the verses Wordsworth composed in the immediate aftermath of the ode, showing how these poems draw on the Fancy, in disregard of the poet's reservations about the adoption of this creative faculty by members of Hunt's circle, to pursue a path beyond Imagination and its involvement with the vicious circle of war and peace. Though the gentle, yielding tones of *The White Doe* would seem to have been silenced, with Wordsworth, in anticipation of renewed hostilities in Europe, expressing support for a revival of those 'martial qualities' that 'are the natural efflorescence of a healthy state of society' (*MY* II. 323), the still small voice that represents the victims of war and that looks forward to the cessation of conflict can yet be heard. That, in 1816, the founding of The Society for the Promotion of Permanent and Universal Peace should pass unrecorded by Wordsworth is of note, but notwithstanding the allusions to Cintra and Pasley that re-emerge in correspondence from this year, echoes of that non-violent counter-spirit continue to resound.

Thoughts and Prayers: Waterloo and the Rhetoric of Sacrifice

On Friday, 19 April 1793, two months after Britain's entry into the war against revolutionary France, devout church-goers, in observance of a decree issued by King George III for a day of fasting and national 'humiliation', uttered prayers 'for the pardon of our sins' and for God's 'Blessing and Assistance on THE ARMS OF HIS MAJESTY, by Sea and Land'.[9] Wordsworth emerges in this period as a complex, contradictory, and shadowy figure: at the beginning of the year he had published two volumes of verse with the liberal publisher Joseph Johnson and had come dangerously close to outing himself as the 'Republican' author of an incendiary attack on the Anglican clergyman and former revolutionary sympathiser Richard Watson, the Bishop of Llandaff.[10] At the same time, in need of funds to support the French mother of his illegitimate child, Wordsworth had petitioned his uncle William Cookson for a curacy in Harwich, Essex, a petition that his uncle declined on account of his nephew's near-treasonable infatuation with republican politics. It was this rejection that most likely prompted the composition of Wordsworth's attack on Watson.

That the poet would have joined in with the prayers for victory in the spring of 1793 seems unlikely, yet the counter-factual image of a young man, recently installed in a provincial parish, imploring divine aid in 'our warfare against an Enemy to all Christian Kings, Princes and States' is perhaps not so difficult to imagine.[11] Certainly the role of parish priest was easy enough for Wordsworth's fellow traveller in France, and possible fellow republican, Robert Jones to adopt. When, in the early autumn, Wordsworth visited Jones in Plas-yn-Llan, Wales, he would have heard his friend intoning state-sanctioned prayers for the triumph of legitimacy over atheism and republicanism. How the radical author of the *Letter to the Bishop of Llandaff* might have responded to such prayers, delivered in the region presided over by the detested subject of this letter, is recorded in Book 10 of *The Prelude*:

> It was a grief,
> Grief call it not, 'twas anything but that,
> A conflict of sensations without name,
> Of which he only who may love the sight
> Of a Village Steeple as I do can judge,
> When in the Congregation, bending all
> To their great Father, prayers were offered up
> Or praises for our Country's Victories,
> And, 'mid the simple worshippers, perchance,
> I only, like an uninvited Guest
> Whom no one owned, sate silent, shall I add,
> Fed on the day of vengeance yet to come?[12]

The shift in perspective, from the ardent Jacobin who, in the wake of the Duke of York's defeat at the Battle of Hondschoote on 6 September, 'Exulted in the triumph of my soul/When Englishmen by thousands were o'erthrown' (ll. 260–1) to the shamed recollection of one who 'sate silent' when 'prayers were offered up' for 'victories' (l. 270–3) and who, more alarmingly at a time of regular calls for collective fasting, *fed* on the prospect of 'vengeance', drives home the point that 'conflict' (l. 265) was an internal matter for Wordsworth. Like that other 'uninvited guest', the ancient mariner who, in Coleridge's poem, loiters on the margins of a ceremony in which individuals pledge allegiance to each other and to God, the poet is presented here as a man at odds with himself and with the world. Perhaps too, as Kenneth Johnston has suggested, there is a memory here of that missed and, for national, religious, and political reasons, impossible ceremony – the wedding service that would have united the English Protestant radical, William Wordsworth, with the French Catholic royalist, Annette Vallon. When in February 1793, as *The Prelude* records, Britain joined in the war against France, the 'ravage of this most unnatural strife' (X, l. 249) was thus experienced by Wordsworth as 'a civil war dividing his own family'.[13]

Considering the connection established between the outbreak of war and the observance, or lack of observance, of prayers in 1793, it seems fitting that Wordsworth should choose to commemorate the end of war in 1815 with a poem intended for a day of national thanksgiving. Wordsworth, by now a confirmed supporter of the Anglican establishment, may well have attended St Oswald's Church in Grasmere on 2 July 1815 joining in with prayers for the 'Glorious Victory obtained over the *French* on Sunday the Eighteen of June, at Waterloo'. Six months later, on Thursday, 18 January 1816, the day set aside for a general national thanksgiving, the former republican may also have uttered '*Amen*' in response to calls for the 're-establishment [...] of legitimate authority and moral order among the distracted nations of Europe'.[14] Wordsworth, no longer a silent witness to collective expressions of triumph, appears on the basis of this evidence and on the sentiments of joy expressed in his 'Thanksgiving Ode' and its accompanying shorter poems to be ardent and assured in his enthusiasm for the defeat of imperial France.

A no less pressing concern for Wordsworth was the troubling matter of the battle's devastating human costs. Whereas the Duke of Wellington's dispatch estimated that around 14,000 British and Hanoverian soldiers were killed, wounded, or missing, subsequent reports stated that the resulting toll was near double this figure.[15] Writing in the wake of William Cobbett's denunciation of the 'delirium' of the victory celebrations and his related attacks on the establishment press,[16] the *Morning Post* on 11 July 1815 averred that 'the magnitude of the loss is eagerly laid hold of by certain factious writers [...] in order to dim the lustre of the triumph, and damp the general joy', adding further that 'If our sacrifices have been great, the splendour of our triumph, and the benefit to be derived from it, correspond well with their magnitude'. For the writer in the *Morning Post* metaphors of light and scale, derived from the rhetoric of the sublime, work to efface the efforts of radical scepticism to 'frown', in a calculated redeployment of Samuel Johnson's *The Vanity of Human Wishes*, 'on war's unequal game/Where thousands bleed to raise a single name'. Substituting the affective charge of 'thousands bleed' for the politically contentious 'wasted nations' in the original poem, the writer affirms that, contra Cobbett, 'the gallant men whose loss we deplore have not died on glory's barren bed'.[17] Outside the metropolis, a related sense of coming to terms with the blood toll of victory is demonstrated by a statement from the *Caledonian Mercury* on 26 June: 'Such a victory could not, of course, be purchased, without a great sacrifice of men.'[18] Like the *Morning Post*'s insistence that 'sacrifice was unavoidable' the *Mercury*'s 'of course' gives an indication of the extent to which the principle of giving up life for a higher purpose provided a rationale for the shocking consequences of war.

What is revealed by such statements is the equivocal position of the dead soldier in myths of national integrity. As *homo sacer* (Agamben: the person who may be killed yet not sacrificed) and as scapegoat (Girard: the one who bears the burden of societal violence), the body of the violated soldier both conceals and reveals the principle of exclusion on which civil society is founded.[19] To adapt Neil Ramsey's analysis of the destabilising tendencies of the military memoir, in the as yet unpublished 'The Discharged Soldier', the depiction of 'the soldier as a suffering individual', rather than as the 'idealised and sacrificial representative of the nation', risked exposing the principle of exclusion on which the myth of the nation as fortress home is founded.[20] In the summer of 1815, as thousands of wounded and destitute servicemen wandered by the towns and villages of Britain in search of hospitality, the face of the excluded other became all too apparent, in consequence of which a discourse was needed to ensure that the demand for recognition did not overstep the bounds of propriety. As a measure of the effectiveness of sacrificial ideology in helping individuals to embrace the 'lustre of the triumph', and as a sign of how far the Wordsworths' sympathies had evolved since the 1790s, it is useful to consider a statement of Dorothy Wordsworth, from a letter written on 28 June on the day that news of Waterloo reached Grasmere. In the first part of the letter, composed in the afternoon, Dorothy writes: 'The particulars of the battle of the 18th are dreadful. The joy of victory is an awful thing, and I had no patience with the tinkling of our Ambleside bells upon the occasion'. By 11 o'clock at night, however, Dorothy's initial recognition of the stark contrast between dreadful 'particulars' and heedless 'tinkling' has been replaced by a clear expression of alignment with the dominant national mood: 'Before I go to bed I must tell you that, saving for the lamentable loss of so many brave men, I have read the newspapers of tonight with unmingled triumph' (*MY* II. 242). With dread qualified by the effects of parenthetic displacement ('saving for'), soothing alliteration ('lamentable loss'), and adjectival assurance ('brave men') the on-message reader is at last able to sleep.

In addition to the establishment press, Dorothy's notice of the sound of church bells gives indication of another means by which the state sought to translate the stark acknowledgement of slaughter into the ardent satisfaction of sacrifice. During the months of July and August churchmen across the nation, sermonising in support of the Waterloo

Subscription, the charitable fund created to assist the 'families of the brave men killed, and of the wounded sufferers', were keen to remind their congregations of 'how dearly their deliverance has been bought, and what sacrifices have been made to obtain it'.[21] The majority of Anglican sermons delivered in this period typically adopted the dominant Tillotson sermon model of exordium, exegesis, and peroration: a finely wrought, argumentative style intended to guide congregations to a shared conclusion.[22] Key to this model was the creation of a sense of identification with the victims of war in which anaphoric imperatives, supported by subordinate declarations of unity between contrasting pronouns, issue in terminal demonstrations of possessive unity, as shown in the following extract from a sermon by Daniell Mathias, delivered at St Mary's Church, Whitechapel, on 13 August:

> And for God's sake, let not us of the same kindred—let not us, nearly allied as we are, proudly allied as we are, to those who have achieved the victory, which will give the *world* repose, and *us* immortal honours; let not us, of the same blood, at any time, much less of this time, when their heroic deeds are present to our eyes—let not us, of the same household, be forgetful of what our brothers were obliged to suffer and endure on that signally auspicious and yet wound-inflicting and life-destroying day.[23]

Having constructed a syntactical and grammatical 'alliance' (p. 18) between 'us' and 'our brothers', Mathias goes on to draw attention to the plight of those left injured, bereaved, and destitute as a result of the battle. Significantly, at the forefront of the clergyman's mind are the proposals presented in Parliament to raise an appropriate monument to the British dead and wounded. Sensitive to the possibility that such a monument might, if unaccompanied by acts of charity, encourage widows, orphans, and wounded soldiers to meditate on the sharp disparity between their feelings of grief and privation and the jubilatory mood of their fellow citizens, Mathias ventriloquises the character of a 'mutilated' veteran, standing before a 'towering column' or 'wide-expanding arch' (p. 19): 'to erect these trophies I fought and bled: they are cemented by my blood, and they are made thus conspicuous by the loss of my precious limbs—and I have gained nothing but infirmity, poverty, and vagrancy!' (p. 20). As one might expect, given the charitable focus of the sermon, Mathias's solution to this exposure of the human costs of Waterloo is couched in the language of debit and credit: 'you owe it to them who are no more, to heal and assuage the wounds and the sufferings, which this memorable day has inflicted! It is the debt of gratitude [...] which it is your bounded duty to repay!' (p. 20). Having established syntactical commonality with the dead and wounded of Waterloo the rector concludes his sermon by assuring his flock that the resulting 'Peace', which 'they' delivered, will provide 'exemption from all the distresses, vexations, and expenses, which are incident to a state of warfare!' (pp. 20–1).

Representative of the reach of this understanding of wartime sacrifice as the exchange of life and limb for a collective purpose is the Reverend Peter Roe's assurance to his Yorkshire congregation that 'many who fell at Waterloo were translated to heaven [...] for ever to celebrate a victory, not of a temporal nature, but over the world, the Devil, and the flesh!'[24] In similar vein the Scottish Episcopalian minister Robert Morehead argued that just as the suffering of those killed and wounded at Waterloo had 'elevated our country to her highest pinnacle of success and glory' so it 'becomes us to dissipate private sorrow in public triumph, and in the triumph of greater things beyond mortality!'.[25] Warning against the 'selfishness of grief' Morehead paints an exulted, sublime image of the British dead, inhabiting 'lofty' offices in heaven from which they will 'delight [...] to fan the fires of patriot daring' (pp. 205–6). In what amounts to a synthesis of the liturgical and secular understandings of the equation of height and majesty Morehead makes much of the raising up of those who 'fell' at Waterloo, arguing that just as 'Their names will ever remain inscribed on the pillar of their country's renown' so 'it becomes us to lift the character of our souls to the level of that majestic height on which our country stands, and to the still higher level of the Gospel' (pp. 206–7). The outcome of Waterloo, in this case, goes beyond the mercantile and, as some commentators observed, perniciously secular peace envisaged by Mathias to embrace the principle of the Church militant: a globalised Anglican mission delivering truth and salvation to the oppressed peoples of the world.

The sense in which the ravages of battle were placed in the service of church and state was cemented further on Thursday, 18 January 1816, the day set aside for a service of general national thanksgiving. Despite the fact that the prayer forming the centrepiece of this service requested that 'the remembrance of past injuries be blotted out by mutual good offices', and that 'the miseries of War be forgotten in the charities of reconciliation',[26] recollections of suffering nevertheless played a key role in forging a sacrificial understanding of Waterloo as, in Whitehall, William Howley, the Bishop of London, superintended the placing of captured Imperial Eagles at the foot of the altar in the Royal Chapel by an escort of guardsmen 'yet pale from the wounds received in the field of glory'. Alluding at once to the spoils of war as well as to the symbolic status of the men's injuries the Bishop concluded that in the 'trophies of these brave men' the country 'may justly be said to have obtained [...] from the mercy of Heaven an adequate compensation' for its 'privations', 'labours', and 'losses'.[27] In more rapturous vein, Archibald Alison exhorted his congregation to give thanks to God for guiding the nation to a victory made 'rich in glory by the blood of the faithful and the brave'. Pursuing the evangelising message of his fellow Episcopalian and sometime protégé Robert Morehead, Alison concluded his sermon with a plea to the Lord to accept the faithful's 'sacrifice' and to make of them 'the asserters of thy eternal *justice*' and the 'messengers of thy *mercy* to the world!'.[28]

Though generally well received, pro-Waterloo sermonising was not immune to criticism. In November 1815, a hostile review of Daniell Mathias's sermon asserted that 'of all the topics for discussion which lie within the widely-extended circle of politics, there are none, most unquestionably, so diametrically repugnant to the plain tenants of the sacred profession, as war and its concomitant horrors'.[29] Echoing Cobbett's critique of the baleful consequences of the Allied victory, the writer condemns Mathias for 'dazzling' his congregation with the 'pseud glories of the combat, and by the glare of victory, to divert the attention from the gross infringement of national rights which was the original cause of its achievement' (p. 524). Recognising the ease with which the rhetoric of the sublime and the poetics of romance conspired to shield the public from the sordid realities of conflict, some preachers did, in fact, come dangerously close to questioning the state-sanctioned understanding of the Allied victory as an act of divine Providence. In a thanksgiving sermon entitled 'Thoughts on Universal Peace', one of the leading Scottish churchmen of the nineteenth century, the Reverend Thomas Chalmers, warned that 'there is a feeling of the sublime in contemplating the shock of armies' and that literature assists in the aggrandisement of war; poetry, in particular, is singled out for lending 'the magic of its numbers to the narratives of blood' and for throwing 'treacherous embellishments' over scenes 'of legalized slaughter'.[30] Those clergymen who, in their Waterloo and thanksgiving sermons, utilised the language of the sublime were, in Chalmers's view, guilty of perpetuating a bellicose ideology founded on the misapprehension of legalised slaughter as holy sacrifice. That such opinions would remain unheeded by those in power who wished to capitalise on Waterloo's status as a symbol of national unanimity is confirmed when one considers the 600 or so 'Waterloo Churches' raised in thanks to God for Britain's victory over Napoleon following the Church Building Act of 1818.

'Thanksgiving Ode, January 18, 1816': The Poetics of Sacrifice

When, in the closing months of 1815, Wordsworth began to compose poetry inspired by the Battle of Waterloo, the problem of how to square the appalling realities of combat with the sublime abstractions of providential theology would prove no less pressing. In the same issue of the *Critical Review* in which the attack on Mathias appeared, a review of Walter Scott's *The Field of Waterloo* made much of that poem's failure to portray 'that scene of melancholy magnificence, that gorgeous Golgotha of the nineteenth century' (p. 457) with 'befitting state and dignity' (p. 459). The poetry that Wordsworth went on to produce in the autumn and winter of 1815–16 is distinguished by a sharp awareness of the extent to which Waterloo placed pressure on the ability of the poet and, indeed, of poetry itself to pronounce on the excessive violence of modern conflict.[31] Those bards who, like Scott and the laureate Southey, attempted to place a providential gloss on the devastation were, as most contemporary reviews confirmed, unintentionally exposing the limitations of their creative abilities whilst also undermining their claims to cultural authority.

The sonnets that Wordsworth composed for John Scott's journal *The Champion* give ample demonstration of how concerned the poet was to avoid making the same mistakes. As these poems, with their interest in questions of permanence and in the transcendence of everyday life, confirm, Wordsworth wished to avoid charges of cultural opportunism. Thus, 'The Bard, whose soul is meek as dawning day', bases its claim to 'worthily rehearse the hideous rout' (l. 12) on the poet's sense of removal from the contradictory freight of 'our time' (l. 9), finding support for its assertion of authoritative disengagement in the self-abnegating poetics of Edmund Spenser, while its companion piece, 'Intrepid sons of Albion!—not by you', finds in the notion of the soldier's wilful embrace of death a related sense of release from quotidian self-interest. The latter poem opens with a declaration of praise for those British heroes who, distinguished by their love of life from 'that impious crew', nevertheless embrace 'death […]/When duty bids you bleed in open war' (ll. 7–8). The sestet builds on the octet's delicate negotiation of the perils and pleasures of the British soldier's being for death – a satisfaction with extinction that touches on the life-denying callousness of Gallic materialism – by qualifying its opening claim, 'Heroes, for instant sacrifice prepared' (l. 8), with the assurance that such men are 'Yet filled with ardour, and on triumph bent,/Mid direst shocks of accident' (ll. 10–11). Life, in other words, persists amid annihilation, ensuring that those soldiers who might otherwise be perceived as the passive objects of 'slaughter' (l. 12) are shown labouring, even unto death, for a noble cause. The sense in which such men 'slight not life' (l. 5) yet offer themselves gladly for the sake of their country is given further liturgical significance in the closing image of the 'sacred Monument', the raising of which, echoing Christ's words on the cross (John 19.30: 'it is finished' or *consummatum est* in the Latin Vulgate),[32] is said to 'consummate the event' (ll. 13–14).

The purported marmoreal support for these lines deserves some additional consideration. By conceiving the sestet as an inscription for a monument Wordsworth entered a debate that had preoccupied the country since the news of Waterloo was announced in late June. Although in Parliament general support was given to Lord Castlereagh's proposal for the raising of a 'triumphal arch or pillar [...] in honour of the splendid victory of Waterloo', there remained some uncertainty as to which individuals should be commemorated by such a monument, with opinion polarised between those who, like Prime Minister Lord Liverpool, believed that the focus should fall exclusively on the Duke of Wellington and those opposition members, such as Charles Watkin Williams Wynn, who wished to see 'the name of every man who had fallen [...] inscribed on the monument'.[33] Outside of Parliament a Committee of Taste, led by Charles Long, Richard Payne Knight, and Sir George Beaumont, was convened to assess plans and designs for a monument; among the more outlandish plans submitted to the Committee was Andrew Robertson's proposal for a vast, granite Parthenon, to be erected on Primrose Hill near the Regent's Park Canal. The Parthenon was to show Minerva and Neptune contending for 'who shall produce the greatest heroes for great Britain', with Minerva vying for Wellington and Neptune for Nelson. The structure included a cemetery for veterans, a cenotaph for the fallen, and space for the names of every serviceman killed in the conflict. In the end, the commission was awarded to William Wilkins and John P. Gandy's plan for an 'ornamental Tower' in Regent's Park – an ambitious plan that failed, due to financial constraints, to materialise.[34]

Whether Wordsworth, through his connection with Sir George Beaumont, was motivated by ambitions to see his work literally inscribed in stone is unclear, but the fact that plans for the tower were abandoned confirms the sense in which Wordsworth's national voice was at a remove from the culture it would govern. Like the numerous common soldiers, whose 'sacrifices' would also remain unrecorded in the general clamour of 'victory sublime',[35] the failure of the sonnet to gain official recognition would serve as an unfortunate reminder of the poet's marginal status. When the poem was eventually published in *The Champion* on 4 February 1816 the debate in Parliament had fractured further as, amid the calls for towers, parthenons, and pantheons, some ministers speculated as to whether the building of a new church, dedicated to the memory of the fallen, should not make a more fitting tribute. When, on 18 January, congregations gathered to give thanks to God for the defeat of French imperialism, calls for an ecclesiastical tribute to the Waterloo dead had begun to gather pace.

It was during this period Wordsworth began work on a more ambitious Waterloo poem, a lengthy 'dramatised ejaculation' 'supposed to be composed, on the morning of the thanksgiving, uttering the sentiments of an *individual* upon that occasion' (*MY* II. 324). The resulting 'Thanksgiving Ode' gave voice not only to a developing sense of poetic authority gained, paradoxically, as a result of cultural exclusion but also to a vexed sense of the disjunction between private and state-sponsored perspectives on the deprivations of war. Unlike Castlereagh, whose assurance to Parliament of the unprecedented nature of this 'transcendentally bright' victory included scant admission of its devastating human toll,[36] Wordsworth, extending the theological concerns of his recently completed sonnets and mindful, perhaps, of the apparent ease with which fellow poets, such as the high-minded laureate Southey and the populist Scott, had described the scale of death and wounding as the unfortunate but necessary cost of British triumph, was careful, in this determinedly contemplative poem, issued from a 'low and undisturbed estate' (l. 342), to give apt expression to just how hard won that triumph had been.

Accordingly, the ode begins by distinguishing itself from those voices that would seek to portray Waterloo as the exclusive result of British military prowess, ungoverned by divine intent. Asserting that Britain has won not 'By the vengeful sword' but 'by dint of Magnanimity' (ll. 57–8), Wordsworth downplays the executive role of the Duke of Wellington that, to date, had formed the focus of most Waterloo poems, parliamentary speeches, and quite a number of thanksgiving sermons. As the ode strives to remind its audience, 'the sole true glory' (l. 83) belongs to God to whom thanks are due not that 'we have vanquished—but that we survive' (ll. 90–1). In the cautiously expressed lines that follow, Wordsworth, recalling the scenes of wartime devastation evoked in the 'Salisbury Plain' verses of the early 1790s, ascribes the blame for 'Wide-wasted regions—cities wrapped in flame [...] desolated countries' and 'towns on fire' (ll. 98–103) to French impiety before adding, by way of a veiled critique of his youthful contributions to radical anti-war sentiment, that the real violation enacted by the 'impious crew' ('Intrepid sons of Albion!', l. 8) was not on persons and property but on 'the life of virtue in mankind' (l. 106). Writing in 1816 as an avowed patriot, far removed from the radical of 1793 who sat in estranged silence when prayers were first raised for English victory, the poet expresses pride in the efforts of his countrymen but only to the extent that such efforts proclaim the will of God. Echoing Mathias's allusion to Genesis 31:3 ('And the Lord said unto Jacob, Return unto the land of thy fathers [...] and I will be with thee'), the poet frames patriotic pride within the discourse of divine submission. Alluding further to Isaiah 37:35 ('For I will defend this city to save it for mine own sake, and for my servant David's sake. Then the angel of the LORD went forth, and smote in the camp of the Assyrians') Wordsworth implies that God granted Britain the *'exterminating sword'* as a reward for its steadfastness in the prosecution of 'Evil'.[37] In representing itself as the humble instrument of divine 'Providence' the nation is protected too from 'these lingerings of distress' – economic, social and political deprivations, as well as traumatic recollections of death and injury – that would threaten to 'veil' the splendour of this great 'moral triumph'; but 'obedience to spontaneous measures', with its implicit reminder of the unregulated form of the ode, also has a role in persuading a people to abandon 'Guilt and Shame' and 'Woe' and so to don 'the radiant vest of Joy' (ll. 125–36; *passim*).

The call for self-limitation in the aftermath of victory extends also to the private sphere. In what amounts to a shocking disavowal of the assertion of poetic creativity over the militant power of Napoleon, as described in the crossing of the Alps passage in *The Prelude*, 'Imagination, ne'er before content,/But aye ascending, restless in her pride [...] Stoops to that closing deed magnificent,/And with the embrace is satisfied' (ll. 163–7).[38] Though the heavily stressed 'Stoops' goes some way to reclaiming some of the Imagination's lost potency it fails to distract from the overarching drive to self-effacement in the face of a higher power. When these lines are read in the light of the youthful poet's assertions of praise for the power of imagination, it is hard not to regard them as a form of creative sacrifice, a gesture akin to the numerous corporeal sacrifices enacted on the field of battle. Yet, as the lines that follow make clear, Wordsworth strives also to show that loss for the sake of a noble cause leads to a greater gain: the incorporation of that which was lost within the inexhaustible frame of the divine. As the conclusion to the poem insists, for a being of 'sovereign penetration' (l. 296), the sight of victory 'Though sprung from bleeding war, is one of pure delight' (l. 305).[39] This emphasis on the sublimation of war's material foundation extends to the effacement of the poem's origins in a system of cultural production. Having seemingly abandoned previous efforts to see his verse inscribed in stone, Wordsworth now conceives his country's praise and, by extension, his own poem as a 'transcendental monument' (l. 213), a 'work' not 'of hands' but of 'the soul', an immaterial trophy reaching 'To highest Heaven' (ll. 215–16). More cannily, perhaps, the poem refers here to those calls in Parliament for the building of a new church, 'A pile that grace approves, and time can trust' (l. 229), while also deferring to those favouring the observance of regular thanksgiving ceremonies in Westminster Abbey. Turning from the trope of light to the power of sound, the poem envisages, with a glance towards Burke's *Reflections on the Revolution in France*, how within such sacred space bonds of 'sweet and threatening harmony' (l. 244) will unite 'The living generations with the dead' (l. 240), transforming unwholesome memories of death and wounding (l. 254) into 'potent symphonies' of 'victory and praise' (ll. 251–2).[40]

As if prompted by these disturbing echoes of the underlying matter of war, Wordsworth turns in the next section of the ode to a sustained justification for the losses of Waterloo. Drawing on Jeremiah 27:8 ('that nation will I punish, saith the LORD, with the sword, and with the famine, and with the pestilence, until I have consumed them by his hand'), the poem reminds its audience that it is God who 'guides the Pestilence', the 'Earthquake', and 'the fierce Tornado' (ll. 260–71; *passim*).[41] The effects of sublime devastation, in other words, are authorised by the divine. 'But', the poem goes on notoriously to assert, 'thy most dreaded instrument/In working out a pure intent/Is Man—arrayed for mutual slaughter, —Yea, Carnage is thy daughter!' (ll. 279–82). William Hazlitt, writing a review of a performance of *Coriolanus* published in December 1816 in the *Examiner*, just a few months after the appearance of Wordsworth's poem, seized upon the grammatically ambiguous pronouncement as evidence of how 'the language of poetry naturally falls in with the language of power' (*CWWH* IV. 347–8). Hazlitt's somewhat stunned appreciation of Shakespeare's depiction of the seductive excitement of tyranny may therefore be understood as an attempt to come to terms with Wordsworth's public endorsement of the triumph of 'Legitimacy'. For Hazlitt, the shock occasioned by the publication of the 'Thanksgiving Ode' makes sense if the 'principle' of poetry is conceived as *naturally* 'aristrocratical', 'anti-levelling', 'dazzling', and excessive. Quoting Shakespeare and Wordsworth in succession he writes:

> It shows its head turreted, crowned, and crested. Its front is gilt and bloodstained. Before it 'it carries noise, and behind it leaves tears'. It has its altars and its victims, sacrifices, human sacrifices. Kings, priests, nobles are its train-bearers, tyrants and slaves its executioners. — 'Carnage is its [*sic*] daughter.' — Poetry is right-royal. (*CWWH* IV. 347–8)

Hazlitt's respectful yet troubled response to Wordsworth's demonstration of the language of power was counteracted in 1819 by Shelley's savagely parodic *Peter Bell the Third*:

> Then Peter wrote odes to the Devil; —
> In one of which he meekly said: —
>   'May Carnage and Slaughter,
>   Thy niece and thy daughter,
>   May Rapine and Famine,
>   Thy gorge ever cramming,
>   Glut thee with living and dead!'[42]

A few years later Lord Byron, less shocked and perhaps less surprised by manifestations of Lakean apostasy, recalled the offending lines in a passage on the Battle of Waterloo in *Don Juan*:

> 'Carnage' (so Wordsworth tells you) 'is God's daughter:'
> If *he* speak truth, she is Christ's sister, and
> Just now behaved as in the Holy Land.[43]

In a note to the passage Byron comments: 'this is perhaps as pretty a pedigree for Murder as ever was found out by Garter King at Arms. — What would have been said, had any free-spoken people discovered such a lineage?'[44] Defending Byron's critique of Wordsworth's lines in an essay published in *Fiction, Fair and Foul* (1880), John Ruskin would conclude that 'the death of the innocent in battle carnage' is not 'His "instrument for working out a pure intent," as Mr. Wordsworth puts it; but Man's instrument for working out an impure one'.[45] That Wordsworth was himself troubled by 'Carnage is thy daughter' is implied by the alteration of the lines in the 1845 *Poems* to the doctrinally inoffensive

> But Man is Thy most awful instrument,
> In working out a pure intent;
> Thou cloth'st the wicked in their dazzling mail,
> And for thy righteous purpose they prevail.[46]

As well as providing a less contentious account of the relations between wartime suffering and divine providence, by cleverly identifying the agents of destruction with the forces of impiety the revised lines perform the additional trick of obviating the Allies from the slaughter of Waterloo. Thus, while falling short of an outright volte face, the ode's final incarnation facilitates the providential rationale for carnage that, in 1816, largely because of maladroit expression, had been a cause of such justifiable outrage.

But while opposition writers were understandably exercised by the poem's manifest callousness, it should be borne in mind that the ascription of carnage to the will of God was not out of line with church doctrine. In 1794, the Reverend Samuel Humfrays, referring his congregation to Isaiah 34.6 ('The sword of the LORD is filled with blood'), had declared: 'This then is the true Faith, that we believe and confess, that War with all its train of Miseries, Rapine, Conflagration, and Carnage is the *Act of God*'.[47] More immediately the text was invoked in the course of a thanksgiving sermon by the Scottish Canadian minister John Bethune:

> He himself put the sword into their hands, he regulated their marches, he breathed courage and ardour into their soldiers, made them indefatigable in labour, invincible in battle; and caused terror and consternation to go constantly before them. The Christian, walking in the meridian light of the Gospel, perceives the hand of God conducting these conquerors through fields of blood and carnage.[48]

As the rousing cadences of Bethune's prose demonstrate, religious justifications for wartime suffering came perilously close to evoking that 'something' in war that 'the heart enjoys'. Though far removed from the 'treacherous embellishments' condemned by Thomas Chalmers, Wordsworth's apparent endorsement of the violence of battle nevertheless bears a disturbing family resemblance to the euphoria of destruction evoked in religious discourse. That Wordsworth was, throughout his career, fascinated by his own propensity to seek delight in scenes of destruction is shown also in the resemblance between the bracing disclosure of 'Yea, Carnage is thy daughter!' and those passages, previously discussed, in which the prospect of dissolution is linked with the sublime. Yet, even as he is drawn to the annihilating threshold of human imagining, Wordsworth does not lose sight of that other 'something' that reins in destructive desires. In 'Home at Grasmere', 'The Recluse', and *The White Doe of Rylstone*, deliverance from over-identification with violence is found in the sanctification of nature; in the ode, as we have seen, it is found exclusively in God: the 'current of this matin song' lies 'deeper [...] Than aught dependent on the fickle skies' (ll. 53–5).

What is often overlooked in readings of the ode's apparent endorsement of carnage is how other poems in the Thanksgiving volume attempt to address the human costs of war. In the collection's concluding poem, 'Elegiac Verses', a heavenly spirit, while taking account of 'Unpitied havoc' and 'Victims unlamented' (l. 14), promises to 'wash away' the 'stains' of a 'perturbèd earth' (ll. 1–4). The spirit accordingly sprinkles 'soft celestial dews/Thy lost maternal heart to reinfuse!' and, 'Scattering this far-fetched moisture from my wings', cleanses the 'secret springs [...] stained so oft with human gore' (ll. 23–6).[49] Like Horace's Bandusia, mortal stains are temporary; through divine intervention blood is turned to water and the sacred river is rejuvenated. In 'Ode. Composed in January 1816', which follows the title poem, an epigraph from Horace's ode to Censorinus reaffirms the lasting worth of poetry, while the verse itself envisions a post-war era of bucolic calm and 'festive beauty' (l. 28).[50] Wordsworth's fantasia portrays a peaceable realm in which warriors with 'crimson banners proudly streaming,/And upright weapons innocently gleaming' (ll. 45–6), are attended by white-robed maidens. The vision recedes, but the poem goes on to imagine unfading tributes of the 'silent art' (l. 81), 'expressive records of a glorious strife [...] Trophies on which the morning sun may shine,/As changeful ages flow' (ll. 94–8). Whereas conflict belongs to the turbulent course of history, art resides with eternity. But greater still than the tributes provided by sculpture are the transcendent records of elevated writing. Thus, the ode concludes with a hymn of praise to the 'Pierian sisters' and, in particular to Mnemosyne, for too long an exile from 'consecrated stream and grove' (l. 102), and a hope that 'I, or some more favoured Bard' (l. 115) may, from 'some spotless fountain' (l. 111), write verse that will secure a lasting memory of Britain's martial triumphs.

In Chapter 5 I return to the consideration of how the image of the sacred fount provides a debateable source of restitution in the aftermath of war, but here we should note how the volume's return to classical sources casts the image of lasting peace as dreamy and fanciful, a vision of national concord rendered dubious as a result of its promiscuous comingling of the sacred and the profane – St George and the Muses vying for authority in a disenchanted world. A counterpart to the 'Thanksgiving Ode', 'Ode. Composed in January 1816' is intended to sweeten that poem's grim affirmation of providential suffering and to consolidate the poet's authority; but just as, in relation to the former, the vision of bodily resurrection is held in delicate tension with the awareness that the prospect of 'martyred Countrymen' garlanded in 'amaranthine wreathes' (ll. 42–4) cannot be maintained outside 'Fancy in her airy bower' (3), so, in relation to the latter, at the poem's close an admission of temporal impermanence and a sequence of conditionals ('for a moment meet my soul's desires/That I [...] may hear [and] may catch' the 'noblest' of Mnemosyne's 'lyres'; ll. 113–17) qualifies the poet's bid for national recognition.

This last point returns us to consideration of the poem's form. In March 1816, Wordsworth informed John Scott that he had composed an 'irregular

Ode' upon the subject of the Thanksgiving, 'the longest thing of the Lyrical Kind, I believe except Spenser's Epithalamion, in our language' (*MY* II. 284). In a subsequent letter to Southey, Wordsworth explains that because the ode is meant to express the feelings of an individual on this occasion rather than 'the sentiments of a multitude', a regular stanza was rejected. Making a virtue of his position as a poet declaiming on national affairs from the cultural margins, Wordsworth notes that formal irregularity may be excused 'where the occasion is so great as to justify an aspiration after a state of freedom beyond what a succession of regular Stanzas will allow' (p. 284). Having placed in tension the Pindaric and Horatian impulses that animate the English ode, thus torn between uttering the voice of a multitude and aspiring after a state of freedom, the verse, on account of the fact that the 'occasion' *is* informed by 'the sentiments of a multitude', becomes the vehicle for an alienated, self-baffling lyric 'I'. That sense of self-contestation is deepened when one considers how the 'Thanksgiving Ode's allusion to Spenser's wedding song is sustained not merely at the level of formal irregularity but also in terms of the poem's temporal organisation, which like the *Epithalamion* follows the course of the sun's rising and setting. Observing the nation's celebratory rituals from a distance, the poet is at once a part of this time yet excluded from it, able to reflect the events that occur on this day yet unable to fully inhabit them. One might go further and recall the similarities with the position of the speaker in 'The Rime of the Ancient Mariner'. In both instances, the liturgical ceremony that would heal the catastrophic disruption of God and Man is overshadowed by a figure who, having sundered himself from that communion, is condemned to watch from outside.

For over thirty years the 'Thanksgiving Ode' performed an uncertain role in Wordsworth's self-fashioning. In Chapter 5 I will have more to say about the significance of the placing of the ode and its attendant verses in Wordsworth's collected poems, but to round off this discussion of how the ode's formal qualities are linked to the poet's personal concerns it is worth paying some attention to how the poem came to be revised. In 1820 the poem was divided into fourteen irregular stanzas, perhaps in hope of mitigating the effects of the expressive freedom that, in 1816, had stood as a marker of the poet's cultural disenfranchisement. In appearance, the newly sequenced ode drew the verse into the ambit of hymnal regularity, thereby lending the ode the illusion, at least, of uttering sentiments representative of a multitude. Placed in the four-volume 1820 *Miscellaneous Poems* as the concluding poem of the Sonnets Dedicated to Liberty, the 'Thanksgiving Ode' could now be read as the culmination of a twenty-year sequence of patriotic verses providing ample justification of the poet's claim to speak, as Milton and Spenser had before him, on behalf of the national interest. The bid to be accepted as the voice of authority was resumed again in the early 1840s when the decision was taken to remove lines 163–288, recasting them as a separate poem titled 'Ode. 1815'. Opening with the image of 'Imagination' stooping before 'the Victory, on that Belgic field', and including the redacted version of the lines assigning carnage to the will of God, the new poem effectively takes on the burden of containing the expressive instability that, in 1816, had prevented the 'Thanksgiving Ode' from attaining the status of a public pronouncement on Britain's triumph at Waterloo. In its significantly curtailed form, the 1845 'Thanksgiving Ode', which followed 'Ode. 1815' as the finale of the 'Poems Dedicated to National Independence and Liberty', no longer bore the imprint of those affecting personal transgressions that, at the time of the poem's composition, gave proof of the poet's separation from the affairs of state. Now, as poet laureate, having dispersed those uncomfortable reminders of an identity at odds with itself, Wordsworth could at last be assured of his right to speak on behalf of a multitude.

Love in the Time of War

Carnage remains, however, stubbornly resistant to bardic transformation, sullying alike the prospect of peace, the belief in a God of justice and mercy, and the right of the poet to pronounce on matters of state. Of those contemporaries who took issue with the ode's seeming endorsement of the destructive power of the divine it is Byron who offers perhaps the most illuminating perspective: '"Carnage" (so Wordsworth tells you) "is God's daughter":/If *he* speak truth, she is Christ's sister.'[51] What Byron's satire draws out, in stressing the peculiarity of the gendering of carnage, sheds additional light on Wordsworth's early fascination with the pleasures and pains of war. In Book 10 of *The Prelude*, Wordsworth follows the account of his uneasy responses to Anglican victory prayers with an extended description of how, in France, 'Domestic carnage now filled all the year' (l. 329). He then goes on to describe the effects of the Terror in terms that seem to have, as Kenneth Johnston suggests, a deep, personal resonance: like William and Annette, in line 331 the 'maiden' is separated 'from the bosom of her love' and, in the following line, in anticipation of the possible fate of Annette and Caroline, 'the mother' is taken 'from the cradle of her babe'.[52] In lines 327–45 the image of the motherless child is sustained in the description of the revolutionaries as children of 'heinous appetites', toying with a 'windmill', which, 'at arm's length', they 'front against the blast [...]/To make it whirl the faster'. Since Wordsworth was not present for the birth of his child, one wonders to what extent the poem's earlier allusions to the 'solid birthright' of a republic 'Redeem'd according to example given/By ancient Lawgivers' (ll. 186–8) is informed by feelings of guilt and concern for ensuring the legitimacy of his progeny. Might illegitimacy, in both the familial and the political senses of the word, be responsible for conflict at all levels of society? By way of an answer to this question Wordsworth's 'Thanksgiving Ode' contends the illegitimate child is, nevertheless, a daughter of God and that when viewed from a providential perspective the devastation she wreaks upon on the world may be understood as the 'working out' of 'a pure intent' (l. 280).

The connections between marriage, restoration, and peace that the ode's echoes of the *Epithalamion* facilitate have, of course, their personal dimensions. Eric C. Walker has speculated that Wordsworth, in alluding to Spenser's poem, may well have wished to tacitly acknowledge the recent wedding of Caroline Wordsworth-Vallon. Born in December 1792, on the cusp of hostilities between Britain and France, Caroline could well have figured in the poet's mind as an emblem of domestic discord, one that extended to the division between Britain and France.[53] Despite the fact that Wordsworth failed to attend his daughter's wedding (echoes here of the failed act of union with Annette) the marriage that took place on 28 February 1816 might have appeared as symbolic confirmation that the traumatic breaks and missed encounters of 1792–3 had at last been healed. When, in 1820, some years after peace was concluded with France, the Wordsworths at last made their journey to France, reuniting father and child, and the never-to-have-been husband and wife, might there have been a moment in which Wordsworth looked on his daughter, now herself a wife and mother, as at once the bearer of conflict *and* as a principle of restitution? In the sonnet 'After Visiting the Field of Waterloo', written in the same year, the poet announces: 'We felt as Men should feel,/With such vast hoards of hidden carnage near,/And horror breathing from the silent ground' (ll. 12–14).[54] Here, Wordsworth appears to compensate for his previous unfeeling response to the carnage of Waterloo. But there is, I think, a deeper resonance to the poet's sobering response to the gross matter of war. As noted previously, in 1793 Wordsworth experienced 'a conflict of sensations' (*Prelude* Book X, l. 265) as church congregations uttered prayers for the vanquishing of a nation that once had offered the promise of liberty, fraternity, and equality. As the friend of a Girondist, and as the lover of a royalist, the returnee 'felt/The ravage of this unnatural strife' (ll. 249–50) as a form of internal warfare, crossing the boundaries between revolution and legitimacy, loyalty to the cause and loyalty to the nation. Amidst this whirlwind of feelings, Wordsworth remembers how he 'Exulted in the triumph' of his soul 'When Englishmen by thousands were o'erthrown' (ll. 260–1). When, twenty-two years later, the poet made his visit to the scene of the French Revolution's defeat, the encounter with the ground that literally blurred the boundaries between bodies, nations, and ideologies no doubt provoked a memory of these earlier, treasonous affects. But in addition to addressing feelings of 'Guilt' at having once gloried in the spectacle of war, when these lines are read in light of the Horatian ascription of violence to carnal desire (*Nam fuit ante Helenam cunnus taeterrima belli/causa*) it is possible that Wordsworth speaks no less of the 'Shame' (ll. 127) issuing from acts of love.[55]

In that same year, Wordsworth returned to 'Laodamia', intending to revise that poem's troublesome conclusion. In the first printed version of the poem, Laodamia, thwarted in her efforts to detain the shade of her departed warrior husband, is 'Delivered from the galling yoke of time/ And these frail elements to gather flowers/Of blissful quiet mid unfading bowers' (ll. 161–3).[56] Urging readers to judge 'gently' of one 'who so deeply loved' (l. 158), the poem was altered in 1820 to preclude the exercise of 'weak pity' for one who had loved 'in reason's spite', leaving the widow 'doomed to wander in a grosser clime,/Apart from happy Ghosts'. As recounted by Benjamin Robert Haydon, who was party to a reading of the poem following Wordsworth's return from the Continent, the alteration was prompted by Mary who persuaded her husband that Laodamia 'had too *lenient a fate* for loving her Husband *so absurdly*'.[57] We may speculate on the extent to which Mary's 'petition' was driven by feelings aroused by the no doubt awkward encounter with Annette Vallon just a few weeks before. Did the fate of *that* abandoned woman rekindle thoughts of how love should submit to duty in times of war? If so, what are we to make of Mary's response to the reading of the poem? According to Haydon while Wordsworth repeated the verse in 'his chaunting tone, his wife sat by the Fire quite abstracted, moaning out the burthen of the line, like a distant echo. I never saw such a complete instance of devotion, of adoration'.[58] Satisfaction may be found in self-abnegation, and there is a sense in which Mary's moans speak at once of the burden of pleasure as well as the burden of suffering, but the inarticulacy echoes too the inability of the poem to resolve its feelings towards the woman who, out of desire for her husband, seeks his restoration. If, in 1820, Laodamia is roundly condemned for her failure to love as a woman should love during war, the verse yet retains a shadow of sympathy for those who cannot submit wholly to the silencing of desire. Something of that lament for rebellious human will survives in the poem's closing image of the 'spiry trees' growing from the warrior's tomb, which, 'when such stature they had gained/That Ilium's walls were subject to their view,/The trees' tall summits wither'd at the sight;/A constant interchange of growth and blight!' (ll. 171–3). In Pliny's *Natural History*, from which the account derives, the long-lived trees testify to Protesilaus's bitterness towards his fate, a manifestation of discontent at odds with the ascription of selfless devotion to a higher cause. In Wordsworth's poem they serve too as a reminder of the gulf between natural life and the 'unfading bowers' of eternity and as a figure for the love that persists in reason's spite.

The conflict between natural impulses and higher reason is sustained in 'Dion', a poem that shares with 'Laodamia' an origin in classical literature and complements that poem's interest in the relationship between *oikos* and *polis*. Furthering the paradox that the home, in order to be preserved, must be sacrificed on the altar of service to the state, Dion, the liberator of Sicily and student of Plato, is presented in Wordsworth's poem as aloof from sexual yearning and, at the same time, as curiously transgendered. Echoing the poem's beautiful opening description of a swan, gliding in luminescent splendour 'without visible Mate/Or Rival save the Queen of night' (ll. 16–17), 'Long-exil'd Dion' (l. 42) marches at the head of his triumphant army in 'still magnificence' (l. 23).[59] The image of heroic self-sufficiency is overshadowed, however, by intimations of domestic division. As Eric Walker observes, in Plutarch's *Lives* rumours abound that Dion 'liked not his marriage, and coulde not live quietlie with his wife', thus highlighting the 'incommensurability of marriage and the very peace it is taken to signify'.[60] Wordsworth, as if in recognition of this incommensurability, omits the scene of loving reunion that for Plutarch at least works partially to affirm the restoration of peace after war, preferring instead to consolidate the vision of Dion's swan-like, solipsistic austerity. Yet, as the poem goes on to affirm, the equation of peace and conjugality is not so much denied as transferred to another register. With no wife to greet him, Dion himself takes on the role of the bride as, 'crown'd with flowers of Sicily/And in a white, far-beaming, corslet clad' (ll. 43–4), the military procession is transformed into an event not a million miles away from the vision of happy espousal underwriting the 'Thanksgiving Ode'. Thus, married to the state, Dion through 'rites divine' (l. 53) is raised to the level of a 'very Deity' (l. 60). There is, perhaps, in a yet unwritten version of 'Dion' the potential for peace to be reimagined not as the gender-normative union of man and woman but as a fluid, or queered, state of perpetual self-invention. But in the poem that is to hand, the depiction of the warrior-hero as the virginal bride resonates only to the extent that it signifies, in Keatsian fashion, a mode of unravished self-government.

In its published form the poem proceeds to temper the image of pious autonomy by casting Dion as a leader whose 'self-sufficing solitude' is matched by 'majestic lowliness' (ll. 32–3), but the source material, which represents the hero as 'a sower man' beset by 'a certain hawtiness of mind and severitie', vies with this description. Moreover, as the poem goes on to reveal, the softening influence of Platonism has failed to prevent Dion from ordering the assassination of his rival Heraclides. From hereon the verse descends into nightmare as, manifested in the form of a vengeful phantom, Dion is confronted by the memory of his crimes. Presented as the obverse of Dion's ethereal beauty, the 'hideous' (l. 87) spectre, dressed in 'woman's garb' (l. 88), takes shape in the poem as a parodic representation of female domestic virtue, her compulsive sweeping a cipher for the failure of peace to eradicate the taint of bloodshed. With 'angry perturbations,—and that look/Which no philosophy can brook!' (ll. 119–20), Dion's dream of glory is brought to earth, providing the lesson that God defends only the statesman 'Whose means are fair and spotless as his ends' (l. 143). The poem's homiletic ending cannot, however, quite subdue the unsettling vision on which it is founded. The marriage that would bring an end to war is shown in 'Dion' to be fractured, jeopardised by the failure of the warrior-leader to prevent the return of the excluded feminine other as an avenging ghost. As a line from the unrevised fair copy confirms, in love after war 'Peace, even Peace herself, is fugitive' (l. 36).

Ceaseless Fire

An extract from a letter written by Dorothy Wordsworth in January 1817 provides ample proof of the extent to which the Wordsworths had become aware of the material hardships facing ordinary people in the aftermath of war. From her window in Halifax (Dorothy had been staying with the Rawsons since October 1816), she reflects on the extent to which the decline in manufacturing has affected the poor: 'Things cannot go on in this way. For a time whole streets—men, women and children may be kept alive by public charity; but the consequence will be awful, if nothing can be manufactured in these places where such numbers of people have been gathered together'. The sight of such distress brings to mind an observation of the Wanderer: 'I see "many rich sink down as in a dream among the poor"'.⁶¹ Looking back on the deprivations of the 1790s the Wanderer looks forward no less to the socio-economic precarity of the late 1810s, deepening the sense in which, for rich and poor alike, war is experienced as the unexceptional condition of everyday life. In Chapter 5, through a reading of the River Duddon sonnets in relation to Peterloo, I will resume this discussion of Wordsworth's response to the maintenance of hostilities in post-war society, but to conclude this chapter I want to consider a final ode from the Thanksgiving collection.

Overlooked in critical accounts of the volume, 'Who rises on the banks of Seine' straddles the line in Wordsworth's classificatory system between Imagination and Liberty. Assigned to the former category in 1820 before being moved to the latter in 1827, the ode was originally placed as the penultimate poem of the Thanksgiving volume. What is interesting about the poem is how it utilises the resources of the irregular ode – variable rhyme and stress patterns, sudden turns and rapidly shifting imagery – to mimic the protean course of the French Revolution and the irresolution of its opponents. In its opening movement the Revolution is personified as a beguiling enchantress, promising peace, love, and joy to those attracted by the shelter of her 'wide-spread wings' (l. 4). By line 5, however, the abrupt movement from pentameter to trimeter, combined with the insertion of the qualifier 'But' and the enervating effects of the repeated present participles ('But they are ever playing,/And twinkling in the light,—/And if a breeze be straying,/That breeze she will invite', ll. 5–8), exposes the Revolution as a creature of fancy, a Miltonic temptress leading men astray. The effect of mass, hypnotic delusion is carried over into lines 9–11 through an anaphoric sequence of introductory conjunctions and simple present tense verbs ('And stands on tiptoe [...]/And calls a look of love [...]/And spreads her arms', ll. 9–11), which cause the assembled principalities to 'melt' (l. 13). Transformed by the end of the sequence into an armoured dragon, the Revolution poses a threat to the integrity of a series of morally charged abstract nouns. As Justice, Faith, and Hope seem to diminish in the face of her polluted sovereignty (ll. 33–6), history itself appears to succumb to the effects of the poem's narcotic repetition as shame following shame and woe supplanting woe become 'the only change that time can show' (ll. 39–40). Picking up on the mood of futility conveyed by these lines, the poet laments 'How long shall vengeance sleep? Ye patient Heavens, how long?' (l. 41), only to counter this complaint with the fierce denunciation of 'Nations wanting virtue to be strong' and 'daring not to feel the majesty of right!' (ll. 44–5).

By the poem's midpoint the mood of despair at the cyclical insufficiency of the global resistance to France appears so pervasive as to preclude even the possibility of victory. Between lines 46 and 60 the desire of the nations to seek for external aid, whether from 'Saints above' (l. 52) or from quasi-pagan 'wishes' (l. 49), is condemned as the source of a kind of spiritual ennui. At this point, having exhausted the observance of national sloth and languor in the face of manifest evil, one might expect the ode to move into a final phase of righteous indignation before a final assertion of the triumph of the just and the true. However, what Wordsworth offers up by way of a conclusion to the poem falls significantly short of this expectation. Opening with a refutation of the power of the 'Supreme Disposer' (l. 61), Napoleon, to overturn the rule of law and justice held as a governing principle 'since the first framing of societies' (l. 64), the endorsement of the social contract that would defend mankind from 'the power of wrong' (l. 68) feels somewhat half-hearted. By far the most persuasive aspect of the ode is its preceding account of how nations succumb to the temptations of secular redemption and then, through failing to offer a coherent counter-response to that temptation, give way to despair. Placed before 'Elegiac Verses', 'Who rises on the banks of Seine' could be read as a contrivance of defeatism prior to that concluding poem's affirmative response. Yet in many ways it is the former poem that best captures the mood of social and political instability that prevailed in Britain following Napoleon's defeat. Mapping the rapid turns of post-war elevation and inertia onto its erratic rhetorical patterning and desultory conclusion, the ode perhaps served more fittingly than the 'Thanksgiving Ode' as a poem that spoke to and of the times.

CHAPTER 4

'Returning, Like a Ghost Unlaid'
Peter Bell *and* The Waggoner

Wordsworth: 1818–1819

Troubled long with warring notions,
Long impatient of thy rod,
I resign my soul's emotions
Unto thee, mysterious God!
—'Inscriptions to Be Found in, and near, a Hermit's Cell'[1]

It is hard to imagine a bleaker outlook for the advancement of Wordsworth's literary reputation than that which presented itself in 1818. Preoccupied with campaigning for the Lowther brothers, alarmed by the Jacobinical stirrings of the local press, harried by political opponents, and beset with financial concerns and worries for the education of his three children, the composition of poetry became, for the most part, a secondary concern. Neither *The White Doe*, the two-volume *Poems*, nor the 'Thanksgiving Ode' had helped to improve Wordsworth's standing with the reading public, so it is perhaps hardly surprising that inspiration for the completion of a major literary work had begun to recede. Yet it would be wrong to assume that no poetry of note was produced during this period as, from the beginning of the year through to the spring of 1819, Wordsworth composed occasional verses that explore his feelings of creative frustration, fears of cultural irrelevance, and sense of embattlement. In this regard, the composition of 'Inscriptions, Supposed to Be Found in, and near, a Hermit's Cell' can be read as an exploration of the sense of cultural autonomy that the writing and publication of the political pamphlet *Two Addresses to the Freeholders of Westmorland* just a few months later would place in doubt. Aligned neither to patron or to place, voiced in the character of a social outsider, these imaginary inscriptions convey, variously, a preoccupation with the evanescence of thoughts (I), the fall of monuments into 'shapeless ruin' (l. 28) (II), the vanity of human wishes (III), and a plea to God for deliverance from 'warring notions' (IV, l. 1, and V). Unpublished in 1818, the inscriptions would eventually find a place in the

1820 Duddon collection, printed between the sonnet 'On the Death of His Late Majesty' and the translation of 'The Prioress's Tale'.² In this new context the verses float free of the personal concerns that animated their composition, defusing, in the case of 'IV. Near the Spring of the Hermitage', the urgency of their questioning:

> What avails the kindly shelter
> Yielded by this craggy rent,
> If my spirits toss and welter
> On the waves of discontent? (ll. 5–8)

Only in submission to God can relief be found from the contradictions of literary patronage, but the use of litotes and the conditional and the delayed object at the end of this inscription – 'Thus dishonouring not her station,/Would my Life present to Thee,/Gracious God, the pure oblation/Of Divine Tranquillity!' (ll. 12–15) – belies somewhat the sturdiness of the hermit's resolve. Peace in this formulation retains its status as the unrealisable horizon of human understanding, a point of quiet oblivion beyond the reach of history.

The successful election of the Lowthers to the East and Lonsdale wards at the beginning of July did little to relieve the troubled tempers of the Broughamites, and on the eighteenth Wordsworth worried that 'a military force' (*MY* II. 475) would have to be deployed to quash the spirit of rebellion. A concern that war might erupt within civil society came, as we shall see in the next chapter, to preoccupy Wordsworth in this period. The idea that the peace of 1815 might need to be defended informs two flower poems that appeared at the beginning of the new year. Like the daisy poems of 1802 and 1815, the snowdrop stands as a symbol of peaceful renewal, albeit, in this case, of renewal under duress. As meteorological and political storms whipped across Westmorland, the snowdrop provides a lesson in quiet resistance, offering gentle testimony to the triumph of the 'Chaste' in a time of inflated passions ('To a Snow-drop, Appearing Very Early in the Season').³ As illustrated by the opening lines of 'Sonnet. On Seeing a Tuft of Snowdrops in a Storm', a congruence of anti-Byronic and anti-Broughamite feeling, tinged with memories of those 'high instincts' before which 'mortal Nature' trembles 'like a guilty Thing surpriz'd',⁴ informs the poem's celebration of the meek:

> When haughty expectations prostrate lie,
> And grandeur crouches like a guilty thing,
> Oft shall the lowly weak, till nature bring
> Mature release, in fair society
> Survive, and Fortune's utmost anger try [...] (ll. 1–5)⁵

Observing how the snowdrops' 'helmets' (l. 6) brave the winter blasts, the sonnet goes on to draw a striking comparison with the resistance of the 'Emathian phalanx' to the 'immortal Theban band' (ll. 11–12), a union of the 'frail' (l. 5) against overwhelming odds. More militant in tone than 'To the Daisy' and its accompanying poems, the connotations of passive endurance are all but voided by the poem's allusions to classical epic and noble self-sacrifice.

Reviewing in 'Malham Cove' the collapse of worldly ambitions, Wordsworth could find, 'mid the wreck of IS and WAS', reasons enough to bemoan a career marked by 'Things incomplete and purposes betrayed' (ll. 11–12).[6] The elegiac mood is sustained in two sonnets composed in the spring of 1819: 'I watch, and long have watch'd, with calm regret' and 'Aerial Rock—whose solitary brow', poems concerned with aging and creative decline. But while these sonnets, along with the 'Inscriptions', presented an image of the poet as baffled, betrayed, and disillusioned, in other poems from this period figures of transient beauty and neglected import provide a way forward, offering a 'shield of Tranquillity' to withstand the 'suffering tumult'.[7] As the year progressed, and questions of political and religious vexation ceded to matters cultural and aesthetic, Wordsworth would discover in 'The Haunted Tree' a way to convert the image of a 'time-dismantled Oak' (l. 7) into 'a vision of English authority',[8] resistant in the nobleness of its decay to the self-indulgent luxuriance and Levantine eroticism of Keats, Shelley, and Byron.[9] Composed in the late spring or early summer, it seems likely that the writing of this poem was prompted by the hostility directed at *Peter Bell* and *The Waggoner* – a hostility fomented, in large measure, by the Cockney School.

Tim Fulford and Jeffrey Cox have both written persuasively about the effects of the contest between the Lake and Cockney schools on Wordsworth's late poetry.[10] The discussion that follows does not add to this debate but seeks, rather, to read these narrative poems in relation to the debates about peace, war, and poetic creativity that have animated this study thus far. Drawing initially on the largely derogatory responses of the periodical press to these poems, the chapter aims to show how the radical experimentation of poetry devised in the 1790s and early 1800s chimed with the concerns expressed in later years for the weak, the embattled, and the neglected, suggesting the persistence of an interest in ontological levelling well into the period of apparent conservative decline. If the poet as a Tory campaigner fashions himself as the aggrieved victim of Jacobinical force, or as a voice in the wilderness, warning of the sensual poison of contemporary culture to an audience of none, the poetry that came to public attention in this period presents a rather more complex picture. In Chapter 2 I considered the representation of peace in *The White Doe of Rylstone* in terms of the participatory relationship between human and non-human beings. In this chapter I return to this consideration, paying attention to the ways in which these tolerant, playful, and essentially good-humoured poems rebut the image of the late Wordsworth as a peevish and obdurate prophet of gloom. An idea that the Thanksgiving volume held in abeyance thus returns to burden Wordsworth's post-war imagination, providing an impression, however short-lived, of a world at peace with itself.

Peter Bell: Engaging the 'Animal Within'

In his fine discussion of *Peter Bell*, Jeffrey Cox makes the point that when 'a poem enters into the world, no matter when it was written, readers see it as speaking to both the present moment and contemporary writers'.[11] As we shall see, discussion of *Peter Bell* and *The Waggoner*, poems drafted, respectively, in 1798 and 1806, but not published until 1819, invites consideration of some counter-factual histories, such as when, in 1814, on the cusp of issuing the *Excursion*, Wordsworth imagined a volume of narrative poems comprising the *White Doe of Rylstone*, *Peter Bell*, and *The Waggoner*. It is interesting to continue to speculate on how this volume might have been read and understood in the immediate post-war period, and in this chapter I will give some thought to how, as a collection, these 'late' early poems speak to a range of actual and possible concerns.

Consideration of contemporary reviews provides a useful entry point for this discussion. As Cox notes, the savaging of *Peter Bell* and *The Waggoner* was at least partially informed by feelings of betrayal. That, by 1819, the Lake School had demonstrably rescinded its support for democratic principles, with Southey established as poet laureate, Coleridge transformed into an apologist for Church and State, and Wordsworth outed as a Tory hireling, was a source of rancour for second-generation radicals. The furore against *Peter Bell*, drummed up by Wordsworth's antagonists and manifested in the form of parodies and scathing reviews, could be read as a form of tribute, a last-ditch attempt by former admirers to laugh the lost leader into self-realisation and self-reform, or at least to maintain silence.[12] But if this were the message that was delivered to Rydal, it was not the message that Wordsworth received. Writing to John Monkhouse, Sara Hutchinson observed that the abusive reviews, pre-empted by the appearance of John Hamilton Reynold's parody, had the unintended effect of encouraging sales of *Peter Bell*, enough to demand a second edition of the poem within a fortnight of its publication. Prompted by this unexpected commercial success, but at the same time irked by the poem's critical reception, the supreme offence of which was a public recitation of another parody in the house of Thomas King, the local Broughamite (*MY* II. 543), Wordsworth consented 'to publish *The Waggoner*, just to give them another bone to pick'.[13] Declaring ignorance 'of the critiques to which you allude' Wordsworth informed Hans Busk that it 'is now 20 years since the "Duncery" of the periodical Press first declared war against me; and they have kept it up with laudable perseverance' (*MY* II. 547). In addition to the Thomas King affair, Wordsworth must have been aware of the far-reaching influence of the Cockney School on account of the reprinting of Keats's review of Reynold's poem in the *Kendal Chronicle*.[14] He may also have known about Leigh Hunt's scathing judgement on *Peter Bell* in *The Examiner*, which spoke of 'another didactic little horror' of Wordsworth's while denouncing its 'half-witted prejudices' and its 'philosophy of violence and hopelessness'.[15]

The last phrase is resonant. In November 1815, at a time when 'Freedom' had been made 'a pretence for old aggression' Hunt was advocating a return to the 'calm green amplitudes' of peace and humanity.[16] That Wordsworth's Waterloo sonnets represented a threat to this vision was made clear by Hunt in an article for the *Examiner* in which he denounces the poet's appropriation of Milton's 'oppressiveness of ambition' to advance a poetics and politics of 'power'.[17] Far removed in its austere grandeur from the playful luxuriance of Hunt's writings, Wordsworth's compositions from this period become a cypher for the collusion of violent imaginings and authoritarian governance. When, in the summer of 1819, Hunt resumed his attack on the poet he no doubt saw in Peter's zeal for brutality and subsequent Methodist conversion an echo of Wordsworth's support for the divinely sanctioned violence of Waterloo. In both cases, the sinner, whether conceived as an individual or as the nation, is redeemed rather than reformed, set upon the path of righteousness following a life-changing katabasis.

Founded on 'bewitching principles of fear, bigotry, and diseased impulse', Hunt sees in Wordsworth's tale a depiction of the forces of reaction that would retard the cause of peace, justice, and liberty.[18] But as Cox suggests, he may also have responded to Wordsworth's critique of 'supernaturalism', a rejection of the 'realm of Faery',[19] in favour of 'the humblest departments of daily life' that, following Wordsworth's earlier slights on Hunt's *Descent of Liberty* and Keats's *Endymion*, could have been read as an assault on the adolescent extravagancies of the Hampstead poets.[20]

When, in the poem's Prologue, the narrator briefly entertains the wish to transcend 'treasons, tumults', and 'wars' (l. 27) it is possible that Hunt detected an element of parody, as if prior to settling for the embrace of the quotidian the poem were attempting to mimic the means by which a member of the Cockney School would seek to escape the ineluctable reality of historical violence. *Peter Bell* does in truth work hard to engage with the experience of conflict in everyday contexts, but to read the poem as a dour rejection of the politics and poetics of romance is to miss the extent to which by means of sly humour and subtle self-reflexivity the poem presents its own, beguiling, alternative to the fatalistic acceptance of life as perpetual war. Narrated from the point of view of an aging poet, 'unfit' for 'high argument' (ll. 839–40), *Peter Bell* discovers in its frequent avowals of mental and physical infirmity a perspective from which to subvert the claims of 'ambitious Youth' (l. 133), finding in its belatedness a platform for playful assertions of cultural authority. Conceived in youth, but speaking from a position of decrepitude, *Peter Bell* makes a virtue of its arrival in 'an age too late' (l. 132), deploying a limping, halting narrator, subject to disease, injury, and breathlessness (ll. 191–5), to advance a subtly subversive message. For while the depiction of Peter's religious conversion confirms Hunt and other liberal readers in their suspicion of Wordsworth's paternalism – and Wordsworth, as an opponent of Methodism, is no doubt guilty of hypocrisy in this part of the poem – there remains a strong element of radicalism in his determination to 'dance' and 'play' (l. 841) with readerly expectations, particularly in regard to the blurring of ontological categories, but perhaps also as a means to re-envision the possibility of a world of justice and thus a world of peace.

Contemporary reviews of *Peter Bell* make repeated mention of the poem's perceived absurdities, insisting in the words of the *Literary Gazette* that 'no talent can render that pathetic which is essentially ludicrous, nor great which is decidedly vulgar, not delightful which is glaringly disgusting'.[21] Unsurprisingly, many of these reviews took exception to the poem's lack of propriety in attributing moral feeling to an ass. Reflecting on Peter Bell, 'a common everyday sort of animal' and his 'rare' companion, the *Edinburgh Monthly Review* states that 'so great are the respective claims to notoriety of these worthy characters, that we are, for a time, at some loss to determine to which of them the name of hero ought to be given' before concluding that an ass is 'too far beneath us in the scale of nature, to permit our sympathizing in its history'.[22] With its 'mild, reproachful look' (l. 471) and capacity for grief, the donkey certainly conveys greater emotional intelligence than his obdurate human counterpart, but perhaps more radically the behaviour of this creature speaks to that larger sense of 'life' (ll. 611–12) in which the poem's core value resides. In *Wordsworth and the Poetry of What We Are*, Paul H. Fry writes of Peter's stubborn refusal to acknowledge the donkey's claim on his affections, preferring to dwell in stonehearted denial of creaturely affinity.[23] Thus, at war with nature, Peter proceeds to abuse the animal, the outcome of which is a retardation of the co-operative, seamless alliance and fluent, unbroken movement of man and beast that had been displayed in 'The Idiot Boy'. Peter does, however, eventually demonstrate a capacity for empathy, and from the moment when he works with the creature to pull the dead man from the stream, the jerky, disjunctive movement that is the result of this asymmetric warfare falls into comforting lockstep. The rhetoric of mineral resistance to change, and of flinty indifference to suffering, manifested in the journeying couple's numerous stops and pauses, as well as in the poem's metrical and syntactical violence ('He dealt a sturdy blow', l. 460; 'But I will *bang* your bones', l. 485), is now gracefully softened. As the lines describing Peter's transformation relay, the *life* of *Peter Bell* consists in the dissolving of physical and emotional 'hardness' (ll. 326–7), such that distinctions between human and animal, the secular and the divine, are relaxed:

> His nerves, his sinews seem'd to melt;
> Through all his frame was felt
> A gentle, a relaxing power!
>
> Each fibre of his frame was weak,
> Weak all the animal within,
> But in its helplessness grew mild
> And gentle as an infant child,
> An infant that has known no sin. (ll. 1014–20)

Peter, in his newfound mildness, thus joins with the patient and long-suffering creature in the imitation of Christ, able alike to 'feel the soul of Nature,/And see things as they are' (ll. 814–15). Like the 'little chapel' that 'With greenest ivy overgrown' dies 'insensibly way/From human thoughts and purposes', Peter Bell bows 'to some transforming power' (ll. 904–10), his identity as a sinner extinguished as he melts into life.

That such a quasi-pagan solution to the problem of sin should be countenanced by Wordsworth highlights, no doubt, the poem's distinction from its nearest intertext, 'The Rime of the Ancient Mariner'. As Bernard Groom has argued, *Peter Bell* affirms that conversion to Christianity may be achieved without recourse to the 'supernatural' or to a 'mythical heaven' or, we might add, through atonement after the death of nature.[24] In *Peter Bell*, the donkey is harried and oppressed but is spared the fate of the albatross. The representative of creation lives on and, as a result, the progress of Peter from sin to redemption can take place within a time and space that is recognisably of this world, far removed from the postlapsarian dead zone depicted in the 'Rime'. The story of Peter's transformation maps nicely onto his progress from brute superstition to Christian knowledge, as shown in the distinction between the lurid rhetorical fancies aroused by the images in the pool where the body of the donkey's dead master lies and the plainly expressed conviction of sin expressed at the poem's close:

> Is it the moon's distorted face?
> The ghost-like image of a cloud?
> Is it a gallows there pourtray'd?
> Is Peter of himself afraid?
> Is it a coffin,—or a shroud?
>
> A grisly idol hewn in stone?
> Or imp from witch's lap let fall?
> Or a gay ring of shining faeries,
> Such as pursue their brisk vagaries
> In sylvan bower, or haunted hall?
>
> Is it a fiend at a stake
> Of fire his desperate self is tethering?
> Or stubborn spirit doom'd to yell
> In solitary ward or cell,
> Ten thousand miles from his brethren?
>
> Is it a party in a parlour?
> Cramm'd just as they on earth were cramm'd—
> Some sipping punch, some sipping tea,
> But, as you by their faces see,
> All silent and all damn'd! (ll. 541–60)

'Like one intent upon a book—/A book that is enchanted!' (ll. 563–5), the seemingly unending flow of conjecture causes Peter to become fixated, 'turned to iron [...] Meet statue for the court of Fear' (ll. 567–8). In 'Part Second' the scene finds a counterpart in the story of a man who, conning the pages of a 'pious book' (l. 792), becomes obsessed with a single 'ghostly word' (l. 806), a '*word*—which to his dying day/Perplex'd the good man's gentle soul' (ll. 804–5) and 'Did never from his lips depart' (l. 807). Disconnected from narrative, the enchanted word becomes an empty signifier, leaving both men, like the mariner, disconnected from community. By contrast, when Peter receives the word of God, it is experienced as pure sound 'resounding from the woody glade [...] clamorous as a hunter's horn', re-echoing 'from a naked rock' (ll. 990–2). Far removed from the 'loud and dreadful sound' that heralds the mariner's return to land,[25] the Word received by Peter is articulate and enlivening, an emanation of divine breath relayed through the voice of the Methodist preacher. Overcome with 'joy' (l. 1009), melting into tears (l. 1010), the 'animal within' (l. 1017) is reunited with the 'flock' (l. 995), rescued from deathly isolation by a potent act of grace. As 'nature, through a world of death,/ Breathes into him a second breath' (ll. 1123–4), Peter, drawn to fellowship with the meanest objects in creation, now sees deeply into the life of things and, as a result, participates meaningfully in the life beyond self.

The difficulty, however, with the Christian reading of *Peter Bell* is that it overlooks the extent to which the transcendental dimension is troubled by the poem's investment in imaginative excess. As the chapel sinks into decay, overwhelmed by natural growth in scenes anticipating the destruction of Rylstone Hall, we are reminded of how the world of matter, associated earlier in the poem with the 'wild fantastic' (l. 727) scenes of pagan superstition, resembles the sentient landscape depicted in the boat-stealing episode in *The Prelude*. In both cases, transgression is met with admonition as rocks morph into weird oppressive forms that 'change countenance' and 'look' at the guilty individual (ll. 734–5). Deliverance from this valley of associative fears comes with the ascent of the travellers to a realm of sublime clarity, a 'high and open plain [...] shining like the smoothest sea,/In undisturbed immensity' (ll. 745–9). Yet even here, a solitary leaf, dancing in the 'sportive wind' (l. 754) serves, along with other fragments of the real – the drops of blood from the donkey's wound, the 'rumbling sound' (l. 877) caused by miners detonating an underground explosive – to remind the potter of his 'wickedness' (l. 760). That these associative fragments can be traced to 'common occurrences', as Groom suggests,[26] in no way diminishes their affective power, and while their placing in the poem is no doubt intended to depict the potter's journey from pagan fancy to Christian imagination, their material richness resonates more strongly than the 'blank' (l. 751) written word.

If Peter's journey from brute superstition to Christian faith is meant as a gentle rebuke to the supernatural excesses of Coleridge's 'Rime', it is a journey that struggles to subdue that poem's lingering potency. Even as, in the abandonment of 'high argument', Wordsworth seeks a mundane alternative to Coleridgean 'Spirits of the Mind' (l. 966), the emphasis in *Peter Bell* on the uncanny sentience and vibrant inter-connectivity of plant, mineral, and animal being pushes the poem back in the direction of its sublated pre-Christian origins. Partaking alike in the animal's wounded condition – the aged narrator is 'sore from a slight contusion' (l. 193), while Peter is 'crippled sore in his narration' (l. 1085) – poet, potter, and beast are united in a world of suffering, akin to the Buddhist notion of Dukkha. Small wonder that contemporary critics should have objected to the poem's mulelike determination to level the hierarchy of being while simultaneously failing to see the strangeness of the spirituality concealed by the strategic invocation of Methodism and the public concessions to Anglican orthodoxy. Frequently denounced as puerile, simplistic, and absurd, *Peter Bell* provokes readers into believing that a beast can mourn (l. 468), 'shake with joy' (l. 606), and 'rightly spell' (l. 697). As the *Eclectic Review* would go on to say of *The Waggoner*, in seeing all things 'as possessing equal claims upon his sovereign attention',[27] Wordsworth's 'late' narrative poem promotes a form of radical simplicity, advancing the belief, to adapt a formulation of Ian Bogost, that 'things can *be* many and various, specific and concrete, while their *being* remains identical'.[28] It is to the examination of this peaceful life, founded in a shared sense of being, that this chapter now turns.

The Waggoner: 'All Together, as We Go'

Reviewing *Peter Bell* and *The Waggoner* in June 1819 the *Theatrical Inquisitor* pointed out that Wordsworth's 'excessive egotism [...] occasions him to attach a degree of importance to the merest trifle which comes from his hands'.[29] A few weeks later, the *Eclectic Review* declared that Wordsworth lacks a sense of the 'ludicrous', explaining that his 'imagination' is 'so accustomed to exert itself with intense interest upon things comparatively mean and trifling [...] that no adequate feelings shall be left for all that is in itself grand, or important, or captivating; and the relative magnitude of this latter class of objects shall be lost in the estimate of the mind, for want of a standard of measurement'.[30]

Twenty years earlier, in *Lyrical Ballads*, Wordsworth had parodied precisely this zeal for measurement, observing how an enthusiasm for calibration worked to forestall the attainment of the sublime – 'He says he is three score and ten,/But others say he's eighty' (ll. 7–8) – before showing how, to the 'gentle reader' (l. 75), ignoble quanta yields immeasurable returns: 'thanks and praises seemed to run/So fast out of his heart, I thought/They never would have done' (ll. 98–100). Thus, 'Simon Lee' ends not with the delivery of a 'tale' (l. 76) but with a deathly outpouring of tears, a spontaneous evacuation of the heart brought on by the severing of the 'tangled root' (l. 94) that binds the old man to life and labour.[31] But just as, in the late 1790s and early 1800s, readers of *Lyrical Ballads* failed, typically, to grasp Wordsworth's fun with measurements, estimates, and relative magnitudes, so in 1819 readers found themselves troubled by the ways in which *Peter Bell* and *The Waggoner* confound category distinctions. Class, of course, is a resonant term here, suggesting at once the categorisation of things that have qualities or attributes on common as well as a system of ordering based on social and economic status. As is well known, Wordsworth's aggrandisement of huntsmen, potters, and waggoners violated class in both senses of the word and was widely perceived as a Jacobinical assault on social hierarchies. Hazlitt's observation of 1825 is apposite here: despite the poet's well-publicised conservatism, and indeed in a contravention of the attack made in 1818 on the 'right-royal' poetics of the 'Thanksgiving Ode', Wordsworth's muse remains essentially a 'levelling one', a manifestation of the revolutionary principle of 'equality' (*CWWH* IV. 214–21). What is interesting about the *Eclectic Review*'s response to *The Waggoner* is how class anxieties, in the ideological sense, are linked to concerns about Wordsworth's narrowness of attention and how a focus on the mean and the trivial prevents the mind from maintaining ontological distinctions, such as the difference between the great and the small, the elevated and the low, and the sublime and the ridiculous. Here's what *The Eclectic Review* goes on to say:

> In the extensive horizon of his capacious intellect, all distant interests it should seem are dwarfed, while, as he lies recumbent, a shrub, or a blade of grass, acquires from nearness a microscopic magnitude occupying the whole field of vision. Or perhaps, in the profound abstraction of his contemplative solitude, princes and potters, heroes and donkeys, would pass before him in the landscape as things of scarcely perceptible difference of configuration, and as possessing equal claims upon his sovereign attention. Under such circumstances, a *simplicity* would soon come to pervade all the associations of ideas excited by external objects, which would forbid the impertinent intrusion of the ludicrous. (p. 63)

Reminiscent of Kant's description of how best to 'get the full emotional effect from the magnitude of the pyramids',[32] Wordsworth, in getting 'too close' to the object of his attention, gets lost in the detail and, as a result, loses a sense of the difference between the vast and the small, the exalted and the low – which, for this reviewer, amounts to saying that in his 'simplicity' Wordsworth is unable to discriminate between the sublime and the ridiculous.

That Wordsworth, in 1819, presented a challenge to readers wishing to square Wordsworthian bathos with Wordsworthian sublimity is nicely illustrated by the *Monthly Review*. Struggling to get a measure of *The Waggoner*, the writer notes sardonically that 'Throughout the piece [...] we detect a sly covert sort of irony, an *under-tone* of playfulness, smiling at the mock heroics of the author; and preserving that difficult but exact spirit of bombast, which betrays a consciousness of misapplied sublimity, without rendering it quite gross and ridiculous' before going on to single out examples of the poem's tonal inelegance.[33] Possibly conceived under the spell of *Don Juan*, the first two cantos of which had been praised in a previous issue of the journal for blending 'the witty and the sublime, the sarcastic and the pathetic, the gloomy and the droll [...] with such power of union',[34] the review captures something of the flavour of Byron's own attacks on Wordsworth, which ranged wildly from mockery of the 'simple WORDSWORTH' in *English Bards and Scotch Reviewers* to the dismissal of the 'unintelligible' *Excursion* in Canto I of *Don Juan*.[35] For Byron, Wordsworth emerges as a baffling provocateur: on the one hand, an 'apostate from poetic rule' for whom 'Christmas stories tortured into rhyme/Contain the true essence of the sublime';[36] on the other, the high-minded creator of a 'system to perplex the sages'.[37] In *Don Juan* Canto III, Byron, as if wishing to settle the question of how best to classify Wordsworth, devotes two stanzas to maligning *The Waggoner*, condemning the poem as 'scumlike', a product of 'bathos' vast abyss' (stanza. 100. ll. 892–3.). Attuned, perhaps, to the poem's Miltonic echoes, Byron regards Wordsworth as the Jack Cades of song, a 'vulgar' renegado and devotee of the 'little' (stanza. 99. l. 885; 100. 895.), whose parodic reframing of *Paradise Lost* falls far short of the satiric grandeur of *Absalom and Achitophel* and the elegant suavity of *The Rape of the Lock*.

Like Byron, the *Monthly Review* struggles to put Wordsworth in his place: there is a note of genuine perplexity underpinning the review's mock praise of the poet as 'the Prince of Poetical Burlesque' (p. 39) and a suspicion that *The Waggoner* might indeed be 'joyful' and 'ingenious' (p. 37). Elsewhere, as if seeking to resolve the questions raised by this writer, the *British Critic*, in one of the few appreciative reviews of the poem, determined that Wordsworth shows 'by a subdued under-tone of humour, by a playful hint', that he is indeed 'master of himself, aware of the real rank of his subject, and not parsing it with disproportionate zeal'.[38] Repeating precisely the terms used by the *Monthly Review* to debunk *The Waggoner*, the review counters that writer's sardonicism by insisting that 'this is a new class of poetry' (p. 466), distinguished from works 'of a more stimulating kind' (p. 465) by the exercise of 'moral sympathy and human fellow-feeling' (p. 469), only to conclude that 'the nature of the subject will be a stumbling block to many; it is easy to call it "a poem on the discharge of a drunken waggoner," and to ask whether that is fit matter for poetry, to be gravely written by a philosophical poet, or seriously read by full-grown men' (p. 479). As these reviews unwittingly reveal, the question of whether *The Waggoner* is playful or serious, sublime or ridiculous, appears undecidable; the undecidable question then becomes a provocation, a reminder of all that makes Wordsworth disproportionate, indiscriminate, and, ultimately, unclassifiable.

The story of how *The Waggoner* came to print comes with its own share of accidents, conflicts, and absurdities. From its inception in 1806 to its publication in 1819, the poem's fate is interwoven with loss of one sort or another. At its core there is the catastrophe of John Wordsworth's drowning aboard the wreck of the *Earl of Abergavenny* in February 1805, a loss registered in the elegiac 'Rock of Names' passage.[39] The tone of the poem that Wordsworth composed a year later in which these lines were initially incorporated is light and playful, but the focus on the forging and breaking of happy allegiances bears the trace of that other, once cheerfully forged but now sadly despoiled, 'file': 'W. W., M. H., D. W., S. T. C., J. W., S. H.'.[40] Through its association with the death of John, the departure of Coleridge, and, later, in 1812 the unexpected loss of Wordsworth's daughter Catharine, *The Waggoner* bears the imprint of a poet's grief. But there is mischance too in the poem's journey from manuscript to print. Paul Betz has documented the history of the poem's several promised incarnations, from the anticipated publication with *Peter Bell* in 1809 to the proposed collected narrative poem volume of 1814, but on at least one occasion the existence of the poem itself had come under threat. As Charles Lamb observed in a letter of May 1815, during one of Wordsworth's visits to London, '[h]as Wordsworth told you that coming to town he lost the manuscript of the 'The Waggoner' and 'Peter Bell' and two hundred lines of a new poem, and that he is not certain he can by any means recover a correct copy of them'.[41] Though the manuscript was subsequently discovered, *The Waggoner* seems never to have fully overcome a link with textual precarity. In an intriguing aside, Betz notes that 'the recent theft of a *Prelude* manuscript from the carrier's cart' may have been 'a factor in the dislike that Wordsworth expresses at the end of the epilogue for the small carts that replaced Benjamin's waggon' (pp. 14–15). John Williams has suggested that Benjamin's cumbersome conveyance, with its unwieldy team of fellow travellers making slow, halting progress across difficult terrain, could be read as a cypher for the author's difficulties with 'The Recluse'.⁴² The suggestion is intriguing, not least because of the ways in which *The Waggoner* freights its own progress with teasing allusions to other works by Wordsworth, his aspiration to be read as a grand, national poet in the Miltonic manner, and his self-defeating attraction towards the slight and the fanciful. Anxieties concerning the progress of 'The Recluse' no doubt weighed heavily on Wordsworth's mind in the winter of 1805–6, but there is, I think, a more particular concern informing the development of *The Waggoner*.

As documented in *The Prelude*, the writing of the 'philosophic Song' (1. l. 230) had long been established as a priority for Wordsworth, but the desire to write 'a narrative Poem of the Epic kind' (*EY* 594) on 'some British theme, some old/Romantic tale, by Milton left unsung' (A-B Stage *Prelude* 1, ll. 179–80) had not entirely abated. As throughout January Wordsworth corrected the first eight books of *The Prelude* thoughts of the as yet unfulfilled promise of 'The Recluse' may well have informed the development of *The Waggoner*.⁴³ But the latter poem's fascination with the raising and dashing of epic expectations, a narrative of decline corresponding to the projected tales of fallen empires outlined in *The Prelude*,⁴⁴ suggests that the ghost of that other, abandoned, work provided the more immediate and specific stimulus. Might there be a connection here between those eight books and the 'eight sorry Carts' (l. 827) that appear at the end of the poem as the 'Unworthy Successors' (l. 828) of Benjamin's 'lordly Wain' (l. 822)?

The idea of *The Waggoner* as a mock-heroic reflection on the unfulfilled ambitions of a would-be writer of epic takes force when we consider the positioning of the poet within the poem. *The Waggoner* opens with a description of the end of a 'burning' day in June (l. 1), echoing the establishment of solstitial time found in 'The Ruined Cottage' and 'Resolution and Independence'. The lumbering entrance of Benjamin and his Wain into this 'close and hot' (l. 14) environment is contrived carefully to complement the air of dreamlike suspension linked with this time of year (*stitium*: stoppage). Redolent of the opening lines of Gray's 'Elegy Written in a Country Churchyard' ('That far-off tinkling's drowsy cheer', l. 26; 'And drowsy tinklings lull the distant folds'),⁴⁵ the poem focuses glancingly on that other, mute inglorious Milton, the 'simple waterdrinking Bard' who lives 'where the DOVE and OLIVE-Bough/Once hung' (ll. 58–9). A former tavern, Dove Cottage stands in the poem as a device to evoke the source of Benjamin's temptation and fall while alluding playfully to Wordsworth's self-positioning as a poet in the Homeric tradition. The link between the strenuous, halting progress of the waggon ('Many a stop and stay he makes,/Many a breathing fit he takes', ll. 36–7) and the intermittent development of 'The Recluse' should again be noted here, along with the allusions to *Paradise Lost*, Genesis, classical tragedy, and epic.[46] But though the introduction no doubt establishes a connection between Benjamin's soon-to-be outmoded labour and the poet's attempts to bring to completion 'a poem so vast in conception, so ponderous that he would never complete it',[47] it is important to note too that much of the interest of the ensuing tale is derived not from a leaden sense of a failure of Imagination but from an enlivened delight in the ability of Fancy 'to quicken and to beguile the temporal part of our nature', to create effects that 'are surprising, playful, ludicrous, amusing, tender, or pathetic, as the objects happen to be appositely produced or fortunately combined' (*Prose* III. 36–7). Recognising this quality in the poem, Edward Quillinan noted that the 'introductory passage about the glow worms was intended to shew the principle on which it was composed & to put the reader in the state of mind favourable for the perusal of a poem of fancy—It is all fancy'.[48] Revised in 1836 in an attempt to recapture the tone of the 1806 manuscript version of the poem, the glow-worm passage chimes with 'The Pilgrim's Dream' as a restatement of the benignant influence of the lowborn and neglected, but also as an endorsement of the value to human life of artistic play. Thus, though rooted in grief, disappointment, and frustration, the poem seeks to recover, through the 'rapidity and profusion' and the 'felicity' with which 'thoughts and images' are 'linked together', a tonic impression of life released from care. Perhaps further, the poem grants insight into how it might feel were the poet to take a lesson from Ovid instead of Homer, discovering in drunkenness an escape not only from the daily grind but a shimmer of how one might live in a world released from war. The allusion to the Dove and Olive-bough is in place to remind us not only of the defeated ambitions of an epic poet but of the covenant which brings about a peaceful relationship between God and his creation. That such a covenant can be recovered only in a moment of intoxicated bliss, reminiscent of Noah's drunken attempt to recover the lost innocence of Eden (Genesis 9. 20–4), in no way detracts from the poem's ability to give voice to the yearning to have done with the social, political, and, indeed, ontological divisions on which conflict is founded.

Was the dedication to the alcoholic Charles Lamb, one of the poem's earliest and most appreciative readers, meant to serve as a covert warning of the dangers of narco-poesis? Certainly Lamb seems to have recognised 'a kind of shadowing affinity between the subject of the narrative and the subject of the dedication';[49] but, as Anya Taylor has noted, Wordsworth the water-drinker is acutely sympathetic of the plight of the afflicted Benjamin, treating his hero with dignity and respect and avoiding condemnation.[50] Henry Crabb Robinson, who, along with Lamb, was treated to an early reading of *The Waggoner*, records how Wordsworth 'praised Burns for his introduction to Tam O'Shanter—By bringing together all the circumstances which can serve to render excusable what is in itself disgusting—Thus interesting our feelings and making us tolerant of what could otherwise be not endurable'.[51] Crabb Robinson goes on to express admiration for the poem's 'grace and [...] delightful [*del to* passages] of description and elegant playfulness', noting how the description of 'the dancing and joy in the Ale house' is informed by 'the Spirit of kindness and indulgence Wordsworth praises in Burns Tam O'Shanter'.[52]

If Wordsworth felt that the austere moralising of *Peter Bell* was best suited to its dedicatee Robert Southey, then what was the dedication to Lamb meant to signal if not the suspension of moral judgement out of a spirit of kindness and indulgence? In *A Letter to a Friend of Robert Burns* Wordsworth gave formal expression to these sentiments, decrying James Currie's fault-finding *Life* while defending Burns's 'charitable indulgence' of 'vicious habits' in his depiction of Tam O'Shanter's drunkenness (*Prose* III. 124). Published in May 1816, shortly after the Thanksgiving volume and informed, perhaps, by memories of Lamb's self-excoriating 'Confessions of a Drunkard' of 1813, the letter reflects also on *The Waggoner*'s Burnsian combination of 'primary instincts' and 'convivial exaltation', in which, 'though there is no moral purpose, there is a moral effect' (124). Here, in a manner far removed from the vatic detachment of the 'Thanksgiving Ode', Wordsworth writes approvingly of the poet who, 'penetrating the unsightly and disgusting surfaces of things, has unveiled with exquisite skill the finer ties of imagination and feeling' that bind the addicted 'to practices productive of so much unhappiness to themselves, and to those whom it is their duty to cherish;—and, as far as he puts the reader in possession of this intelligent sympathy, he qualifies him for exercising a salutary influence over the minds of those who are thus deplorably enslaved' (*Prose* III. 124–5).

If, then, in *The Waggoner* there is a target of approbation, it seems rather to be Wordsworth than Lamb as, recalling Milton's *Elegia Sexta*, the poem pokes fun at the moralising Homerian who, 'drinking soberly from a pure spring', writes 'about wars, and a heaven ruled over by Jove who has outgrown his boyhood, about heroes who stick to their duty and princes who are half gods'.[53] The poet of *The Waggoner* writes too of wars and of the deleterious effects of god-like power, but the perspective adopted by this poet is more attuned to 'the felicities of love and wine' and thus more sympathetic to the 'conditions of others' than the angry writer of epic (*Prose* III. 124). In Benjamin's mock-heroic journey we encounter a 'poetic self', not unlike Burns, and a hero, not unlike Tam O'Shanter, who, following initial resistance to temptation, gives way to the 'spirit of pleasure', discovering in the shelter of the village inn, 'while the storm is roaring, and heaven and earth are in confusion' and 'the night is driven on by song and tumultuous noise', a vision of humanity 'blended into one proud and happy composition of elated spirits' (124).

That *The Waggoner* serves to convey an image of the peaceable society, however flawed and however temporary, is nicely illustrated by the passage describing Benjamin's encounter with the wandering sailor and his wife and child. The meeting follows a description of a storm. Inspired by a passage in Thomson's 'Autumn', nature is presented here at war with itself. Harried by rain falling like 'drops of lead' (l. 157), advancing on a road that is 'batter'd' and 'shatter'd' (ll. 184–5), the battle-weary travellers eventually arrive at the grave of King Dunmail: 'He who had once supreme command,/Last king of rocky Cumberland;/His bones, and those of all his Power,/Slain here in disastrous hour!' (ll. 207–10). Indicative of that old abandoned 'British theme', the waggoner passes 'through this narrow strait,/(Stony and dark and desolate)' (ll. 211–12) in recollection, perhaps, of the Spartan defence of Thermopylae, only to be halted by the voice of a woman, pleading for shelter. Reminiscent of the encounter with wartime suffering depicted in 'The Female Vagrant' but differing in the ease with which hospitality is extended and the alacrity with which it is accepted, the poem represents Benjamin as a model host, willing to accommodate the woman and her baby unconditionally and without expectation of return. The woman's sheepish acknowledgement of her hitherto unnoticed sailor husband draws attention to the disparagement with which wandering servicemen and their families were commonly viewed, but Benjamin, true to the goodness of his nature, is no less willing to provide shelter for this man.

The sights and sounds of a 'Merry-night' (l. 305) at the Cherry Tree lure the travellers to the poem's primary scene of temptation. The description of the evening's entertainments, which struck a chord with Crabb Robinson, do indeed owe a debt to Burns, but there are echoes too of the dizzying sights and sounds of London, as described in Book 7 of the recently dispatched and almost lost *Prelude*. Corresponding to that description, the pub scene in *The Waggoner* draws energy from a critical mass of present participles, single, double, and off-centred rhymes, closed and open couplets, anaphora, accumulated exclamation marks, and jumbled category distinctions:

> This was the outside proclamation,
> This was the inside salutation;
> What bustling—jostling—high and low!
> A universal overflow!
> The tankards foaming from the tap!
> What store of cakes in every lap!
> What thumping—stumping—overhead!
> The thunder had not more been busy:
> With such a stir, you would have said,
> This little place may well be dizzy! (ll. 229–338)

Evoking the jubilant cacophony of an evening of serious drinking, the passage conveys the sense of a world in which, subjected to the mad, associative logic of intoxication, even the most lifeless objects join with the collective spirit: 'The very bacon shows its feeling,/Swinging from the smoky ceiling!' (ll. 343–4). What the comedy of the poem reveals, both at the level of form and at the level of content, is the power of 'affective' bodies, due to their participation in modes of common 'substance', to enter into strange and unforeseen alliances.[54] If in the London book of *The Prelude* the relation of 'self-destroying, transitory things' is tempered by the disciplinary logic of 'Composure and ennobling harmony' (l. 740–1), here the delight in drunken fancy appears to be unconstrained. The poem, however, does provide an intimation of the disaster that is to come, as Benjamin, forgetful of 'care' (l. 355) and 'strife' (l. 357), is compared to 'A Caesar past the Rubicon!' (l. 356).

As narcotic forgetfulness descends on the travellers (shades here of Homer's lotus-eaters), the mood of collective 'bliss' (l. 373) is interrupted by the sudden entrance of the sailor with 'A ship of lusty size;/A gallant stately Man of War,/Fix'd on a smoothly-sliding car' (ll. 381–3). Convention has it that the sailor functions in the poem as a satanic tempter, ushering Benjamin into the inn before he has had a chance to exercise his judgement.[55] This may be true, for like the devil (and, for that matter, Lord Byron) the man has a 'limp' (l. 379), but his presence in the poem also highlights the condition of those who, having placed their lives in the service of the state, were denied adequate medical and social care.[56] Like many other disabled naval veterans of the period, the sailor supplements his living by displaying a handcrafted model warship, in this case a representation of Nelson's flagship, the *Vanguard*. A popular subject for sentimental painters and graphic satirists alike, the disabled sailor proceeds to regale his audience with a vivid account of the Battle of the Nile. Attuned to the satirist's stark depiction of aggressively enterprising penury rather than to the sentimental portrayal of a member of the deserving but objectified poor, Wordsworth, as John Williams points out, frames the sailor's tale as an opportunity to debunk the 'virtual beatification', less than a year after his death, of Admiral Lord Nelson.[57] That Nelson should be toasted as 'England's pride and treasure,/Her bulwark and tower of strength' (ll. 423–4), by a profligate member of the fleet highlights the means by which hero-worship could be deployed to provide distraction from the hardships of war. Presented as a 'Showman' (l. 395), the sailor, whose performance appears again to be related to *The Prelude*'s account of the disorderly showiness of the metropolis, highlights Nelson's own capacity for self-promotion – a capacity that Wordsworth had criticised in 'The Character of the Happy Warrior'. Motivated perhaps by a sense of the contrast between the rectitude of his brother John, whose death passed virtually unnoticed to the world at large, and the dubious morality of this highly publicised martyr to a vainglorious cause, the sailor's account of the Battle of the Nile is appropriately extravagant, making use of 'uncouth terms of art' (l. 401) ('A sight that would have rous'd your blood! [l. 406]) and desacralised biblical language ('Let this be Land, and that be Sea', l. 409), to expose the tawdry elevation of its subject.

Commenting on this passage, Theresa Kelley draws attention to the narrator's subsequent gloss on the battle, which with its pointed allusion to the conflict between Satan and God in *Paradise Lost* ('The dismal conflict, and the might/And terror of that wondrous night!', ll. 419–20), debunks still further 'the heroic sublime'.[58] But the Miltonic allusion also reveals the trace of that unwritten epic poem on some British theme. As filtered through the poem's quasi-Shandian depiction of the model ship, the Battle of the Nile becomes, in Susan Stewart's sense, a fetishized object, a locus for 'an experience which the object can only evoke and resonate to, and can never fully recoup'.[59] Echoing the means by which the model and its supplementary narrative 'plays in the distance between the present and [...] experience as it might be "directly lived"',[60] the poem shows how the representation of war 'creates a longing that of necessity is inauthentic because it does not take part in lived experience'.[61] Trading on the promise of restoration ('You'll find much in little here!', l. 394), the sailor's promise of the real, 'And you shall see her in full trim;/I'll set, my Friends [...] every inch of sail upon her [...] masts, sails, yards,/He names them all' (ll. 396–401), with its punning allusion to Corporal Trim's exposition of the Battle of Namur, exacerbates rather than resolves the breach between representation and the 'ultimate experience', intensifying the audience's longing for war as the lost horizon of everyday life.[62]

As I have argued throughout this study, although Wordsworth's poetry participates, to some extent, in the pleasure of destruction, it works at the same time to scrutinise and expose the mechanisms that enable such participation. In *The Waggoner*, the linking of alcohol-induced reverie, nostalgia, and showmanship with the techniques of excitement and aggrandisement deployed in popular histories, ballads and songs, prints, paintings, and commemorative plates goes some way towards deflating the manufacture of consent that precluded rational debate about Nelson's standing as a national hero. When, after concluding his narrative by pledging a draft to 'England's pride and treasure' (l. 423), the 'battered tar' (l. 433), having led Benjamin by example to quaff a 'deep, determined, desperate draught' (l. 432), leaves the inn 'a hero, crown'd with laurel' (l. 435), his actions, appearance, and honours function as a traducing of Nelson's own, narcotic, appeal. To have published such an expose of the fostering of pro-war sentiment in 1806, within a year of Nelson's death, would have been foolhardy, but in 1819, as positive appraisals and commemorative wares continued to command attention in British culture, publication could be seen as a no less contentious gesture. That Benjamin succumbs to temptation, joining in with the devil's draught, is a demonstration of the power of populist media to institute a culture of agreement inoculated against dissent. Against the promotion of this form of reactionary levelling, Wordsworth's poem makes a small but defiant stand, offering in its quirkily inverted representation of state-sponsored war culture a parodic point of critique.

But as I have intimated, levelling of another kind takes place in the poem, offering at least the potential for readers to gain a sense, albeit momentarily, of how life could be lived after war. Theresa Kelley, invoking Charles Lamb's praise for the poem's 'spirit of beautiful tolerance', argues that *The Waggoner* is informed by 'the most obvious values of the beautiful—benevolence [...] and social coherence'.[63] Kelley goes on to advance a reading of the poem that highlights its investment in images of shelter and rest, noting how those victims of wartime displacement – the mendicant sailor and his family – are protected from the storm: a vision of natural life safe from sovereign violence. *The Waggoner*'s elegiac conclusion does indeed provide a beautiful alternative to those traces of sublime terror that seem, at times, to threaten the poem's progress, but the spirit of tolerance exhibited in these lines seems to me to exceed the category of the beautiful, at least insofar as Kant determines the beautiful as that which 'concerns the form of the object'.[64] To retrieve the sense in which *The Waggoner*'s drive for inclusivity reaches beyond the rigid opposition of the beautiful or 'bounded' object and the sublime or 'unbounded' object, we need to return to *The Waggoner*'s activation of the poetics of fancy, as advanced in the Preface to *Poems* of 1815, and to the interest displayed in the ascription of consciousness to non-human beings and inanimate objects, which the poem shares with *The White Doe of Rylstone* and with *Peter Bell*. In both cases, I suggest, peace is discovered not in the antagonistic labour of self-realisation, still less in that labour's silent aftermath, but in the sensual comingling of beings and things.

Involved and Restless All

Throughout its course, *The Waggoner* provides glimpses of this shared, collective life: the team of horses that acts as a chorus, responding with 'one mind' (l. 133) when the going is legitimate, halting 'reluctantly' (l. 326) when it is not; the mastiff that offers a 'monitory growl' (l. 430) when Benjamin joins in the toast to Nelson. Evidence abounds in the poem for the ability of creatures and even objects to exhibit human emotion, but the notion of a communal delight in being, first glimpsed at the Cherry Tree, is explored fully in Canto Third when, in the aftermath of the drinking session, the pace of the waggon, and of the poem, is dramatically accelerated. Working now as an assemblage of human and non-human actants – Benjamin and his waggon, the sailor and his wife and child, the model warship, an ass, the mastiff, and the team of horses – the waggon mounts 'to a higher height/And higher still' (ll. 467–8), pursuing a 'greedy flight' (l. 468) beyond the reach of conventional wisdom. As the team coasts 'the silent lake' (l. 473) the sense of collective joy becomes infectious, prompting the narrator to partake in 'Their inspiration' and 'Share their empyreal spirits' (ll. 474–5). Thus, with 'enraptured vision' (l. 476) informed by 'fancy' (l. 477), the narrator paints a series of 'shifting pictures—clad in gleams':

> Of colour bright as feverish dreams!
> Earth, spangled sky, and lake serene,
> Involved and restless all—a scene
> Pregnant with mutual exaltation
> Rich change, and multiplied creation! (ll. 478–83)

The single and double rhymes, metrical variations, and closed and run-on lines support the impression of a complex inter-animation of contrasting elements, providing a template for the lines that follow as, with 'tears of rapture', 'profound entreaties, and hand-shaking', the disparate company unites in 'solemn, vacant, interlacing' (ll. 486–8), prior to tethering the sailor's ass and model ship to the rear of the waggon.

In the events that follow, the commitment to categorical blurring is sustained as Benjamin, reflecting on the happy conjunction of human, animal, model, and machine ('we make a kind of handsome show!', l. 518) and echoing the observations made by the narrator earlier in the poem, compares this newly created assemblage to a ship with 'canvas spread' (l. 522). Benjamin's nautical reverie, along with his account of the 'enjoyment' of the owls of Windermere, 'Mocking the Man that keeps the ferry' (ll. 560–9, *passim*), speaks to the awakening of a creative power, shared not only by humans – sailors, waggoners, and poets alike – but by all things. The allusion here, of course, is to the Boy of Winander and to the owls that, with 'mimic hooting', usher in the sensation of an accord between mind and nature.[65] In a manner distinct from the meditative sobriety of the water-drinking bard, the pilot of the wain, inspired by alcohol-induced conviviality, indulges in a spontaneous overflow of playful, ludicrous, and tender combinations. Benjamin's delight in this poetics of fancy reaches its zenith at the canto's conclusion when, absorbed by the sailor's Quixotic combat with the mountain tops, he beholds 'among the stars':

> [...] a dancing—and a glancing;
> Such retreating and advancing
> As, I ween, was never seen
> In bloodiest battle since the days of Mars! (ll. 579–83)

In 'Eve's lingering clouds extend in solid bars', a sonnet composed in 1807 but not published until 1819 where it stands as the concluding poem of *The Waggoner* volume, the 'rich show' (l. 11) of 'Jove—Venus—and the ruddy crest of Mars' (l. 5) reflected on the surface of Grasmere lake offers to 'fancy' (l. 10) a vision of 'tranquillity' (l. 14), at 'happy distance from earth's groaning field,/Where ruthless mortals wage incessant wars' (ll. 7–8).[66] If, by way of contrast to this poem's assertion of Neoplatonic order, Benjamin's vision of cosmic conflict suggests an inherent disorder in the universe, a case can be made too for regarding primal strife not solely as a destructive force but as a form of creative delirium. In that rhyming whirl of present participles, more akin to Ovidian intoxication than Homeric sobriety, the poem locates its pleasurable core as, no longer split between material flux and transcendental constancy, the world above and the world below meld in vibrant accord.

In this account of dynamic, universal entent, Wordsworth may have recalled his early engagement with Spinozian thought, which in *Lyrical Ballads* and the preliminary drafts for 'The Recluse' had informed the pantheistic notion of the 'life of things'. But Spinoza's description of a world in which objects struggle to maintain their integrity through the ceaseless forging of confederations with other objects bears no less on the political significance of *The Waggoner*. As advanced in the *Political Treatise*, the shifting world of conative encounters functions like a 'commonwealth' to realise the potential of its constituents in a manner that is beneficial to the well-being of the whole.[67] Distinct from the Hobbesian notion of peace as the absence of war, which entails the perpetuation of a conception of being characterised by perpetual strife, Spinozian peace orients itself in relation to a state of harmony defined not by the externally imposed agencies of Law, Monarchy, or State Religion but by 'a free people'.[68] In this mode of temporary assemblages and fraught alliances, antagonism is recognised and accepted but is itself placed in a tensional relation with other countervailing modes, chiefly with the desire for self-regulation. Benjamin's waggon, with its constantly morphing set of alliances, provides as apt an illustration as any of how such a commonwealth might function, for when tensions erupt peace is restored by the action of the meek, reacting against the imposition of sovereign power in the interests of the whole:

> That instant was begun a 'fray
> Which called their thoughts another way;
> The Mastiff, ill-conditioned carl!
> What must he do but growl and snarl,
> Still more and more dissatisfied
> With the meek comrade at his side?
> Till, not incensed though put to proof,
> The Ass, uplifting a hind hoof,
> Salutes the Mastiff on the head;
> And so were better manners bred,
> And all was calmed and quieted. (ll. 539–49)

Kicked by the peace-loving ass, the warmongering mastiff thus learns his place in the team, but as is the fate of most alliances, the community of the waggon must soon come to an end.[69]

Canto Fourth opens with a flight of fancy and a shift from the tenebrous visions of the night to the lucent displays of the rising dawn. Tracking the journey of the 'Muse' (l. 595) over Raven Crag, the River Greta, and St John's Vale, and from there to Skiddaw and Nathdale Fell, the poem registers 'glimmering' mountain tops and 'glittering' streams – momentary sights which, while shrouded in mist, 'the merry sun/Takes delight to play upon' (ll. 681–2). The journey north from Grasmere to Thirlmere is a journey too to the Rock of Names. Excised from the 1819 publication, the lines commemorating the meeting place between Wordsworth and Coleridge overshadow this journey, lending an air of expectant disappointment to the descriptions of the morning's transient joys. The absent presence of Coleridge at the poem's conclusion is a reminder no less of how poems belonging to the category of Fancy are, for Wordsworth, a guilty pleasure. Insofar as it distracts from the serious business of completing the long philosophical poem, *The Waggoner* runs the risk of attracting the censure of Wordsworth's greatest critic. Nominated at the poem's conclusion as the 'Friend', a loaded designation cementing the poem's connection with *The Prelude*, Coleridge steps out of the shadows to displace Lamb as the poem's primary addressee:

> Accept, O Friend, for praise or blame,
> The gift of this adventurous Song;
> A record which I dared to frame,
> Though timid scruples check'd me long;
> They check'd me—and I left the theme
> Untouch'd—in spite of many a gleam
> Of fancy which thereon as shed,
> Like pleasant sun-beams shifting still
> Upon the side of a distant hill. (ll. 774–82)

What the opening of the canto offers then is a reflection on the momentary pleasure that 'makes my bliss!' (l. 785). Presented to Coleridge almost in a spirit of defiance, responsibility for the poem's creation is attributed not to the great 'I AM' of imaginative potency but to an unbidden vital force:

> Nor is it I who play the part,
> But a shy spirit in my heart,
> That comes and goes—will sometimes leap
> From hiding-places ten years deep [...]
> Returning like a ghost unlaid,
> Until the debt I owe be paid. (ll. 788–93)

The address to the Friend follows the scene in which Benjamin is discovered by his 'Master'. Presented in mock-heroic terms as shielded, like Apollo, from enemy scrutiny by the combined effects of mist and laborious 'exhalation' (l. 678), the Master nevertheless sees through the 'radiant shroud' (l. 722) to perceive the carnivalesque disorder within.

With Benjamin's summary sacking the journey concludes, and with it ends the happy assemblage that presented a peaceable alternative to the rationalised antagonism of alienated labour. With the Master's return comes the re-imposition of hierarchy and a corresponding loss of delight, but also and perhaps more pointedly a diminution of local memory. As the narrator sadly opines, the waggon served as 'A living Almanack', a 'speaking Diary' that 'Gave to the days a mark and name' (ll. 798–801). Related in purpose to the Old Cumberland Beggar, the waggon progressing 'Majestically huge and slow' (l. 807) enables the marking of the seasons, serving as a locus for the maintenance of community over time. When, gazing through the window of the Dove and Olive-bough, the poet observes the waggon's replacement, 'Eight sorry Carts, no less a train!' (l. 827), he sees also the loss of the values of kindness and hospitality that Benjamin offered to the indigent poor. Significantly, the new arrangement lays stress on the isolation of its constituent parts: 'one by one—See, perch'd upon the naked height/The summit of a cumbrous freight,/A Single Traveller—and there,/Another' (ll. 832–5). The disassembly of the waggon and its replacement with a segmented train lead in turn to the exposure, both literally and figuratively, of those victims of modernity – 'the lame, the sickly, and the old;/Men, Women, heartless with the cold;/And Babes in wet and starv'ling plight' (ll. 836–8) – for whom the 'lordly Wain' (l. 822) no longer provides a 'shelter' (l. 841). Wordsworth may be alluding here to the exposure of his own poetic labours to violent contingency. He may also have in mind the reduction of creative spontaneity to the dreary realisation of that tyrannical schema, otherwise known as 'The Recluse'. But imbuing all these fears is the sense of a world given over to the programmatic extinction of mutual satisfaction, self-governance, and enjoyment – the life-denying principles, in other words, of a community at war.

CHAPTER 5

Violent Waters
The River Duddon *and* Ecclesiastical Sketches

After Peterloo

On 30 May 1820 Mary Wordsworth records how she and her husband, pausing in Manchester to change coaches on their journey to Banbury, prior to their departure to Belgium in the second week of July, 'took a walk, and inspected Peterloo; the particulars of the Stations of the Performers, the ground upon which certain feats were wrought, etc., we learned from a Person upon the spot, who had witnessed the whole scene'.[1] At once indefinite and exacting, Mary concludes her account by noting that 'William was not inclined to see anything further'.[2] A few weeks later, the field of Waterloo seemed, at first, to present a similarly uninspiring prospect. Yet, as Dorothy observes in her journal entry for 17 July, while there 'was little to be seen' there was 'much to be felt, —sorrow and sadness, and even something like horror breathed out of the ground as we stood upon it!' (*JDW* III. 29). Responding to Dorothy's impressions, Wordsworth writes in his sonnet 'After Visiting the Field of Waterloo' that even as the field appeared 'joyless, blank, and cold' (l. 6) and 'Meanings [...] could not there be found' (l. 10), still 'we felt as Men *should* feel,/With such vast hoards of hidden carnage near,/And horror breathing from the silent ground!' (ll. 12–14).[3] That Wordsworth found significance in the 'great exploits' of Waterloo (l. 12) but felt disinclined to retrieve meaning from 'certain feats' at Peterloo is unsurprising. Writing to Viscount Lowther the previous autumn Wordsworth had made clear his opposition to 'the revolutionary projects' of those 'active Reformers' who sought to arouse 'public disapprobation of the conduct of the Manchester Magistrates' (*MY* II. 558), and as late as December 1820 he felt moved to remark critically on the conduct of a Leicestershire bookseller, 'a notorious Jacobin and Incendiary, and Usher of a school', who had appointed a teacher of radical principles 'who had given the "Manchester Massacres" as a Theme for his Boys' (*MY* II. 657).

Civilian pilgrimages to European battlefields were, by 1820, a common enough occurrence, but what the Wordsworths' visit to Peterloo unintentionally reveals is the striking congruity between sites of national and international conflict. That both sites could be regarded as notable additions to the tourist's itinerary, transformed from bloody, corporeal events to theatrical set-pieces, compounds the sense in which Peterloo was conceived, in the autumn of 1819, as the ironic counterpart of Waterloo.[4] That the massacre was, at least in part, perpetrated by soldiers who had served at Waterloo, and that at least one of the victims, John Lees, had also fought in that battle, underscored the relationship still further.[5] On the journey to Manchester Wordsworth, afflicted by the eye disease that would dog him for the remainder of his life, and that was most likely transmitted by soldiers returning from the fight against Napoleon in Egypt, remained 'silent and looked ill'.[6] According to Mary, the poet's spirits were roused only by the sight of the race ground at Manchester, populated by an 'immense concourse of persons—10,000, as we were afterwards told. The race was just over, and the stream of life that was flowing down from the mass which still seemed stationary, was a sublime sight'.[7] Pre-echoes of this vision were heard the previous summer when, for instance, the radical reformer and journalist Archibald Prentice observed the stream of gaily clad people moving 'slowly and orderly' down Mosley Street on their way to the hustings.[8] Yet, with its emphasis on fluidity and stasis, an optical illusion reminiscent of Wordsworth's encounter with the 'stationary blasts' of the Gondo gorge,[9] Mary's account may also be read as a proleptic response to Samuel Bamford's memorable description of the breaking of the dense, compacted crowd at St Peter's Field: 'For a moment the crowd held back as in a pause; then was a rush, heavy and resistless as a headlong sea; and a sound like low thunder, with screams, prayers, and imprecations from the crowd-moiled, and sabre-doomed, who could not escape'.[10] Here, two versions of the sublime may be compared and contrasted. While Bamford draws on Homeric tropes of catastrophic terror, engulfing the crowd in a tsunami-like wave of destruction, Mary's emphasis on the poised 'stream of life' recalls the observations of the river Duddon that had preoccupied Wordsworth the previous year. By informing her vision with a related affirmation of unity amidst change, Mary endeavours to reverse the current, recasting an 'immense concourse of persons' as a flowing yet stationary mass, in sight of an end that is forever delayed. Those 'certain feats' of which the Wordsworths learn but are reluctant to envision are here effectively consigned to temporal oblivion, annulled by an intelligence in thrall to the recovery of a pre-political society. Witnessed only in glimpses and notably only when on holiday, the Wordsworthian social ideal is characterised nevertheless by a sense of historical indeterminacy, a state in which the distinctions between peace and war become difficult to discern let alone sustain.

Drawing on such observations, this chapter argues that while Wordsworth's direct references to Peterloo may be few and predictably conservative, his indirect referential engagements with 'treasons, tumults', and 'wars' in poems published in the aftermath of Peterloo reveal a thoughtful and unpredictable engagement with the place of conflict in civil society.[11] The principal focus of the chapter is on a single collection, *The River Duddon, a Series of Sonnets: Vaudracour and Julia and Other Poems. To Which Is Annexed, a Topographical Description of the Country of the Lakes, in the North of England*. That, in 1820, Wordsworth regarded *The River Duddon* as the culmination of a five-year period of sustained creativity, and that the volume was intended to serve as a pacific coda to the bellicose imaginings of the Thanksgiving volume, is made clear by an advertisement informing the reader that 'This publication, together with "The Thanksgiving Ode," January 18 1816, "The Tale of Peter Bell," and "The Waggoner," completes the third and last volume of the Author's Miscellaneous Poems'.[12] As observed in Chapter 3, purchasers wishing to add the collection to the 1815 two-volume *Poems* and the aforementioned works are provided with an alternative title page, 'Poems by William Wordsworth: Including The River Duddon; Vaudracour and Julia; Peter Bell; The Waggoner; A Thanksgiving Ode and Miscellaneous Pieces. Vol. III', and a tipped-in spine label: 'Wordsworth's/Poems/Including the/ River Duddon/Vol. III'.[13] Bringing together within one binding poems and prose writings composed during the period of the revolutionary and Napoleonic wars (*Peter Bell, Vaudracour and Julia*, the guide to the Lakes), verses written in the wake of Waterloo (the 'Thanksgiving Ode' and related poems), the post-Peterloo sonnets and other 'Miscellaneous Pieces' concerned with governance, morality, and war, the rare third volume of Wordsworth's *Poems* offers a sustained commentary on the historical origins of political violence while seeking, through meditation on the natural histories of rivers, mountains, and lakes, the grounds for a peaceable, albeit reactionary, alternative.[14]

Composed, for the most part, a year in advance of Peterloo, but appearing in its disruptive wake, the *Duddon* sonnets' depiction of peace turns out to be strangely dissonant, even warlike, reflecting the poet's suspicion that social tensions, hitherto kept in check by the maintenance of hostilities with a foreign antagonist, were about to spill over into outright civil war. How is it that a sequence of poems, contrived to celebrate the enduring presence of a native British river, should come to be associated with conflict? Pastoral waters ought, ideally, to bring peace to troubled souls but Wordsworth's engagement with the fluvial tradition rarely conforms to expectations, in part because of his inveterate self-scrutiny, which intensifies in the later poetry to the point where confident declarations of inviolable truth are stirred by underswells of doubt, insecurity, and self-contestation. Inspired by Coleridge's aborted plans for 'The Brook', a poetical essay on 'men, nature, and society' that took 'a stream, traced from its source in the hills [to the sea]' as its subject,[15] *The River Duddon* can be read as a tributary of Wordsworth's own great unrealised project: 'The Recluse'. In the autumn of 1804, a few weeks prior to resuming work on the expanded version of *The Prelude* – a poem that begins and ends with the sound of running waters – Wordsworth, accompanied by Dorothy, undertook a tour of the Duddon valley. The tour inspired the writing of a sonnet, 'To the River Duddon', a poem that offers oblique commentary on the wayward progress of 'The Recluse' ('paths renew'd/By fits and starts [...] through this passage cleave/Attended but by thy own Voice', ll. 7–13), while providing a source for the 1820 sequence.[16] Wordsworth's declaration of autonomy and purposefulness rises again in the *Duddon* sequence's opening sonnet but, as I go on to argue, the rhetoric of self-confidence is undercut by recollections of that which has been left undone, as well as by intimations of bloodshed, war, and sacrifice stirred up by allusions to sacred founts and rivers belonging to the classical tradition.

The River Duddon speaks, then, to the memory of a lost totality, its activation of hostile currents preventing the realisation of harmony, synthesis, and reconciliation. As a 'late work', in the sense identified by Adorno and Said, the collection aspires towards completion but is baffled at every stage by the late poet's ingrained self-reflexivity, resulting in a style that is 'bristling, difficult, and unyielding'.[17] But the cultivation of self-consciousness is not the only source of trouble in *The River Duddon*. Julia S. Carlson has observed that the organising principle of the sonnet sequence bears some resemblance to Joseph Priestley's charts and Friedrich Strass's *Stream of Time* – large-format chronological 'maps', which sought to impose graphic order on the messy contingency of human history (Figures 3 and 4).[18] Inscribed beneath an epigram from Horace's Ode 3.29, '*Fluminis ritu Feruntur*', or 'flows away like a river',[19] Priestley's *Chart of Biography* (1764) depicts history as a succession of discrete, yet interconnected, 'spaces of time', floating 'on the surface' of an 'immense river [...] without beginning or end'.[20] In *A Description of a New Chart of History* (1769), Priestley

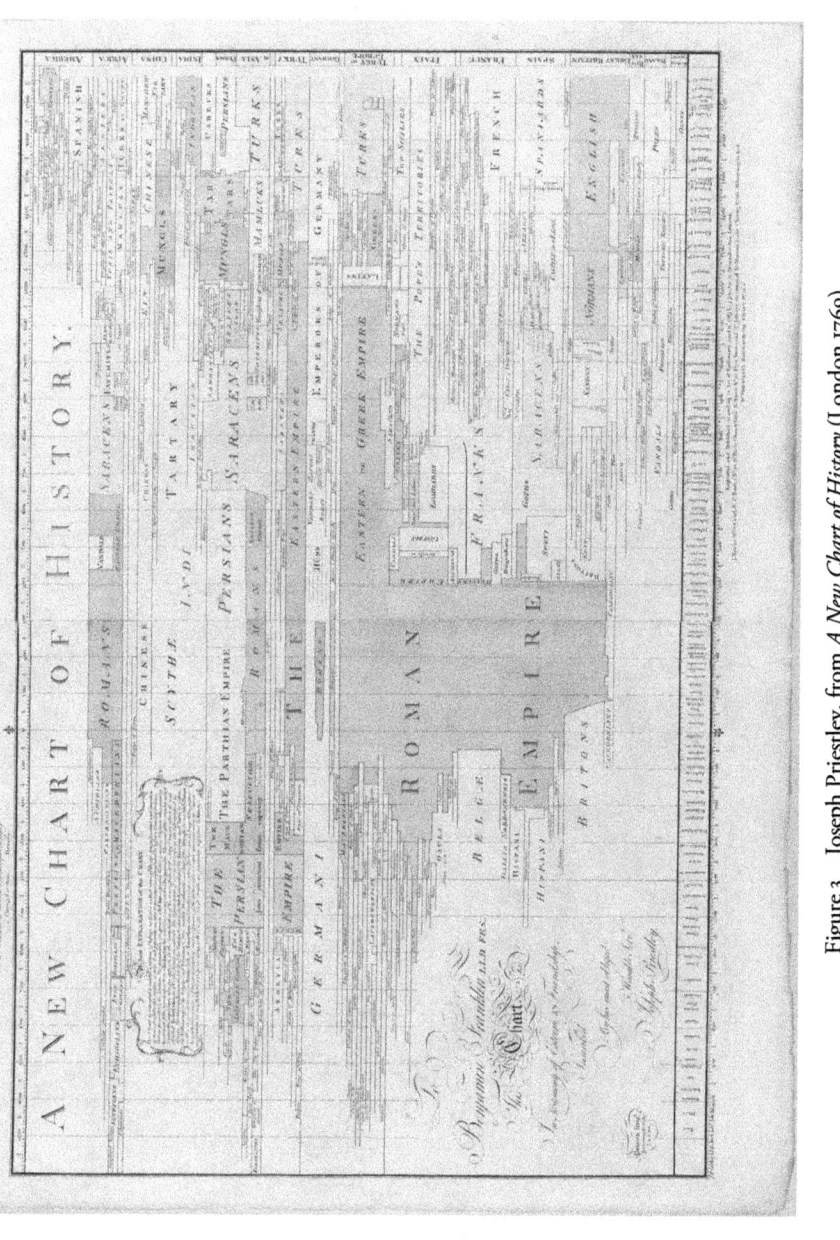

Figure 3 Joseph Priestley, from *A New Chart of History* (London 1769).
Source: Engraved and published by Joseph Priestley.
64.8 cm × 97.8 cm. Public domain.

150 *The River Duddon* and *Ecclesiastical Sketches*

Figure 4   Friedrich Strass, *Der Strom der Zeiten* (*The Stream of Time*) (1804). Source: Berlin: Garde. 13 cm × 70 cm. Public domain.

anticipates the response of a notional reader of this chart, dismayed by the 'torrents of human blood' that distort and disfigure its surface, belying its claims to order, uniformity, and constancy. Acceding to the perspective of the 'Most high', for whom wars and revolutions are always 'subservient to most benevolent purposes', Priestley assures his reader that such disruptions have, on the whole, been 'extremely favourable to the progress of knowledge, virtue, and happiness' and that 'it will not be long before this world assumes another, and more agreeable aspect; and that the chart of history some centuries hence, will not be intersected and disfigured, in so shocking a manner, as it has been in centuries past'.[21]

Alluding, in the *Duddon* sequence's well-known conclusion, to Horace's 'yet on it glides, and on it will glide, rolling its flood forever',[22] Wordsworth observes the progress of human history from a position of a-temporal constancy, not unrelated to Priestley's divine point of view:

> For, *backward*, Duddon! as I cast my eyes,
> I see what was, and is, and will abide;
> Still glides the Stream, and shall for ever glide;
> The Form remains, the Function never dies [...] (Sonnet XXXIII, ll. 3–6)

Yet, while the poem observes human limits from a transcendental perspective, the sequence that precedes it retains the sense of how small pockets of unmeasured time, held in discordant specificities, introduce those 'sly/ And sure encroachments of infirmity' (Sonnet IX, l. 13) that bring all life to an end. In this sense, *The River Duddon* is perhaps more in tune with the gloomy and uncertain pronouncements on futurity that can be found in William Bell's translation of Strass's *Descriptive Guide to the Stream of Time* (1810). Rejecting the 'stiff regularity' of Priestley's lines in favour of a literal rendering of time's riverine course, 'more agreeable in its variations to the nature of the abstract notion', Strass nevertheless struggles to address the problem of contingency, which threatens always to reconfigure the shape and course of history.[23] Acknowledging this problem, Bell provides the reader with a 'short space' at the end of the chart 'for the introduction of any great events, which may occur in the two succeeding decenniums; and indeed from the probable instability of the present state of things'. Writing in 1812, at the height of the Peninsular War, Bell sees no immediate end to 'the present afflicting contest'; the prospect of 'a general and stable peace' remains no more than a possibility.[24] We might imagine the purchaser of Strass's chart inscribing 'Waterloo' in 1815 to rebut Bell's pessimism, only to inscribe 'Peterloo', somewhat ruefully, just a few years later.

In the final part of the chapter, I trace the re-emergence of these violent waters in the three-volume *Poems* (1820), the four-volume *Miscellaneous Poems* (1820), and *Ecclesiastical Sketches* (1822). Criticism that focusses on the links between these collections is rare, surprisingly so given the ways in which, between 1818 and 1822, Wordsworth devotes himself to the development of a poetics of riparian nationalism, a project culminating with the pan-European reflections of *Memorials of a Tour on the Continent, 1820* (1822), which I go on to examine in the next chapter.[25] In all of these collections, the motif of the river journey provides the poet with a means to measure and endure the vicissitudes of time: pursuing, in *The River Duddon*, the course of a 'native Stream' from source to sea; connecting, by virtue of their location in the three- and four-volume editions, the *Duddon* sonnets, and the Thanksgiving poems; comparing, in *Ecclesiastical Sketches*, the historical assent of the Anglican Church to a 'cloud-fed spring' destined for that 'Eternal City—built/For the perfected Spirits of the just!'; celebrating, in *Memorials of a Tour on the Continent, 1820*, those 'unconquerable' streams that witnessed the rise and fall of revolutionary and Imperial France.[26] Alert to how traumatic memories of war resurface in *The River Duddon*, the collected *Poems*, and in *Ecclesiastical Sketches*, this chapter contends that sensitivity to the contested histories of rivers, a pervasive motif in contemporary nature writing, from Claudio Magris's *Danube* to Robert Macfarlane's *Underland*, is nothing new: Wordsworth has known, all along, that sacred founts are laved in blood.

September Songs: 1815–1819

To initiate this reading of *The River Duddon* I want first to consider two poems composed by Wordsworth in the immediate aftermath of the events in Manchester. Commentary on Romantic poetry and the Peterloo Massacre owes much to Jerome McGann, whose 1979 article 'Keats and the Historical Method in Literary Criticism' proclaimed, to the consternation of critics as varied in approach as Paul Fry, Nicholas Roe, and Vincent Newey, that 'To Autumn' 'is an historically specified fiction dialectically called into being by John Keats as an active response to, and alteration of, the events which marked the late summer and early fall of a particular year in a particular place'.[27] Sharing common ground with Marjorie Levinson's Marxian critique of Wordsworth's 'repression' of material contradictions in the landscape of 'Tintern Abbey',[28] McGann's reading of 'To Autumn' was widely interpreted as a wholescale denunciation of the high Romantic lyric and its purported evasion of history. Yet what is striking about the criticism written in response to McGann's provocation is the corresponding narrowness of its attention, which with the exception of some notable discussions of Shelley's *Masque of Anarchy* and associated poems remained almost solely focussed on providing subtle defences of Keats's politics and poetics. In the articles, essays, and books that emerged in this period and that attempted to engage with Peterloo there are hardly any mentions of poetry by Wordsworth, a surprising omission given that Wordsworth wrote two poems in the autumn of 1819 that may be read, along McGannian lines, as 'an active response to, and alteration of, the events' at St Peter's Field.[29] For reasons that will become clear, the poems in question, 'September 1819' and 'Upon the Same Occasion', included in *The River Duddon* volume, deserve closer attention.

Composed during a period when Wordsworth, disabled by a severe attack of trachoma and concerned by 'the revolutionary projects' (*MY* II. 558) of the Broughamites, was beginning to reassess his role as a poet and cultural authority, 'September, 1819' seems, at first, to present an image of peace and plenitude far removed from the shocks occasioned by the Manchester massacre:

> The sylvan slopes with corn-clad fields
> Are hung, as if with golden shields,
> Bright trophies of the sun!
> Like a fair sister of the sky,
> Unruffled doth the blue Lake lie,
> The Mountains looking on. (ll. 1–5)[30]

As idealised and idealising as Keats's complementary portrayal of autumn – at the start of September Dorothy records how 'torrents of rain' had caused severe damage to the corn (*MY* II. 554) – the mood of peace and plenty, enhanced as much by the prosodic assurances of *rime coué* as by the imagery of pastoral seclusion, is subtly challenged by the inclusion of those 'golden shields' (l. 2). These spoils of war assembled under the name of Apollo, god of the sun, of healing, and of poetry, present a strikingly troubling image. The impression of internal dissonance is compounded further still when one recalls Nicholas Roe's discussion of the allusion to the goddess Ceres in Keats's ode. Noting the resemblance between Keats's personification of the season and the female deity of justice, liberty, and autumnal abundance depicted on the Peterloo banner, Roe argues persuasively that the ode participates in a radical re-reading of classical mythology, drawing on Ceres' associations with husbandry, cultivation, and 'common' law to mount a quiet denunciation of the pernicious effects of the Corn Laws in solidarity with the protestors in Manchester.[31] Composed like Keats's poem in a time of economic deprivation and state oppression, 'September, 1819' is, by contrast, ruthlessly combative, marshalling images of armoured fruition to quell political unrest. Where Keats's poem grants the vibrant delights of spring, in order to celebrate the mellow, attenuated pleasures of autumn, Wordsworth offers stark criticism, asserting that the autumnal tone is 'more profoundly dear/Than music of Spring' (ll. 11–12):

> For *that* from turbulence and heat
> Proceeds, from some uneasy
> Seat in Nature's struggling frame,
> Some region of impatient life;
> And jealousy, and quivering strife,
> Therein a portion claim. (ll. 13–18)

In opposition to the constitutional unrest of spring, an echo of the Hobbesian *bellum inter omnia* advanced in the 'Topographical Description of the Country of the Lakes',[32] the poem thus establishes autumn as a season of 'soft harmony' (l. 26) unchecked by internal conflict. Yet, because such seasonal concord is predicated on the suppression of 'impatient life' and 'quivering strife' it becomes increasingly difficult to sustain a distinction between the institution of the peaceable state and the primal antagonism from which it is said to emerge. To extend this Hobbesian notion further, autumn is presented in Wordsworth's poem as a state of exception, founded on, or facilitated by, the threat of violence against that singular, self-constituting multitude that would jeopardise the power of the sovereign to maintain the distinction between internal and external peace.

In the pendant poem 'Upon the Same Occasion' a related attempt is made to shift the focus of attention towards 'undiscordant themes' (l. 21).[33] In concert with the poet's Waterloo poetry, the verse is as much about Wordsworth's aspiration to be acknowledged as a national bard, overcoming faction and dissent in the name of a higher, literary principle as it is about the wish for release from internal division. Sustaining the meditation on aging and poetic decline introduced in the previous poem, 'Upon the Same Occasion' initially makes light of the poet who, beset by the lively din of 'social Warblers gathering in/Their harvest of sweet lays' (ll. 11–12) and 'conscious that my leaf is sear,/And yellow on the bough' (ll. 14–15), can yet find 'cheer' (l. 13) in the prospect of bestowing his 'myrtle wreaths' (l. 16) on the head of some younger bard. The mood of quiet acceptance changes, however, in the fourth stanza, as the poet turns to address those contemporaries who, gripped by 'vernal extasies,/And passion's feverish dreams' (ll. 23–4), would 'enervate and defile' (l. 30) the analeptic labour of the Apollonian bard. It is possible that Hunt and Keats, poets readily associated with 'vernal extacies' and the 'snares of soft desire',[34] are the target of these lines, but as Carl Ketcham suggests it seems more likely that Wordsworth has Lord Byron in mind, whose recently published *Don Juan*, Canto 1 had lampooned Wordsworth and his fellow Lake poets.[35] In addition to striking back at Byron for this public attack, Wordsworth might also have wished to single out the poet for his ambivalent response to the defeat of Napoleon and for his support of radical political causes. Tellingly, in the poem's concluding stanzas Wordsworth invokes as model for the post-Peterloo bard the ancient Greek poet Alcaeus who supported the nobles in the civil war in Mytilene and whose 'fierce vindictive song' was the scourge of the leaders of the people, known as 'Tyrants' (ll. 37–41). Combining sympotic and lyrical impulses, Alcaeus, together with Horace, is thus presented as an exemplar of the 'deathless powers' (l. 25) of poesy, assessing and overcoming moral and political corruption through the adoption of a timeless, dispassionate perspective.

In maintaining this perspective, Wordsworth resumes the vatic tone adopted in his earlier post-war autumnal sonnet 'September 1815'.[36] Composed shortly after the victory at Waterloo, the octave registers a sense of an oncoming period of austerity and of the likelihood of a forthcoming civil war, culminating with the advice to '"Prepare/Against the threatening Foe your trustiest shields"' (ll. 7–8). In the sestet, the forewarning of conflict is countered by the image of a 'season potent to renew,/Mid frost and snow, the instinctive joys of song, —/And nobler cares than listless summer knew' (ll. 12–14). In these lines the threat of destruction is incorporated within a rhythmic seasonal cycle, one that allows conflict to be refigured as a 'potent' source of creative, moral, and political renewal. What remains unclear is how the bracing destruction of mid-year lassitude may be aligned with the 'soft harmony' (l. 26) that, in 'September, 1819', transcends 'Nature's struggling frame' (l. 15), allowing the spirit 'to mount above/The anxieties of human love' (ll. 22–3). Moreover, as the manuscript of 'Upon the Same Occasion' graphically displays, the two models of poetry outlined in these verses – one divinely inspired and politically legitimate, the other profane and alarmingly radical – would seem to be struggling for primacy.[37] Close attention to the manuscript reveals that in place of the fifth stanza denouncing those poets who would 'enervate and defile' their sacred 'function', Mary had inadvertently copied the fifth stanza of 'September, 1819', which had been intended not only as an affirmation of the voice of eternal harmony over and above the conative strife of nature but also as a corrective to the vagaries of contemporary taste. Crossed out in the manuscript, the lines nevertheless ghost the characterisation of those young contemporaries who, as a result of indulging their rebellious passions, would lose sight of the eternal, thereby committing themselves to the relentless assaying of discordant themes.

A small detail in the manuscript adds to the complexity of this vision. In place of 'function' in line 28, Mary has inserted the word 'Patron'. But who are the poets who would disclaim their patrons, 'pleas'd with what is aptliest framed/To enervate and defile'? In this first version of the poem the target no longer seems to be Byron and the Cockney School; instead, the focus turns to Wordsworth himself who, throughout the month of September, had been engaged in frantic correspondence with Lord Lowther regarding the consequences for Westmorland of the political disturbances in Manchester. Might it be the case that Wordsworth through seeking to condemn those 'kindred souls' who, enamoured of 'feverish dreams', would neglect their higher vocation was, in truth, holding a light up to that part of himself that felt drawn towards the indulgence of aberrant desires in defiance of the bonds of patronage? Nothing in the published record provides support for this suggestion, but still one wonders how far Wordsworth detected in the writings of his young contemporaries an echo of his early and perhaps undiminished fascination with sexual and political transgression.

Currents of Disturbance: Sounding War in *The River Duddon*

The desire to transform discordant themes, discovering in the process the extent to which such themes shape one's identity, is present in *The River Duddon* too. Wordsworth casts his sequence as a response to Coleridge's aborted long poem 'The Brook', a work intended to rival Cowper's *Task* in providing 'equal room and freedom for description, incident, and impassioned reflections on men, nature, and society' while yet supplying 'in itself a natural connection to the parts, and unity to the whole'. Recalling the plan for 'The Recluse', Coleridge states that his own essay on 'men, nature, and society' was to have taken for its subject 'a stream, traced from its source in the hills [to the sea]'.[38] In the postscript to *The River Duddon* Wordsworth freely admits his borrowing of this unifying motif but states that his work differs from 'The Brook' on account of 'the restriction which the frame of the Sonnet imposed upon me, narrowing unavoidably the range of thought, and precluding, though not without its advantages, many graces to which a freer movement of verse would naturally have led'.[39] By embracing formal restrictions Wordsworth is able, as Daniel Robinson explains, to partially fulfil the promise of 'his and Coleridge's shared vision'.[40] But in revisiting these, as yet, unrealised works, through the medium of the loco-descriptive river poem, Wordsworth also, necessarily, recalls the genre's elegiac aspects. Thus, as much as *The River Duddon* seeks to make good on the youthful poet's promise to complete a work addressing 'men, nature, and society', the combination of formal 'narrowing' and thematic revisiting cannot help but place the sequence in relation to a greater and, seemingly, lost object. *The River Duddon*, I would suggest, is therefore couched, from the outset, as a work of melancholy.

Writing in *Wordsworth's Poetry, 1815–1845* of the failure of *Ecclesiastical Sketches* to encompass the contested history of the Anglican Church, Tim Fulford observes that the sonnet form's 'narrow room' is 'too isolated and too static to allow the sequence to articulate historical struggle' and that its primary 'architectonic metaphor—the holy river—remains too gestural to compensate for this deficiency'.[41] Recalling the strained endeavour of sonnet XXXIII to encompass 'what was, and is, and will abide' (l. 4), one might concur that *The River Duddon* fails no less to forge a collective narrativisation of the relations between man, nature, and society that a 'large-scale poetic structure' would have accomplished.[42] But while it is fruitful to read *The River Duddon* as a fallen version of 'The Recluse', the publication of the sequence in the wake of Peterloo suggests a relationship not merely with a lost object but with an impossible object. In Wordsworth's autumnal poems, as we have seen, the attempt to establish a realm of post-war harmony is jeopardised by the return of images of internal strife. And in the *Duddon* sequence's orchestration of local and national history the progressive narrative is shadowed by memories of conflict: from the 'unprotected' man 'nurs'd/In hideous usages, and rites accurs'd' (VIII, ll. 5–7; *passim*), to the 'sovereign Thames', freighted with 'Commerce' or 'triumphant War' (XXXI, ll. 12–14). Thus, as much as Wordsworth pursues the ideal of a peaceable society, seeing in the Duddon's journey to 'Eternity' an image of how the 'tumultuous' workings of history may at last be 'left behind' (XXXII, ll. 10–14; *passim*), the poetry speaks repeatedly of the impossibility of attaining this goal.

Regarded in this light, Wordsworth's refusal to reflect on the significance of St Peter's Field may be understood as a manifestation of perplexity at the blurring of distinctions between allies and enemies, citizens and soldiers, but also as a sign of the poet's unwillingness to register the work of *stasis* in determining that which is political and that which is unpolitical.

Nevertheless, as the *Duddon* sonnets reveal, aspects of civil discord are manifest throughout the sequence, consuming not merely the city but also nature. For if, according to Agamben, 'civil war is a projection of the state of nature into the city' then the converse must also be true; that is, we should not be surprised to see descriptions of natural life (*zoē*) – the physical realm of rocks, rivers, earth, and plants – marked by the effects of a dissolving *bios politikos*.[43] If this statement about the violent transformation of nature seems counterintuitive, it is important to remember that the pastoral tradition that Wordsworth recalls in his poetry is forged in a context of civil discord. In showing through the *Duddon* sequence how the significance of rivers is informed by the effects of war, Wordsworth positions himself in relation to Horace and Virgil, sharing their anxieties about the politicisation of nature.[44]

The opening sonnet identifies three established and, by implication, overworked poetic precedents: Horace's spring of Bandusia (ll. 1–4); the Persian fountains that, in the wake of Sir William Jones's imitations of Nezami, had become a stock feature of literary orientalism (ll. 5–6), and the 'Alpine torrents' (ll. 7–8) that had featured in Wordsworth's earlier loco-descriptive poetry, as well as in Book VI of the unpublished *Prelude*, and that Byron had since imitated to considerable acclaim in Canto III of *Childe Harold's Pilgrimage* and in *Manfred*.[45] Against these well-worn, exotic, and populist precedents, dismissed through a series of verbal negations, the poet declares a wish to 'seek the birth-place of a native Stream' (l. 8) so that his verse may 'flow [...] pure, vigorous, free, and bright' (l. 13), unencumbered by generic expectations. Yet, despite the confident turn, the octave's accumulation of literary sources signals an understanding of the fraught relations between imitation and innovation and, further still, displays a shrewd awareness of the submerged violence of the pastoral tradition. Key to both insights is the significance of the opening allusion to Horace's Ode 3.13, a poem that seems to have held a lifelong fascination for Wordsworth.[46] Horace's verse takes the form of a dedicatory address to a *fons Bandusiae*, an obscure spring believed to be located in the grounds of Horace's Sabine estate.[47] As translators and commentators have pointed out, Horace is attempting in this poem to elevate a Roman fountain and, by extension, Roman verse to the distinguished position occupied by Greek springs and Greek pastoral poetry.[48] Thus, the *fons Bandusiae* will emerge as a rival to Arethusa, Castalia, and Hippocrene, and Ode 3.13 as a worthy successor to the feted river songs of Theocritus and Callimachus. However, just as Horace's assertion of literary authority is qualified by its acknowledgement of Greek models of inspiration, in particular the modest 'holy fountain' in Callimachus' *Hymn to Apollo*,[49] so Wordsworth's description of native purity is sullied by its engagement with Horace. The priority of that 'rocky spring' may not be envied, but the sonnet must be forged within its 'shades' (ll. 1–2).

More pressing still, for both poets, is the problem of how to maintain the sense of the pastoral mode, with its associations of peace, obscurity, and retirement. In stating that the Duddon and his poem about the Duddon is 'pure' Wordsworth displays his awareness of the contentious or mixed status of Horace's stream, which on the eve of a rustic festival is set to be stained by the blood of a sacrificial kid, a product of the 'wanton herd' (l. 8), whose 'budding horns' mark him out for 'Battles and love' (ll. 4–5).[50] Although line five may be understood as a reference to benign battles of love (*et venerem et proelia*) the kid's status as a symbol of Callimachean eroticism is itself sacrificed to the ode's larger concern with literary authority. For, rather than dwelling on or indeed dismissing the ignoble taints of blood, sacrifice, and war, the Horatian pastoral seeks to sublimate violence, thereby transforming itself into something greater than a Callimachean hymn to rural delights. In Erwin Panofsky's sense, Ode 3.13 exemplifies the aim of pastoral to 'resolve' instances of individual suffering through incorporation within larger structures of artistic harmony.[51] Thus, though blood may spoil the waters, the stream's consecration as one of the 'famous fountains' (l. 13) ensures that no lasting harm is done.

While Horace, like Callimachus, demonstrates the ability of art to triumph over destruction by portraying the blood of the sacrificial kid as, at worst, a temporary sullying of the sacred spring, and of the poem itself as capable of encompassing the bifurcated themes of love and war, the elevation of the humble brook in pastoral lyric is brought about as a reaction to the bellicose legacy of the epic tradition. In George Chapman's translation of *Iliad*, Book XXI, for example, Achilles battles with enemies in the whirling currents of the Xanthus:

> The siluer-gulphed deepe
> Receiu'd them with a mightie crie: the billowes vast and steepe,
> Ror'd at their armours; which the shores, did round about resound:
> This way, and that, they swum, and shriekt; as in the gulphs they drownd.[52]

Blinded by fury, Achilles escalates the slaughter, prompting the river, in the shape of a man, to protest against the accumulation of bodies that choke its currents with 'mortalitie'.[53] But still Achilles fights on, accelerating the combat to a struggle between man and river, thereby revealing how 'simple natural life' is politicised as 'bare life' through exposure to death.[54]

Echoing the concerns of his classical antecedents, Wordsworth's sonnet sequence offers glimpses of a post-war world, of that which remains after the apocalyptic struggle of man, nature, and society. In Sonnet VIII, for example, a series of Keatsian rhetorical questions, seemingly addressed to the ghost of an ancient warrior – 'What aspect bore the Man who rove or fled [...] to this dark dell?', 'who first in this pellucid Current slaked his thirst?', 'Was the Intruder nurs'd/In hideous usages, and rites accurs'd,/ That thinned the living and disturbed the dead?' (ll. 1–8) – is answered by silence: 'the earth, the air is mute', only the 'murmuring' stream provides a 'soft record' of a capacity to 'heal and to restore,/To soothe and cleanse, not madden and pollute!' (ll. 9–14). And in Sonnet XXIII, otherwise known as 'Sheep-Washing', the sequence returns to the relations between violence and purity addressed by Horace, only here, instead of receiving a slaughtered kid, the Duddon's 'laving currents' perform 'prelusive rites' (l. 3) so that the dales-men may shear their sheep. Moreover, should the 'Duddon's spotless breast receive/Unwelcome mixtures' of 'uncouth noise' (ll. 9–10), from 'barking dogs', boyish 'clamour', and fearful 'bleatings' (ll. 7–8), 'the pastoral river will forgive/Such wrong' (ll. 10–11). The 'stains' produced by such 'sports' are 'fugitive' and nature will be sustained in 'quiet equipoise' (ll. 13–14). Alert to the potential for furore encoded in the etymology of 'noise', Wordsworth in both poems presents the river as a form of sound baffle, a means of dampening the potential for tumult inherent in the pastoral mode.

In Sonnet XIII, 'Open Prospect', however, the soothing influence of the river in 'Sheep-Washing' is curtailed by a 'dread swell of sound' that cuts through the 'stiff lance-like shoots of pollard ash' (ll. 6–7). Rather than muffling the sounds of war, the river is itself a source of discord, emitting 'angry' notes (l. 11) that the nearby households must drown out by means of 'mantling ale' and laughter (ll. 12–13). Still, in this poem, the turn in line 9 towards the social realm cannot wholly conceal the echoes of pre-pastoral violence encoded in the octave's allusion to *Aeneid*, III, lines 24–82. Specifically, the 'lance-like shoots' recall the densely packed myrtles, 'rough with many a spear' (l. 32), which Aeneas, seeking to establish a homeland in Thrace, uses to build a canopy for a sacrificial altar.[55] In Wordsworth's translation of Virgil's poem the harvesting of the green shoots reveals 'a dire portent, [...] wond'rous to be told!' (l. 36):

> No sooner was the shatter'd root laid bare
> Of the first Tree I struggled to uptear,
> Than from the fibres drops of blood distill'd,
> Whose blackness stain'd the ground. (ll. 37–40)

Aeneas tries a second time to tear the stalks from the earth and is met again by the sight of blood seeping from the torn bark. A third attempt elicits a 'mournful groan' (l. 56) and a warning to the hero to desist from his labours. The voice belongs to Polydorus, a victim of Achilles in the war against the Trojans, whose sword-pierced body, transformed into sanguineous 'myrtle lances' (l. 54), testifies to the co-implication of pastoral retirement and the reciprocal activity of death and wounding. For if rivers, plants, earth, and air serve as indelible registers of human suffering, must the *patria* itself be implicated? Is there no sacred space on which violence does not encroach?

Elsewhere, in *The River Duddon* volume, the Hobessian notion of nature at war with itself is manifested in 'The Brownie's Cell', which with its description of battle-wrought stars, 'winds combating with woods', and 'Lands delug'd by unbridled floods' (ll. 61–70) recalls the account of discordant nature as an augur of civil strife presented by Virgil in *Georgics* I: in advance of Caesar's assassination the sun is hid in 'dusky gloom'; Etna shoots out 'balls of flame and molten rocks'; the Alps rock with 'unwonted terrors'; the Eridanus, king of rivers, washes away whole forests, sweeping cattle and stalls alike across the plains; the sky is marked by lightning and 'blazing comets'.[56] A time will come when the farmer, tilling the soil with 'crooked plough', will uncover 'javelins eaten up with rusty mould, or with his heavy hoe shall strike on empty helms, and marvel at the giant bones in the upturned graves', but for now the 'crooked pruning-hooks are forged into stiff swords' and the world is convulsed by the thirst for annihilation.[57] The best that can be hoped for, as Virgil anticipates in *Eclogues* I, is a pastoral zone rescued from conflict: 'Happy old man! Here, amid familiar streams and sacred springs, you shall court the cooling shade' (ll. 46–58); but for every farmer who lives to till the soil, another must die so that the soil may be nourished, and thus there is no sacred spring that is not defiled by blood.[58]

In Sonnet XXVIII Wordsworth seeks to correct this assumption. The inspiration for the verse comes from the site of a disused Quaker burial ground, known locally as the Sepulchre, situated on the east bank of the Duddon about a mile above Ulpha Bridge. Amidst these 'retired domains', the poem records, there is no evidence of 'lance opposed to lance' (ll. 1–2) and, notably in light of the bleeding soil alluded to in sonnets VIII and XIII, no account of turf stained 'purple from the veins/Of heroes fall'n, or struggling to advance' (ll. 3–4). The ground, that is, bears no trace of epic fight or, more pointedly, of 'power usurp'd' (l. 13). 'Yet', the sestet confirms, the 'blank earth' shelters the remains of 'the loyal and the brave' who, though 'neglected and forlorn', receive the 'tribute' of 'passing Winds' and the 'praise' of torrents, 'inspiring [...] glad acknowledgment of lawful sway' (ll. 6–14). Composed between March and December 1819, the sonnet may be read as a pointedly anti-conspiratorial gesture, using Virgilian meditations on pastoral exceptionalism and the outcome of 'doubtful combat' (l. 5) to inform a reactionary judgement of the current state of affairs. For if, like St Peter's Field, the earth is now unmarked, it serves, nevertheless, as confirmation of a power greater and more enduring than the human capacity for revolt. Still, the objects of this praise remain unregistered, and the voices of the winds and of the river are strictly inarticulate, suggesting that pacific heroes must remain exiles from signification.

The characteristic pattern of affirmation via negation is sustained at the sequence's close. In Sonnet XXXI the Duddon is released from the picturesque hold of 'flower-enamelled lands', 'blooming thickets', and 'rocky bands' allowing the river to flow in 'radiant progress' towards the Irish sea (ll. 1–4). Following a densely plotted series of negated verbs – 'Not hurled [...] Lingering no more [...] nor [...] held' – in line 5 the heavily accented *'now'* signals the Duddon's possession of the tidal flats, allowing it to sweep in 'unfettered' majesty over 'smooth flat sands' (ll. 5–6). The river is presented from hereon in terms of the natural sublime, its grandeur unsullied by transient picturesque forms, by baroque rhetorical constructions, or by fears of mortality.[59] The octave, composed in advance of the sestet between December 1818 and March 1819, makes comparison between the Duddon and the 'sovereign Thames' (l. 12). United in 'Stately mien' (l. 12), the concluding lines depict the latter river 'Spreading his bosom under Kentish downs,/With freighted Commerce or triumphant War' (l. 14).[60] As the penultimate sonnet makes clear, the 'Majestic Duddon' may be 'allied' (Sonnet XXXI, ll. 12) to the 'sovereign Thames' but is ultimately immunised from the oppositional logic that defines the capital river's supremacy.[61] Thus, in Sonnet XXXII, the octave composed during the same period as the previous sonnet's sestet confirms that 'no cannon thunders to the gale' and 'no haughty pendants cast/A crimson splendour' upon the waves (ll. 1–2); and in like manner, in the sestet, written in advance of the octave between December 1818 and March 1819, the 'Wanderer' (l. 7) and the 'Poet' (l. 9), taking the river's progress towards the sea as their model, resign the 'strange vicissitudes' (l. 6) of mortal life, 'Prepared, in peace of heart, in calm of mind/And soul' to 'mingle with Eternity!' (ll. 13–14). Peace, therefore, is presented at the close of *The River Duddon* as a release from the alternation between opposing or contrasting things, specifically from the constitutional violence – 'Commerce' *or*

'War' – in which the *polis* is forged. Of significance here is the fact that the lines most preoccupied with conflict – the sestet of XXXI and the octave of XXXII – were both written after the violent events in Manchester. Benjamin Kim observes that in its original form Sonnet XXXI provided a much neater and far less worldly ending to the sequence.[62] The revised sestet of XXXI therefore introduced a disjunctive element that the octave of XXXI was designed to resolve, as if in recognition of the impossibility of preventing the alliance of warlike and pacific rivers.[63]

As the final sonnet in the sequence confirms, the attempt to pacify antagonism can succeed only by accepting and upholding a mode of life that, by virtue of its release from death, is no longer subject to politicisation. Looking back on his journey, the poet of Sonnet XXXIII, 'Conclusion', sees 'what was, and is, and will abide;/Still glides the Stream and shall for ever glide;/The Form remains, the Function never dies' (ll. 4–6). In the continuity of being through past, present, and future tenses, in the paradoxical logic of 'For, *backward*, Duddon' (l. 3) and 'Still glides' (l. 5), and in the assertion of life living on, not as bare life but as eternal Platonic Form, Wordsworth releases the stream and the literary work in which the stream is enshrined, from the exclusionary/inclusionary logic of the *polis*. From another perspective, however, the attempt to protect nature from death merely replaces one form of co-optation – the political – with another, namely, the religious. For just as the peaceable fount is retroactively produced through the violent suspension of the political, so that 'life' which lives on is made conditional on the inclusive exclusion of death through 'faith's transcendent dower' (l. 13). In line 9 the distinction between the acceptance of mortality and the declaration of that 'something', which 'from our hands have power/To live, and act, and serve the future hour' (ll. 10–11), is, accordingly, signified through a protracted pause: 'We Men, who in our morn of youth defied/The elements must vanish;—be it so!' (ll. 8–9). The terminal clause that enables the poem to accept the necessity of non-existence and that serves also to enable progression beyond the potentially fatal pause is reminiscent of the '*now* expands' clause of Sonnet XXXI and, in like manner, signals the poem's commitment to the upholding of internal division as a key element in the furtherance of life. By marking a reciprocal relation between nullity and activity, the clause paves the way for the iambic insistence of the transient verbs in line 10, which seek fulfilment in a deferred object, 'the future hour' (l. 10) in which 'We feel that we are greater than we know' (l. 14).

Thus, the conclusion to *The River Duddon* performs the work of a lemniscate, melding the river's origin and tendency in seamless continuity.

Of all the poems in this sequence, therefore, Sonnet XXXIII appears successfully to withstand the irresistible encroachment of political violence in the peaceable kingdom, surveying these encroachments from the perspective of a benevolent future in which, as Priestley anticipated, war is no more. Yet, as intimated above, death is included within the poem's constitution, echoing the call to self-sacrifice that impels the Happy Warrior:

> Who, doom'd to go in company with Pain,
> And Fear, and Bloodshed, miserable train!
> Turns his necessity to glorious gain;
> In face of these doth exercise a power
> Which is our human nature's highest dower;
> Controls them and subdues, transmutes, bereaves
> Of their bad influence, and their good receives [...][64]

Like the Duddon poet, the Happy Warrior 'looks forward' to 'noble deeds' (l. 75) that, sanctified by 'Heaven's applause' (l. 83), grant 'fame' beyond the bare life of 'a dead unprofitable name' (ll. 79–80). Notably, the transmutation of 'Pain,/And Fear, and Bloodshed' (ll. 13–14) is accomplished by means of bereavement, a privation that yields 'nature's highest dower' (ll. 16–17). To adapt Steven Miller's unsettling analysis, the poem may be read as a defence of the 'dignity of war-and-death against the incursion of violence worse than death'.[65] For it is precisely because war 'imposes and upholds death' as 'both sacrifice and limit' that life is protected from annulment,[66] whether that annulment is conceived as the effect of the death drive or, in the sense outlined earlier, as a consequence of the failure to transmute loss so that it may be placed in the service of life. What Sonnet XXXIII shares with 'Character of the Happy Warrior' is the realisation that conflict subsists within the contours of the real so that life may be preserved from the urge to return to a state of inertia. A poem proclaiming peace thus internalises war so that life may be saved from a fate worse than death – a point of cancellation seen in a '*backward*' glance, an extended pause, a river that is 'Still'.

Binding *The River Duddon*

Bound within *The River Duddon* and, ultimately, within the boards of a collected edition, the conclusion to the *Duddon* sequence speaks of a peace that is always to come, a peace that, by virtue of its inability to coincide with the here and now, maintains life at the threshold of extinction. Those material thresholds – the boundaries that determine how books and poems flow in and out of each other – take on a special significance in the case of the afterlife of *The River Duddon*. In its original form, as the alternative title page makes clear, the *Duddon* sonnets were intended to be bound with 'Vaudracour and Julia; Peter Bell; The Waggoner; A Thanksgiving Ode and Miscellaneous Pieces', thus forming the third volume of Wordsworth's collected *Poems*. Copies of this elusive three-volume edition are by no means uniform. In addition to the third volume having no connection with the classification system used in 1815, compilers of the edition did not always follow the recommended order as, in some cases, *The Waggoner* precedes *Peter Bell*.[67] One constant is the positioning of the *River Duddon* at the start of the third volume and the placing of the 'Thanksgiving Ode' at the end. Importantly, the poet's collected works are bookended by collections that provide alternately oblique and direct perspectives on the disruptive effects of war and peace.

That war might be ineradicably related to peace is highlighted when one considers how a reader of the three-volume *Poems* would have been able to encounter the *River Duddon* volume as a conduit between two expressive odes.[68] Might the 'Ode: Intimations of Immortality' that concludes the second volume of *Poems* and the 'Thanksgiving Ode' that concludes the third be more closely connected than first appears? In Chapter 3 I observed how counter-currents of guilt, shame, and grief lurk beneath the surface of Wordsworth's most notorious public poem. What the three-volume *Poems* inadvertently reveals is just how closely the 'Thanksgiving' ode, in its concern with loss and restoration, in its engagement with the passage from corporeal to incorporeal being, and, as noted earlier, in its efforts to supplant the transient glee of the French Revolution, repeats the central concerns of the 'Immortality' ode. In each of these poems the emphasis falls on those primal sympathies – love of nature and love of country – 'that spring/Out of human suffering' and 'In the faith that looks through death' (ll. 184–9; *passim*). The immortalising sentiments of *Duddon* Sonnet XXXIII sits naturally between these poems, metonymically invoking, in the circulatory relationship between the 'cloud-born stream' and 'the Deep',[69] a sense of the silent horizon of peace as the origin and tendency of life.

Yet, despite their points of formal and thematic contact, the odes differ in the extent to which their respective explorations of collective and individual renewal are informed by the circulatory economy of sacred waters. In a manner that corroborates readings of the later poetry that stress the subordination of nature to religion, the celebration of those brooks and fountains that, in the 'Immortality' ode, afford 'soothing thoughts' (l. 186) to 'the philosophic mind' (l. 189), appears to have been effaced in the 'Thanksgiving' ode's claim that the 'current of this matin song' lies 'deeper […] Than aught dependent on the fickle skies' (ll. 53–5).[70] However, when considered as a whole and in relation to those poems that precede it in the three-volume edition, the Thanksgiving volume does not entirely abandon its connection with the fluvial tradition. Prefiguring the Horatian concerns of 'Upon the Same Occasion', 'Ode. Composed in January 1816', for instance, expresses the hope that the 'Pierian sisters […] exiled too long/From many a consecrated stream and grove' (ll. 100–3) will return to 'meet my soul's desires!/That I, or some more favoured Bard' (ll. 114–15), may, from 'some spotless fountain' (l. 111), be inspired to immortalise Britain's military success.[71] But from this return to the classical notion of the water-drinking bard as a voice for the expression of martial triumph, the Thanksgiving volume also derives impulses of a more pacific order, informed in part by the positioning of these poems within the three-volume edition. A reader adhering to the recommended order of binding would, for example, encounter the 'Thanksgiving Ode' on the back of 'Eve's lingering clouds', the concluding sonnet of *The Waggoner* volume, which, with its Neoplatonic vision of 'waters, steeled/By breezeless air to smoothest polish' to reflect cosmic harmony, provides a tranquil alternative to 'earth's groaning field,/Where ruthless mortals wage incessant wars' (ll. 7–8).[72] Though the sonnet's investment in pagan Fancy is ultimately superseded by the ode's accession to Anglican sobriety, and by the ill-judged attempt to rationalise carnage as the working out of divine intent, the Thanksgiving volume, as well as the three-volume *Poems*, ends nonetheless with a resumption of this whimsical mood, envisaging in 'Elegiac Verses, *February* 1816' an act of spiritual cleansing 'to wash away' (l. 5) the 'rivers stained so oft with human gore' (ll. 26–7).[73] Having restored the 'secret springs' of Nature's 'lost maternal heart' (l. 22) with 'celestial dews' (l. 21), the poem concludes with the image of 'Discord […] chained for ever to the black abyss!' (ll. 28–32), an emblem of the long-desired peace that, were it to be attained, would negate the sense of longing on which pastoral is founded. Hence the close of the poem, which with 'vision closed in darkness infinite' (l. 36), offers the promise that Wordsworth's thirty-year engagement with the poetics of conflict and resolution will be concluded.

Shortly after the publication of the *Duddon* volume the newly expanded *Poems* was made redundant by the appearance, in four volumes, of Wordsworth's *Miscellaneous Poems*, which dispersed the contents of the third volume under the classificatory headings first used in the 1815 edition. Shrewdly priced at 32 shillings, the new collection allowed purchasers to catch up on the favourably reviewed *Duddon* volume as well as almost all of Wordsworth's published works from *An Evening Walk* and *Descriptive Sketches* of 1793 to *The White Doe of Rylstone* of 1815, and from the 1816 Thanksgiving volume to *Peter Bell* and *The Waggoner* of the previous year. *Miscellaneous Poems*, writes Peter Manning, therefore 'looked backward to an earlier work' as well as 'forward to a larger audience', attempting to 'defy the fall' in Wordsworth's reputation by making the poetry not only affordable but also reinvigorated as a result of its rearrangement into 'new configurations that recast the significance of the poems' and, by extension, the image of the poet.[74]

The new arrangement does indeed reveal some interesting correspondences: the third volume bookends 'Sonnets Dedicated to Liberty' with *The White Doe* and the 'Thanksgiving Ode'; the fourth volume, which opens with the *Duddon* sonnets, concludes with 'Epitaphs and Elegiac Poems', in which category 'Elegiac Stanzas, Suggested by a Picture of Peele Castle, in a Storm', 'To the Daisy', 'Invocation to the Earth' (aka 'Elegiac Verses, *February* 1816'), and 'Ode—there was a time when meadow' form the edition's finale. Manning argues persuasively that the collection seeks to instantiate a sense of the English national character as one forged in 'peace' and 'fearful innocence',[75] upholding the anti-revolutionary sentiments that emerged in the 1802 patriotic sonnets, that informed the 'Immortality' ode, and that culminated in the 'Thanksgiving Ode'. But we may also trace within this arrangement a sense of how war threatens constantly to unsettle this narrative, shadowing its portrayal of gentle resistance to internal and external threats with stark reminders of the intentional and unintentional costs of war. In this edition we move, then, from a lament for the devastating aftermath of civil struggle (*The White Doe*) to a strangely unnerving declaration of triumph over the French Revolution (the 'Thanksgiving Ode'), to a sonnet series querying the establishment of the ensuing peace (*The River Duddon*), to end, after passing through 'Poems of Sentiment and Reflection', 'Poems on the Naming of Places', 'Inscriptions', and 'Poems Referring to the Period of Old Age', with a sequence of poems directly and indirectly concerned with the effects of grief in times of war ('Peele Castle', 'To the Daisy') and the promise of post-war restoration ('Invocation to the Earth', 'Ode—there was a time when meadow'). Running through this final volume, the passage from the Bandusian spring (*Duddon* Sonnet I, l. 1) to 'the mournful murmur' of the sea ('To the Daisy', l. 54), and from the 'rivers stained so oft with human gore' ('Invocation to the Earth', ll. 26–7) to 'the mighty waters rolling evermore' ('Ode—there was a time when meadow', 170), shows how, for Wordsworth, dreams of pastoral completion are riven always and forever by fears of discordant returns.[76]

Outflow: Enduring Peace in *Ecclesiastical Sketches*

> All my lovely rapids are crammed with corpses now,
> no channel in sight to sweep my currents out to sacred sea—
> I'm choked with corpses and still you slaughter more,
> you blot out more! Leave me alone, have done—
> captain of armies, I am filled with horror!— *the River Xanthus protests to Achilles*[77]

To end this chapter, I turn to a collection that reflects on its formal and thematic relationship with *The River Duddon* and that attempts, through renewed engagement with the fluvial tradition, to reach a peaceful settlement by surveying the conflicted course of mortal history from the standpoint of the divine. Initiated shortly after the Wordsworths' return from the continent in the autumn of 1820, *Ecclesiastical Sketches* projects its history of the 'progress and operation of the Church in England' onto a river journey inspired directly, as the volume's introductory sonnet makes clear, by the 'strictly-measured pace' (I. I. ll. 4) of the *Duddon* sequence.[78] Shifting attention from the geophysical to the divine, Wordsworth locates the origins of this 'holy River' (l. 10) not on some 'cloud-fed spring' (l. 2) but on 'the heights of Time' (ll. 9–10), anticipating its terminus in the 'Eternal City', unstained and unpolluted by the accretions of history (III. XXVIII. ll. 11–12). Moving thus from the natural to the figurative, *Ecclesiastical Sketches* offers a view of history that, while acknowledging the pathos of human suffering, endeavours to regard such pains as providentially decreed. Like all battles fought in the name of Christian truth, the carnage that would pollute the sacred fount is cleansed by the hand of God.

To advance this proposition, however, the sequence must first take account of those lingering traces of militancy that would maintain the primacy of Imagination over 'Heaven's high will' (I. XI. l. 3). The introductory poem therefore correlates the tempering of poetic authority with the sacrificial origins of Christian faith, channelling the dormant combativeness that inspired the Duddon poet towards a gentler end:

> I, who descended with glad step to chase
> Cerulean Duddon from his cloud-fed spring,
> And of my wild Companion dared to sing,
> In verse that moved with strictly-measured pace;
> I, who essayed the nobler Stream to trace
> Of Liberty, and smote the plausive string
> Till the checked Torrent, fiercely combating,
> In victory found her natural resting place [...] (ll. 1–8)

Presented as a tussle between subjective freedom and organisational control, the sestet submits, finally, via the heavily accented 'smote' of 'the plausive string', to the triumph of the latter over the former. Yet just as, in the octave, the aggressively foregrounded 'I' is displaced by the supervening authority of the blessed river and by the impersonality of the third person pronoun, so the rhetoric of militancy gives way to dismissal of those who, driven by 'lawless force' (ll. 11–12) – a possible slight at Byron's sensationalist appeal? – become the unworthy recipients of laurels. Foregoing the transient delights of popular acclaim for Milton's 'Immortal amaranth' (l. 14; *Paradise Lost* III. ll. 352), the poet no longer regards the river as a 'wild' (l. 3) subject to be 'checked' (l. 7) by the disciplinary pace of metre and rhyme but as a 'sacred Well' (I. II. l. 3), from whence flows, in divine measure, wisdom, justice, and order to a world overcome by 'savage' (l. 4) contestation.

Commenting on 'Nuns fret not at their Convent's narrow room', Joseph Phelan has observed how the choice of Milton's 'heavily rule-governed Petrarchan or "legitimate" sonnet' becomes 'an iconic representation of the poet's own freely chosen confinement; both his acquiescence in the rules of form and his minor creative infractions of them acquire an almost immediate moral and political resonance, reinforcing or counterpointing the poem's explicit discussion of the relative merits of liberty and submission to authority'.[79] Seeking to moderate the unruly course of poetic liberty in the opening sonnet of *Ecclesiastical Sketches* Wordsworth aligns conformity to literary tradition with allegiance to the Anglican Church, discovering, through the consecration of the pagan fount, a Christian solution to the problem of mortal strife, whether this strife be conceived in terms of the turbulent history of the Church or the contest between freedom and control that afflicts the would-be national poet. As the sequence proceeds, however, it becomes evident that peaceful resolution of corporate and singular struggles for recognition cannot take place in this world. Whether charting the sacrificial practices of the Druids, Roman persecution, the ravages of the Picts and Scots, the Saxon, Danish, and Norman conquests, the Crusades, the abuses of the Papacy, the dissolution of the monasteries, the Wars of the Roses, the Gunpowder Plot, or the curiously elided history of the English Civil War, the peace that Wordsworth anticipates is informed by the violence on which it is founded.[80]

Nonetheless, woven into this history of pain are threads of gentle resistance, lines of beatific calm that defy the ceaseless course of destructive change. Echoing the Catholic sympathies of *The White Doe of Rylstone*, Wordsworth writes appreciatively of the peace to be found in monastic seclusion and, though wary of the motivations that prompt the belligerent to forsake their arms in favour of 'cloistered privacy' (I. XXI. l. 6) and the sybaritic to indulge in fantasies of 'voluptuous indolence' (I. XXIII. l. 3), celebrates Bede as one who, rejecting 'penitential cogitations' (I. XXI. l. 9) and rusticated indolence alike, discovers in the 'Perpetual industry' (I. XXII. ll. 8) of 'a hallowed seat/Of Learning' (l. 6) a means to honour the glory of God. Wordsworth returns to this theme in Part 2, in a series of poems describing the dissolution of the monasteries. In 'Abuse of Monastic Power' and 'Monastic Voluptuousness' he mounts a predictably unfavourable attack on 'cloistered Avarice' (II. XII. ll. 5) and 'Unhallowed' revelries (II. XIII. l. 2), singling out in the latter poem 'Venus disguisèd like a Nun' and 'Bacchus, clothed in semblance of a Friar' (ll. 3–4) as instances of the corrupting effects of alcohol abuse in cloistered communities. Notably in thrall 'to madding Fancy dear' (l. 11), the debauched conventuals do not, however, stand as the sole representatives of the sequestered life. In sonnets XV and XVI, Wordsworth writes sensitively of the effects of the dissolution of the monasteries on the lives of devotees, young and old, who have been forced to leave their homes. Thus, the description of the worldly nun of XIII is matched in XV by the portrait of a 'lovely Nun' (l. 1) who, pursued by 'unrelenting mandates' (l. 5), 'Goes forth—unveiling timidly her cheek/Suffused with celestial hue' (ll. 5–6). Though raised above the taint of mortal longing, the comparison with Iris, personification of the rainbow and messenger of the gods – 'An apparition more divinely bright!/ Not more attractive to the dazzled sight/Than wat'ry glories in the stormy brine' (II. XV. ll. 10–12) – suggests that Wordsworth, no less than the figures decried in 'Monastic Voluptuousness', is drawn by pagan Fancy.

The path that connects pagan superstition and Catholic idolatry in *Ecclesiastical Sketches* strays, not infrequently, beyond the straight and narrow. In XVII 'Saints' and XVIII 'The Virgin', for example, Wordsworth laments the hardening of the heart that is a consequence of iconoclasm, going so far, in the latter sonnet, as to bemoan the toppling of those images of Mary that 'mixed and reconciled' in visible form a 'mother's love with maiden purity' (ll. 12–13). Considering the poet's comparison between the constricted form of the sonnet and the nun's narrow cell it is perhaps hardly surprising that traces of Catholic sympathy should be detected in these verses. In the image of the fallen Mother, blending 'high and low, celestial with terrene' (l. 14), Wordsworth may well have discovered a fitting analogue for his own attempts to marry the visible and the invisible. But perhaps more so, in the prospect of despoiled beauty, the poet could retrieve something of the nostalgia for Catholic worship that, in *The White Doe*, had merged with the desire for peace. In sonnet XX, 'Imaginative Regrets', and in sonnet XXI, 'Reflections', Wordsworth describes a global lamentation for the collapse of the Holy Roman Empire, a global grief extending from the Tiber to the Ganges and Nile sufficient in force to qualify the disclosure of papal 'trumpery' (II. XXI. l. 6) and fraud (II. XX. l. 10). Significantly, the 'dolorous groan' (II. XX. l. 4) issues not merely from 'justly honoured' sages (l. 2) but 'from all the ghostly Tenants of the wind,/Demons and Spirits' (ll. 3–4) joined in mourning for this 'dominion overthrown' (l. 5), suggesting that shock for the loss of Rome transcends national and religious allegiances to affect the world itself, and all that lies beyond.

But something more than high Anglican nostalgia animates Wordsworth's sympathetic response to the fall of Rome. In Part 1 of the sequence, sonnet XII, 'Monastery of Old Bangor', opens with a quotation from the sixth-century Brythonic poet, Taliesin: '*The oppression of the tumult—wrath and scorn—/The tribulation—and the gleaming blades*' (ll. 1–2). Dismissing the 'impetuous spirit' that inspired these bellicose sentiments, the sonnet goes on to declare: 'Ours shall mourn/The *unarmed* Host who by their prayers would turn/The sword from Bangor's walls' (ll. 3–5). Voicing support for non-violent resistance to anti-Christian oppression, the sonnet joins with other poems in the sequence in support of the 'gentle life' that 'spreads round holy spires' (II. I. 'Cistertian Monastery', ll. 12) causing 'Fierceness and rage' to 'melt away' (I. XXIV. 'Danish Conquests', ll. 6–8). Yet, as the Bangor sonnet sestet makes clear, all things in time must give way to loss, burning to 'senseless ashes' (l. 9) or dying 'like steam' (l. 10):

> Only perchance some melancholy Stream
> And some indignant Hills old names preserve,
> When laws, and creeds, and people, all are lost! (ll. 12–14)

Derived in large part from a passage in Samuel Daniel's *The Collection of the History of England* (1618), Wordsworth appears to have been struck by a vision of devastation, extending not only to the extinction of a people but to 'the open destruction, and desolation of the whole Country, whereof in the end they extinguished both the Religion, Lawes, Language, and all, with the people and name of *Britaine*'. As Daniel goes on to explain, the 'subversion' of Britain

> concurred with the universal mutation, which about that time happened in all parts of the world; whereof, there was no one Countrey or Province but changed bounds, inhabitants, customes, language, and in a manner, all their names [...] Wherefore, we are now here to begin with a new Bodie of people, with a new State, and government of the Land, which retained nothing of the former, nor held other memory but that of the dissolution thereof: where scarce a Citie, Dwelling, Riuer, Hill, or Montaine, but changed names.[81]

Holding no 'other memory but that of the dissolution thereof', global Christianity is thus birthed in desolation, registering the shock of the new in the pain of historical erasure; however militant we might deem Wordsworth's account of the rise of Anglican hegemony, there are instances of pathos enough in the *Ecclesiastical Sketches* to confirm that the poet remained attuned to the spiritual value of that which had been expunged to facilitate this rise. Catholicism is certainly one of those lost objects that the poet appears to mourn during this history, but there are glimmers too of that older, palpitating life that haunted the earlier work. Most notably, in Part 2, sonnet XIV reflects movingly on the dissolution of the monasteries – 'The tapers shall be quenched, the belfries mute' (II. XIV. l. 3) – only to discover, amidst their ruins, a revival of profane life as, within 'choirs unroofed by selfish rage':

> The warbling wren shall find a leafy cage;
> The gadding bramble hand her purple fruit;
> And the green lizard and the gilded newt
> Lead unmolested lives, and die of age. (ll. 5–8)

Thus, peace is found in the lattice-like connectivity of animate and inanimate beings, aspects of nature linked by adjectival attributes, tending towards a peaceful end.

Elsewhere, in Part 3, sonnet XVII, 'Old Abbeys', the contemplation of 'ruin, beauty', and 'ancient stillness' (l. 3) inspires toleration for 'the infirmities/And faults of others' (ll. 7–8) and distrust of the 'hidden ill' that prompts the inquisitive to 'break Time's charitable seals' (ll. 10–11). Addressing the ruins, the poet declares: 'Once ye were holy, ye are holy still;/Your spirit freely let me drink and live!' (ll. 13–14), allowing discord to dissolve in fanciful certitude. Here, then, is that other sacred fount – a source of pure, poetic imagining, unsullied by the demands of doctrinal rigour. In these moments we might almost forgive the ideological fervour that allows Wordsworth at the end of the sequence to describe the 'living Waters, less and less by guilt/Stained and polluted' (III. XXVIII, ll. 11), brightening as they roll towards that eternal city, 'built/For the perfected Spirits of the just' (ll. 13–14). Though the river journey allows us to float 'at ease' as nations efface nations, and 'Death gathers to his fold/Long lines of mighty Kings' (ll. 6–9), it reveals too how past traumas insist on the present and how peace may be found, if only fleetingly, amidst the ruins of the world.

CHAPTER 6

Wordsworth after Byron
Memorials of a Tour on the Continent, 1820

Rest and Recreation

What better way to mark the beginning of the end of the post-Napoleonic depression than to take a holiday? And what better way for Wordsworth to draw his own experience of post-war austerity to a close than by undertaking the long-deferred reunion with the daughter of his former lover? Wordsworth's visit to Peterloo marked the opening stage of a journey that would interweave memories of personal struggles with the bitter and as yet unresolved history of the wars against revolutionary and Imperial France. Last seen walking on a beach in Calais in 1802, Caroline, now a married woman in her late twenties, met her father in Paris, towards the end of the continental tour that the Wordsworths took in the summer and autumn of 1820. The meeting, at which Caroline's mother, husband, and two little girls were also present, passed without any apparent awkwardness or bitterness; from the diaries of Mary Wordsworth and Henry Crabb Robinson we learn that time was spent sightseeing, with visits to the Champs Elysee, the Louvre, the Tuileries, and the Jardin des Plantes.[1] There is no evidence to suggest that Wordsworth was in any way haunted by memories of his previous visit to Paris when, as a young radical, he surveyed the events of the Revolution with a mixture of ardency and alarm. One other meeting in Paris does, however, give a clue to the complexity of feelings experienced by the poet during this period. As if to make up for the missed encounter of 1792, Wordsworth called on his old friend Helen Maria Williams not once but twice. On one of these occasions, he recited from memory her sonnet 'To Hope', the closing lines of which speak of a heart made weary by longing for release from grief and misfortune. A poem of muted acceptance, 'To Hope' bids farewell to 'Fancy's radiance' (l. 7) and the 'dear illusions' (l. 10) that once charmed the eye.[2] And in this manner, Wordsworth's holiday draws to an end, a holiday that included, among its must-see sights, the fields of Peterloo and Waterloo and that, as we shall now see, provided a means for the older poet to come to terms not only with a conflicted past but also with a conflicted present.

Holidays after war have an air of the ridiculous about them. In Lamb's account of the 1814 peace celebrations, the parks of London provide the setting for a summer-long period of drunkenness, promiscuity, and misrule.[3] In the high-spirited summer of 1815, we learn from Southey that Wordsworth, of all people, caused a commotion when, dressed as a Spanish Don, he accidently kicked over a kettle of boiling water intended for the punch that was to be consumed, in celebration of Waterloo, on the summit of Skiddaw.[4] From the same period, the *Morning Chronicle* reported that in Britain's seaside resorts '[p]astime, in all its diversities, is the order of the day. Droves of donkeys, freighted with youth and Beauty, and clouds of vehicles, as richly filled, scour the rides from morn to eve— while the promenades and libraries teem with all the charms and elegance of fashion'.[5] In *Sanditon*, Jane Austen comments acidly on the growth of the seaside leisure economy that afforded distraction from rising prices, high taxation, and social unrest. A man of grand designs, the entrepreneurial Mr Parker foregoes the house of his forefathers – 'an honest old place' – for a new home with a view of the sea:

> 'You will not think I have made a bad exchange, when we reach Trafalgar House—which by the bye, I almost wish I had not called Trafalgar—for Waterloo is more the thing now. However, Waterloo is in reserve—& if we have encouragement enough this year for a little Crescent to be ventured on—(as I trust we shall) then, we shall be able to call it Waterloo Crescent—& the name joined to the form of the Building, which always takes, will give us the command of Lodgers.'[6]

As the language of triumph percolated into the language of tourism – one thinks back to Dorothy's dismissal of the *Bellerophon* moment – so the cultured traveller sought to distinguish him or herself from the common herd.[7] For those in the know, and the Wordsworths were most certainly of that class, the spoils of victory would be spent not sojourning in a 'small, fashionable Bathing place',[8] of the kind that, in Austen's story, had come to be associated with the sickly aftermath of war, but rather in pursuit of those enlivening pleasures that defended individuals and nations alike from the enervating tide of post-war melancholy.

The collection of poems in which Wordsworth sought to capture these pleasures, written mostly in the form of snapshot sonnets, and arranged in sequence like a family album, was developed a year after the holiday came to an end. In this volume, Wordsworth charts a journey across France,

Belgium, Switzerland, and Italy, a literary grand tour that reads, at once, as an attempt to appease the ghosts of the tour that the poet undertook in earlier, revolutionary, times and to come to terms with other, more recent, but no less insistent concerns. Written during the phase of intense compositional activity that resulted in *The River Duddon* and *Ecclesiastical Sketches*, *Memorials of a Tour on the Continent, 1820* follows a similarly riparian course, charting the histories – personal as well as collective – evoked by journeys made along and beside the Rhône and the Rhine. Critical readings of *Memorials*, which are rare, have pointed to the air of solemnity and, at times, pomposity that can be found in the collection; but such readings miss the surprising variety of tones, as well as the capacity for irony, even prankishness, that these poems exude.[9] True, the tendency towards sententiousness, pat expressions of grandeur, and leaden phraseology, qualities that have come to define the 'later style', are evident in *Memorials*, but we must also be alert to the ways in which the poetry seeks to challenge the drive towards the unreflective foolishness of late middle age. Considered as a lyrical travelogue, *Memorials* is not unaware of its status as a contribution to the burgeoning literature of post-war tourism, at once delighting in the exercise of newfound freedoms – to travel, to revisit, and to reclaim sights associated with the delusions of youth – even as it works to distance itself from a culture given over to the parroting of an outmoded style. That style, which will eventually be recognised as Romantic, is associated in *Sanditon* with the hyper-cultivated silliness of the leisured classes: in Sir Edward Denham's deployment of 'all the usual Phrases' to evoke the '*undescribable* Emotions' excited by the sea; in his ill-informed enthusiasm for Scott and Burns; in the 'fancy, the love of Distinction & the love of the Wonderful' that impels the hypochondrial Parkers in all their speculative endeavours.[10]

Wordsworth, no less than Austen, is aware of how the currency of Romanticism has become devalued. *The White Doe*, as we have seen, gives evidence of an early inclination to have done with the 'sovereign impulses of illimitable Ardour' and to cultivate a style more in keeping with the 'prosaic Decencies of life'.[11] Then, the targets had been the epic romances of Scott and Southey; now, the target is the transgressive exoticism of Byron, Shelley, and the Cockney School. Although, in the course of their journey across Europe, the Wordsworths found some traces of the poet's influence on the reading habits of British tourists – Dorothy notes quotations from 'Matthew' and 'Yarrow Visited' in the hotel album at Chamonix – for the most part it is Byron whose works 'inspired by the landscapes of the Continent had now become a part of the public experience of those landscapes'.¹² At Chillon Castle, Dorothy discovered, by way of complement to the place's history of 'sickening sorrow', 'tyranny', and 'recent war', a copy of Byron's poem in their apartment's sitting-room.¹³ But this overt sign of Byron's hold on the popular imagination is superseded by the uncited but no less commanding influence of *Childe Harold's Pilgrimage*. As is well known, Byron's description of the Swiss alps in Canto III cemented in the public mind an association between *Child Harold* and a love for the natural sublime that, for all its indebtedness to Wordsworth's 'Tintern Abbey' and 'Immortality' ode, was regarded as more successful, because more recognisably refined, than the singular productions of the Lake Poet. That, in retracing his earlier, revolutionary, journey Wordsworth was also treading ground ceded to Byron was a source of some considerable rancour, resulting, as we shall see, in forms of thematic and stylistic combativeness that echo the collection's broader engagement with Europe's war-torn history.

The predicament of writing 'After' the event—after oneself, after Byron, and after war—has been elegantly described by Peter Larkin:

> 'After,' in acknowledging the claim of the other in time, admits also that the present moment may be threateningly unique, that a climax, almost by definition, cannot continue on the same level. A postclimactic sphere must be consolidated, even by inviting meditation on loss, old age, or on death, the pure past.¹⁴

To find oneself the subject of the 'past's own proleptic expectations, its persistent self-forwardings', Larkin continues, is to 'arrive at, not a greater self-coincidence, but a more intense degree of reserve. It is a nostalgia compelled to absorb in its present plight (the plight of ageing) the past's desire to terminate there as an inheritance'.¹⁵ In related vein, Robin Jarvis notes how 'the layers of self-allusion in the 1820 *Memorials*', to past experiences and to past retellings of these experiences, 'implicitly acknowledge the frailty of the linguistic shrine they aspire to become'.¹⁶ At stake in these readings of the late poetry is the sense in which the production of new writing, even as it embraces 'a deliberately calm, attenuated voice [...] so as not to compete with the past', risks the desecration of previously erected monuments to self-recollection.¹⁷ In *Memorials*, as I argue in this chapter, the tensions exposed by the poetics of unself-rivalry are made more acute by the collection's belatedness to *Childe Harold*. To adapt Peter Manning's account of Wordsworth's subsequent continental sequence, the 'Memorials of a Tour in Italy, 1837', the 1820 *Memorials* may be read 'as a deliberate anti-*Childe Harold*'.¹⁸ Informed by the wish to submit 'to the terms of a private inheritance, to enclose himself in a predefined after-experience, to enact the postsublime', Wordsworth must strive to confirm that he is the rightful legatee of that inheritance.[19]

The reading of *Memorials* that follows attempts, then, to account for the volume's curious mixture of confidence and uncertainty. Despite the work performed by the collection's marmoreal title, Wordsworth struggles to allay the taint of superfluity that has come to be associated with the discourse of tourism. Moreover, as an observer of sights linked with a personal history of enmity and disloyalty, the poet aspires towards a self-accord, both unthreatened by and unthreatening towards the return of discordant memories that, to avoid silence, must yet accept and engage with the formative power of linguistic and historical violence. Manifested in the poetry's descriptions of quiescent cities, haunted battlefields, sanguine rivers, and blasted castles, the poet works also to distinguish his voice from the readymade expressions that, thanks to Scott and Byron, had made of Europe's past and present a playground for the elicitation of heightened sentiment. To affirm the priority of the poet's self-positioning while avoiding the reactivation of the early poetry's visionary power is, of course, not easily achieved, and indeed, for a majority of readers, it is the studied attention to the diminution of such power that accounts for the pallid mediocrity of the later work. The discussion that follows qualifies this view on two counts: first, by drawing attention to the ways in which *Memorials* works to enact the post-sublime; second, by showing how, in the effort to temper the militant stirrings of the visionary imagination, the poet discovers what remains of the gentle voice of Fancy, not as it appears in the spoiled society of Sanditon but as it used to be heard before the time of speculation. In this voice of quiet resignation, linked with the acceptance of the disappearance of determinate words and things and of all that has come to characterise the fabricated identities of those who, unaffected by social and economic precarity, prosper in the wake of loss, Wordsworth hears the placid but intractable soundings of the melancholy ends of war.

Calais, Again

Memorials of a Tour on the Continent, 1820 begins, however, not with the voice of quiet resignation but with a bad joke in sonnet form. Often cited as one of the worst poems ever written by Wordsworth, and sometimes used as evidence of the aging poet's indifference to social and artistic decorum, 'Fish-Women.—On Landing at Calais' – the title alone reads like a challenge to standard notions of good taste – is perhaps the most unprepossessing opening to a collection of poems by a notable writer ever to appear in print. Certainly, this is how the matter struck Francis Jeffrey who judged the poem to be emblematic of Wordsworth's 'emphatic inanity' and 'singular [...] feebleness of thought',[20] a judgement that chimed with the opinion of the reviewer for the *Literary Chronicle* for whom the poem was 'silly' and 'absurd', representative of a collection in which 'we cannot quote a single stanza worthy of notice'.[21] Why, then, would a poet so recently preoccupied with establishing a position of authority in the public imagination descend to such tactics? Could it be, as the collection's dedicatory sonnet advertised, that 'Fish-Women' was intended solely for the amusement of the poet's 'Dear Fellow-Travellers', that devoted coterie in whose 'enjoyment' the Muse 'confides' (l. 10)?[22] Or might the apparent lapse in judgement be taken as a mischievous assault on contemporary reading tastes?

Let us consider the first possibility. Intended as poetic illustrations for Dorothy's journal account of the tour, the exercise rapidly took on a life of its own, resulting in a fully fledged collection that went to press towards the end of the month.[23] 'Fish-Women' takes inspiration from the following passage:

> Landed on the shores of France at ½ past one. What shall I say of CALAIS? I looked about for what I remembered, and looked for new things, and in both quests was gratified. With one consent we stopped to gaze at a groupe—rather a *line* of women and girls, seated beside dirty fish-baskets under the old gateway and ramparts—their white nightcaps, brown and puckered faces, bright eyes etc. etc. very striking. The arrangements—how unlike those of a fish-market in the South of England! but the cleanly, tight dress of these females prevents all disgust in looking at *them*; however you may dislike the smells from their slovenly baskets, and even in the countenance of these fish-women, the very lowest of the people, there is something of liveliness, of mental activity, interesting to me, an Englishwoman, fresh from home. Others however, if they have perceived, hardly remember this—and much of it may have been the gift of my own fancy. Every one is struck by the excessive ugliness (if I may apply the word to any *human* creatures) of the fish-women of Calais, and *that* no one can forget. (*JDW* II. 9–10)

With its slow, tentative drift from curiosity-piqued admiration of 'liveliness' and 'mental activity' in 'the very lowest of the people' to brusque disavowal of their combined visual effect – 'Every one is struck by the excessive ugliness [...] of the fish-women of Calais' – Dorothy's account, though seeming initially to admire and sympathise with these representatives of 'Low and rustic life',[24] ends by confirming the notion that, in matters of taste, bourgeois disgust trumps jacobinical fellow-feeling. Thus, radical sympathy is exchanged for worldly *hauteur* and brand Wordsworth is made fit for public consumption.

The sonnet written by way of illustration to these impressions begins and ends with a suave tip of the hat to the educated reader, relying on a shared sense of classical knowledge to advance its satirical intent:

> 'Tis said, fantastic Ocean doth enfold
> The likeness of whate'er on Land is seen;
> But, if the Nereid Sisters and their Queen,
> Above whose heads the Tide so long hath roll'd,
> The Dames resemble whom we here behold,
> How terrible beneath the opening waves
> To sink, and meet them in their fretted caves,
> Withered, grotesque, immeasurably-old,
> And shrill and fierce in accent!—Fear it not;
> For they Earth's fairest Daughters do excel;
> Pure unmolested beauty is their lot;
> Their voices into liquid music swell,
> Thrilling each pearly cleft and sparry grot—
> The undisturbed Abodes where Sea-nymphs dwell!

But for Jeffrey, the representative of the educated elite, the joke falls flat as the poet, 'supposing that Nereids may possibly be like the Calais fish-women' and 'judiciously remarking, how terrible it would be to dive and meet such tenants of the submarine caves', assures himself, 'without assigning any reason', that the Nereids excel in beauty 'Earth's fairest Daughters' and 'therewithal clothes them in every quality of form and voice'. Intended to be of a 'gay, lively cast', the poem becomes, for Jeffrey, an indication of Wordsworth's tonal flat-footedness and, crucially, of his failure to meet the needs of a cultivated readership.[25]

The above points seem, at first glance, to be uncontroversial. But closer attention, both to the sonnet and its literary relations, might prompt us to reconsider, and perhaps even appreciate, if not the success of the joke then at least the invention that underlies its creation. The opening couplet turns on a fondly mocking allusion to the primordial Titan's water-encompassing powers and to the tradition of analogical thought, described by Pliny, that maintained a belief in the correspondence between things found in the sea and things found on land. By forcing the contrast between the grotesque fish-women and the beautiful Nereids the poet alludes both to a 'common opinion' sustained in classical and early modern thought and to a detail found in Hogarth's *The Gate of Calais, or the Roast Beef of*

Figure 5 William Hogarth, *The Gate of Calais, or the Roast Beef of Old England* (1749). Source: Engraved by William Hogarth and Charles Mosley. Print. 38.5 cm × 46 cm. Public domain.

Old England (1749).[26] In a note added to the poem in 1836 Wordsworth attempts to excuse himself of the charge of ungallantry to the 'worthy Poissardes' – meaning 'vulgar, low woman' and, from association with 'poisson', more pointedly 'fishwife' – by taking 'shelter under the authority of my lamented friend, the late Sir George Beaumont who, a most accurate observer, used to say of them, that their features and countenances seem to have conformed to those of the creatures they dealt in'.[27] Beaumont, who would have been familiar with Hogarth's painting and its widely circulated engraving (Figure 5), may have pointed out to Wordsworth the detail of 'an amused fish-woman' gloating over 'a large skate with a face resembling her own'.[28]

By focussing on this arresting correspondence, the poem attempts to provide an amusing critique of the *beau idéal*, while pushing the extent of analogical thought to its absolute limit. Yet still, even in jest, there is scope for flattering confirmation of the distinction between fishwife's 'withered' condition and the sea-nymph's 'unmolested beauty'. Conceived, perhaps, as a witty compliment to the female members of the holiday party, the sonnet speaks also of the distinction between discordant earthly sounds – 'shrill and fierce in accent!' – and the 'liquid music' of the Nereids. Poetry, the sestet implies, will be found not in nature but in mythological imagining.

There remains, however, something deliberately forced about the sonnet's display of classical learning, as if the poet were poking fun at a propensity for studied contrivances. In this respect Jeffrey's incredulity at the poem's failure to assign a reason for the sudden turn in line 9 comes close to the mark: might the sonnet be working deliberately to undermine the taste for Ovidian exoticism that had briefly interested Wordsworth and that had most recently come to be associated with Keats, Hunt, Shelley, and Byron? The idea that the contrast between fish-women and nereids may have been fashioned as a satirical barb against Keatsian paganism takes shape when one considers how the description of 'liquid music [...] Thrilling each pearly cleft and sparry grot' mimics the fanciful expressions and overwrought sensuality of *Endymion*.[29] However, as Tim Fulford and Jeffrey Cox note, Keats's ornate diction and use of classical similes owes much to Wordsworth's own earlier experiments in the classical mode, most notably the stylised description of 'pagan Greece' from Book IV of *The Excursion* (ll. 847–87; l. 846).[30] In addition to stock mentions of naiads, oreads, and zephyrs, together with an allusion to the 'beaming Goddess' Diana (l. 865), this passage includes one of only four uses of the word 'grotesque' in Wordsworth's poetry: 'Withered Boughs grotesque,/ Stripped of their leaves and twigs by hoary age' (ll. 875–6), and it may be that 'Fish-Women' recalls this depiction of natural decay so as to sharpen the critique of pagan idolatry that, in *The Excursion*, ran the risk of waylaying the ascent to Christian truth through overindulgence in the sensual poetics of classical 'Fancy' (l. 853).

But while 'Fish-Women' presents a challenge to the contemporary vogue for classical fancy and, indeed, to Wordsworth's role in supporting this vogue, a more immediate, and perhaps stronger, explanation can be found in the sonnet's personal and political contexts. The port of Calais had long been conceived in the Wordsworthian imagination as an indicator of personal and political friction. In the summer of 1802, the town became a locus for meditations on the fragility of peace, the corruption of liberty, and the potential for hope. Then, the opposition between the sublimity of the 'senselessness of joy' that characterised the poet's experience of France in 1792 and the 'hollow', alienated feelings of the present appeared insurmountable;[31] in 1820, one might have expected Wordsworth to commemorate his return to France with a poem announcing the fulfilment of his hopes for the return of liberty's 'Fair seasons' ('To a Friend, Composed near Calais'. l. 14), a verse that would testify to the healing of wounds, the restoration of harmony, and the establishment of peace, a poem that would declare in tones of reserved self-satisfaction not only the end of war but also the end of the striving for visionary distinction that was born out of war. But 'Fish-Women' is not that poem. With its cultivated disparities of tone and jarring themes, this late poem is markedly less than sublime, but it is also something more than ridiculous.

This distinction gains force when attention returns to the question of how the poem is situated in relation to the discourse of post-war tourism. In a manner akin to the recently published *Doctor Syntax in Paris, or, a Tour in Search of the Grotesque* (1820), 'Fish-Women' seems to play on the contrast between the categories of the grotesque, the beautiful, and the sublime to substantiate unsubtle points about French impropriety, overfreighting the distinction between the withered victims of sexual disease and their 'unmolested' counterparts in Britain. But so wildly conceived is the distinction between these categories and their respective exemplars that one cannot help but entertain the idea that Wordsworth may, after all, be setting out deliberately to parody the expectations of the cross-channel travel genre. If we reject the crude dichotomies of Hogarth for the playful antimonies of Sterne, then the sonnet may be read not simply as a fatuous reiteration of conventional xenophobic misogyny but, rather, as a sophisticated reflection on the ways in which humour is used to discharge, while at the same time reinforcing, anxieties about national identity. More serious than it first appears, 'Fish-Women' participates artfully in a long history of Anglo-French antagonism, a history that links Hogarth's *Gates of Calais* with anti-French visual satire. For as Wordsworth would have been aware, Hogarth's depiction of fish-women with faces of 'leather' and soldiers 'ragged and lean' was an established trope of anti-gallic sentiment, dating back to the Seven Years' War and deployed most recently and effectively as an aid to recruitment in the war against revolutionary and Napoleonic France.[32] *Memorials of a Tour on the Continent* begins, then, with a deceptively stark refocillation of wartime propaganda, its underlying subtleties revealed only when the poem's context is attended to and when read in the light of the volume as a whole.

From Bruges to Waterloo

While the opening verse proclaims its strangeness as a challenge to readers seeking confirmation of the ennobling sites to be encountered on a continental tour, the two sonnets that follow seem, at first, to be more conventionally framed. Offering delicately poised reflections on the compensatory beauty of Bruges as seen at dusk, neither comedy nor violence appears to trouble the smooth surface of these poems, yet closer inspection reveals the presence of currents that run against the mood of settled calm. In the first sonnet, the 'sunless hour/That slowly introduced peaceful night/Best suits with fallen grandeur' offers to the poet's 'sight' a prospect of 'magnificence' to guard against 'the injuries of time, the spite/Of Fortune, and the desolating storms of future War' (ll. 3–10; *passim*). Written in response to Dorothy's impression of the city, the poem offers a complementary vision of 'tender melancholy' and 'self-sustained' beauty (*JDW* II. 17–19). As is typical for Wordsworth, the adaptation of the Petrarchan sonnet, while maintaining the basic rhyme scheme, enjambs the octave and the sestet, allowing the poem to advance in an even, continuous manner, thereby sustaining the thematic emphasis on resistance to time and change at the level of form. At the close of the verse, as the poet seeks to stave off the return of night, peace is figured as 'gentle' and 'silent', a vision of fleeting 'grace' embodied in 'the forms/Of Nun-like Females' who 'with soft motion glide' (ll. 11–14). Here, then, is an image of concord, informed by notions of idealised feminine beauty, to contrast with the discordant clamour and appearance of the fish-women of Calais. As 'Fish-Women' deploys clashes of sight and sound to forward its argument, a set of thematic antitheses mirrored formally in the clear division of octave and sestet, end-stopped lines, and conventionally placed volta, so 'Bruges' works by blurring these conventions, presenting an impression of seamless continuity through the sustained use of enjambment and anaphora (four lines begin with the preposition 'Of', further underling the importance of maintaining relations between verbal entities) and near-strict adherence to iambic pentameter. An abrupt turn is introduced, however, in the middle of line 10 as, faced with the return of desolation, the poet implores the 'Power of Darkness' to 'Advance not—spare to hide,/[…] these mild hues;/Obscure not yet these silent avenues' (ll. 10–12). Via the imperative mood Wordsworth reintroduces negation into the poem and with it a premonition of the notion that peace on earth cannot be sustained.[33]

Serving as counterpoint to the grotesque opening poem, the first Bruges sonnet presents an image of purity briefly havened from the depredations of history and an idea of peace figured as post-discursive silence. The second sonnet endeavours to maintain this vision, dissolving the distinction between the secular and the divine through the portrayal of the city as 'one vast Temple' (l. 10). Reminiscent of the Westminster Bridge sonnet, the poem depicts Bruges as a harmonious entwining of the 'popular' (l. 3) and the 'devout' (l. 4), the 'vulgar' (l. 7) and the 'consecrated' (l. 9). Within this space 'jarring passions' (l. 13) are effaced, the potential for violence quelled by 'mutual respect' (l. 11) and 'forbearances sedate' (l. 12).

The poem again marries content and form by moving with 'swan-like ease' (l. 6) between octave and sestet and in this case by erasing all trace of the formulaic volta. Yet, even here, as 'nobler peace than that in deserts' is 'found' (l. 14), the sonnet cannot avoid falling back on the Longinian rhetoric of conflict as, in line 5, the 'Spirit of Antiquity' 'Strikes at the seat of grace within the mind' (l. 5), the violent implications enhanced by the placing of three intervening clauses between the subject and the main verb. Thus, as Theresa Kelley has suggested, while the later Wordsworth engages with the category of beauty to smooth over formal divisions within poetry and political divisions within society,[34] he does so with the full awareness that beauty, and its cognate peace, may be approached within the contested medium of language but can never fully be realised.

This consideration of Wordsworth's efforts to reach beyond the economy of discursive violence while acknowledging the necessity of warring antitheses leads me to the central concern of this chapter. In the Autumn and Winter of 1821, when Wordsworth composed the bulk of the *Memorials*, domestic peace seemed, indeed, to be a distant dream. Although debates about the significance of Waterloo had begun to recede, the aftershocks of Peterloo remained a source of concern, prompting a detailed riposte to the charge of apostasy in a letter to James Losh (*LY* III. 96–9) and an angry swipe at Charles Lloyd for his role in fuelling Hazlitt's attack on Wordsworth's involvement in Westmorland politics in the November issue of 'Table Talk, No. XII—On Consistency of Opinion' (*LY* III. 106–8). As the poet sought to distance himself from former radical friends, he was moved at the same time to offer succour to his fellow apostate Robert Southey, whom Lord Byron had recently accused of slander. Beset by political and reputational assaults, Wordsworth may well have abandoned himself to the process of recollecting gentler, peaceable times to stave off vexation. And there is a sense in which the composition of piecemeal poems, following the course of a journey, may have worked as a form of self-regularisation, providing a way forward at a time of stress.

The fact that Byron should reappear on the horizon during the writing of these poems is not without significance. Relations between Wordsworth and Byron had deteriorated since the evening of Waterloo when, during a dinner at Samuel Rogers's house, the poets had argued about the desirable outcome of the battle. Wordsworth would go on to voice grave reservations about the 'bold bad Bard Baron B' (*MY* II. 283), stating that the 'farewell' poems and verses on Napoleon gave evidence the 'man is insane' and that, in the third canto of *Childe Harold*, he had been 'poaching on my Manor' (*MY* II. 394). In January 1820, piqued no doubt by the dedication to *Don Juan*, with its attack on Southey, the Tory 'renegade', and jibe at Wordsworth's 'place in the Excise',[35] Wordsworth intensified his criticism of Byron by claiming that the poem would 'do more harm to the English character, than anything of our time' (*MY* II. 579). A year later, disturbed by the attacks and counterattacks of the Satanic School controversy, Wordsworth may have seen the *Memorials* as an opportunity to extend the civilising mission of *The River Duddon* and the *Ecclesiastical Sketches*, only in this case by using the framing device of the continental tour to counter Byron's pernicious hold on public taste and to confirm the triumph of the Tory and Anglican establishment against the resurgence, in the wake of Peterloo, of republican and atheist dissent.

That, by the time preparation for *Memorials* was underway, Byron's powers of imitation as much as his moral and political beliefs were a source of concern to Wordsworth is evident in Tom Moore's account of a meeting with the poet in Paris towards the end of the continental tour. At this meeting Wordsworth reanimated his charge against Byron's '*antithetical* manner' (*MY* II. 385), before going on, as Moore recounts, to list

> Byron's plagiarisms from him; the whole third canto of *Childe Harold* founded on his style & sentiments. The feeling of natural objects, which is there expressed not caught by B.[yron] from Nature herself, but from him [Wordsworth], and spoiled in the transition. 'Tintern Abbey' the source of it all [...] with this difference, that what is naturally expressed by him, has been worked by Byron into a laboured and antithetical sort of declamation.[36]

When read in this light, *Memorials* can be seen as an attempt on Wordsworth's part to reclaim ground yielded to his more successful contemporary. As we have seen, however, the effort to present *Memorials* as a work of synthesis, offering unity and harmony in place of antithesis, gets off to a bad start, and despite the efforts of the two Bruges sonnets, *Memorials* is unable, fully, to revoke its own stake in the poetics and politics of violent opposition.

The impression of a baffled, self-contradicting work is highlighted still further when one considers how closely the collection maps the course of *Childe Harold's Pilgrimage*, Canto III. While such a comparison may, at first, seem aberrant, a brief consideration of these works reveals some compelling similarities. Like Byron's poem, *Memorials* follows the tourist route, as set out in popular guides to Northern Europe published after Waterloo, combining evocations of riparian beauty and alpine sublimity with pronouncements on war, religion, and contemporary politics. No less than Byron, Wordsworth uses the device of the poetic journey to explore questions of memory, creativity, and the persistence of self over time. And just as Byron begins and ends his poem with an address to an absent daughter, so Wordsworth comes to frame his collection, albeit belatedly, as a means of reaching out to an estranged child.[37] Though there are, of course, obvious points of formal and ideological difference between the two works, *Memorials*, I propose, is a collection that turns out to be unexpectedly Byronic, and perhaps not least when setting out to distinguish itself from Byron.

The poets' respective treatments of the field of Waterloo may be taken as cases in point. Scott and Southey, and eventually Byron, would all make trips to Waterloo within a year of the battle having taken place; Wordsworth, however, did not visit the field until 1820. The vision of triumph hymned in the Thanksgiving volume was therefore a work of pure imagination, informed by factual accounts but divorced from personal contact. Byron would wait until the *Vision of Judgement* and *Don Juan* to announce his official disdain for Wordsworth's invocation of divine support for the 'Carnage' of Waterloo, but *Childe Harold*'s unflinching presentation of the indiscriminatory fate of bodies on the field ('Rider and horse,—friend, foe,—in one red burial blent!'; stanza 28, l. 252), along with the claim that 'Waterloo with Cannae's carnage vies' (stanza 64, l. 608), provided an immediate, albeit oblique, form of attack.[38] Initiated by the arresting announcement 'Stop!—for thy tread is on Empire's dust!' (stanza 17, l. 145), the arrival at Waterloo jolts *Childe Harold* out of the contemplative mode, supplanting ruminations on the nature of poetic creativity and the benefits of the *via contemplativa*, for a series of rapidly shifting perspectives on the waste and ruin of war. In pronouncing the Juvenalian 'Stop!', Byron may well have had been seeking to arrest the seemingly endless flow of celebratory verses that followed in the wake of the battle, with Scott, Southey, and Wordsworth having published some of the more notable and, in Wordsworth's case, notorious examples, but by setting the grandeur of Marathon against the carnage of Cannae, he was seeking also to ensure that Waterloo would not serve as a mythical point of origin for the Holy Alliance.

Located as the fourth poem in the *Memorials* sequence, Wordsworth's arrival at Waterloo is no less jolting than Byron's, coming as it does after the two poems celebrating the pacific harmonies of Bruges. Sustaining the intention to develop a sequence of poems to complement Dorothy's prose account of the tour, the resulting sonnet, 'After Visiting the Field of Waterloo', takes inspiration from the observation that, aside from 'a few monuments erected to the memory of the slain', the field displays 'no other visible record of slaughter' (*JDW* II. 29). Five years have passed since the battle, and the traces of the dead have been covered by 'luxuriant crops' (29). Like the dark inverse of 'Tintern Abbey', Dorothy's description affords scant delight from the restoration of natural beauty. Struck by the disparity between the ripening corn and the effacing of the material evidence of battle ('The ruins of the severely contested chateau of Hougamont [*sic*.] had been riddled away since the battle, and the injuries done to the farm-house repaired'), Dorothy ventures 'a charge of ingratitude against the course of things, that was thus hastily removing from the spot all vestiges of so momentous an event'. Still, even as 'Nature's universal robe of green, humanity's appointed shroud' obliterates the memory of the fallen, there is 'much to be felt;—sorrow and sadness, and even something like horror breathed out of the ground as we stood upon it!' (29). It is to this restoration of feeling in the face of scenic paucity that the sonnet responds, recognising in Dorothy's disappointment with Waterloo the moment when, with an eye made quiet by the power of disharmony, we see into the death of things.

What Wordsworth sees in the field, but more specifically in Dorothy's account of the field, is an opportunity to repeal Byron's attack on the apparent callousness of the attribution of 'Carnage' to divine providence. The difficulty addressed by this sonnet is to acknowledge the 'sorrow and sadness' of Waterloo while maintaining a sense of its grandeur. Accordingly, Wordsworth adapts the argumentative form of the Petrarchan sonnet to accommodate sharp distinctions of perspective and tone while sustaining an impression of unity. Seeking to counter Byron's rendition of Waterloo as, at once, a mock-heroic version of Marathon and a site of irredeemable loss, Wordsworth begins by forging a blunt contrast between a 'Winged Goddess' (l. 1) dispensing 'glittering crowns and garlands' (l. 4) on the 'far-famed Spot' (l. 5) and the dreary prospect of the present-day field. In the gap between 'She vanished' and '—All was joyless, blank, and cold' (l. 6), the sonnet foregrounds the incongruity between the din of bardic triumphalism and the mute intractability of the site on which that vision is raised. In offering a concession to the radical critique of Waterloo, Wordsworth comes close to undoing the imaginative labour of the 'Thanksgiving Ode', which had endeavoured to sublimate the horror of mass slaughter by raising it to the status of divine sacrifice. Furthering this process of undoing, the two conditional formulations that comprise the octave accept the field's resistance to 'Meanings' (l. 10), only to transform this acceptance into the self-righteous derivation of an 'ought' from an 'is':

> If the wide prospect seemed an envious seal
> Of great exploits; we felt as Men *should* feel,
> With such vast hoards of hidden carnage near,
> And horror breathing from the silent ground! (ll. 11–14)

At the poem's close, however, the alliterative 'hoards of hidden carnage near,/And horror breathing from the ground' intensifies Dorothy's use of the voiceless glottal fricative ('something like horror breathed out of the ground as we stood upon it!'), the uncanny suggestion of breath issuing from the dead serving as a grotesque counterpoint to the moralising endorsement of cognitive inadequacy. Intended as a defence of the lines that had so offended Hazlitt, Byron, and Shelley, the reiteration of 'carnage' works to check the arrogance associated with inflated visionary perspectives on Waterloo but by doing so forces an encounter with the battle's excessive human cost. As with the opening sonnet, this is not the first time that the collection has risked offending its audience with a vision of the grotesque. Yet here, once again, Wordsworth appears to be surprisingly in accord with the disruptive aesthetic of Lord Byron. At the same time, it should be noted that Byron is often surprisingly sympathetic towards Wordsworth's pursuance of unity and calm. To develop this claim, I should like to return, via a reading of the description of the Napoleonic character in *Childe Harold* Canto III, to the question of Byron's fascination with antitheses and his attempts, in the Swiss stanzas, to utilise Wordsworth to overcome this fascination.

'But This Is Not My Theme': Byron after Wordsworth

Responding to Medwin's charge that he was indebted to Wordsworth in *Childe Harold*, Byron had this to say: 'Very possibly [...] Shelley, when I was in Switzerland, used to dose me with Wordsworth physic even to nausea; and I do remember then reading some things of his with pleasure'.[39] To this barbed praise, Byron added that the *Lyrical Ballads* 'jacobinical and puling with affection of simplicity as they were, had undoubtedly a certain merit' and that 'Wordsworth, though occasionally a writer for the nursery masters and misses [...] now and then expressed ideas worth imitating'.[40] Studies of the Wordsworthian influence on *Childe Harold* focus, understandably, on the poem's adaptation of unity with nature tropes derived, in large measure, from 'Tintern Abbey' and the 'Immortality' ode.[41] Again, for good reason, Byron's imitations of Wordsworth's declarations of irenic synthesis are read as temporary staging posts in a poem that works unsparingly and relentlessly to cultivate fraught intensities. Like a

Wittgensteinian ladder, the release from self-contestation that Byron discovers in Wordsworth's poetry must be kicked away if the world is to be seen aright.[42] Where *Childe Harold* is most true to itself, then, is in its portrayal of lives that resist the appeal of beatific quiescence, preferring instead to advance the transformative labour of *energeia*, even to the point of pursuing their being-at-work to a violent end stop.

The life that best represents the paradoxical undoing of the drive to self-completion is, of course, Napoleon: 'There sunk the greatest, nor the worst of men,/Whose spirit antithetically mixt/One moment of the mightiest, and again/On little objects with like firmness fixt' (stanza 36, ll. 316–19). Derived from Pope's Sporus, Dryden's Achitophel, and Milton's Satan, the caricature of Napoleon represents the limit point of Byron's fascination with fiery extremes. By stanza 45, the division between Napoleonic heights and depths, signalled by the unbridgeable distinction between the 'sun of glory' '*above*' and the 'hate of those below' (ll. 400–1), reaches its warlike apogee as, alone on the summit of fame, 'Contending tempests' excoriate the Emperor's 'naked head' (l. 404). From this inverted nadir the poem turns, in stanza 46, to the lower ground of 'Maternal Nature' and the 'blending' of 'beauties' that may be discovered 'on the banks' of the 'majestic Rhine' (ll. 409–11). Moving from the death-dealing abstractions of the masculine sublime to the combinatory vigour of the feminine picturesque ('streams and dells,/Fruit, foliage, crag, wood, cornfield, mountains, vine'; ll. 411–12), Byron follows Ann Radcliffe in ascribing pacific and healing qualities to the Rhineland scenery. The problem, however, is that no sooner has nature been ushered in as a solution to the martial sublime than remnants of that combative history start to return. Thus, at the close of stanza 46, the verse adds to the catalogue of blended beauties the prospect of 'chiefless castles, breathing stern farewells/From grey but leafy walls, where Ruin greenly dwells' (ll. 414–15). With its violent yoking of desolation and vitality, the final line recalls the contestable pomp of ambition that the paean to Nature is meant to resolve. As the verse proceeds, recollections of heroic prowess and fierce destruction are shown, ultimately, to result in the sullying of nature, as figured in the image of the 'discoloured Rhine' that flows beneath the scenes of 'ruin' (stanza 49, l. 441). For Byron, the ability of the 'abounding river' (stanza 50, l. 442) to efface the effects of violence with images of enduring beauty is challenged by the human propensity to despoil 'its fair promise' with the 'sharp scythe of conflict' (ll. 444–7; *passim*). Violence, no less than nature, persists through time, and although the tide may wash down 'the blood of yesterday', leaving the river 'stainless' (stanza 51, ll. 455–6), the waves 'vainly roll' over the 'blackened memory's blighting dream' (ll. 458–9); history, that is, must have the final say.

In the stanzas that follow, Byron attempts to rebut this gloomy conclusion by addressing his absent half-sister Augusta who serves, like Dorothy in 'Tintern Abbey', as a repository for 'love' that is 'pure' (stanza 55, l. 490) and as an emblem of continuity over time and connection across space. The lyric 'The castled crag of Drachenfels' that comes between stanzas 55 and 56 presents an unbaffled, harmonious view of the Rhine that succeeds, for a moment, in erasing the memory of conflict. Associated in German folklore with heroic resistance to political oppression, the ruins of Drachenfels become for Byron a setting for a subtly defiant assertion of the love between brother and half-sister. Here, while casting a slur at establishment prurience, Byron invokes the conclusion of 'Tintern Abbey' explicitly: 'Nor could on earth a spot be found/To nature and to me so dear' (stanza 4, ll. 532–3). With its affirmation of the purity of sibling love, 'Tintern Abbey' provides a fitting touchstone for Byron's lyric, but the description of innocence is cut short by the poem's re-entry, via the ensuing references to the history of conflict at Coblentz, Ehrenbreitstein, and Morat, into the realm of history. What these intrusions of conflict confirm, I would suggest, is the impossibility of sustaining socially prohibited forms of love outside the domain of lyric fantasy. Yet just as the pursuit of political freedom is spurred on by recollections of 'Morat and Marathon […] true Glory's stainless victories' (stanza 64, ll. 609–10) and, more recently, by the actions of the 'brave, and glorious' General Marceau (stanza 57, l. 545), so the prospect of erotic fulfilment is kept in play by literary exempla.

Unable to sustain the quasi-Wordsworthian mood of stanzas 71–75 ('I live not in myself, but I become/Portion of that around me'; stanza 72, ll. 680–1; 'But this is not my theme'; stanza 76, l. 715) the poem turns to address the memory of Rousseau, whose reputation as 'The apostle of affliction' (stanza 77, l. 726) presents Byron with a more appropriate model than Wordsworth. In Rousseau's 'burning page' (stanza 78, l. 742) Byron encounters a propensity for antithesis that matches his own. Thus, whereas 'placid Leman' raises the prospect of a return to 'a purer spring' (stanza 85, ll. 797–800) 'wild Rousseau' remains a 'self-torturing' figure (stanza 77, l. 725). Thoughts of conflict are never far from Byron's mind when describing Leman and the Rhône. Through an allusion to his recently dissolved marriage, Byron sees in the 'swift Rhone', as it 'cleaves his way between/Heights', an image of 'lovers who have parted/In hate' (stanza 94, ll. 879–80). The breaches between river and mountains, husband and wife, are here granted expression through the poet's careful attention to word order, stress patterning, and line breaks while, at the close of the stanza, the double sense of cleave finds issue in the linking of 'Love' and 'rage' (l. 884) and in the alacrity with which 'thwarted' (l. 883) lovers wage 'war' both against each other and 'within themselves' (l. 887).

Through all these descriptions of social, personal, and mental conflict, Byron cannot quite abandon his reawakened fascination with Wordsworth. Like the Solitary, proud declarations of self-bafflement are placed alongside admissions of a gentler, less forceful kind as, at night, the poet 'breathes a living fragrance from the shore,/Of flowers yet fresh with childhood', while 'on the ear/Drops the light drip of the suspended oar' (stanza 86, 811–13). Here, echoing Wordsworth's tribute to Collins, the poem works to slow down time, repeatedly emphasising the stillness of the scene to pave the way for a passage that responds to the 'Immortality' ode:

> 89
> All heaven and earth are still—though not in sleep,
> But breathless, as we grow when feeling most;
> And silent, as we stand in thoughts too deep:—
> All heaven and earth are still [...]

> 90
> Then stirs the feeling infinite, so felt
> In solitude, when we are *least* alone;
> A truth, which through our being then doth melt
> And purifies from self [...]

If, as the poem goes on to confirm, the stillness attained at this point is but the calm before the storm, critics have perhaps read too much into the fiery defiance of the '*one*' word' (stanza 97, l. 910), seeing in the destructive lightning bolt a final return to the antithetical mode.[43] As the remainder of Canto III demonstrates, the poem advances a mood of harmonious interchange that engages with Wordsworth's poetics more subtly than the previously cited stanzas. Though stanza 104 is devoted ostensibly to the recovery of Rousseau's beauties, the language used is imitative of 'Tintern Abbey', albeit this time in a manner that, for being barely noticeable, is more effective than the poem's more blatant borrowings:

> 'twas the ground
> Where early Love his Psyche's zone unbound,
> And hallowed it with loveliness, 'tis lone,
> And wonderful, and deep, and hath a sound,
> And sense, and sight of sweetness [...] (ll. 971–5)

***

> a sense sublime
> Of something far more deeply interfused,
> Whose dwelling is the light of setting suns,
> And the round ocean, and the living air,
> And the blue sky, and in the mind of man [...] (ll. 96–100)

Responding to the music of conjunction in 'Tintern Abbey' – 'And [...] and [...] And [...] and') – the poem bridges those 'gaps' that threaten to mire the fruitful accord of nature in Hobbesian 'devastation' (stanza 95, l. 895), creating a 'hallowed' space of 'something far more deeply interfused'. For a moment, adrift in connectiveness, one might even believe that Byron's poem had reached an accord with itself.

'Backward, in Rapid Evanescence': Wordsworth after Wordsworth

We have seen how *Memorials* seeks to 'glide' or 'smooth' over gaps in expression, breaches in private and public history, and violations of artistic decorum. I have also observed how poems in the collection continue to mine these crises, finding in repeated acts of division the resources for repeated acts of healing. When Wordsworth revisits the Rhine he writes, therefore, with a mind to the restorative qualities of the river while, like Byron, reflecting on the river's share in the bellicosity that informs its historical meaning. To reach this point, however, Wordsworth must first account for the relationship between time, speed, and perception; more specifically, he must isolate the mode of travel best suited to the contemplation of past, present, and futurity. The guidebooks to northern Europe stressed the importance of a comfortable coach. Heeding this advice Byron had commissioned a replica of Napoleon's coach, a 'performative and public act of mimicry' that, according to Clara Tuite, aimed to transform a moment of defeat into 'something of value'.[44] We may imagine a scene: Byron at the carriage window, watching as the Rhine sweeps by, observing in the sequential images of beauty and ruin a resource for renewed acts of creative vigour.

Childe Harold makes no mention of the poet's means of conveyance, but *Memorials* does, and for Wordsworth the medium is the message:

> Sonnet.
> In a Carriage, upon the Banks of the Rhine
>
> Amid this dance of objects sadness steals
> O'er the defrauded heart—while sweeping by,

> As in a fit of Thespian jollity,
> Beneath her vine-leaf crown the green earth reels:
> Backward, in rapid evanescence, wheels
> The venerable pageantry of Time,
> Each beetling rampart—and each tower sublime [...] (ll. 1–7)

Confined to the carriage, unable to arrest the flow of images, the viewer succumbs to giddy narcosis. In this drunken state of being, recalling the queasiness experienced by Dorothy on the journey to Goslar in the winter of 1798, the poet is unable to record spots of time; the ability to memorialise the scenes that reel in 'rapid evanescence' is compromised. In the preceding sonnet the poet recalls the voyage down the Rhine made with Robert Jones thirty years earlier. Then too, the landscapes of the river had appeared and disappeared, offering a baffling succession of sights, to the waterborne voyagers ('who shall count the Towers', 'Author's Voyage down the Rhine (Thirty Years Ago)', l. 6). Relief comes in the sestet when, released from hurry, the 'slack'ning stream' spreads like 'a spacious Mere' (ll. 10–11), affording, through its echo of 'Home at Grasmere', the travellers an opportunity to 'measure/A smooth free course' (ll. 11–12), and so to 'Think calmly on the past, and mark at leisure/Features which else had vanished like a dream' (ll. 13–14). In the view from the carriage, as objects dance in 'Thespian jollity', the heart is 'defrauded' (ll. 2–3). Here, in addition to experiencing the unreadable inanity of an accelerated past, Wordsworth may have in mind the performative intensities of the opening stanzas of *Childe Harold* III. But whereas Harold is jolted from point to point, seemingly unable or unwilling to halt the 'whirling gulf of phantasy and flame' in which he appears caught (stanza 7, l. 58), the inhabitant of Wordsworth's carriage expresses confidence that 'Pedestrian liberty shall yet be mine' (l. 11). As signalled by the interjectory 'Yet why repine?' (l. 9), the volta breaks the flow of enjambement into units of 'fit measure' (l. 14). By means of discretely punctuated verbals and end-stopped lines the traveller is granted the power to 'muse, to creep, to halt at will, to gaze' (l. 12), regaining the 'Freedom which youth with copious hand supplied' (l. 13) by reclaiming ground that would otherwise give way to flux.

Thus prosaically, one foot at a time, the *Memorials* seeks to counter the oxymoronic imperative 'Still must I on' that, in Byron, prevents the attainment of that sustained point of stillness in which time is restored. Nevertheless, as subsequent poems reveal, the dual meaning of stasis, which Wordsworth revealed in the Duddon series and which he struggled to repress, is also present in *Memorials*. By stopping the flow of time, the traveller aspires to peace, but stopping the flow, as Byron and Wordsworth discover at Waterloo, may also lead to strife. How, then, to admit violence into the poetry of nature while holding on to a desire for peace? In the sonnet that follows 'After Visiting the Field of Waterloo' the poet marvels at the beauty of the River Meuse as morning spreads her 'peaceful ensigns' (l. 5), and its contrast with the 'crimson stains' ('Scenery between Namur and Liege', l. 3) that once, at a time when the area surrounding the river was 'War's favourite playground' (l. 3), besmirched its 'cities, heights, and plains' (l. 2). In line 9, in what amounts to a meta-voltaic performance, the 'eyes/Turn from the fortified and threatening hill' (ll. 9–10) to muse on the serenity and stillness of the 'watery glade' (l. 11). Attributed to 'gentle Fancy' (l. 1) rather than Imagination, the shift from traumatic memories of war to scenes of sacerdotal calm is granted a surprising degree of force as a result of the heavily accented 'Turn' (l. 10). Elsewhere, in 'Hymn, for the Boatmen, as They Approach the Rapids, under the Castle of Heidelberg', Wordsworth adopts a six-line tetrameter stanza, rhyming abcbdd, a pattern suited to the poem's description of travellers 'swept along' (l. 2) by 'troubled waters' (l. 6) whose faith is expressed at the stanza's close – 'All our hope is placed in Thee;/Miserere Domine!' (ll. 23–4) – in rhyming couplet certainty. Long established as a symbol of heroic resistance to despotism, most recently during the campaign against Napoleon, the ruins of Heidelberg Castle are a reminder no less of how dreams of peace succumb to the return of war. Thus, 'while through the meadows green' (l. 9), the boatmen are lulled into believing 'the peaceful flood' (l. 10) will endure, their subsequent passage through raving and fretted waters confirms that lasting peace cannot be attained.

In the next sonnet, 'Local Recollections on the Heights near Hockheim', Wordsworth's attention returns to those moments when, 'with breath suspended' (l. 4), strife is 'Abruptly paused' (l. 1). Inspired by a passage 'recorded in the journals of the day',[45] the poem describes the reactions of the Austrian army as they observed the French retreat across the Rhine following their defeat at Leipzig in November 1813. The point of suspension, marked by the full stop at the close of the opening quatrain, leads to a cry of victory as the 'barrier Rhine' (l. 9) flashes before them. Echoing the sinuous course of the 'unconquerable Stream' (l. 14), as well as the 'shock' (l. 11) of the defending nation, the sonnet plays on the tension between movement and stasis, subordinating warring antitheses to the encompassing harmony of the divine. The connection between the account of the 'men who gazed heart-smitten by the view' (l. 10) and the description in stanza 60 of *Childe Harold* III of 'eyes' that 'resign/Their cherish'd gaze upon thee, lovely Rhine!' (ll. 574–5) was later flagged up by the editors of

Byron's *Poetical Works*, who appended the quotation from the 'journals of the day' that Wordsworth had cited in the *Memorials* as a note to the stanza:

> When the Austrians took Hockheim, in one part of the engagement they got to the brow of the hill, whence they had their first view of the Rhine. They instantly halted—not a gun was fired—not a voice heard: but they stood gazing on the river with those feelings which the events of the last 15 years at once called up. Prince Schwartzenberg rode up to the cause of this sudden stop, they then gave three cheers, rushed after the enemy, and drove them into the water.[46]

In citing this passage from 'Local Recollections', the editors seem not to have considered Francis Jeffrey's scathing judgement on the poem:

> If his political sentiments partake of the spirit of the Morning Post, and other classical works of that refined description, we may wonder the less to find him recur to the same sources as the 'perennial fountains' of historic truth. Coming to the heights of Hockheim, near the Rhine, his lyre is awakened by a most notable anecdote, which he candidly admits to rest upon the following newspaper paragraph [quotes 'When the Austrians took Hockheim [...] and drove them into the water']. We presume the *Austrian* soldiers never were in such a fit of sentiment at any other period of the monarchy: Our poet, however, takes it all as equally natural and true; and produces forthwith a Sonnet [...] in which, after describing them as pausing 'with breath suspended, like a listening scout', he exclaims—
>
>> 'O Silence! thou wert Mother of a Shout
>> That thro' the texture of yon azure dome
>> Clove its glad way—a cry of harvest-home
>> Uttered to Heaven in ecstasy devout!'
>
> —which indeed is about as natural in thought and expression, as the historical passage that serves for its groundwork.[47]

Drawn verbatim, either directly from Wordsworth's poem or from Jeffrey's review, the passage's anti-Napoleonic sentiments at first sit strangely with the pastoral delicacy of Byron's verse, yet on further consideration may be read as congruent with the description of the ensanguined Rhine in stanzas 49–51. To Victorian readers, unperturbed by long-forgotten Regency turf wars, the incorporation within Byron's poem of Wordsworth's impressions of fluvial conflict may not have seemed strange at all. Indeed, for the attentive reader, particularly one with a knowledge of the classics, the intertwining of the bucolic and the bellicose on display in *Childe Harold* and *Memorials* may well have been a given.

Seeking in the course of the river an emblem of lasting peace, as Wordsworth had attempted in the Duddon sequence, proves a fraught endeavour in *Memorials*. If, as that sequence's penultimate sonnet affirmed, the Duddon 'mingle[s]', at last, 'with Eternity!' (XXXII, l. 14), the Rhine, by contrast, remains in flux: 'Smooth and green' in one instance (l. 5), 'fretting and whitening' (l. 8) in another, leaving 'men' to 'Wonder that aught of aspect so serene/Can link with desolation' (ll. 4–5). In 'The Jungfrau—And the Rhine at Shauffhausen', from which these contrasting images are taken, the descent of the river into 'madness' (l. 9) is conveyed by the descriptive flood that follows the turn in line 7:

> [...] but on they go
> Fretting and whitening, keener and more keen
> Till madness seizes on the whole wide Flood
> Turned to a fearful Thing, whose nostrils breathe
> Blasts of tempestuous smoke, with which he tries
> To hide himself, but only magnifies:
> And doth in more conspicuous torment writhe,
> Deafening the region in his 'ireful mood.' (ll. 7–14)

As the heavily worked Amherst manuscript confirms, Wordsworth struggled to bring the poem to a satisfactory conclusion and at one point had considered closing with '[Roaring like storms at war with some huge [*alt* vast] wood] Roaring with voice, no time extinguishet[h]/And doth in more conspicuous torm[ent] writhe'. As Geoffrey Jackson points out, 'This leaf (3) was once pasted over DC MS. 177.4 [...] WW completed his revision of lines 13 and 14 by writing at the top what was then the facing page (DC MS. 77.5): "And doth in more conspicuous torment writhe/Defeaning [*sic*] the region in his ireful mood".'[48] Jackson notes also that the word 'writhe' is written twice at the bottom of the page. The impression of the sonnet as itself a physically contorted, squirming production, running in excess of the author's conscious control, is amplified by the closing allusion to the Temple of Mars, from Dryden's translation of 'The Knight's Tale': 'In midst of all the Dome, Misfortune sat,/And gloomy Discontent, and fell Debate,/And Madness laughing in his ireful Mood' (ll. 580–2).[49] Dryden's translation, which Wordsworth had previously criticised for failing to capture Chaucer's 'amiable [...] ennobling and intense passions' (*EY*. 641), lays great store on how, in the state of war, rational discourse gives way to 'Menaces [...] foul Disgrace/And bawling Infamy, in Language base,/Till Sense was lost in Sound, and Silence fled the Place' (ll. 573–5). Recalling Wordsworth's reservations about Dryden's style – 'there is not a single image from Nature in the whole body of his works'

(*EY*. 641) – the quotation from *Palamon and Arcite* provides a fitting conclusion to a poem in which the Rhinefall, 'Turned to a fearful Thing' (l. 10) on account, as Theresa Kelley and Robin Jarvis note, of its complex associations with religious, revolutionary, and imperial terror, has ceased to appear natural.[50]

Mindful of how 'poetically impassioned' language, focussed on 'unpleasing subjects' (*EY*. 641), undermines the corrective labour of the later verse, Wordsworth returns in 'The Fall of the Aar—Handec' to advance an image of natural beauty drawing sustenance from destruction. As flowers breath 'life' and 'joy' (l. 11) from the torrent, so humble worshippers 'nod/Their heads in sign of worship' (ll. 12–13), recognising in the river's 'fierce aspect' (l. 1) an image of the divine. Read by Larkin as a demonstration of how beauty 'assimilates the motion of the torrent and renders life-giving what is otherwise too violent to be available to age', and by Jarvis as a 'pacification of the sublime', the poem continues Wordsworth's interest in the politics and poetics of the torrent.[51] More assured in its quelling of sublime terror than the Rhinefall sonnet, the verse derives much of its placing in the sequence after 'On Approaching the Staub-Bach, Lauterbrunnen'. In this poem, appreciation of the waterfall is jeopardised by the 'wild and savage' song of the local beggars, which as Wordsworth states in an accompanying note, 'reminded me of religious services chaunted to Streams and Fountains in Pagan times'.[52] Identified by Dorothy as 'two women' (*JDW* II. 117–18), the pagan beggars whose song 'with regret and useless pity haunt[s]/This bold, this pure, this sky-born WATERFALL!' (ll. 13–14) represents a further instance of the intrusion of unruly feminine noise within the sober confines of the *Memorials*. Like 'Fish-Women' the sonnet is an exercise in disenchantment, debunking the fanciful associations of 'thrilling melodies' and 'notes shrill and wild' ('no Mermaid warbles [...] no caverned Witch/Chaunted a love-spell [...] more musical', ll. 5–9) by tracing its source to 'the lips of abject Want/And Idleness' (l. 10). Rejecting the intense lyricism that, in 'The Solitary Reaper', had made of the encounter with unrefined song a rich source of 'raptures unconfined' (l. 4), the verse is left with no alternative but to reconfigure itself as an ironic riposte to the desire for release from 'human-kind' (l. 1). As such, even as the final line reinstates an image of the Christian sublime triumphing over pagan fancy and, by implication, the potential return of jacobinical lawlessness, the haunting of otiose enthralment by uncultivated idleness recasts the poem as a self-reflexive commentary on the dashed expectations recounted in countless travel narratives and as a not-so-subtle dig at Byron's hand-me-down account of the pleasures of solitude in *Childe Harold* III.

Forms of War and Peace

For Byron, I have argued, absorption in nature is shown to be an unsatisfactory alternative to the conflictual egotism of the Napoleonic self. And for the poet of *Memorials*, nature provides, at best, only brief respite from the exigencies of war. That said, there are occasions in the collection when readers catch sight of what it might be like to transcend violence, discovering at the silent horizon of human history a locus of enduring calm. Just as, in Wordsworth's memorial to the Swiss patriot Aloys Reding, who opposed the 'flagitious, and too successful, attempt of Buonaparte to subjugate [his] country',[53] the image of the votive stone 'Touched' by the setting sun ('Memorial. Near the Outlet of the Lake of Thun', l. 16) provides a figure for mutability that serves as a glimpse of eternity, so in other poems fragments of permanence flicker in the light of a peace yet to come. As with the memorial to Reding, such fragments are often politicised, recalling in their ruin recollections of heroic resistance to tyranny. In, for instance, 'Fort Fuentes—At the Head of the Lake of Como', a poem commemorating a visit to a site of strategic significance demolished on the orders of Napoleon in 1796, the discovery of a 'sweet-visaged Cherub of Parian stone', 'upheaved by war's sulphurous blast' (ll. 1–2) and now overgrown with 'moss and leaves' (l. 13) with a 'green, gilded snake' twined around its neck (ll. 7–8), serves as a reminder of the Fall, the rejuvenation of nature, and the peace that will return 'When the whirlwind of human destruction' is 'passed away' (ll. 19–20).

In her journal, Dorothy notes the changes wrought on the landscape by the revolutionary and Napoleonic wars, with the replacement of the old, traditional routes, which Wordsworth and Jones had followed in 1790, by the new, military roads constructed by Napoleon, being a particular preoccupation. As John Wyatt observes, the journal 'portrays a damaged environment, chiefly ruined by war'.[54] By the time the Wordsworth party reached the Simplon Pass, the sight of a landscape violently altered as a result of human interventions threatened to destabilise the memory of transcendence that had been documented in *The Prelude*. Whereas at Fuentes the toppled statue of a child could evoke, in spite of the world, an image of divine restoration, elsewhere in Lombardy Wordsworth faced starker and more recalcitrant monuments to the folly of man. In the sonnet describing 'The Column Intended by Buonaparte for a Triumphal Edifice in Milan, Now Lying by the Way-Side on the Semplon Pass', the poet encounters a fit emblem of defeated ambition: a blank, unscripted pillar. Designated as 'Vanity's hieroglyph', the unreadable column nevertheless serves as a 'choice trope' of 'Pride o'erthrown' (ll. 7–8). Rightly scrutinised by Jarvis as a contradictory and perplexing image – how does a bare, uninscribed column work as a complex, verbal trope? – the prostrate stone serves, nevertheless, as a device for alerting the 'Soul' to history's unrecorded 'Crimes' (ll. 11–12).[55] The sonnet's closing heroic couplet recalls the post-verbal 'shrieks' and 'groans' evoked by the field of Waterloo (ll. 13–14), but lifeless matter, no less than nature's 'silence' ('Fort Fuentes— At the Head of the Lake of Como', ll. 18–20), provides a 'hint' (l. 11) of the peace that is to be found in quiet submission to 'Power Divine!' (l. 10). Here, Wordsworth shows how bodies, poems, and memorials alike, predicated on incompletion, gain meaning only by entering a relationship with the divine. In the absence of such a relationship, the work of sublimity falls short of the threshold, persisting only as mute testament to the limits of secular fulfilment. Peace, then, but only for a time.

In tracing the course of war and peace in *Memorials*, I have suggested that Wordsworth deploys shorter lyrics, with an emphasis on the sonnet, to resist the relentless carrying forward that is characteristic of Byron's Spenserian romance. Simply put, the sonnet affords opportunities to combine movement with stasis, showing how, even amid change, points of stillness may be attained. As if to consolidate this notion, Wordsworth introduces to the sequence a poem written in Spenserian stanzas: 'Processions. Suggested on a Sabbath Morning in the Vale of Chamouny'. As the title suggests, the poem evokes memories of Coleridge's 'Hymn before Sun-Rise, in the Vale of Chamouni', but in contrast to Coleridge's irregular blank verse, with its performance of spontaneity, Wordsworth's adherence to the nine-line stanza and ababbcbcc rhyme scheme presents a more disciplined affirmation of the affinity between nature and God. Divided into two halves comprising four stanzas each, the first half centring on descriptions of Persian, Hebrew, Ammonite, and Roman ceremonials and the second focussing on the Catholic procession identified in the poem's title, 'Processions' can be read as an extension of the gradualist history portrayed in *Ecclesiastical Sketches*. Sustaining the collection's emphasis on slowness, stillness, and ease of transition, the poem contrasts the gaudy insistence of pagan rites, denoted by heavily accented present participles ('gushing', 'tilting', 'dancing', 'Striking'; ll. 20–33, *passim*), emotional manipulation ('[The Priests] Provoked responses with shrill canticles', l. 22; 'the haughty claims/Of Chiefs triumphant after ruthless wars', l. 29), and abruptly shifting scenes, with the 'sober litanies' and steady pace (l. 40) of Christian pageantry. Utilising the full expressive potential of the Spenserian stanza, Wordsworth's run-on lines imitate the 'winding' (l. 42) procession 'Of white-robed Shapes, seemed linked in solemn guise/[...] by mysterious ties' (ll. 48–50). Shifting from the description of 'living monuments' (l. 5) of antiquity to 'the living Stream' of Christianity (l. 48), the poem works hard to distinguish its rhetoric of 'seeming' – the procession '*seemed* linked' (l. 49), the spotless figures '*seem*' to be a 'product' of the 'awful Mount (l. 57) – from the protean suggestiveness of pagan imaginings. Drawing on Ovid's *Fasti*, Wordsworth sets the overbearing enthusiasm of heathen ritual against the quiet composure of Christian ceremony, laying stress, by way of a gendered rhetorical economy, on the 'sisterly resemblance' (l. 61) of the votaries to 'everlasting snow' (l. 58), 'virgin-lilies' (l. 59), and 'swans' (l. 60) – 'fair Forms' that 'glide', in recollection of the nun-like figures witnessed at Bruges.

In its determination to downplay the imaginative appeal of pagan ceremonials and to advance the cause of Christian worship, the poem appears to be directed at Shelley, Byron, Hunt, and Keats, the quartet now firmly associated in Wordsworth's mind, thanks in large measure to Southey's recent interventions, with the promotion of radicalism, atheism, and sexual impropriety. Specifically, in its suspicion of the poetics of Ovidian 'metamorphosis' (l. 69), 'Processions' appears to have the pretty paganisms of Keats and Hunt in its sights. The Christian representation of Chamonix might also be read as a pointed response to Shelley's atheistic 'Mont Blanc', and indeed, as Peter Manning suggests, as a rejoinder to the hubristic sublime that is both conjured and guarded against in Book VI of *The Prelude*.[56] But there is a close link, too, with Byron's lines on the Alps in *Childe Harold* III, both at the level of form and at the level of content. In stanza 91, at the close of the most recognisably Wordsworthian section of the poem, Byron writes of the pagan predilection for 'open air' worship:

> Not vainly did the early Persian make
> His altar the high places and the peak
> Or earth-o'ergazing mountains, and thus take
> A fit and unwall'd temple, there to seek
> The Spirit, in whose honour shrines are weak,
> Uprear'd of human hands. Come, and compare
> Columns and idol-dwellings, Goth or Greek,
> With Nature's realms of worship, earth and air,
> Nor fix on fond abodes to circumscribe thy prayer! (ll. 851–9)

In a note to the stanza Byron takes this notion further, offering a provocatively syncretic defence of early Christian, Methodist, and Muslim devotional practices, writing of 'The Mussulmans' that 'the simple and entire sincerity of these men, and the spirit which appeared to be within and upon them, made a far greater impression than any general rite which was ever performed in places of worship'.[57] At first glance, Wordsworth's stanzas appear to emulate Byron's praise of outdoor devotions. Taking inspiration from Dorothy's account of the procession, with its fanciful 'connection' between the white-robed figures and the 'small pyramids of the Glacier' (*JDW* II. 290–1), the poem seems to recast the mountain setting as a vast, natural temple, echoing related descriptions of open-air worship in *The Excursion* and *Ecclesiastical Sketches*. However, while faith inclines the observer to perceive resemblances between natural and spiritual forms, Wordsworth locates a disturbance in this inclination as, 'Trembling', he looks upon 'the secret springs' of that 'licentious craving in the mind/To act the God among external things,/To bind, on apt suggestion, and unbind' (ll. 64–7). Composed shortly after *Ecclesiastical Sketches*, in which the contemplation of the 'beauty' and 'ancient stillness' of Catholic ruins ('Old Abbeys', l. 3) becomes a source of spiritual rejuvenation (ll. 13–14), the prospect of living Catholic worship in 'Processions', with its ghostlike and potentially unending train of resemblances, raises the fear of that tendency of the mind to become untethered not only from reality but also from the divine.

Through recounting the hypnotic effect of these baroque associations, Wordsworth reflects also on Byron's invocation of 'the feeling infinite' (stanza 90, l. 842), which 'sheds a charm,/Like to the fabled Cytherea's zone,/Binding all things with beauty' (ll. 847–50). Blending Wordsworth's 'sense sublime' with echoes of Ovidian eroticism, Byron becomes an exemplar of that tendency of mind to 'bind' and 'unbind', responding with momentary beguilement to passing resemblances while glancing over the deeper, more lasting satisfaction to be gained from sensing the 'mysterious ties' that connect a body of worshippers. With its emphasis on female purity girdling the Catholic Church, 'Processions' attempts to purge itself of Aphroditic connotations, only to signal in the stridency of its closing lines the destructive alure of 'Fable's dark abyss!' (l. 72) and thus to record an enduring threat to the integrity of the Protestant imagination. Only in moments of fluvial stasis, or in the prospect of monumental ruin, can the mind yield an image of that peace that ought, ideally, to reside in the world.

Culture Wars

From beginning to end, *Memorials* bears the imprint of Wordsworth's previous journeys to the Continent, as well as the more recent mark of Byron's revisioning of the earlier poetry. Framed by this double consciousness,

Wordsworth's late collection endeavours to come to terms with itself, hindering the journey to peace by highlighting the disparity between personal and public histories and the brittle lines between lyric enchantment and ironic realism. The journey from Rydal to Lucerne, which for the most part followed the 1790 route, albeit in the reverse direction, folds back no less on the republican and atheistic stirrings that, at the outbreak of war, had placed Wordsworth as one who 'sate silent' when 'prayers were offered up' for Allied 'victories' (1805 *Prelude*, X. l. 270–3). Patriotic declarations are threaded throughout *Memorials*, but the collection's allegiance to the values of the post-war British establishment is most clearly displayed in the 'Ode to Enterprize', a verse that announces the end of history's 'convulsive throes', a reign of terror urged by the 'Pharaohs of the earth, the men of hardened heart' (the allusion to Napoleon is clear) (ll. 94–108; *passim*) and the coming of a new age of peace, born from the ascendency of Britain's beneficent imperial mission. Offering itself as an annex to the sequence (the 1820 volume concludes in fact with 'Desultory Stanzas upon Receiving the Preceding Stanzas from the Press', a postscript poem adverting to the delicate negotiation of biographical settlement and visionary resurgence that, for critics writing after Hartman, constitutes the central interest of the collection), the ode seeks to align the sublime transports of philosophers and poets with the aspirations of Britain's venture capitalists who, carried by 'a thousand thousand sails' (l. 143), will establish global peace through international trade.

The ode's upbeat conclusion is shadowed, however, by the unsettled air of three preceding sonnets, the first of which, 'Sky-Prospect—From the Plains of France', picks up on the collection's cautionary soundings on the over-exercise of Fancy. Observing the clouds, the poet discerns shapes resembling 'proud Ararat' (l. 2), the 'Ark' (l. 3), a 'Lion's shape' (l. 4), and a 'huge Crocodile' (l. 5), but such innocent conjuring yields to the prospect of a 'blazing Town' at risk of 'destruction' (ll. 7–8). Despite the efforts of the volta to correct such alarmist 'shows' (l. 12), the sonnet remains troubled by its insight into the propensity of the poet to allow the 'Mimics of Fancy' to upbraid the 'servile map of history'.[58] The following poem, 'On Being Stranded near the Harbour of Boulogne', conveys similar alarm at the travelers being cast 'back upon the Gallic shore' (l. 1), unable to depart from the beach on which Napoleon, the 'dreaming Conqueror' (l. 8), forged his plans for the invasion of Britain. Set against this image of military folly is Wordsworth's peaceful 'project' (l. 4). A completed work, contrasting with the '*unfinished*' Napoleonic pillar that the party visited prior to embarkation, *Memorials* is presented here as an enduring counter-monument to the 'vanity and arrogance' of the would-be conqueror (*JDW* II. 332–3). But the verse's attunement to the wave-like returns of historical contingency belies the rhetorical confidence of the terminal Shakespearian affirmation: 'These local reflections ne'er can cloy/Such ground I from my very heart enjoy!' (13–14). The line dividing the territorial ambitions of poet and emperor turns out, after all, to be written in the sand.

Wordsworth's journey closes at Dover, and in the sonnet that commemorates this return the reader is alerted to the proto-tabloid clamour that 'past/Thro' Europe', disturbing the poet's holiday with 'blast[s]' of 'Faction' and 'turmoil' ('After Landing—The Valley of Dover'; ll. 2–3). The news that 'filled our hearts with grief for England's shame' (l. 4) is the Queen Caroline affair. If Lord Byron emerges in this context as a somewhat detached supporter of the queen, Wordsworth's formal opposition is, if anything, more difficult to describe. At the beginning of the trial, Wordsworth, together with Coleridge, Crabb Robinson, and Sara Hutchinson, was professedly liberal in his attitude; however, by the end of the summer, sensing how the queen's cause had been taken up in radical circles, his feelings had hardened. Still, throughout this period, Wordsworth did not venture explicit condemnation of the queen. Writing to Lord Lonsdale in October 1820, Wordsworth declared that he had had 'little opportunity' to know anything of 'public affairs' and that, in respect of the queen, 'we deem ourselves truly fortunate in having been out of the country, at a time when an inquiry at which all Europe seems scandalised, was going on' (*MY* II. 642–3).

Protestations of distance and detachment are at odds, however, with the side of Wordsworth that maintained a steady fascination with this *cause célèbre*; indeed, if anything, the poet seems to have been drawn to the queen, finding himself, even at a distance, in uncomfortable proximity with her scandal-beset body, as the following extract, taken from a letter to Mary, despatched from London in June 1812, confirms:

> R. H- was at some distance from me, and I had no conversation with her. She is a fat unwieldly Woman, but has rather a handsome and pleasing Countenance, with an expression of hilarity that is not however free from Coarseness. This was a large Assembly, saw few pretty women, and many most disgusting objects; one I encountered of a tolerable face and features, but in her native bosom so huge and tremendous, that had you seen her enter a room in that condition I am sure the soul of modest womanhood in you would have shrunk almost as with horror. Her Breasts were like two great hay-cocks or rather hay stacks, protruding themselves upon the Spectator, and yet no body seemed to notice them— (SNL, p. 104)

Nobody, that is, except Wordsworth. How is the impartial Spectator expected to remain detached when faced with such 'Coarseness'? At Lugano, in 1820, William and Mary slept in a room formerly occupied by the queen. As recounted by Crabb Robinson, this room was connected to one occupied by her suspected Italian lover, Bartolomeo Pergami.[59] The impression of a man attracted, whether by accident or design, to the spectacle of royal *déshabillé* is confirmed by James Stephanoff's *Trial of Queen Caroline*, a small watercolour capturing the moment on the final day in the House of Lords when the Pains and Penalties Bill was effectively quashed. There, Zelig-like, amid a crowd of onlookers, appears the head of Wordsworth, staring at the scene of the queen's vindication, while Henry Brougham, Lord Lonsdale's detested opponent in the 1818 Westmorland election, lords it up in his role as the queen's chief advocate.[60]

Composed shortly after the trial, 'After Landing' appears, at first, to provide a fitting conclusion to *Memorials* as, elevated by 'rural stillness' (l. 14), the poet's 'Spirit' reaches 'a calmer height' (l. 13), freed from the fractious rumour mill encountered in Europe. The concluding lines of the sonnet thus work to transform the poetics of discord that, throughout the collection, have threatened to undermine the establishment of enduring peace. But although 'Peace' in line 5 signals a decisive turn from those 'noisy followers of the game/Which Faction breeds' (ll. 1–2), with its connotations of tumult, servitude, and loveless reproduction, the lines that follow are peculiar, to say the least:

> Peace greets us;—rambling on without an aim
> We mark majestic herds of Cattle free
> To ruminate—couched on the grassy lea,
> And hear far-off the mellow horn proclaim
> The season's harmless pastime. Ruder sound
> Stirs not; enwrapt I gaze—with strange delight [...] (ll. 5–10)

Inspired by a passage in Dorothy's journal, 'The scattered cattle quietly selecting their own food was a cheering and home-feeling sight' (*JDW* II. 335), the sight signifies for William the distinction between continental over-cultivation and native spontaneity, which becomes, in turn, a not entirely coherent image of the difference between English and European ideas of liberty. Whereas, on the Continent, English tourists, prompted by the 'Newsman's blast' (l. 3), become slaves to the 'game' – and here one wonders whether Byron, a sometime friend of Queen Caroline, is implicated in their number – at home the travellers are free to follow their inclinations, 'rambling on without an aim' (l. 5). However, in the wayward associations provoked by 'majestic herds of Cattle free/To ruminate' the distinctions between high and low become muddied: are the cattle a breed apart from the Faction that breeds? Does nature blindly consume, or do these creatures possess a capacity for higher thought? In its strained attempts to curtail such thoughts, the poem's bid for sublimity falls into bathos, unable to shake off the unintended comedy afforded by those elevated cows chewing the cud while thinking deeply of England's glory. Moreover, what are we to make of the 'mellow horn' and the 'Season's harmless pastime'? Throughout this passage, with its emphasis on 'the sight of animals enjoying life', Wordsworth may have in mind Cowper's description of the 'harmless sport' of Eden.[61] But in this 'sin marr'd' realm,[62] does the hunting horn really present a safe alternative to the 'Ruder sound' of news-driven tumult?

Perhaps the conclusion of *Memorials*, with its echoes of the tonal awkwardness of 'Fish-Women', provides fit testimony to the vein of misogynistic strangeness that runs throughout the collection. Intended to consolidate a sense of native harmlessness, at odds with continental faction, 'After Landing' appears, on closer inspection, to be as fractured in composition as many of the volume's avowedly more combative companion pieces. Whether centred on images of riparian calm, feminine beauty, or alpine stillness, peace, for Wordsworth, remains elusive, his attempts to quell the intrusions of historical violence, both past and present, threatened at every turn by descents into formal and thematic antagonism. If Wordsworth's return to England, to peace and to conjugality, was meant to be read in triumphant contrast to the account of exile and marital antagonism depicted at the close of *Childe Harold* III, it is a triumph riven with the very tensions – historical, political, sexual, and artistic – that traverse Byron's poem. In its very unlikeness, Wordsworth's late poetry is perhaps more Byronic than it can afford to admit.

At Dover, Again

As previously noted, envois to daughters, lost and found or at the risk of loss, conclude *Childe Harold's Pilgrimage* Canto III and *Memoirs of a Tour on the Continent, 1820*. But perhaps 'conclude' is not the right word. Certainly, in Wordsworth's case, the several attempts to draw the sequence to a fit conclusion – 'After Landing', followed by two 'annexed' pieces, bearing their own title pages, 'Ode to Enterprize' and 'Desultory Stanzas' – suggest the poet's reluctance to pronounce his memoirs at an end. Thus, during the course of the radical reshaping of *Memorials* as the first instalment of 'Itinerary' sonnets for the 1838 sonnet volume, Wordsworth announced to Henry Crabb Robinson that 'There will be one add^l Son: which I composed yesterday for a conclusion to the class of our Continental Tour in –20–' (*LY* III. 522). Titled 'At Dover', the poem was originally included in a letter to Dora with the postscript: 'Suggested by a passage in your journal, and sent as a peace-offering, at your dear Mother's request'.[63] Most likely arising from the conflict between father and daughter prompted by Dora's decision that year, against Wordsworth's wishes, to accept the marriage proposal of Edward Quillinan,[64] the sonnet that brings the 1838 continental sequence to an end deserves consideration:

> From the Pier's head, musing—and with increase
> Of wonder, long I watched this sea-side Town,
> Under the white cliff's battlemented crown,
> Hushed to a depth of more than Sabbath peace.
> How strange, methought, this orderly release
> From social noise—quiet elsewhere unknown!
> A Spirit whispered, 'Doth not Ocean drown
> Trivial in solemn sounds? Let wonder cease.
> His overpowering murmurs have set free
> Thy sense from pressure of life's common din;
> As the dread voice that speaks from out the sea
> Of God's eternal Word, the voice of Time
> Deadens—the shocks of tumult, shrieks of crime,
> The shouts of folly, and the groans of sin.

Wordsworth, of course, has visited this scene before, specifically in 1802 when the poet returned from Calais following his meeting with Annette and Caroline Vallon. In the sonnets 'Composed in the Valley, near Dover, on the Day of Landing' and 'September, 1802', feelings of individual and national appeasement are conjoined with uncertain results. The latter poem, in particular, with its ambivalent attitude to the proximity of France, separated by the narrowest of water margins ('I shrunk, for verily the barrier flood/Was like a Lake, or River bright and fair', ll. 5–6), highlights the extent to which dalliance with transgression blurs individual, national, and moral boundaries: 'yet what power is there!/What mightiness for evil and for good!' (ll. 7–8). Looking towards the coast of France, 'drawn almost into frightful neighbourhood' (l. 4), God alone knows how 'Nations', like selves, 'shall be great and free' (ll. 13–14).

The personal and public traumas expressed in 1802 and re-encountered in 1820 are decisively met in 1838 by the overpowering voice of Christian duty, the liberating outcome of which is truly catastrophic. For with its unequivocal submission to 'the dread voice that speaks from out the sea/ Of God's eternal Word', (ll. 11–12) 'At Dover' embraces a severance not only from the 'shocks' of human affairs but also from the aimless temporality, the 'hourly din' (l. 10) that taints visionary 'wonder' (l. 2) with natural doubt (ll. 5–7).[65] From a creative perspective this renders 'At Dover' not only unsatisfactory but also estranging, for in its wish to establish lasting peace through submission to the eternal Word the poem speaks also of a desire to get to the end of poetry. As the allusion to *Lycidas* implies, while for Milton 'the dread voice is past/That shrunk' (ll. 132–3) the stream in which, according to Ovid, the river god Alpheus sought union with the nymph Arethusa, for Wordsworth the resounding of that voice suggests, over and above its obvious moral implications, a desire to do away with the very tradition that allows for the imaginary circumvention of sexual, moral, and creative constraints – the source, in other words, of poetic Fancy.[66]

If the strength of Wordsworth's greatest poetry is a consequence of its openness to wonder, then the lesson of 'At Dover', by contrast, invites no such response; its Christianising authority is absolute. What the poem requires from its reader, therefore, is not interrogative freedom but irrational obedience. By drawing the 'Spirit' that oversees the passing shows of being into the frame of sensible experience, the freedom to question is exchanged for the illusory integrity of blind accession. Such a gesture is truly deadening, for the voice of God speaks as well of a loss of receptivity, of the openness to time that informs the Romantic imagination. Long associated with the recovery from physical and mental strife and with the return of inspiration, the fount of Arethusa, which, as *The Prelude* recounts, Wordsworth advised Coleridge to drink from during his stay in Sicily, is stilled.[67] Thus, 'At Dover' marks the retreat from a vital source of creation and the embrace of a thanatoid peace, beyond the reach of poetry.

After Wordsworth

Let us cultivate the poetry of peace. Let Wordsworth and Montgomery supersede Campbell and Scott. *The Peace Almanac and Diary, for 1846.*[1]

Carnage Is God's Daughter

The International Peace Congress, held in 1843 and then, from 1848, at yearly intervals until the outbreak of the Crimean War in 1853, raised awareness among some cultural commentators of the responsibility placed on poets to promote the cause of peace. In these debates, Wordsworth was sometimes couched as the poet of 'calm' and 'peaceful scenes', opposed to those poets of 'passion' who, like Campbell, Scott, or Byron, would leave readers 'restless and uneasy', oppressed in mind by 'images of terror and sublimity' rather than soothed by descriptions of 'flowers that grow unscathed amidst all the tumult of waters'.[2] Thus, pitching Byron's stanzas on Waterloo against Wordsworth's lines on the Falls of the Aar, a student writer for the *Grange Magazine* sought to enlist the laureate as a celebrant of universal peace, forgetting that Wordsworth, in determining Carnage as the daughter of God, had perhaps done more than Byron to disturb the peace that, as many correspondents noted, had been maintained in Europe for over thirty years.[3]

Though widely maintained in the 1840s, the view of Wordsworth as the poet of peace did not go unchallenged. Thomas De Quincey's essay 'On War', first published as the lead article in *Macphail's Edinburgh Ecclesiastical Journal and Literary Review* in February 1848 and then republished in a revised and expanded form in *Selections Grave and Gay* during the first year of the Crimean War, is prefaced by an 'Explanatory' note in which the author misquotes the offending lines from the 'Thanksgiving Ode' with approval, and perhaps even with relish:

> Most heartily, and with my profoundest sympathy, do I go along with Wordsworth in his grand lyrical proclamation of truth not less divine than it is mysterious, not less triumphant than it is sorrowful—viz., that

amongst God's holiest instruments for the elevation of human nature, is 'mutual slaughter' amongst men, yes, that 'Carnage is God's daughter' [*sic*] [...] The instruments rise in grandeur, carnage and slaughter rise in holiness, exactly as the motives and interests rise on behalf of which such awful powers are invoked. Fighting for truth in its last recesses of Sanctity, for human dignity systematically outraged, or for human rights mercilessly trodden under foot—champions of such interests, men first of all descry, as from a summit suddenly revealed, the possible grandeur of bloodshed suffered or inflicted. (*WTDQ* XX. 31)

For De Quincey, Wordsworth is the poet of war, providing unashamed support to the notion that when blood is shed in battles 'fought for godlike truth, for human dignity, or for human rights' (*WTDQ* XX. 33) war may be raised to the level of the Sublime.

As the essay proceeds, the challenge of this opening claim is granted conceptual respectability by way of the philosophical doctrine of necessitarianism. Robert Hopkins has pointed out that the essay's definition of conflict as 'a physical necessity arising out of man's nature when combined with man's situation' and as 'moral necessity [...] under which it becomes lawful to say that war *ought* to exist, as a balance to opposite tendencies of a still more evil character' (*WTDQ* XVI. 271) owes much to Kant, whose essays on 'Perpetual Peace' and 'Idea for a Universal History' De Quincey had translated in the mid to late 1820s.[4] Echoing Kant's pessimistic sense of antagonism as the lamentable but necessary means which nature employs to accomplish the advancement of human society, De Quincey states provocatively that 'like other scourges in the divine economy, war purifies and redeems itself in its character of a counterforce to greater evils that could not otherwise be intercepted or redressed'. The destructive horror of war must be countenanced, in other words, on the grounds that it serves as a 'balance to opposite tendencies of a still more evil character' (*WTDQ* XVI. 272). Among the evils that De Quincey itemises in his 'Explanatory' preface are the Peace Societies that would, if 'their power kept pace with their guilty purposes, work degradation for man by drawing upon his most effeminate and luxurious cravings for ease' (*WTDQ* XX. 31). For De Quincey, again with implicit reference to Kant, the moral integrity of the nation, like that of the manly individual, occurs through conflict. Paradoxically it is only through participation in ceaseless antagonism with others that individuals and nations may secure a coherent sense of identity.

De Quincey's remarks on the connections between war and identity were echoed elsewhere in debates in the run-up to the Crimean War. In November 1852, two months after the Duke of Wellington's death and thirty-seven years after the Battle of Waterloo, an anonymous writer in *Blackwood's* set about bemoaning the effects of the prolonged state of peace: where once a nation affirmed its strength on the field of battle, now it sets to dreaming; where once a nation distinguished itself in battle, now it is characterised by 'a studied contempt of loyalty – a bitter hatred of the aristocracy [...] a loud systematic derision of courage, self-devotion, and patriotism—an identifying of national honour with national wealth—a dogged pursuing of self-interest—a habit of considering ease and comfort as the *summum bonum*'.[5] The writer goes on to decry those 'lounging pleasantly on prize sofas from the Great Exhibition [while] reading the story of [Wellington's] Campaigns [...] There would have been more of life in that hour of Waterloo—more self-knowledge—more awakening of noble faculties in your soul [...] than in a long and wrinkling course of remunerative Mammon-worship'. This, the writer observes, in anticipation of Matthew Arnold's 1853 Preface to *Poems*, is 'an unheroic age'.[6] For *Blackwood's* the epitome of the 'unheroic' age is the Manchester manufacturer, Liberal MP, peace activist, and advocate of free-market capitalism, Richard Cobden. Cobden, who had played an active role in the international peace congresses of the late 1840s, and who introduced into the House of Commons a motion calling for the formation of treaties by which disputes could be adjudicated by impartial arbitrators (a motion that was defeated), had argued vociferously against the pessimistic view of war as a necessary evil. Claiming that war was against the interests of European mercantile society Cobden went on to court controversy as a fierce critic of British intervention in the Crimea. When looking, for instance, at Britain's commercial links with Russia and Turkey he compares the expanding nature of Anglo-Russian commerce with the limited scale of business with Turkey. Put simply, war against Russia makes bad financial sense.[7]

The *Blackwood's* writer's critique of Cobden's pacificism, which regards international diplomacy, legislation, and trade as the antidotes to barbarity, finds an analogue in De Quincey's 'On War', which offers, by way of an attack on the universalising tendencies of the commercial spirit, a rigorous defence of national self-interest:

> Every nation's duty, first, midst, and last, is to itself. No nation can be safe from continual (because insensible) losses of ground, but by continual jealousies, watchings, and ambitious strivings to mend its own position. Civilities and high-bred courtesies pass and ought to pass between nations; *that* is the graceful drapery which shrouds their natural, fierce, and tiger-like relations to each other. But the glaring eyes, which express this deep and

inalienable ferocity, look out at intervals from below those gorgeous draperies [...]' (*WTDQ* XVI. 277)

The idea that war can be abolished through an act of political will appears to De Quincey to be not only '*romantic*' (*WTDQ* XX. 31) but also atavistic. For, he argues, 'Banish war as now administered, and it will revolve upon us in a worse shape, that is, in a shape of predatory and ruffian war, more and more licentious' (XVI. 279). In anticipation of Freud's theorising in his 1933 essay 'Why War?', De Quincey regards hostility towards others as a safety valve for the discharge of internal violence, a defence against the return to some more 'lawless *guerrilla* state' of war. Were war to be forbidden, he continues, 'the only result of that prohibition would be to throw back the exercise of war from national into private and mercenary hands; and *that* is precisely the retrograde or inverted course of civilisation' (XVI. 279). War, therefore, is intrinsic to civilisation. As civilisation progresses, so war is 'exalted [...] from a horrid trade of butchery into a magnificent and enlightened science [...] cleansed from all horrors except those which [...] no longer stand out as reproaches to [man's] humanity' (*WTDQ* XVI. 288).

In the revised 1854 essay, picking up on his earlier comments on the transformation of war into an 'exalted' science, De Quincey commends war as 'an organ of respiration—for breathing a transcendent atmosphere, and dealing with an idea that else would perish—viz., the idea of mixed crusade and martyrdom, doing and suffering, that finds its realization in a battle such as that of Waterloo' (*WTDQ* XVI. 708). When this claim is read alongside the concluding section of the recently published *The English Mail-Coach* it becomes clear that De Quincey is seeking, like Wordsworth before him, to present Waterloo as the battle to end all battles, the apocalyptic finale to the endless cycle of victory and defeat that constitutes the pattern of human history.[8] That Waterloo cannot put an end to the ceaseless violence of national realisation is, nevertheless, the message that 'On War' drives home with remorseless insistence – a point enforced by the declaration of war in the Crimea.

Not long after De Quincey announced his sympathy with Wordsworth's controversial address to the Deity, a fellow survivor of the Romantic second generation would present an opposing perspective. In the 1849 reprint of the 1835 postscript to his anti-war poem, 'Captain Sword and Captain Pen', Leigh Hunt, in a passage that may well have prompted De Quincey to double down on his support for 'Carnage is thy daughter' for the 1854 version of 'On War', mounts an extended attack on Wordsworth's notorious lines. Bearing a dedication to Lord Brougham, the abolitionist, peace campaigner, and opposition contestant in the 1819 Westmorland election, 'Captain Sword and Captain Pen' can itself be read as a satire on Wordsworth's artistic and political decline, from the Jacobin champion of the rural poor and advocate of domestic tranquillity to the Tory campaigner and strident apologist for Waterloo. Overlooked in critical accounts of English Romanticism, the poem, as I have argued elsewhere, amplifies the central tropes of the anti-war poetry of the 1790s, in particular the attention given to the death and wounding of women and children and the destruction of the home, that Wordsworth, Southey, and Coleridge, once ardent in their opposition to war, would seek in their later years to discretely elide.[9] Following an extended quotation from a note documenting, in excruciating detail, the effects of war on civilians in Southey's 1797 ode 'To Horror', a poem that Hunt, in an earlier effort to embarrass Southey, had reprinted in the *Examiner* in 1816 as part of the series of 'Specimens of Early Jacobin Poetry', the postscript leaps forward to cite Wordsworth's offending lines from the 'Thanksgiving Ode', using the contrast between an expression of radical outrage and a declaration of instrumentalist acceptance, to destabilise the relation between 'then' and 'now' on which the poet's bid for cultural respectability depended.

If, in the 'Thanksgiving Ode', 'Carnage is thy daughter', together with the submission of Imagination to history's higher calling, was meant to confirm a necessitarian view of Waterloo, Hunt believed otherwise. In the 1849 postscript, serious fun is had with 'Carnage is thy daughter', to the point where the line's intended sublimity tips into the ridiculous:

> Men get rid of smaller evils which lie in their way—nay, of great ones; and there appears to be no reason why they should not get rid of the greatest, if they will but have the courage. We have abolished inquisitions and the rack, burnings for religion, burnings for witchcraft, hangings for forgery (a great triumph in a commercial country), much of the punishment of death in some countries, all of it in others. Why not abolish war? Mr Wordsworth writes no odes to tell us that the Inquisition was God's daughter; though Lope de Vega, who was one of its officers, might have done so—and Mr Wordsworth too, had he lived under its dispensation. Lope de Vega, like Mr Wordsworth and Mr Southey, was a good man, as well as a celebrated poet: and we will concede to his memory what the English poets will, perhaps, not be equally disposed to grant (for they are severe on the Romish faith) that even the Inquisition, *like War*, might possibly have had some utility in its evil, were it no other than a hastening of Christianity by its startling contradictions of it. Yet it has gone. The Inquisition, as War may be hereafter, is no more. Daughter if it was of the Supreme Good, it was no immortal daughter. Why should 'Carnage' be,—especially as God has put it in our heads to get rid of it?[10]

And further:

> Nobody tells us, when we attempt to put out a fire and to save the lives of our neighbours, that Conflagration is God's daughter, or Murder God's daughter. On the contrary, these are things which Christendom is taught to think ill of, and to wish to put down; and therefore we should put down war, which is murder and conflagration by millions.[11]

Hunt's 'unbounded' faith in progress and co-operation over the dead stop of 'Elemental necessity', finds its prosodical cognate in a piling up of rhetorical questions, qualifying clauses, illustrative quotations, and a potentially endless stream of supplementary notes and prefaces ('A Few More Words'; 'Further Remarks'), which have the effect of forestalling the drive to closure on which the necessitarian view of war is predicated.[12] Seeking to reanimate the spirit of playfulness that Wordsworth and De Quincey's late romanticism rescinds, Hunt's prose is directed towards a future that remains subject to change. From within this open-ended space, a space that can accommodate condemnation of the grisly excess of war – its violent intrusions into the bodies and minds of the innocent from which the prose does not flinch – as well as hope for the amelioration of 'this beautiful and most capable world',[13] Hunt speaks to the possibility of an alternative future for romanticism: a future no longer determined by the struggle for bare life, but by the promise of liberation.

A Desolation, a Simplicity

As if in response to Hunt's recollections of the liberatory potential of romanticism, in 1851 the appearance of Christopher Wordsworth's *Memoirs of William Wordsworth* drew renewed attention to the poet's radical years, describing Wordsworth's ardent hope, at the commencement of the French Revolution, that 'All ancient abuses were to be swept away; and a golden age of universal peace was about to succeed in its place: "Bliss was it in that dawn to be *alive*,/But to be *young* was very heaven!"'.[14] Drawing extensively on passages from the recently published *Prelude*, the memoir works hard to present Wordsworth's political trajectory as a development from Jacobin misadventure to loyalist acceptance, a narrative assisted by the 'late' poem's high Anglican and conservative reorientation. Among the passages Wordsworth reworked for the published version of the *Prelude* was a remnant of the '1300 lines' (*EY* 214) of blank verse that, in the spring of 1798, had marked the beginnings of that long philosophical poem, 'The Recluse'. Placed at the conclusion of Book 4 in manuscripts of the *Prelude* since 1804, 'The Discharged Soldier', with its unnerving account of a late-night encounter with a diseased and benumbed veteran of Britain's colonial wars, corresponds to the 'object' of 'The Recluse' 'to give pictures of Nature, Man, and Society' (*EY* 212), providing, along with the tale of Margaret's wartime fate, a spur for the activation of the poet's hopes for the dawn of universal peace.

Despite some unnecessary cuts to the description of the soldier in the original poem, the shock of the encounter with the 'ghastly figure' (IV. l. 434) is largely undiminished in the thirteen-book *Prelude*. However, following cuts and revisions in the 1830s, the poem that appeared in print in 1850 is much less striking than the 1798 *Recluse* and AB- and C-Stage *Prelude* versions – and perhaps deliberately so. What accounts for the later poem's strange diminution of affect? In all early versions of 'The Discharged Soldier' attention dwells on the contrast between the pacific assurances of the passage's opening scene and the disturbing encounter with the veteran. As the body of the poet, moving slowly along the moonlit road, draws from the surrounding stillness a 'restoration like the calm of sleep', his mind restored in turn to a state of Arcadian calm, the mood of tranquil 'self-possession' is abruptly disturbed by the sight of 'an uncouth shape' at a chance turning of the road. Such is the unnerving effect of this alien encounter that the poet retreats to the safety of a hawthorn bush.[15] Thus 'unseen' (l. 40), the poet initially surveys the soldier rather than engaging with him in a free and open communicative exchange, thereby replicating how society conspires to conceal itself from the knowledge of its violent origins. As the poem goes on to reveal, the discharged soldier turns out to be a double for the poet, his stillness, solitude, and air of 'half-absence' (l. 140) challenging the mood of 'self-possession' (l. 34) established by the opening lines, yet conforming, at the same time, to the poet's subsequent attitude of detached spectatorship, a subject position that protects the poet from the perils of over-identification. Appearing as neither one thing nor the other – 'Half-sitting, and half-standing'; 'faded yet entire'; 'half detached' (ll. 53–9; *passim*); 'sublime' yet 'unmoved' (ll. 139–42; *passim*) – the veteran persists in a state that appears estranged from the world. Flickering between gross, excessive physicality ('He was in stature tall,/A foot above man's common measure tall,/And lank, and upright', ll. 41–3) and spectral indeterminacy ('His legs were long,/So long and shapeless that I looked at them/Forgetful of the body they sustained', ll. 45–7), the man's form, as Mark Offord has argued, withdraws from even as it presents itself as an object of sympathy.[16]

When the poet eventually overcomes his 'specious cowardice' (l. 83) to greet the 'Stranger' (l. 85) and hence to draw him into a communicative relationship, the soldier relays his 'history' (l. 93) in a manner that appears deliberately to fall short of what might be expected of a wartime tale. Unmoved and with a 'stately air of mild indifference' (l. 96), the soldier abstains from vivid accounts of epic struggle and heroic self-sacrifice, preferring instead to recount a 'simple fact': that he had been dispatched to 'the tropic isles' from whence he had returned 'some ten days past' and, with 'what little strength he yet had left/Was travelling to regain his native home' (ll. 97–103; *passim*). The history is notable for its lack of stirring detail and for the teller's characteristic absence of affect, a dissociation from historical experience that may be read either as an elision of the harrowing truths of colonial warfare or as evidence of 'an alienation almost beyond imagining'.[17] Yet, despite the soldier's seeming 'indifference' to 'what he had endured/From war, and battle, and the pestilence' (ll. 136–7), the verse resonates with ominous murmurs, issuing from the brook (l. 11), from the soldier himself (l. 69 and l. 78), and again from the brook (l. 134). In *Paradise Lost*, murmuring is often used to signify insinuation and discontent: the demonic assembly murmurs approval for Mammon's counter-revolutionary speech (2. l. 284), and at the end of Book 4, Satan flees from Gabriel, 'murmuring' his defiance of the archangel's vision of heavenly judgement (l. 1015).[18] In concert with these unsettling, low frequency sounds, suggestive of inchoate, unvoiced disaffection, the veteran is disturbed by the howling of a 'chained mastiff' (l. 80; l. 130; l. 134), a war dog in 'his wooden house' (l. 80) who '"every second moment rang a peal/Felt at my heart"' (ll. 131–2). This, the soldier's only overt admission of psychological distress, becomes a cypher for how violence re-emerges in civil society, erasing the boundary between war and peace.

Subsisting at a remove from coherent expression, the sonic landscape of 'The Discharged Soldier' introduces dissonance into the world and, as such, sets a challenge: how can the noise of war, which brings conflict into the very fabric of nature, be silenced? The answer to this question is to be found in the poem's mounting concern with rehabilitation: to bring an end to the tumult and furore that infects the world, the 'murmuring voice of dead complaint' (l. 78) must be given a home. In the first instance, this imperative is treated as an artistic problem: how can that which is formless be made to harmonise with that opening mood in which meditative calm walks in lockstep with metrical harmony? The issue of how murmurings of complaint and howls of anger and frustration can be accommodated within a poem estranged from beauty, harmony, and self-possession is brought vividly to point when the poet declares: 'Long time I scann'd him with a mingled sense/Of fear and sorrow' (ll. 67–8). Relating observance of a document or thing to the analysis of poetic metre, 'scann'd' deepens the sense in which the soldier who, until greeted, remains 'Fixed to his place' (l. 76), and whose stillness disturbs the poet ('His shadow/Lay at his foot and moved not', ll. 71–2; 'I wished to see him move', l. 76), resists the business of placing one foot in front of the other so that order may be secured. Just as 'scann'd' is contracted to conform to the iambic pattern, so the soldier's recalcitrant body must be brought into step so that harmony can be restored to the world.

In a second, more literal sense, the soldier, to avoid further disturbance to the peaceful locale, must be moved forward and placed in a home. Thus, the poet and the soldier, discovering no prospect of rest in the village whose doors and windows remain 'silent' (l. 78; l. 107) and whose occupants are asleep – emblems of the worldly indifference to historical violence with which the poem is concerned – make their way to the dwelling of a labourer who, crucially, 'will not murmur should we break his rest' (l. 112). But while the focus of the poem broadens to encompass the conditions of charitable relief that ought to pertain by right for Britain's servicemen, the soldier appears, almost to the end, stubbornly resistant to the poet's offer of hospitality, to the extent that his claim to 'trust' solely 'in the God of Heaven/And in the eye of him that passes me' (ll. 161–2) could be heard as a refusal of the general economy of the gift that inscribes any act of hospitality within an economy of debt. The awareness of the impossibility of pure hospitality overshadows the poet's aside to the cottager: 'beneath your roof/This night let him find rest, and give him food—/The service if need be I will requite' (ll. 151–52), and subtly informs the 'reviving interest' (l. 167) with which the veteran, having at last accepted the offer of a bed for the night, thanks the poet for his pains.

In a challenging reading of the poem's conclusion, Offord qualifies Alan Bewell's claim that 'the poem follows the stations of an Enlightenment line of progress, from the "natural man" to "civilized and cultural humanity"', by arguing that the veteran, in his 'ghastly mildness' (l. 161), restates something of that uncouth being that cannot be accommodated within a social care system founded on 'mimetic sympathy'.[19] As if in recognition of the troubling persistence of the soldier's unhoused condition, the version of the poem that appeared in print in 1850 goes some way towards moderating the lengthy account of the veteran's disturbingly liminal appearance: no longer 'half-sitting, and half-standing' nor 'cut off [...] and more than half detached/From his own nature', the discharged soldier steps much sooner from the realm of the uncanny into the reassuring frame of the sentimental tale, in accordance with which the poet, prompted by 'pity' (l. 426), announces his intention to lead him to shelter.[20] On arrival at the cottage, the entreaty to offer 'charitable care' to 'a poor friendless Man' (l. 450–51) results in the 'speedy' unbarring of the door (l. 461), a gesture that speaks to the reassuring reciprocity of demand for and delivery of care that ought to pertain in a just society. But where previously Wordsworth had allowed space for the soldier's 'strange half-absence' and tone of 'weakness and indifference' to shadow the poem's conclusion, in the final version, the itinerant is all too swiftly placed behind closed doors. The suspicion that the 1850 version might, after all, be seeking to silence those dissonant notes that, from 1798 to 1820, had exposed the structure of exception on which domestic peace is founded, would seem, then, to be born out. In much the same way as the 1839 manifesto poem, 'The Power of Sound', had sought, via the crowning affirmation of the eternal WORD, to banish 'life's visionary stir', to silence 'man's noisy years', and thus to quell the 'rapturous strife' that had prevented the 'Immortality' ode from accomplishing its release from heretical discord, so the 1789 'Discharged Soldier' is made quiet not so that radical discord may be accommodated but so that it may be contained.[21]

In working towards this conclusion, the 1850 poem also seeks to erase a teasing ambiguity that had troubled all previous versions of the tale. As the published version makes clear, Wordsworth is keen to distinguish 'benign Solitude' (l. 357) from the condition of barren isolation experienced by the victims of war. In 1798 the soldier embodies 'A desolation, a simplicity/ That [appertained] to solitude' (l. 64); in 1850 the run-on line is altered to the thematically conventional and tonally underwhelming 'To which the trappings of a gaudy world/Make strange background' (ll. 402–03). If, in the original poem, the soldier's solitude provides an analogue to the exhausted poet who remembers the 'importance of his theme' (l. 143) but feels it no longer, what the published poem clarifies, but to the cost of the revealing ambiguity of the original, is how relief from stasis, considered as a phase of poetic inactivity, is diminished by bringing soldier and poet too swiftly to the conclusion of their journeys and by allowing the latter to depart 'with quiet heart' to a 'distant home' (l. 468).

What can be hoped for in a world that fails to perceive in the rehabilitation of the discharged soldier a reflection of its desire to persist in a state of endless war? In a passage from *The Arcades Project* Benjamin writes: '[a]s long as there is still one beggar around there will still be myth.' And so long as myth is maintained in the world, violence will continue.[22] Commenting on Benjamin's fragment, Adorno evokes the image of a child, lulled to sleep by the assurance that, warned off by the family dog, 'to the gate the beggar flees'.[23] In this allegory of the logic of the included/excluded other on which the stability of bourgeoise society depends, the beggar is never completely expelled; 'only with the last beggar's disappearance would myth be appeased'. Nevertheless, Adorno continues, concealed within the allegory is the hope that the reign of mythic violence will one day come to an end, leaving the beggar to 'find refuge in his homeland, freed from exile on earth'. Might the discharged soldier's trust in God, retained in the 1850 poem, testify to such hope? Despite the attempt to remodel the soldier's unknowability, to render the uncouth shape fit for social exchange, the persistence of this appeal to the coming of the Messianic Kingdom, and so to the suspension of the law that sustains poverty, suffering, and exile, retains its enigmatic charge.

***

As the contest between Hunt's and De Quincey's versions of Wordsworth's wartime afterlife should remind us, while the late poet sought to present his lifework in reified form as an unbroken historical continuity, to the extent, as Peter Larkin suggests, of devising strategies to discharge the potential of new writing to invalidate the proleptic expectations of the past, forces seeded in the poet's forelife would ensure that pulses of an older, contested history would continue to be felt in the present. One such example is the 1845 poem 'Suggested upon Loughrigg Fell'.[24] Much admired by contemporary readers, the verse was inspired by the poet's observation of a mountain daisy, casting the shadow of its 'star-shaped' (l. 5) crown on the smooth surface of a nearby stone. The sight raises thoughts of the 'pure sympathy' (l. 18) of nature and art, albeit framed as a work of fancy, granted fleetingly and only to those who subordinate their creative powers to the will of God. The 'faith' that, in 'Lines Written in Early Spring', had once impelled the poet to attribute consciousness to 'every flower' that 'breathes', and that continued to inform much of Wordsworth's poetry in the 1800s and 1810s, appears now to have dwindled to a contrived display of conjectural whimsy:

> So fair, so sweet, withal so sensitive,
> Would that the little Flowers were born to live,
> Conscious of half the pleasure which they give;
>
> That to this mountain-daisy's self were known
> The beauty of its star-shaped shadow, thrown
> On the smooth surface of this naked stone!
>
> And what if hence a bold desire should mount
> High as the sun, that he could take account
> Of all that issues from his glorious fount!

> So might he ken how by his sovereign aid
> These delicate companionships are made;
> And how he rules the pomp of light and shade;
>
> And were the Sister-power that shines by night
> So privileged, what a countenance of delight
> Would through the clouds break forth on human sight!
>
> Fond fancies! wheresoe'er shall turn thy eye
> On earth, air, ocean, or the starry sky,
> Converse with Nature in pure sympathy;
>
> All vain desires, all lawless wishes quelled,
> Be Thou to love and praise alike impelled,
> Whatever boon is granted or withheld. (ll. 1–21)

But if here Wordsworth exhibits a sceptical attitude to the 'Fond fancies' that animated his earlier daisy poems, moved perhaps by consciousness of the conservative views of those who accompanied the poet on his ascent of the fell – Archdeacon Julius Hare, the moral philosopher William Archer Butler, and the former 'staunch Berkeleyan' Sir William Hamilton[25] – there remains in the poem's affirmation of 'delicate companionships', and in its protracted evocation of the possible ('Would that [...] That to [...] were known [...] And what if [...] that [...] could [...] So might [...] And were [so] would'), a remembrance of that other world in which transient, profane life can at last recover its happiness.

Notes

Introduction

1 Here, I am influenced by Andrew Stauffer's erudite and moving account of the Victorian enthusiasm for placing botanical inserts in printed books: 'Found (and plucked) as flowers, saved (and then lost) as souvenirs, found again through chance encounters, and speaking primarily of loss (of the past, and of one's own mortality) when found – these bookish flowers signal both preservation and absence, their *fort-da* alternations seemingly overcharging them with nostalgia's recursive narratives'. *Book Traces: Nineteenth-Century Readers and the Future of the Library* (Philadelphia, PA: University of Pennsylvania Press, 2021), p. 53. Citing Michel de Certeau's commentary on history writing as 'a labor of death and a labor against death', Kevis Goodman writes in related vein of the elegiac status of historiography: 'It is a "labor against death" because the historiographer claims the epistemological compensation of knowledge and the aesthetic reward of historical form, but "of death" because de Certeau recognises that this recompense is always compromised, that conveying the past is also betraying it'. *Georgic Modernity and British Romanticism* (Cambridge: Cambridge University Press, 2004), p. 109.
2 Wordsworth, 'The Solitary Reaper', ll. 19–20. *'Poems, in Two Volumes', and Other Poems, 1800–1807*, ed. Jared Curtis (Ithaca, NY: Cornell University Press, 1983), pp. 184–5.
3 Stevie Smith, *The Holiday* (London: Virago, 1981), p. 31.
4 Wordsworth to Henry Crabb Robinson, 6 April 1826. LY I. 440. Lamb's observation is taken from the *Correspondence of Henry Crabb Robinson with the Wordsworth Circle*, ed. Edith J. Morley, 2 vols. (Oxford: Oxford University Press, 1927), I. 151–2.
5 'Ode. The Morning of the Day Appointed for a General Thanksgiving. January 18, 1816', ll. 163–7; *passim*. *Shorter Poems, 1807–1820*, ed. Carl H. Ketcham (Ithaca, NY, and London: Cornell University Press, 1989), pp. 180–9. See Simon Bainbridge's illuminating commentary on this passage in *Napoleon and English Romanticism* (Cambridge: Cambridge University Press, 1995), pp. 176–7, and 'Wordsworth, War and Waterloo', in *Wordsworth, War and Waterloo*, ed. Simon Bainbridge and Jeff Cowton (Grasmere: The Wordsworth Trust, 2015), pp. 16–28.

6 *Diary, Reminiscences, and Correspondence of Henry Crabb Robinson*, ed. Thomas Sadler, 3 vols. (London, 1869), III. 321–2.
7 Wordsworth to James Losh, 11 March 1798. *EY* 212.
8 *Last Poems, 1821–1850*, ed. Jared Curtis (Ithaca, NY, and London: Cornell University Press, 1999), pp. 59–60.
9 *Last Poems, 1821–1850*, ed. Curtis, p. 22.
10 William Shakespeare, *The Complete Sonnets and Poems*, ed. Colin Burrow (Oxford: Oxford University Press, 2002), p. 511.
11 A thoughtful and exacting account of Hegel's account of war and self-fashioning can be found in Michael J. Shapiro, *Violent Cartographies: Mapping Cultures of War* (Minneapolis, MN: University of Minnesota Press, 1997), pp. 41–5.
12 For commentary on how eighteenth-century thinkers distanced themselves from 'the codes of 'patriotism and honor that had imbued most previous writings on war', leading to 'the reframing of war as violence, suffering, and carnage', see Madelaine Dobie, 'The Enlightenment at War', *PMLA* 124.5 (2009), pp. 1851–4 (p. 1852).
13 Jean-Jacques Rousseau, 'The State of War', in *The Basic Political Writings*, 2nd edn., trans. Donald A. Cress (New York: Hackett, 2011), pp. 253–65 (p. 256). Published in 1761, appearing in English translation in the same year, and republished in 1767, 1774, and 1795, Rousseau's abstract of Abbé Saint-Pierre's 1713 treatise *Projet pour rendre la paix perpétuelle en Europe*, and his posthumously published critique of the *Projet*, shows further the extent of Rousseau's simultaneous admiration for and suspicion of absolutist and utopian plans for universal perpetual peace. See 'The Plan for Perpetual Peace, on the Government of Poland, and Other Writings on History and Politics', in *The Collected Writings of Rousseau*, ed. Roger D. Masters and Christopher Kelly; trans. Christopher Kelly and Judith Bush, 14 vols. (Hanover: University Press of New England at Dartmouth College, 2005), XI. 25–49.
14 Ibid., p. 254. For excellent commentary on the aporia at the heart of Rousseau's account of peace, war, nature, and the social contract see Chris Washington, 'Romantic Postapocalyptic Politics: Reveries of Rousseau, Derrida, and Meillassoux in a World without Us', in *Romanticism and Speculative Realism*, ed. Chris Washington and Anne C. McCarthy (New York and London: Bloomsbury, 2019), pp. 133–56.
15 Immanuel Kant, *Critique of Judgement*, ed. and trans. Walter S. Pluhar (Indianapolis, IN: Hackett Publishing, 1987), p. 122.
16 Ibid., p. 320.
17 Ibid., p. 122.
18 Immanuel Kant, 'Perpetual Peace, A Philosophical Sketch' (1795), in *Political Writings*, 2nd edn., ed. H. S. Reiss, trans. H. B. Nisbet (Cambridge: Cambridge University Press, 1991), pp. 93–130 (p. 93). Kant's essay appeared in English, first in 1796 in an edition published by Vernor and Hood and then in 1798 in *Essays and Treatises on Moral, Political, and Various Philosophical Subjects, by E. Kant* […], trans. J. Richardson, 2 vols. (London, 1798–9). For discussion

of the English reception of Kant's essay see Monika Class, *Coleridge and Kantian Ideas in England, 1796–1817: Coleridge's Responses to German Philosophy* (London: Bloomsbury, 2012), pp. 93–120.
19 Peter Melville, *Romantic Hospitality and the Resistance to Accommodation* (Waterloo: Wilfred Laurier University Press, 2007), p. 86.
20 Ibid., p. 87. Derrida's commentary on the trace of violence in Kant's 'Perpetual Peace' can be found in *Adieu to Emmanuel Levinas*, trans. Pascale-Anne Brault and Michael Naas (Stanford, CA: Stanford University Press, 1999), pp. 88–101. See also 'Hostipitality', *Angelaki* 5.3 (2000), pp. 3–18, and *Cosmopolitanism and Forgiveness*, trans. Mark Dooley and Michael Hughes (London and New York: Routledge, 2001).
21 Thomas Beddoes, 'Kant: Zum Ewigen Frieden', *Monthly Review* 20 (1796), pp. 486–90. For discussion of Beddoes's reading of Kant's essay, see Class, *Coleridge and Kantian Ideas in England, 1796–1817*, pp. 99–101. The background to the distinction between negative and positive peace is advanced by Johan Galtung, 'Violence, Peace, and Peace Research', *Journal of Peace Research* 6.3 (1969), pp. 167–91. John Bugg presents a detailed and persuasive reading of how the movement for positive peace was advanced by Romantic period writers and activists in *British Romanticism and Peace* (Oxford: Oxford University Press, 2022). For general discussion of the representation of peace in English writing see R. S. White, *Pacifism and English Literature: Minstrels of Peace* (Basingstoke: Palgrave Macmillan, 2008).
22 Debates on the comparative merits of Wordsworth's early and late poetry were initiated by Richard Hutton in a paper delivered to the Wordsworth Society in 1882: 'The Earlier and Later Styles of Wordsworth', in *Wordsworthiana: A Selection from Papers Read to the Wordsworth Society*, ed. William Angus Knight (London, 1889), pp. 61–78. With the passing exception of Edith Batho's vigorous defence of Wordsworth's late poetry in *The Later Wordsworth* (Cambridge: Cambridge University Press, 1933) and Geoffrey Hartman's and William Galperin's thoughtful and occasionally provocative pronouncements on selected late poems, the idea that Wordsworth's later poetry marked a falling off from the visionary power of the early work has remained largely unchallenged. Two recent studies, Tim Fulford, *Wordsworth's Poetry, 1815–1845* (Philadelphia, PA: University of Pennsylvania Press, 2019) and Jeffrey C. Robinson, *Poetic Innovation in Wordsworth's Poetry, 1825–1833: Fibres of These Thoughts* (London: Anthem Press, 2019), look set to significantly modify this idea. See Geoffrey H. Hartman, *Wordsworth's Poetry, 1787–1814* (New Haven, CT: Yale University Press, 1964), pp. 325–8, and the essays on the late verse collected in *The Unremarkable Wordsworth* (Minneapolis, MN: University of Minnesota Press, 1987): 'Blessing the Torrent', pp. 75–89; 'Words, Wish, Worth', pp. 90–119; 'Diction and Defence', pp. 120–8. See also William H. Galperin, *Revision and Authority in Wordsworth: The Interpretation of a Career* (Philadelphia, PA: University of Pennsylvania Press, 1989).
23 See Tim Fulford, *Landscape, Liberty and Authority: Poetry, Criticism and Politics from Thomson to Wordsworth* (Cambridge: Cambridge University Press, 1996),

p. 163. On Coleridge's opposition to war in the 1790s and his change to a prowar position in the 1800s see Dorothy A. Stansfield, 'A Note on the Genesis of Coleridge's Thinking on War and Peace', *The Wordsworth Circle* 17.3 (Summer 1986), pp. 130–34; Charles de Paolo, 'Kant, Coleridge and the Ethics of War', *The Wordsworth Circle* 16.1 (1985), pp. 3–12.

24 The number of books that engage with the turn towards conservatism in Wordsworth's politics is vast, but James K. Chandler, *Wordsworth's Second Nature: A Study of the Poetry and Politics* (Chicago: The University of Chicago Press, 1984) and Fulford, *Wordsworth's Poetry, 1815–1845*, while very different in focus and approach, understand that Wordsworth's engagement with contemporary political affairs cannot be reduced to a case study of radical apostacy.

25 'Fragment ["There is an active principle alive in all things"]', ll. 1–15 (*c.* 1798–1800). *'Lyrical Ballads', and Other Poems, 1797–1800*, ed. James Butler and Karen Green (Ithaca, NY, and London: Cornell University Press, 1992), pp. 309–10. The material is adapted after 1800 for *The Excursion*, Book IX, ll. 1–152.

26 For the historical background to the emergence of organised peace societies in Britain in the late eighteenth and early nineteenth centuries see J. E. Cookson, *The Friends of Peace: Anti-war Liberalism in England, 1793–1815* (Cambridge: Cambridge University, 1982) and Martin Ceadel, *The Origins of War Prevention: The British Peace Movement and International Relations, 1730–1854* (Oxford: Oxford University Press, 1996), chapter 6.

27 The phrase is used by Wordsworth in correspondence with Francis Wrangham, 26 April 1814. *MY* II. 144.

28 William Hazlitt, 'Character of Mr Wordsworth's New Poem, *The Excursion*'. Originally published in three parts in *The Examiner*, 21 August 1814, 28 August 1814, and 2 October 1814. *CWWH* XIX. 9–25 (18).

29 'Strangeness' is the quality that Hartman ascribes consistently to Wordsworth's late poetry. See *Wordsworth's Poetry, 1787–1814*, p. 331, and *The Unremarkable Wordsworth*, p. 83.

30 'The effect even of genuine sublimity, therefore, is impaired by the injudicious frequency of its exhibition, and the omission of those intervals and breathing-places, at which the mind should be permitted to recover from its perturbation or astonishment'. From a review of Southey's *Thalaba*, *The Edinburgh Review* 1 (October 1802), p. 70. Cited by Jerome C. Christensen, *Romanticism: At the End of History* (Baltimore, MD: Johns Hopkins University Press, 2000), p. 113.

31 *'Poems, in Two Volumes', and Other Poems, 1800–1807*, ed. Curtis, pp. 65–9.

32 Epigraph added in 1815. As quoted in *'Poems, in Two Volumes', and Other Poems, 1800–1807*, ed. Curtis, p. 65.

33 Jacques Khalip, 'Dead Calm: The Melancholy of Peace', *The New Centennial Review* 11.1 (Spring 2011), pp. 243–75 (p. 251).

34 Khalip discusses the contours of this feeling at length in 'Dead Calm: The Melancholy of Peace', invoking Christensen's 'temporality of peace' in which 'postwar survival' becomes 'a continuation of wartime, a conservative mode

of exhausted living that "presupposes no future of its own" and generates no capacity for progress. Such peace convalesces – it hopes for the return of a time that was, a time of "robust, belligerent health"', p. 249. Quotations from Christensen, *Romanticism: At the End of History*, p. 7.

35 Immanuel Kant, *Religion and Rational Theology*, ed. Allen Wood and George di Giovanni (Cambridge: Cambridge University Press, 2001), p. 202.

36 The broadly positive responses of British authors to the announcement of the Peace of Amiens are described by J. R. Watson in *Romanticism and War: A Study of British Romantic Period Writers and the Napoleonic Wars* (Houndmills: Palgrave Macmillan, 2003), pp. 84–90.

37 Despite the chalk-emblazoned coaches, festive transparencies, and painted signs, concerns remained that the peace would lead to a slackening of the nation's moral character. From the signing of the peace preliminaries onwards, journalists sympathetic to Pitt's view that the war against France had taken on an ideological character and should thus be prosecuted with the utmost severity lest the nation sink into degeneracy maintained their influence. See, for example, John Bowles, *Reflections at the Conclusion of the War* (London, 1801): 'when the paroxysm of joy, which has been produced by the unexpected arrival of a most ardently desired event shall be over, it will be found that the Peace, which is the subject of so much exultation, is at best but a bold and hazardous experiment', p. 2. While an uneasy alliance of radicals, Foxites, and pro-Addington Tories remained resolute in their defence of the social, economic, and moral benefits of the peace, the pro-war faction continued to express dissatisfaction with the terms of the peace. As one preacher gloomily pronounced, 'the arts of peace [...] are not without their snares. If they promote the comforts, they also minister, and often fatally, to the luxuries, and the vices of mankind [...] it is well if they do not enervate the corporeal and mental faculties, or alienating the affections from higher and nobler objects, direct them to sordid and unworthy concerns'. Samuel Butler, *The Effects of Peace on the Religious Principle Considered. A Sermon, Preached in the Chapel of Berwick, on Tuesday, June 1, 1802, Being the Day Appointed by Proclamation for a General Thanksgiving* (Shrewsbury, 1802), p. 18. That national antipathies might be exacerbated rather than vanquished by the peace was also widely expressed. Thus, for example, the author of *A Review of the French Revolution* complained of 'the fatal mischiefs occasioned by long peace and prosperity' that 'by spreading corruption through the whole community' must lead to civil war. William Cameron, *A Review of the French Revolution* (Edinburgh and London, 1802), pp. 1–2. For a nuanced account of how writing of the period gave vent to fears that the end of the peace would grant license to the forces of reaction to double down on the repression of revolutionary politics, see Jeffrey N. Cox, *Romanticism in the Shadow of War: Literary Culture in the Napoleonic War Years* (Cambridge: Cambridge University Press, 2014), pp. 26–7; pp. 56–7. See also John Bugg's scholarly defence of the Peace of Amiens and his sympathetic readings of the literature of the peace in chapter 2 of *British Romanticism and Peace*.

38 Between December 1801 and April 1802, Wordsworth returned to the composition of 'The Pedlar', from which these lines, added to the MS D addendum in 1799, are taken. Omitted from the 1802 version of 'The Pedlar', the lines eventually become *Excursion*, IV, ll. 1207–98. Transcription of Additions to 'The Ruined Cottage', MS. D, 68ᵛ, ll. 1–28; *passim*. *The Ruined Cottage and The Pedlar*, ed. James Butler (Ithaca, NY: Cornell University Press, 1979), p. 374. The 'one life' passage from MS. D 64ʳ, ll. 1–27, was added to the 1799 *Prelude*, ll. 446–64. *The Prelude, 1789–1799*, ed. Stephen Parrish (Ithaca, NY: Cornell University Press, 1977).

39 Gregory Leadbetter, 'The Lyric Impulse of *Poems, in Two Volumes*', in *The Oxford Handbook of William Wordsworth*, ed. Richard Gravil and Daniel Robinson (Oxford: Oxford University Press, 2015), pp. 221–36 (p. 227).

40 Fears of enervation attendant upon the end of war are endemic in religious, political, and philosophical writings of the period. Jacques Derrida's commentary on Levinas, from which the notion of peace as the 'silent horizon' of speech is taken, is perhaps the most recent example of how critical thought attempts to negotiate the idea that 'war dies out only at the end of discourse'. Derrida, *Writing and Difference*, trans. Alan Bass (London: Routledge & Kegan Paul, 1978), p. 117.

41 Ibid., p. 37.

42 For further discussion of the liberatory potential of Fancy in Romantic poetry see Jeffrey C. Robinson, *Unfettering Poetry: The Fancy in British Romanticism* (Basingstoke: Palgrave Macmillan, 2006). Robinson maintains that for Wordsworth in the 1815 Preface, Fancy, for all its 'considerable vitality', remains in the shadow of Imagination (p. 31).

43 Note on 'The Thorn'. *'Lyrical Ballads', and Other Poems, 1797–1800*, ed. Butler and Green, pp. 350–2 (p. 351).

44 Ibid., 33.

45 Ibid., 36.

46 Kelly Grovier, '"Shades of the Prison House": "Walking" Stewart, Michel Foucault and the Making of Wordsworth's "Two Consciousnesses"', *Studies in Romanticism* 44.3 (Fall 2005), pp. 341–66 (p. 345). As Grovier recounts, Wordsworth met 'Walking' Stewart in Paris in the autumn of 1792. Impressed by his 'eloquence' 'on the subject of nature', Wordsworth, according to De Quincey, agreed that Stewart was 'by instinct' 'a true philosopher', p. 344.

47 David Fairer, *Organising Poetry: The Coleridge Circle, 1790–1798* (Oxford: Oxford University Press, 2009), pp. 53–4.

48 'Lines Written a Few Miles above Tintern Abbey, on Revisiting the Banks of the Wye during a Tour, July 13, 1798', ll. 82–3. *'Lyrical Ballads', and Other Poems, 1797–1800*, ed. Butler and Green, pp. 116–20.

49 For Spinoza, 'the actual essence of the thing [res]' is that 'each thing strives [conatur] to persevere in its being'. Benedict de Spinoza, *Ethics*, ed. and trans. Edwin Curley (London: Penguin, 1996), III. p. 6 (p. 75). *Conatus* thus names a power that is shared by human and non-human entities. As Jane Bennett comments, 'Spinoza's conative bodies are also associative' or 'social bodies, in the

sense that each is, by its very nature as a body, continuously affecting and being affected by other bodies'. Further, since 'modes' are assemblages or mosaics of 'simple bodies' it no longer makes sense to think of individual things as autonomous, inviolable singularities. See *Vibrant Matter: A Political Ecology of Things* (Durham and London: Duke University Press, 2010), pp. 21–2. 'Lines Written in Early Spring', ll. 17–18. *'Lyrical Ballads', and Other Poems, 1797–1800*, ed. Butler and Green, p. 76.

50 Spinoza, *Ethics*, Lı. p. 97 (p. 41).
51 Marjorie Levinson, 'A Motion and a Spirit: Romancing Spinoza', *Studies in Romanticism* 46.4 (Winter 2007), pp. 367–408 (p. 377). Here it is worth noting 'Walking' Stewart's later political writings, which set radical critique of the 'feuds and wars of local and selfish interest' and advocacy of equality and freedom within eccentric and increasingly authoritarian proposals for social reform. See John Stewart, *The Apocalypse of Human Perfectuability [sic.], to Consummate the Great Science of Man and Nature, as Revealed in the Opus Maximum* (London, 1808), pp. 11–12. For commentary on the development of Stewart's thought see Gregory Claeys, '"The Only Man of Nature That Ever Appeared in the World": "Walking" John Stewart and the Trajectories of Social Radicalism, 1790–1822', *Journal of British Studies* 53.3 (July 2014), pp. 636–59.
52 *'Poems, in Two Volumes', and Other Poems, 1800–1807*, ed. Curtis, pp. 238–9.
53 'Nam fuit ante Helenam cunnus taeterrima belli/causa'. 'Satire 1', 3, ll. 107–8. *Horace: Satires*, trans. Emily Gowers (Cambridge: Cambridge University Press, 2012), p. 40.
54 In *The Writing of the Disaster*, Maurice Blanchot provides a suggestive account of the event that 'takes no account of being or not-being [...] it is the advent of what does not happen, of what would come without arriving', of that which is 'outside being'. Maurice Blanchot, *The Writing of the Disaster*, trans. Ann Smock (Lincoln, NE: University of Nebraska Press, 1995), p. 5. In Blanchot's sense, peace remains 'outside being' because the very possibility of being has been denied. For commentary germane to this discussion see David Collings, 'Blank Oblivion, Condemned Life: John Clare's "Obscurity"', in *Romanticism and Speculative Realism*, ed. Washington and McCarthy, pp. 75–92 (pp. 83–4).
55 See John Milton, *Paradise Lost*, ed. Alastair Fowler (London: Longman, 1971), Book IV, ll. 260–8 (l. 268); William Cowper, *The Task and Selected Other Poems*, ed. James Sambrook (London and New York: Longman, 1994), Book VI, ll. 759–77 (l. 770).
56 *The Fenwick Notes of William Wordsworth*, ed. Jared Curtis (Tirril: Humanities-Ebooks, 2007), p. 113.
57 For reflections on the role of the apostle during the end of days, relevant to this discussion, see Giorgio Agamben, *The Time That Remains: A Commentary on the Letter to the Romans*, trans. Patricia Dailey (Stanford, CA: Stanford University Press, 2005), p. 68.
58 *'Poems, in Two Volumes', and Other Poems, 1800–1807*, ed. Curtis, pp. 608–14.

59 *The Letters of John Wordsworth*, ed. Carl H. Ketcham (Ithaca, NY: Cornell University Press, 1969), p. 112.
60 Here I am influenced by Spinoza's veiled critique of Hobbes in *Political Treatise*, trans. Samuel Shirley (Indianapolis, IN, and Cambridge: Hackett, 2000), p. 62. The far-reaching implications of this critique are explored by Antonio Negri in 'Peace and War', in *Empire and Beyond*, trans. Ed Emery (Cambridge: Polity, 2008), pp. 53–63.
61 Walter Benjamin, *Toward the Critique of Violence: A Critical Edition*, ed. Peter Fenves and Julia Ng (Stanford, CA: Stanford University Press, 2021), p. 50.
62 Ibid., pp. 57–8. For further discussion of the relationship between language, conflict resolution, and divine violence in Benjamin's thought see Judith Butler, *The Force of Non-violence: An Ethico-political Bind* (London and New York: Verso, 2020), pp. 122–41.
63 Giorgio Agamben, *Idea of Prose*, trans. Michael Sullivan and Sam Whitsitt (Albany, NY: SUNY Press, 1995), pp. 81–2.
64 Ibid., p. 82.
65 Helmut Illbruck, *Nostalgia: Origins and Ends of an Unenlightened Disease* (Evanston, IL: Northwestern University Press, 2012). See also Philip Shaw, 'Longing for Home: Robert Hamilton, Nostalgia and the Emotional Life of the Eighteenth-Century Soldier', *Journal for Eighteenth-Century Studies* 39.1 (2016), pp. 25–40.
66 Agamben, *Idea of Prose*, p. 82.
67 For insight into the relations between wartime suffering and social care relevant to this discussion, see Neil Ramsey, *Romanticism and the Biopolitics of Modern War Writing* (Cambridge: Cambridge University Press, 2022).
68 *The Augustan Review* 1 (May–December 1815), pp. 343–56 (p. 345).
69 *Quarterly Review* 14 (October 1815), pp. 201–25 (p. 208).
70 Paul Fussell, *The Great War and Modern Memory* (Oxford: Oxford University Press, 1975/2000), p. 79.
71 'The Poet for 1916'. *Hull Daily Mail* 9360 (5 October 1915), p. 6. In Britain, the war years were marked by a growth of interest in Wordsworth's patriotic poetry, initiated in 1914 by Frederick Samuel Boas's essay *Wordsworth's Patriotic Poems and Their Significance Today* (London: The English Association, Pamphlet 30, 1914), followed by Arthur H. D. Acland's *The Patriotic Poetry of William Wordsworth: A Selection* (Oxford: Clarendon Press, 1915) and Albert Venn Dicey's *The Statesmanship of Wordsworth: An Essay* (Oxford: Clarendon Press, 1917).
72 Edmund Blunden, *Undertones of War* (Harmondsworth: Penguin, 1982), p. 245.
73 Wordsworth, 'I would not strike a flower', ll. 1–12. '*Lyrical Ballads', and Other Poems, 1797–1800*, ed. Butler and Green, pp. 312–14.
74 '*Poems, in Two Volumes', and Other Poems, 1800–1807*, ed. Curtis, pp. 77–9.
75 Simon Bainbridge, *British Poetry and the Revolutionary and Napoleonic Wars: Visions of Conflict* (Oxford: Oxford University Press, 2003), p. 97. As Bainbridge and Philip Martin have noted, Wordsworth's poem responds also to Robert Southey's 'The Sailor's Mother' (1799), a poem that itself responds

to the figure of the intermediary in 'Old Man Travelling'. Bainbridge argues that Wordsworth's description of the sailor's mother, 'Majestic in her person [...] And like a Roman matron[...]' (ll. 6–7), 'fulfils exactly the function that the "good old cause" of English republicanism will serve in the sonnets' and that the poem refigures the sailor's mother 'for the period of the invasion threat'. It should, however, be noted, that the date of composition situates the poem as a response to the peace, rather than as an expression of that 'ancient Spirit' on which England's defence will depend. See pp. 96–7. Also, Philip Martin, *Mad Women in Romantic Writing* (Brighton and New York: Harvester Press and St Martin's Press, 1987), p. 76.

76 'The Barberry-Tree', l. 113. *'Poems, in Two Volumes', and Other Poems, 1800–1807*, ed. Curtis, pp. 576–9.

77 *'Poems, in Two Volumes', and Other Poems, 1800–1807*, ed. Curtis, p. 137.

78 See Ovid, *Metamorphoses*, trans. A. D. Melville (Oxford: Oxford University Press, 1986), Book 5, pp. 116–18.

79 Timothy Morton, *Hyperobjects: Philosophy and Ecology at the End of the World* (Minneapolis, MN, and London: University of Minnesota Press, 2013), pp. 146–7.

80 For an account of the fate of the volume's 'advertisement' and the likely decisions that led to the printing of the Virgilian motto on the title page see: *'Poems, in Two Volumes', and Other Poems, 1800–1807*, ed. Curtis, pp. 26–7.

81 Brian Folker, 'Wordsworth's Visionary Imagination: Democracy and War', *ELH* 69.1 (Spring 2002), pp. 167–97 (p. 180).

82 *'Poems, in Two Volumes', and Other Poems, 1800–1807*, ed. Curtis, pp. 271–7.

83 Marjorie Levinson, *Wordsworth's Great Period Poems: Four Essays* (Cambridge: Cambridge University Press, 1986), pp. 83–9.

84 'Calais, August 15th, 1802', l. 11. *'Poems, in Two Volumes', and Other Poems, 1800–1807*, ed. Curtis, pp. 158–9.

85 Michel Foucault, *Society Must Be Defended: Lectures at the Collège de France, 1975–76*, ed. Mauro Bertani and Alessandro Fontana, trans. David Macey (London: Penguin, 2003), p. 51.

86 Eric C. Walker, *Marriage, Writing and Romanticism: Wordsworth and Austen after War* (Stanford, CA: Stanford University Press, 2009).

87 Readings of the Calais sonnets that bear on this discussion include: Alan Liu, *Wordsworth: The Sense of History* (Stanford, CA: Stanford University Press, 1989), pp. 428–36; Stephen C. Behrendt, 'Placing the Places in Wordsworth's 1802 Sonnets', *Studies in English Literature, 1500–1900* 35.4 (1994), pp. 641–57; Judith W. Page, *Wordsworth and the Cultivation of Women* (Berkeley, CA: University of California Press, 1994), pp. 54–76; Bainbridge, *British Poetry and the Revolutionary and Napoleonic Wars*, pp. 99–119.

88 'To a Friend, Composed near Calais, on the Road leading to Andres, August 7th, 1802', l. 4; l. 11. 'It is a beauteous evening calm and free', l. 12. *'Poems, in Two Volumes', and Other Poems, 1800–1807*, ed. Curtis, pp. 156–7; pp. 150–1.

89 Judith Page observes how the strong and, for Wordsworth, uncharacteristic, line break at the end of line 8 ('A sound like thunder – everlastingly./ Dear Child! Dear Girl! that walkest with me here [...]', ll. 8–9) 'divides the child from the divinity of the scene created in the octave'. By means of this formal separation and the allusion to the sacrificial and eschatological significance of 'Abraham's bosom', 'Wordsworth not only disavows his paternity in this sonnet, but he also symbolically kills the child'. *Wordsworth and the Cultivation of Women*, pp. 64–5.
90 Ibid., pp. 162–3.
91 *Morning Post* 10774 (16 April 1803), pp. 2–3.
92 *'Poems, in Two Volumes', and Other Poems, 1800–1807*, ed. Curtis, pp. 157–8.
93 Ibid., p. 150.
94 Ibid., pp. 164–5.
95 Ibid., pp. 166–7.
96 Ibid., p. 170.
97 Ibid., p. 171.
98 Ibid., p. 173.
99 See the transcription and photographic reproduction of MS. D (DC MS. 76) in *Home at Grasmere. Part First, Book First, of The Recluse*, ed. Beth Darlington (Ithaca, NY: Cornell University Press, 1977), p. 413.
100 *The Excursion*, ed. Sally Bushell, James A. Butler, and Michael C. Jaye (Ithaca, NY, and London: Cornell University Press, 2007).
101 Spinoza, *Ethics*, 'Definition of the Affects', XII (p. 106).
102 John Wilson, 'Essays on the Lake School of Poetry. No. 1. Wordsworth's *White Doe of Rylstone*'. *Blackwood's Edinburgh Magazine* III (July 1818), pp. 369–81 (pp. 380–1).
103 Ibid., p. 381.
104 'The Force of Prayer; or the Founding of Bolton Priory. A Tradition', l. 1. *The White Doe of Rylstone*, ed. Kristine Dugas (Ithaca, NY, and London: Cornell University Press, 1988), pp. 147–9 (p. 147).
105 *Shorter Poems, 1807–1820*, ed. Ketcham, p. 188.
106 P. B. Shelley, 'Verses Written on Receiving a Celandine in a Letter from England', ll. 57–8; l. 30. *Selected Poems and Prose*, ed. Jack Donovan and Cian Duffy (London: Penguin, 2016), pp. 132–3.
107 *Shorter Poems, 1807–1820*, ed. Ketcham, pp. 200–1 (p. 200).
108 'Occasioned by the Same Battle. *February* 1816', l. 10. *Shorter Poems, 1807–1820*, ed. Ketcham, p. 172.
109 For the idea of the peaceable commonwealth, see Spinoza, *Political Treatise*: 'For peace is not just the absence of war, but a virtue which comes from strength of mind: for obedience is the steadfast will to carry out orders enjoined by the general decree of the commonwealth', p. 62. This notion is explored further in Chapter 4.
110 *Ecclesiastical Sketches*. Part II. 'XIV. Dissolution of the Monasteries', l. 4. *Sonnet Series and Itinerary Poems, 1820–1845*, ed. Geoffrey Jackson (Ithaca, NY, and London: Cornell University Press, 2004), p. 171.

111 'After Visiting the Field of Waterloo', l. 14. *Sonnet Series and Itinerary Poems, 1820–1845*, ed. Jackson, p. 361.
112 *TWDQ* XVI. 269–88 (278).

Chapter 1 Conscripting 'The Recluse'

1 Among prominent Whigs, opposition to the restoration of the Bourbon monarchy was confined to a minority of Foxites and liberals, such as Charles Grey and Henry Holland. Surprisingly, the notable radical member Samuel Whitbread declared cautious support for the restoration. See Rory Muir, *Britain and the Defeat of Napoleon, 1807–1815* (New Haven, CT, and London: Yale University Press, 1996), p. 328.
2 For discussion of the spectrum of attitudes to Napoleon's abdication and the ensuing peace see Stuart Semmel, *Napoleon and the British* (New Haven, CT, and London: Yale University Press, 2004), pp. 147–58.
3 *Monthly Magazine* 37 (July 1814), p. 553. Quoted in Semmel, *Napoleon and the British*, pp. 156–7.
4 *The Times* 9178 (25 March 1814), p. 3.
5 *The Excursion*, ed. Bushell, Butler, and Jaye, p. 37. All quotations from *The Excursion* are from this edition. Wordsworth sought formal permission for the dedication to Lord Lonsdale on 14 June 1814. *MY* II. 148–9.
6 See Jeffrey N. Cox's detailed and exacting account of how Shelley, Byron, Hazlitt, and members of the Cockney School responded to *The Excursion* in *William Wordsworth, Second-Generation Romantic: Contesting Poetry after Waterloo* (Cambridge: Cambridge University Press, 2021).
7 *Collected Letters of Samuel Taylor Coleridge*, ed. Earl Leslie Griggs, 6 vols. (Oxford: Oxford University Press, 1956–71), IV. 574–5.
8 John Finch persuasively argues that these poems make up the 1,300 lines of the long poem that Wordsworth initiated in 1798. See 'Wordsworth, Coleridge, and "The Recluse," 1789-1814', doctoral thesis (Ithaca, NY: Cornell University, 1964) and *Bicentenary Studies in Memory of John Alban Finch*, ed. Jonathan Wordsworth (Ithaca, NY: Cornell University Press, 1970), pp. 14–15.
9 See *'Lyrical Ballads', and Other Poems, 1797–1800*, ed. Butler and Green, pp. 309–16.
10 *The Prelude, 1789–1799*, ed. Parrish.
11 Hazlitt, 'On the Late War', 3 April 1814, *CWWH* VII. 72–6 (72). Hazlitt's determination to discover hope in the Solitary's despair foreshadows the redemptive view of failed revolutionary action announced in Walter Benjamin's 'Theses on the Philosophy of History'. Commenting on Benjamin's idea of historical redemption, Giorgio Agamben writes: 'What cannot be saved is what was, the past as such. But what is saved is what never was, something new [...] in historical redemption what happens in the end is what never took place. This is what is saved'. 'Walter Benjamin and the Demonic: Happiness and Historical Redemption', in *Potentialities: Collected Essays in Philosophy*, trans. Daniel Heller Roazen (Stanford, CA: Stanford University Press, 1999), p. 158.

12 *Home at Grasmere*, ed. Darlington, l. 169. Unless stated otherwise, quotations from this poem are taken from the MS. B manuscript.
13 *The Speculative Turn: Continental Materialism and Realism*, ed. Levi Bryant, Nick Srnicek, and Graham Harman (Melbourne: re-press, 2011), p. 3.
14 The title given to the final draft of the poem. See the transcription and photographic reproduction of MS. D (DC MS. 76) in *Home at Grasmere*, ed. Darlington, p. 413.
15 Kenneth R. Johnston, *Wordsworth and 'The Recluse'* (New Haven, CT, and London: Yale University Press, 1984), pp. 88–9.
16 Note on 'The Thorn'. *'Lyrical Ballads', and Other Poems, 1797–1800*, ed. Butler and Green, p. 351.
17 Kevis Goodman, '"Uncertain Disease": Nostalgia, Pathologies of Motion, Practices of Reading', *Studies in Romanticism* 49.2 (Summer 2010), pp. 197–227 (p. 220).
18 Clare's pleasure in listing the objects he perceives in nature can be understood in terms of ontography, a term used in object-oriented ontology to describe the many and varied forms of being and their interconnectedness. For Ian Bogost, 'Ontographical cataloging hones a virtue: the abandonment of anthropocentric narrative coherence in favor of worldly detail'. See *Alien Phenomenology, or What It's Like to Be a Thing* (Minneapolis, MN, and London: University of Minnesota Press, 2012), pp. 41–2.
19 Book IV. l. 321; l. 774.
20 Derrida's critique of Levinas is apposite here: 'according to Levinas, nonviolent language would be a language without the verb *to be*, that is without predication. Predication is the first violence.' *Writing and Difference*, pp. 146–8. The deconstruction of the performative-constitutive distinction is explored by Derrida in 'Signature Event Context', in *Margins of Philosophy*, trans. Alan Bass (Chicago: University of Chicago Press, 1982), pp. 307–30.
21 Johnston, *Wordsworth and 'The Recluse'*, pp. 231–2.
22 Here I am inspired by Theresa Kelley's persuasive commentary on these lines in *Wordsworth's Revisionary Aesthetics* (Cambridge: Cambridge University Press, 1988), pp. 44–5.
23 Derrida, *Writing and Difference*, p. 130.
24 'Among the chief of these reasons [why "apparent tautology" is a beauty of the "highest kind"] is the interest which the mind attaches to words, not only as symbols of the passion, but as <u>things</u>, active and efficient, which are themselves part of the passion.' Note on 'The Thorn'. *'Lyrical Ballads', and Other Poems, 1797–1800*, ed. Butler and Green, p. 351.
25 Goodman, '"Uncertain Disease": Nostalgia, Pathologies of Motion, Practices of Reading', p. 225.
26 All quotations from the 1808 'Recluse' poems are taken from *'The Tuft of Primroses', with Other Late Poems for 'The Recluse'*, ed. Joseph F. Kishel (Ithaca, NY, and London: Cornell University Press, 1986).
27 Goethe's response to Luke Howard's *Essay on the Modifications of Clouds* (1804) is quoted by Mary Jacobus in 'Cloud Studies: The Visible Invisible',

in *Romantic Things: A Tree, a Rock, a Cloud* (Chicago and London: Chicago University Press, 2012), p. 25.
28 'To the Clouds' (1842), ll. 87–94. *'The Tuft of Primroses'*, ed. Kishel, pp. 63–71.
29 ll. 1601–9; *passim*. *The White Doe of Rylstone*, ed. Dugas.
30 James A. Butler, pre-empting Johnstone's reading of the poem as a litany of architectural ruins in *Wordsworth and 'The Recluse'* (pp. 243–60), writes: 'what was "Perfect Contentment, Unity entire" in *Home at Grasmere* is the victim of "an unrelenting doom" in *The Tuft of Primroses*'; the poem 'records a decay in the physical environment of Grasmere' that is at odds with the earlier poem's confident assertions of rural stability. 'Wordsworth's "Tuft of Primroses": An "Unrelenting Doom"'. *Studies in Romanticism* 14.3 (Summer 1973), pp. 237–48 (p. 244). My reading of the poem's pessimistic account of the Vale differs from Butler's in the extent to which, along with Johnston, I view the drive towards decay and displacement as no less pervasive in 'Home at Grasmere'.
31 Jessica Fay, *Wordsworth's Monastic Inheritance: Poetry, Place, and the Sense of Community* (Oxford: Oxford University Press, 2018), p. 113.
32 Ibid., p. 114.
33 Mary Moorman suggests that Wordsworth may have read St Basil's letters in Latin while staying with his brother Christopher in Lambeth in March 1808. *William Wordsworth: A Biography. The Later Years, 1803–1850* (Oxford: Oxford University Press, 1968), p. 133. However, as Joseph Kishel points out, it is more likely that Wordsworth adapted his account of Basil's biography from William Cave's *Apostolici: or, the History of the Lives, Acts, Death, and Martyrdoms of Those Who Were Contemporary with or Immediately Succeeded the Apostles [...]* (London: 1716), a copy of which was kept at Rydal Mount. See *'The Tuft of Primroses'*, ed. Kishel, p. 21, and Duncan Wu, *Wordsworth's Reading, 1800–1815* (Cambridge: Cambridge University Press, 1995), p. 44. See also Fay, *Wordsworth's Monastic Inheritance*, p. 117.
34 Cave, *Apostolici*, p. 471.
35 Simon Jarvis, *Wordsworth's Philosophic Song* (Cambridge: Cambridge University Press, 2002), p. 130.
36 Cave, *Apostolici*, p. 503.
37 Ibid.
38 Quotations taken from *Descriptive Sketches*, ed. Eric Birdsall (Ithaca, NY, and London: Cornell University Press, 1984).
39 Tellingly, Allan Bank was identified by Wordsworth, in a letter to William Sharp dating from February 1805, with the very forces of despoilation that the poem laments: a 'temple of abomination' that will 'entirely destroy' the village's 'character of simplicity and seclusion' (*EY* 534).
40 See Richard Gravil, 'Wordsworth as Partisan', in *Concerning the Convention of Cintra. A Critical Edition*, ed. Richard Gravil and W. J. B. Owen (Tirril: Humanities-Ebooks, 2009), pp. 17–19, and the essays by David Bromwich, Timothy Michael, and Patrick Vincent in this collection: 'Vicarious Feeling: Spanish Independence, English Liberty', pp. 34–42; 'The State of

Knowledge in "The Convention of Cintra"', pp. 43–52; 'Sleep or Death? Republicanism in "The Convention of Cintra"', pp. 53–62. For the background to this debate see: Gordon Kent Thomas, *Wordsworth's Dirge and Promise: Napoleon, Wellington and the Convention of Cintra* (Lincoln, NE: University of Nebraska Press, 1971), Michael H. Friedman, *The Making of a Tory Humanist: William Wordsworth and the Idea of Community* (New York: Columbia University Press, 1979), James Chandler, *Wordsworth's Second Nature*, pp. 42–4, and Deirdre Coleman, 'Re-living Jacobinism: Wordsworth and the Convention of Cintra', *The Yearbook of English Studies* 19 (1989), pp. 144–61.

41 Quotations from *Concerning the Convention of Cintra* are taken from William Wordsworth, *Concerning the Convention of Cintra. A Critical Edition*, ed. Gravil and Owen, the text for which is derived from *Prose*, I. 220–457. References are to line numbers in the HEB edition.

42 Edmund Burke, *A Philosophical Enquiry into the Origin of Our Ideas of the Sublime and Beautiful*, ed. Adam Phillips (Oxford: Oxford University Press, 1990), p. 122.

43 For discussion of Aristotle's conception of *energeia* see Giorgio Agamben, *The Man without Content*, trans. Georgia Albert (Stanford, CA: Stanford University Press, 1999), pp. 60–7.

44 'Preface' to *Poems, in Two Volumes* (1815). *Prose* III. 31.

45 Ibid., p. 37.

46 Burke, *A Philosophical Enquiry*, p. 53.

47 See 'The State of Knowledge in "The Convention of Cintra"', especially pp. 50–2.

48 'Preface' to *Lyrical Ballads* (1800). *Prose* I. 128.

49 For further discussion of Wordsworth's strained attempts to discriminate between political power and civic virtue in his analysis of the 'military spirit' see Folker, 'Wordsworth's Visionary Imagination: Democracy and War', pp. 194–6.

50 Kelley, *Wordsworth's Revisionary Aesthetics*, pp. 140–1.

51 Adam Ferguson, *An Essay on the History of Civil Society* (New Brunswick and London: Transaction Books, 1980), p. 24.

52 Adam Ferguson, Lecture 89, 9 April 1776. Quoted by David Kettler in his survey of Ferguson's lecture notes in 'Political Education for Empire and Revolution', in *Adam Ferguson: History, Progress, and Human Nature*, ed. Eugene Heath and Vincenzo Merolle (London: Routledge, 2008), pp. 87–115 (pp. 108–9).

53 Sally Bushell, *Re-reading 'The Excursion': Narrative, Response and the Wordsworthian Dramatic Voice* (Aldershot: Ashgate, 2002), p. 88. Voltaire, *Candide and Other Stories*, trans. Roger Pearson (Oxford: Oxford University Press, 2006), p. 4.

54 Mary Favret writes movingly of the relationship between Margaret and the Solitary, observing how the characters' experience of spatial and temporal precarity responds to 'wartime as a particular and recurrent (retraceable)

geopolitical condition, the very ground of an experience that is nevertheless always in some sense removed, re-moved'. *War at a Distance: Romanticism and the Making of Modern Wartime* (Princeton, NJ, and Oxford: Princeton University Press, 2012), p. 29.

55 Spinoza, *Ethics*, III, Definition XII, p. 106.

56 Meditating on the advent of a 'World of Justice', Meillassoux posits that the hope for such a world enables the 'possibility that it could arise as if this hope were the source of it', noting further that the 'as if' of justice, like the 'as if' of the Kant's idea of the beautiful, is no longer to be conceived 'as if the divine had made it happen' but 'as if human hope had made it happen'. From L'Inexistence divine', translated by Graham Harman. Graham Harman, *Quentin Meillassoux: Philosophy in the Making* (Edinburgh: Edinburgh University Press, 2015), p. 269; p. 163.

57 Underlying this reading is Agamben's account of a *post iudicium* world in which life is accepted as 'irreparable' and no longer in need of salvation. In this world without remedy, being is informed by 'the world as it is' rather than oriented towards a realm of transcendental plenitude with which it can never coincide. See Giorgio Agamben, *The Coming Community*, trans. Michael Hardt (Minneapolis, MN: University of Minnesota Press, 1993), pp. 89–90.

58 *Home at Grasmere*, ed. Darlington, pp. 187–99.

59 DC MS. 48. *The Thirteen-Book Prelude*, ed. Mark L. Reed, 2 vols. (Ithaca, NY, and London: Cornell University Press, 1991), II. 427.

60 On Wordsworth's interest in and developing understanding of the idea of the commonwealth, see John Rieder, *Wordsworth's Counterrevolutionary Turn: Community, Virtue, and Vision in the 1790s* (Newark: University of Delaware Press, 1997), pp. 46–52. See also Fulford, *Landscape, Liberty and Authority*, pp. 163–8.

61 Francis Jeffrey, 'Review of *The Excursion*', *Edinburgh Review* 24.47 (November 1814), pp. 1–30 (p. 1); John Herman Merivale, 'Review of *The Excursion*', *Monthly Review* 76 (February 1815), pp. 123–36 (pp. 128–9).

62 Charles Lamb, 'Review of *The Excursion*; a Poem. By William Wordsworth'. *Quarterly Review* 12 (October 1814), pp. 100–11 (p. 105).

63 For detailed commentary on the biblical, Miltonic, and self-referential allusions in this speech, see Brandon Chao-Chi Yen, *'The Excursion' and Wordsworth's Iconography* (Liverpool: Liverpool University Press, 2018), pp. 65–6.

64 Charles Lamb to William Wordsworth, 9 August 1814. *The Letters of Charles and Mary Anne Lamb*, ed. Edwin W. Marrs Jnr, 3 vols. (Ithaca, NY, and London: Cornell University Press, 1978), III. 95–9.

65 Hazlitt, taking a less sympathetic view of the celebrations, observes in his review of *The Excursion* that Wordsworth's 'mind is [...] coeval with the primary forms of things', pointing out that 'Every one wishes to get rid of the booths and bridges in the Park, in order to have a view of the ground and water again'. *CWWH* XIX. 10n. For further discussion of the peace celebrations see Cox, *Romanticism in the Shadow of* War, pp. 161–4.

Chapter 2   Peace Out of Time: *The White Doe of Rylstone*

1. 'We do not think [the poem] his best. The narrative part will be most attentively pursued by readers, and it does not seem to be most successfully accomplished.' [John Scott], 'Mr. Wordsworth's Poems', *Champion* 129 (25 June 1815), pp. 205–6 (p. 205). As a measure of the uncertainty and rapidity of the times, Scott noted the publication of *The White Doe* on 4 June. On 11 June, the *Champion* carried a three-column report from Paris on Napoleon's restoration. A week later, on the day of the Battle of Waterloo, the paper announced that Napoleon was 'generally believed to have left Paris, and to have joined his troops: the awful blow may therefore be hourly expected'. See Richard Gravil, *Wordsworth's Bardic Vocation, 1787–1842* (Houndmills: Palgrave Macmillan, 2003), p. 273.
2. *Collected Letters of Samuel Taylor Coleridge*, ed. Griggs. III. 112.
3. *The Letters of Charles and Mary Anne Lamb*, ed. Marrs. III. 148.
4. Alan Forrest notes that among the measures supported by Parliament to substantiate Waterloo as a locus for national unity was the Church Building Act of 1818, which resulted in some 600 'Waterloo Churches', raised in thanks to the glory of God for his help in defeating the Usurper. 'Contrasting Memories: Remembering Waterloo in France and Britain', *War, Demobilization and Memory: The Legacy of War in the Era of Atlantic Revolutions*, ed. Alan Forrest, Karen Hagemann, and Michael Rowe (Houndmills: Palgrave Macmillan, 2016), pp. 353–70 (p. 367).
5. John Wilson, 'Essays on the Lake School of Poetry. No. 1. Wordsworth's *The White Doe of Rylstone*', p. 369.
6. Ibid., p. 370.
7. Ibid.
8. Ibid., p. 380.
9. Ibid., p. 381.
10. 'Occasioned by the Same Battle. February 1816', l. 10. *Shorter Poems, 1807–1820*, ed. Ketcham, p. 172.
11. Peter J. Manning, '*The White Doe of Rylstone*, *The Convention of Cintra*, and the History of a Career', chapter 8 of *Reading Romantics: Text and Context* (Oxford: Oxford University Press, 1990), pp. 165–94. See also chapter 9 in this study, 'Tales and Politics: *The Corsair, Lara*, and *The White Doe of Rylstone*', pp. 195–216. As Manning suggests, Wordsworth's defence of the poem's 'pure and lofty Imagination' (*MY* II. 276) may also have been prompted by resentment towards the success of Byron's cheaper and far more popular *Corsair*.
12. *The Fenwick Notes of William Wordsworth*, ed. Curtis, pp. 102–3.
13. Christopher Wordsworth, *Memoirs of William Wordsworth*, 2 vols. (London, 1851), II. 313.
14. *Shorter Poems, 1807–1820*, ed. Ketcham, pp. 147–52.
15. Page, *Wordsworth and the Cultivation of Women*, pp. 79–84.

16 *Shorter Poems, 1807–1820*, ed. Ketcham, pp. 151–2. For a suggestive reading of the circumstances that led to the revision of Laodamia's fate, see John Barrell, '"Laodamia" and the Moaning of Mary', *Textual Practice* 10.3 (1996), pp. 449–77.
17 Page, *Wordsworth and the Cultivation of Women*, p. 100.
18 Quotations from *The White Doe*, referenced by canto followed by line number(s), are from *The White Doe of Rylstone*, ed. Dugas.
19 Kelley, *Wordsworth's Revisionary Aesthetics*, p. 154.
20 Jessica Fay has made a persuasive case for linking *The White Doe* to Wordsworth's efforts, in the 'Essay Supplementary to the Preface', to delineate the co-operative relationship between poet and reader. See chapter 1, 'Wordsworth's Creation of Taste' in *Wordsworth's Monastic Inheritance*, pp. 28–62.
21 Hartman, *Wordsworth's Poetry, 1787–1814*, p. 330.
22 Ibid., p. 329.
23 Text taken from *The White Doe of Rylstone*, ed. Dugas, pp. 78–80.
24 Ibid., p. 57.
25 Ibid., p. 58.
26 Fay provides an illuminating reading of how the Spenserian influences acknowledged in 'In trellis'd shed' are developed in *The White Doe*. See *Wordsworth's Monastic Inheritance*, pp. 32–53.
27 *'Lyrical Ballads', and Other Poems, 1797–1800*, ed. Butler and Green, pp. 133–9.
28 'Weak is the will of Man', l. 9. *The White Doe of Rylstone*, ed. Dugas, p. 76.
29 Earlier in the poem, the doe is likened to a ship 'In sunshine sailing far away [...] that hath the plain/Of ocean for her own domain' (ll. 59–66), a smile that, according to Theresa Kelley, responds to Milton's comparison of Satan to the image of a fleet when seen from a distance ('So seem'd/Far off the flying fiend'; *Paradise Lost*, II. ll. 642–3). *Wordsworth's Revisionary Aesthetics*, p. 153. In the 1815 Preface, Wordsworth uses this comparison as illustration of the power of the Imagination. Here, however, the doe's mastery of the ocean yields to an image of loss that, in its self-conscious artistry, implies that Imagination may yet find accord with the powerless, the marginalised, and the dead.
30 Note on 'The Thorn'. *'Lyrical Ballads', and Other Poems, 1797–1800*, ed. Butler and Green, p. 351.
31 Fay, for example, follows Hartman's account of Wordsworth's 'Miltonic' understanding of the 'difference between the Protestant and the Catholic imagination' (*Wordsworth's Poetry, 1787–1814*, p. 326) by claiming that in *The White Doe* Wordsworth 'favours the Protestant model by which truth is reached through individual spiritual effort and, at the same time, denounces the Catholic ritual practices of the rebels and their superstitious attachment to external symbols such as the banner'. *Wordsworth's Monastic Inheritance*, p. 42.
32 On 5 May 1825, in a letter to Lord Lowther, Wordsworth declared his opposition to the Catholic Relief Bill. See *LY* II. 347–8 and *LY* I. 63. In the same month, writing to Sir George Beaumont, he expressed an admiration for the Gospel of St John that, according to Jeffrey Robinson (citing Edith Batho),

'indicates his preference for the Incarnation (Catholic) over that of the Atonement (Protestant) in ethical and by extension poetic thinking'. See *LY* II. 351 and Robinson, *Poetic Innovation in Wordsworth's Poetry, 1825–1833*, p. 246.

33 21 January 1824. *LY* I. 244–5.

34 On doctrinal responses to monastic ruins see Anne Janowitz, *England's Ruins: Poetic Purpose and the National Landscape* (Oxford: Wiley-Blackwell, 1990) and Michael Tomko, *British Romanticism and the Catholic Question: Religion, History and National Identity, 1778–1829* (Basingstoke: Palgrave Macmillan, 2011).

35 John Dryden, *The Hind and the Panther. A Poem, in Three Parts*, l. 1. *The Poems and Fables of John Dryden*, ed. James Kinsley (London: Oxford University Press, 1962), pp. 352–421 (p. 355).

36 Dating from the period when composition on *The White Doe* began, 'Song, at the Feast of Brougham Castle', first published in *Poems, in Two Volumes* (1807), and then classed among 'Poems of the Imagination' from 1815 onwards, the 'Song', like *The White Doe*, takes inspiration from Thomas Dunham Whitaker's account of the life of Henry Lord Clifford in *The History and Antiquities of the Deanery of Craven* (London, 1805). Wordsworth notes that 'Henry, the subject of the poem, was deprived of his estate and honours' by the House of York as an act of revenge for his father's role in the slaughter of the Earl of Rutland, Son of the Duke of York, in the aftermath of the Battle of Wakefield. The poem, which frames a purported translation of a minstrel's song (ll. 5–88), recounts Henry Clifford's years of exile when, after twenty-four years spent living as a shepherd, he became 'softened', and *Other Poems, 1800–1807* into feeling, sooth'd, and tamed' (l. 164). *'Poems, in Two Volumes', and Other Poems, 1800–1807*, ed. Curtis, pp. 259–64. Richard Gravil observes that the 'Song', which shares the 'twice-told' technique of 'Hart-leap Well' and 'The Thorn', sets the minstrel's martial enthusiasm against a concluding sequence of reflective lyricism. Clifford thus becomes the embodiment of military virtue, a happy warrior who, following the restoration of his estates and honours, would go on to distinguish himself at Flodden while yet sustaining 'in lofty place/The wisdom which adversity had bred' (ll. 171–2). Like *The White Doe*, the poem provides a lesson in how the savage passions that lead to sectarian conflict can be tempered by pastoral virtue. See Gravil, *Wordsworth's Bardic Vocation*, pp. 267–73.

37 Tomko argues convincingly that the melding of nature and history in England's Catholic ruins is envisaged by Wordsworth as 'a fountainhead to revitalize the national community', anticipating the Tractarian call for a synthesis of Protestant and Catholic theology in Anglican worship. *British Romanticism and the Catholic Question: Religion, History and National Identity, 1778–1829*, p. 18. For a reading sympathetic to Wordsworth's support for the repurposing of Catholic monastic practices see Tonya Moutray, 'Remodelling Catholic Ruins in William Wordsworth's Poetry', *European Romantic Review* 22.6 (2011), pp. 819–31. See also Fay, *Wordsworth's Monastic Inheritance*, pp. 23–5.

38 For a fuller account of how the poem deploys the feminine category of the beautiful as a corrective to the masculine investment in 'sublime suffering and guilt', see Kelley, *Wordsworth's Revisionary Aesthetics*, pp. 150–6 (p. 151).

39 Transcription of MS. 61, 20ᵛ. *The White Doe of Rylstone*, ed. Dugas, p. 365.
40 The story of how 'the boy of Egremond' met his death in the rocky channel called the Strid in the woods between Bolton and Barden is recounted by Whitaker in *The History and Antiquities of the Deanery of Craven*.
41 For a reading of the doe's role as chronicler of historical trauma, see Barbara Gates, 'Wordsworth's Symbolic White Doe: "The Power of History in the Mind"', *Criticism* 17.3 (1975), pp. 234–45.
42 Bruno Latour, *Aramis, or the Love of Technology*, trans. Catherine Porter (Cambridge, MA: Harvard University Press, 1996), pp. 225–6.
43 The question of whether non-human life can participate in a Levinasian face-to-face encounter, and therefore enter an ethical relationship with the human, is debated by Jacques Derrida in *The Animal That Therefore I Am*, ed. Marie-Louse Mallett, trans. David Wills (New York: Fordham University Press, 2008), pp. 105–18.
44 Walter Benjamin's thinking on the relations between language, nature, and sadness is relevant to this reading. In the essay 'On Language as Such and on the Language of Man', Benjamin speculates that 'all nature would begin to lament if it were endowed with language'. As the conditional sentence implies, were nature able to use language it would express only the sorrow over its inherent linguistic loss. *One-Way Street and Other Writings*, trans. Edmund Jephcott and Kingsley Shorter (London and New York: Verso, 1997), pp. 115–36 (p. 113).
45 Emmanuel Levinas, *Totality and Infinity: An Essay on Exteriority*, trans. Alphonso Lingis (Dordrecht: Kluwer Academic Publishers, 1991), p. 157.
46 Page, *Wordsworth and the Cultivation of Women*, p. 96.
47 For Levinas, 'the contrariety that permits its terms to remain absolutely other is the *feminine*'. Emmanuel Levinas, *Time and the Other (and Additional Essays)*, trans. R. A. Cohen (Pittsburgh, PA: Duquesne University Press, 1986), p. 85.
48 Georg Wilhelm Friedrich Hegel, *The Philosophy of Fine Art*, trans. F. P. Osmaston (London: G. Bell, 1920), III. 16–17. For Derrida, Hegel's commentary on the affective power of music 'demonstrates very well the strange privilege of sound in idealization, the production of the concept and the self-presence of the subject'. *Of Grammatology*, trans. Gayatri Chakravorty Spivak (Baltimore, MD: Johns Hopkins University Press, 1967), p. 12.
49 Jacques Derrida, *Spectres of Marx: The State of the Debt, the Work of Mourning and the New International*, trans. Peggy Kamuf (New York and London: Routledge, 1994), pp. xvii–xviii.

Chapter 3 Thanksgiving after War

1 Wordsworth dined with Byron, Rogers, and Lamb in London on the evening of the Battle of Waterloo. A pencil memorandum by Charles Wordsworth records that 'Ld B [?argued] & seemed to wish that Buonaparte wd be victorious. My Uncle on the Contrary maintained He had no chance whatever if the allies kept together.' Mark L. Reed, *Wordsworth: The Chronology of the Middle Years* (Cambridge, MA: Harvard University Press, 1975), pp. 498–9.

2. *Prelude*, Book III, ll. 279–80. *The Thirteen-Book 'Prelude'*, ed. Reed.
3. Spenser's role in Wordsworth's post-war self-fashioning is examined in Philip Shaw, *Waterloo and the Romantic Imagination* (Houndmills: Palgrave Macmillan, 2002), pp. 153–64.
4. Eight years after the volume's publication, only 164 copies had found purchasers. Duncan Wu notes that in 1834, 220 copies 'continued to gather dust in its publisher's warehouse'. 'Wordsworthian Carnage', *Essays in Criticism* 66.3 (July 2016), pp. 341–59 (p. 342).
5. See Wu, 'Wordsworthian Carnage'; Richard Gravil, 'A "Hideous Rout": Wordsworth's "Thanksgiving Ode" in Context', *The Coleridge Bulletin* 46 (Winter 2015), pp. 59–78; Philip Shaw, 'On War: De Quincey's Martial Sublime', *Romanticism* 19.1 (2013), pp. 19–30.
6. Unless noted otherwise, quotations from the 'Thanksgiving Ode' and other poems printed in the *Thanksgiving* volume are taken from *Shorter Poems, 1807–1820*, ed. Ketcham.
7. For an influential reading of this passage see Bainbridge, *Napoleon and English Romanticism*, pp. 176–7.
8. Bob Tennant notes: 'Purely in the numbers of words published in 1815–16, sermons constitute the largest nonjournalistic literary genre about the Battle of Waterloo'. 'On the Good Name of the Dead: Peace, Liberty, and Empire in Robert Morehead's Waterloo Sermon', *Religion in the Age of Enlightenment* 1 (2009), pp. 251–77 (p. 251).
9. *A FORM OF PRAYER, TO BE USED in All Churches and Chapels [...] upon Friday the Nineteenth of April next, being the Day appointed by Proclamation for a General FAST and Humiliation Before Almighty God [...] By His Majesty's Special Command* (London, 1793), title page. Material in this and the following section has been adapted from 'Wordsworth, Waterloo, and Sacrifice', in *Sacrifice and Modern War Literature*, ed. Alex Houen and Jan-Melissa Schramm (Oxford: Oxford University Press, 2018), pp. 20–48.
10. For a detailed account of Wordsworth's publishing activities in this year see Kenneth R. Johnston, *The Hidden Wordsworth: Poet, Lover, Rebel, Spy* (New York and London: W. W. Norton & Company, 1998), pp. 334–40.
11. *A FORM OF PRAYER* [...], p. 6.
12. ll. 263–74. *The Thirteen-Book 'Prelude'*, ed. Reed. II. 274.
13. Johnston, *The Hidden Wordsworth*, p. 388.
14. *A FORM OF PRAYER AND THANKSGIVING TO ALMIGHTY GOD; TO BE USED [...] on Thursday the Eighteenth of January, Being the Day appointed by Proclamation for a General THANKSGIVING to Almighty God [...]* (London, 1816), p. 10.
15. Waterloo is remembered for its high casualty rate yet, as Tennant remarks, 'the proportion of Anglo-Allied casualties was not unusually heavy – perhaps 35 percent of British personnel were killed or wounded'. 'On the Good Name of the Dead', p. 257.
16. 'NO. I'. *Cobbett's Weekly Political Register* [London, England] 24 June 1815: n.p. *19th Century British Newspapers*. Web. Accessed 8 February 2022.

17 'LONDON'. *Morning Post* [London, England] 11 July 1815: n.p. *19th Century British Newspapers*. Web. Accessed 21 April 2022.
18 'Caledonian Mercury'. *Caledonian Mercury* [Edinburgh, Scotland] 26 June 1815: n.p. *19th Century British Newspapers*. Web. Accessed 8 February 2022.
19 Giorgio Agamben, *Homo Sacer: Sovereign Power and Bare Life*, trans. Daniel Heller Roazen (Stanford, CA: Stanford University Press, 1998), p. 8. See also René Girard, *Violence and the Sacred*, trans. Patrick Gregory (Baltimore, MD: Johns Hopkins University Press, 1977), pp. 81–4 and p. 249. For a subtle and far-reaching reading of the soldier as Girardian scapegoat see Laura Wittman, *The Tomb of the Unknown Soldier, Modern Mourning, and the Reinvention of the Mystical Body* (Toronto: University of Toronto Press, 2011), pp. 98–9.
20 Neil Ramsey, *The Military Memoir and Romantic Literary Culture, 1780–1835* (Farnham: Ashgate, 2011), p. 94.
21 Henry Cotes, *Another Mite for Waterloo. A Sermon, Preached in the Parish Church of Bedlington, in the County of Durham, on Sunday, the Twentieth of August, 1815* (Newcastle, 1815), p. 13.
22 For further detail see Tennant, 'On the Good Name of the Dead', pp. 258–66.
23 Daniell Mathias, *Waterloo Subscription. A Sermon, to Recommend the Same, Preached at St. Mary's Church, Whitechapel, August 13, 1815* (London, 1815), p. 17. Subsequent references in parentheses.
24 Peter Roe, *A Sermon Preached in the Episcopal Chapel of Harrogate, Sunday, July the 30th, 1815, in Behalf of the Sufferers of the Battle of Waterloo* (Knaresbrough, 1815), p. 28.
25 Robert Morehead, *On the Good Name of the Dead, in The Sunday Library; or, the Protestant's Manual for the Sabbath-Day*, 6 vols. (London, 1831), VI. 198–207 (206–7). Subsequent references in parentheses.
26 *A FORM OF PRAYER AND THANKSGIVING TO ALMIGHTY GOD*, p. 10.
27 William Howley, *A Sermon Preached on Thursday, January 18, 1816, Being the Day Appointed for a General Thanksgiving* […] (London, 1816), p. 12. Subsequent references in parentheses.
28 Archibald Allison, *Discourse Preached in the Episcopal Chapel, Cowgate, Edinburgh, Jan, 18, 1816* […] (Edinburgh, 1816), pp. 23–5; *passim*.
29 *The Critical Review* 5.5 (November 1815), pp. 523–8 (p. 523). Subsequent references in parentheses.
30 Thomas Chalmers, *Thoughts on Universal Peace: A Sermon, Delivered on Thursday, January 18, 1816* […] (Glasgow, 1816), p. 28, p. 30.
31 Shaw, *Waterloo and the Romantic Imagination*, pp. 140–64. See also Richard Gravil, *Wordsworth's Bardic Vocation, 1787–1842*, pp. 319–46.
32 *Latin Vulgate (Clementine)*. Web. Accessed 8 February 2022.
33 *House of Commons Debates, 29 June 1815*. Web. Accessed 8 February 2022.
34 Holger Hoock, *Empires of the Imagination: Politics, War, and the Arts in the British World, 1750–1850* (London: Profile Books, 2010), pp. 361–2.
35 'The Bard, whose soul is meek as dawning day', l. 11.

36 *House of Commons Debates, 23 June 1815.* Web. Accessed 8 February 2022.
37 Quotations from *The Bible: Authorized King James Version with Apocrypha* (Oxford: Oxford University Press, 1997).
38 See Bainbridge, *Napoleon and English Romanticism*, pp. 54–94.
39 That an encounter with the abject matter of war might have its own imaginative appeal is seen in the efforts of some ecclesiastics to persuade their congregations to meditate on the sufferings of dead and wounded soldiers. In a few cases the appeal to 'Imagination' in these sermons runs the risk of supplanting the drive towards exultation with a morbid fixation on death and ruin. See, for example, Edward Patteson, *A Sermon Delivered in the Parish Church of Richmond in Surrey, on Sunday the 30th Day of July 1815* [...] (London, 1815): 'Remembering for what purposes we are endued with the powers of imagination [...] let us keep a steadfast eye on the horrors attendant and consequent upon war, until we can appreciate the miseries of those, who actually groan under them', p. 23.
40 See Edmund Burke, *Revolutionary Writings*, ed. Iain Hampshire-Monk (Cambridge: Cambridge University Press, 2014), p. 101.
41 Gravil, *Wordsworth's Thanksgiving Ode in Context*, pp. 17–18.
42 *Peter Bell the Third*, ll. 634–40. *Selected Poems and Prose*, ed. Donovan and Duffy, p. 393.
43 *Don Juan*, Canto VIII, stanza 9. ll. 70–2. *Lord Byron: The Complete Poetical Works*, ed. Jerome J. McGann and Barry Weller, 7 vols. (Oxford: Clarendon Press, 1980–93), V. 367.
44 Ibid., 732.
45 *The Literary Criticism of John Ruskin*, ed. Harold Bloom (New York: De Capo Press, 1965), pp. 371–3.
46 'Thanksgiving Ode', ll. 106–9. *The Poetical Works of William Wordsworth*, ed. Ernest de Selincourt and Helen Darbishire, 5 vols. (Oxford: Clarendon Press, 1940–49), III. 155.
47 Samuel Humfrays, *The Sword Is the Lord's. A Sermon Preached in the Parish-Church of Daventry, January 19th 1794* [...] (Northampton, 1794), p. 13.
48 As quoted in Gravil, *Wordsworth's Thanksgiving Ode in Context*, p. 18.
49 Ibid., pp. 200–1.
50 Ibid., pp. 201–6.
51 *Don Juan*, Canto VIII, stanza 9. ll. 70–2. *Lord Byron: The Complete Poetical Works*, ed. McGann and Weller, V. 367.
52 Johnston, *The Hidden Wordsworth*, p. 390.
53 Walker, *Marriage, Writing and Romanticism*, pp. 73–8.
54 *Sonnet Series and Itinerary Poems, 1819–1850*, ed. Jackson, p. 361.
55 Horace, 'Satire 1', 3. ll. 107–8. *Horace: Satires*, p. 40.
56 Text taken from *Shorter Poems, 1807–1822*, ed. Ketcham, pp. 142–51.
57 *The Diary of Benjamin Robert Haydon*, ed. Willard Bissell Pope, 3 vols. (Cambridge, MA: Harvard University Press, 1963), II. 464. This incident is

discussed by John Barrell in '"Laodamia" and the Moaning of Mary', *Textual Practice* 10.3 (1996), pp. 449–77.
58 *The Diary of Benjamin Robert Haydon*, II, p. 464.
59 Quotations from *Shorter Poems, 1807–1822*, ed. Ketcham, pp. 213–21.
60 Walker, *Marriage, Writing and Romanticism*, p. 80. Walker quotes from Thomas North's 1579 translation that Wordsworth used.
61 As quoted in *MY* II. 355.

Chapter 4   'Returning, Like a Ghost Unlaid': *Peter Bell* and *The Waggoner*

1 'IV. Near the Spring of the Hermitage', ll. 1–4. Quotations from the 1818 inscriptions taken from *Shorter Poems, 1807–1822*, ed. Ketcham, p. 270.
2 William Wordsworth, *The River Duddon, A Series of Sonnets: Vaudracour and Julia and Other Poems. To Which Is Annexed, a Topographical Description of the Country of the Lakes, in the North of England* (London, 1820), pp. 164–72.
3 l. 13. *Shorter Poems, 1807–1822*, ed. Ketcham, p. 279.
4 'Immortality' ode, ll. 149–50. *'Poems, in Two Volumes', and Other Poems, 1800–1807*, ed. Curtis, pp. 269–77.
5 *Shorter Poems, 1807–1822*, ed. Ketcham, pp. 279–80.
6 Ibid., p. 277.
7 'Composed during One of the Most Awful of the Late Storms', l. 12 and l. 1. *Shorter Poems, 1807–1822*, ed. Ketcham, p. 280.
8 Ibid., pp. 281–2.
9 Fulford, *Wordsworth's Poetry, 1815–1845*, p. 186.
10 See Jeffrey N. Cox, *William Wordsworth, Second-Generation Romantic*; Fulford, *Wordsworth's Poetry, 1815–1845*, pp. 177–92.
11 Cox, *William Wordsworth, Second-Generation Romantic*, p. 110.
12 For a review representative of the hostility directed towards *Peter Bell*, see *The Monthly Review* 89 (August 1819), pp. 419–22: 'All past, present, and (probably) future performances, by the same author, must sink into nothing before Peter Bell. No lisping ever more distinctly lisped than the versification of this poem; and no folly was ever more foolishly boasted than that of the writer, whether in style or subject-matter', p. 419.
13 *The Letters of Sara Hutchinson*, ed. Kathleen Coburn (London: Routledge and Kegan Paul, 1954), p. 154.
14 Noted in *MY* II. 543.
15 *The Examiner* 592 (2 May 1819), pp. 282–3.
16 'To Kosciusko, Who Never Fought Either for Buonaparte or the Allies', l. 11. From Leigh Hunt, *Foliage; or, Poems Original and Translated* (London, 1818), p. 58.
17 *Leigh Hunt's Literary Criticism*, ed. Lawrence Houston Houtchens and Carolyn Washburn Houtchens (New York: Columbia Press, 1956), p. 23.
18 *The Examiner* 592 (2 May 1819), p. 282.

19 *Peter Bell*, l. 106. This reference and all subsequent references to the poem are taken from William Wordsworth, *Peter Bell*, ed. John E. Jordan (Ithaca, NY, and London: Cornell University Press, 1985).
20 Cox, *William Wordsworth, Second-Generation Romantic*, p. 124.
21 *The Literary Gazette, and Journal of Belles Lettres, Arts, Politics etc* 119 (1 May 1819), pp. 273–6 (p. 275).
22 *The Edinburgh Monthly Review* 2 (July–December 1819), pp. 654–61 (pp. 656–7).
23 Paul H. Fry, *Wordsworth and the Poetry of What We Are* (New Haven, CT: Yale University Press, 2008), pp. 106–7.
24 Bernard Groom, *The Unity of Wordsworth's Poetry* (London: Macmillan, 1966), p. 128.
25 'The Rime of the Ancyent Marinere' (1798), l. 583. Samuel Taylor Coleridge, *The Complete Poems*, ed. William Keach (London: Penguin, 1997), pp. 147–66.
26 Groom, *The Unity of Wordsworth's Poetry*, p. 130.
27 *The Eclectic Review* 12 (July–December 1819), pp. 62–76 (p. 63).
28 Bogost, *Alien Phenomenology*, p. 12.
29 *The Theatrical Inquisitor, or, Monthly Mirror* 14 (January–June 1819), pp. 447–9 (p. 447).
30 *The Eclectic Review* 12 (July–December 1819), p. 62.
31 *'Lyrical Ballads', and Other Poems, 1797–1800*, ed. Butler and Green, pp. 64–7.
32 Kant, *The Critique of Judgement*, p. 108.
33 *The Monthly Review; or Literary Journal* 90 (September–December 1819), pp. 36–40 (p. 37).
34 *The Monthly Review; or Literary Journal* 89 (May–August 1819), pp. 309–21 (p. 314).
35 *English Bards and Scotch Reviewers*, l. 237; *Don Juan*, Canto I, stanza 90. l. 720. *Lord Byron: The Complete Poetical Works*, ed. McGann and Weller, V.
36 *English Bards and Scotch Reviewers*, l. 236, ll. 245–6.
37 *Don Juan*, Canto I, stanza 4. l. 28.
38 *The British Critic* 11 (January–June 1819), pp. 464–79 (p. 465).
39 MS 1. l. 752. William Wordsworth, *Benjamin the Waggoner*, ed. Paul F. Betz (Ithaca, NY: Cornell University Press, 1981), p. 82. Quotations from the poem are taken from this edition.
40 MS 1. l. 500. *Benjamin the Waggoner*, ed. Betz, p. 82. See Betz's introduction: pp. 9–10.
41 Ibid., pp. 23–4.
42 John Williams, *William Wordsworth* (Houndmills: Palgrave, 2002), p. 118.
43 Reed, *Wordsworth: The Chronology of the Middle Years*, p. 306.
44 In the A-B Stage Book I, lines 186–220, Wordsworth conjures with the idea of an epic poem recounting, variously, the decline of the Roman empire and the persistence of 'Liberty' (l. 197) in the subsequent course of European history. *The Thirteen-Book 'Prelude'*, ed. Reed, I. 111–12.
45 'Elegy Written in a Country Churchyard', l. 6. *Gray, Collins and Goldsmith: The Complete Poems*, ed. Roger Lonsdale (London: Longman, 1969), pp. 103–41 (p. 119).

46 See Betz's comments in the 'Introduction' to *Benjamin the Waggoner*, ed. Betz, p. 4.
47 Williams, *William Wordsworth*, p. 115.
48 Entry from Quillinan's notebook dated 1836. Quoted in *Benjamin the Waggoner*, ed. Betz, p. 29.
49 Letter to Wordsworth, 7 June 1819. *The Letters of Charles Lamb, to Which Are Added Those of His Sister Mary Lamb*, ed. E. V. Lucas, 3 vols. (New Haven, CT: Yale University Press, 1935), II. 249.
50 Anya Taylor, *Bacchus in Romantic England: Writers and Drink, 1780–1830* (Houndmills: Macmillan, 1999), p. 52.
51 As noted by Betz. *Benjamin the Waggoner*, ed. Betz, p. 21.
52 Ibid., p. 22.
53 *Milton: Complete Shorter Poems*, ed. John Carey (London: Longman, 1981), pp. 117–18.
54 Jane Bennett, *Vibrant Matter: A Political Ecology of Things* (Durham and London: Duke University Press, 2010), p. 21.
55 John Williams, *Wordsworth: Romantic Poetry and Revolution Politics* (Manchester and New York: Manchester University Press, 1989), p. 171.
56 For an informed account of the measures adopted by discharged seamen to survive in this period see Simon Houfe, 'Poor Jack: The Mendicant Sailors of Regency London', *Country Life* (3 May 1979), pp. 1381–2.
57 Williams, *Wordsworth: Romantic Poetry and Revolution Politics*, p. 172.
58 Kelley, *Wordsworth's Revisionary Aesthetics*, pp. 147–8.
59 Susan Stewart, *On Longing: Narratives of the Miniature, the Gigantic, the Souvenir, the Collection* (Durham and London: Duke University Press, 1984), p. 136.
60 Ibid., p. 139.
61 Ibid., p. 23.
62 The long history idea of war as a marker of authenticity is explored by Yuval Noah Harari in *The Ultimate Experience: Battlefield Revelations and the Making of Modern War Culture, 1450–2000* (Houndmills: Palgrave Macmillan, 2008).
63 Kelley, *Wordsworth's Revisionary Aesthetics*, p. 146.
64 Kant, *Critique of Judgement*, p. 98.
65 'There was a Boy, ye knew him well, ye Cliffs', l. 10. *'Lyrical Ballads', and Other Poems, 1797–1800*, ed. Butler and Green, pp. 139–40.
66 *Shorter Poems, 1807–1820*, ed. Ketcham, p. 43.
67 Commenting on the idea that 'peace is not just the absence of war, but a virtue [.] enjoined by the general decree of the commonwealth' (Spinoza, *Political Treatise*, p. 62), Willi Goetschel argues that for Spinoza, the active pursuit of peace is coeval with the principle of 'autonomous self-determination' that is central to the *res publica*. *Spinoza's Modernity: Medelssohn, Lessing, and Heine* (Madison, WI: The University of Wisconsin Press, 2004), p. 78. In recent years, the notion of an autonomous, self-regulating multitude has been adapted by Antonio Negri and Michael Hardt as a counterforce to 'global civil war'. See *Multitude: War and Democracy in the Age of Empire* (New York: Penguin, 2004), p. 100.

68 Spinoza, *Political Treatise*, p. 62.
69 As previously noted, Negri, in seeking to break the 'monstrous hybridization of peace and war', argues that it is not peace but 'the constituent cooperation of singular multitudes that creates the common existence of the world'. *Empire and Beyond*, p. 61.

Chapter 5 Violent Waters: *The River Duddon* and *Ecclesiastical Sketches*

1 *The Letters of Mary Wordsworth, 1800–1855*, ed. Mary Elizabeth Burton (Oxford: Clarendon Press, 1955), pp. 55–6. Important historical studies of Peterloo include Donald Read, *Peterloo: 'The Massacre' and Its Background* (Manchester: Manchester University Press, 1958), E. P. Thompson, *The Making of the English Working Class* (Harmondsworth: Penguin, 1968), Robert Walmsley, *Peterloo: The Case Reopened* (Manchester: Manchester University Press, 1969), and the two special issues of the *Manchester Region History Review: Peterloo Special Edition* 3.1 (1989) and *Return to Peterloo*, ed. Robert Poole, 23 (2012). The cultural significance of Peterloo is examined by Charles Tilly, *Popular Contention in Great Britain, 1758–1834* (Cambridge, MA: Harvard University Press, 1995), James Chandler, *England in 1819: The Politics of Literary Culture and the Case of Romantic Historicism* (Chicago: Chicago University Press, 1998), and Anthony Jarrells, *Britain's Bloodless Revolutions: 1688 and the Romantic Reform of Literature* (Basingstoke: Palgrave Macmillan, 2005). See also Mary Fairclough, *The Romantic Crowd: Sympathy, Controversy and Print Culture* (Cambridge: Cambridge University Press, 2013), and Katrina Navickas, *Protest and the Politics of Space and Place, 1789–1848* (Manchester: Manchester University Press, 2015). This chapter draws on material initially presented in 'Wordsworth after Peterloo: The Persistence of War in *The River Duddon ... and Other Poems*', in *Commemorating Peterloo: Violence, Resilience and Claim-Making during the Romantic Era*, ed. Michael Demson and Regina Hewitt (Edinburgh: Edinburgh University Press, 2019), pp. 250–71.
2 The next day the party was joined by a Manchester magistrate who was 'most agreeable [...] quite a gentleman of the right sort of principles. His presence cheered up Wm.' *The Letters of Mary Wordsworth, 1800–1855*, ed. Burton, p. 56.
3 *Sonnet Series and Itinerary Poems, 1820–1845*, ed. Jackson, p. 361. All quotations from *The River Duddon* sonnet sequence are taken from this edition.
4 For further discussion of battlefield tourism, with a focus on Waterloo, see Shaw, *Waterloo and the Romantic Imagination*, pp. 67–82.
5 *Peterloo Massacre, Containing a Faithful Narrative of the Events Which Preceded, Accompanied and Followed the Fatal Sixteenth of August 1819 [...] Edited by an Observer* (Manchester, 1819), p. 124. Anne Jones of Windmill Street informed

the inquest that she had seen 'the cavalry cutting and slashing men on the way to the hustings. After getting to the hustings, they turned their horses round, and rode over the people in all directions, still cutting and slashing [...] One of the special constables came into my house, and with great triumph exclaimed, "This is Waterloo for you, – This is Waterloo"', p. 178.

6 *The Letters of Mary Wordsworth*, ed. Burton, p. 55.
7 Ibid.
8 Archibald Prentice, *Historical Sketches and Personal Recollections of Manchester Intended to Illustrate the Progress of Public Opinion from 1792 to 1832* (London, 1851), p. 159.
9 Book VI, l. 558. *The Thirteen-Book 'Prelude'*, ed. Reed, p. 190.
10 Samuel Bamford, *Passages in the Life of a Radical* (Oxford: Oxford University Press, 1984), p. 152.
11 Quotations from *Peter Bell*, ed. Jordan, l. 27.
12 Wordsworth, *The River Duddon, A Series of Sonnets*, preliminary matter.
13 Ibid., endpapers.
14 For further discussion of this 'most fugitive' publication see Walker, *Marriage, Writing and Romanticism*, pp. 66–7 (p. 66), and Eric C. Walker, 'Wordsworth's "Third Volume" and the Collected Editions, 1815–20', *Papers of the Bibliographical Society of America* 80 (1986), pp. 437–53. See also Brian R. Bates, *Wordsworth's Poetic Collections, Supplementary Writing and Parodic Reception* (Abingdon: Routledge, 2012), chapter 7: '*The River Duddon* Volume and Wordsworth's Canonical Assent', pp. 141–61, and Jalal Uddin Khan, 'Publication and Reception of Wordsworth's *The River Duddon* Volume', *Modern Language Studies* 32.2 (Autumn 2002), pp. 45–67.
15 Samuel Taylor Coleridge, *The Collected Coleridge: Biographia Literaria*, ed. James Engell and W. Jackson Bate, 2 vols. (Princeton, NJ: Princeton University Press, 1983), II. 195–6. For discussion of the influence of 'the Warton school' on the Duddon sonnets see David Fairer, *Organising Poetry*, pp. 95–117, and A. Harris Fairbanks, '"Dear Native Brook": Coleridge, Bowles, and Thomas Warton, the Younger', *The Wordsworth Circle* 6.4 (Autumn 1975), pp. 313–15.
16 *'Poems, in Two Volumes', and Other Poems, 1800–1807*, ed. Curtis, pp. 142–3.
17 Edward W. Said, *On Late Style* (London: Bloomsbury, 2006), p. 12. For a reading of style in late romanticism relevant to this discussion, see Ben Hutchinson, *Lateness and Modern European Literature* (Oxford: Oxford University Press, 2016).
18 Julia S. Carlson, 'Charting the Stream of Time: William Wordsworth and Joseph Priestley'. Conference paper delivered at 'After Wordsworth: Water, Writing'. University of Leicester, 8 January 2021.
19 Horace, Ode 3.29, 'To Maecenas'. *Odes and Epodes*, ed. Niall Rudd, Loeb Classical Library, vol. 33 (Cambridge, MA: Harvard University Press, 2015), p. 214.
20 Joseph Priestley, *A Description of a Chart of Biography; with a Catalogue of All the Names Inserted in It, and the Dates Annexed to Them*, 7th edn. (London, 1778), p. 6, p. 24. For discussion of Priestley and Strass's time charts, see Daniel Rosenberg and Anthony Grafton, *Cartographies of Time: A History of*

the Timeline (New York: Princeton Architectural Press, 2010), pp. 116–47; *passim*. See also Alan Liu, *Friending the Past: The Sense of History in the Digital Age* (Chicago and London: University of Chicago Press, 2018), pp. 176–84.
21 Joseph Priestley, *A Description of a New Chart of History, Containing a View of the Principal Revolutions of Empire, That Have Taken Place in the World*, 4th edn. (London, 1777), pp. 15–19; *passim*.
22 Horace, Epistle 2.43. *Epistles, Satires and Ars Poetica*, trans. H. B. Fairclough, Loeb Classical Library, issue 194, vol. 2 of Horace (Cambridge, MA: Harvard University Press, 1978), p. 265. Wordsworth owned an 1807 edition of Philip Francis's 1746 translation, which renders the line as 'Still glides the River, and will ever glide'. *A Poetical Translation of the Works of Horace [...] by Philip Francis D. D. A New Edition, with Additional Notes, by Edward Du Bois*, 4 vols. (London, 1807), IV. 27.
23 Friedrich Strass, *Descriptive Guide to the Stream of Time; or, General Outline of Universal History, Chronology, and Biography, at One View*, trans. William Bell, 4th edn. (London, 1817), p. 9.
24 Ibid., pp. 34–5.
25 The relations between the *Duddon* sequence and the formation of national identity are explored by Benjamin Kim in 'Generating a National Sublime: Wordsworth's "The River Duddon" and "The Guide to the Lakes"', *Studies in Romanticism* 45.1 (Spring 2006), pp. 49–75. See also James M. Garrett, *Wordsworth and the Writing of the Nation* (Aldershot: Ashgate, 2013), chapter 5: 'The River Duddon Sonnets and the Writing of the Nation', pp. 125–48, and Bates, *Wordsworth's Poetic Collections*.
26 *The River Duddon*, Sonnet I, l. 9. *Ecclesiastical Sketches*, Part 1, 'I. Introduction', l. 2. *Ecclesiastical Sketches*, Part 3, 'XXVIII. Conclusion', ll. 13–14. *Memorials of a Tour on the Continent, 1820*, 'Sonnet. Local Recollections on the Heights near Hockheim', l. 14. Quotations from *Ecclesiastical Sketches* and *Memorials of a Tour on the Continent, 1820* are taken from *Sonnet Series and Itinerary Poems*, ed. Jackson. Andrew Raven comments astutely on how the *Duddon* sequence 'seeks to render explicit Wordsworth's Christian loyalty, augmenting the spiritual power of the poem's final stages with a vision of Duddon Valley's connectedness to the British nation in its entirety'. See Andrew Raven, '"Now Expands Majestic Duddon": Wordsworth's Textual Expansion of the "The River Duddon" and Its Theological Implications', *The Wordsworth Circle* 51.1 (Winter 2020), pp. 20–34 (p. 33).
27 Jerome J. McGann, *The Beauty of Inflections: Literary Investigations in Historical Method and Theory* (Oxford: Clarendon Press, 1985), p. 61. Significant critical responses to McGann's original 1979 article 'Keats and the Historical Method in Literary Criticism' include Paul H. Fry's 'History, Existence, and "To Autumn"', *Studies in Romanticism* 25.2 (Summer 1986), pp. 211–19, and Nicholas Roe, 'Keats's Commonwealth', in *Keats and History*, ed. Nicholas Roe (Cambridge: Cambridge University Press, 1995), pp. 194–211. See also the essays in this volume by Vincent Newey, Michael O'Neill, and Theresa M. Kelley.

28 Levinson, *Wordsworth's Great Period Poems*, p. 48.
29 James Chandler makes brief mention of Wordsworth's response to Peterloo in *England in 1819*, p. 10. More recently, Brian R. Bates has pointed out that the dramatic shift from negative to positive appraisals of Wordsworth's poetry in the wake of Peterloo corresponds with George Canning's bold proclamation that 'November 1819 and March 1820 effectively belonged to different "epochs" in the nation's history'. See *Wordsworth's Poetic Collections*, pp. 143–4.
30 Text taken from *Shorter Poems*, ed. Ketcham, pp. 283–4.
31 See Roe, 'Keats's Commonwealth', pp. 207–9.
32 Wordsworth, *The River Duddon*, p. 249.
33 'Upon the Same Occasion', l. 30. Text taken from Wordsworth, *Shorter Poems*, ed. Ketcham, pp. 284–6.
34 MS of 'Upon the Same Occasion'. *Shorter Poems*, ed. Ketcham, p. 285.
35 In Canto 1 of *Don Juan* Byron attacks Wordsworth as a 'shabby' civil servant (stanza 6. l. 47), as 'unintelligible' (stanza 90. l. 720. and as 'crazed beyond all hope' (stanza 205. l. 1635.). *Lord Byron: The Complete Poetical Works*, ed. McGann and Weller, V. For Ketcham's comments on the allusion to Byron see Wordsworth, *Shorter Poems*, ed. Ketcham, p. 550. Wordsworth's critique of Byron is sustained in another poem from the *Duddon* volume, 'The Pilgrim's Dream; or, the Star and the Glow-Worm'. See Jalal Uddin Khan, 'The Allegories of "The Pilgrim's Dream; or, the Star and the Glow-Worm"', *Studies in Philology* 94.4 (Autumn 1997), pp. 508–22.
36 Wordsworth, *Shorter Poems*, ed. Ketcham, p. 175.
37 DC MS. 86/1. See the transcription in *Shorter Poems*, ed. Ketcham, pp. 284–6.
38 Coleridge, *The Collected Coleridge: Biographia Literaria*, ed. Engell and Bate, III. 195–6.
39 Wordsworth, *Sonnet Series and Itinerary Poems*, ed. Jackson, p. 76. In 1833, Wordsworth uses 'the image of an orbicular body, a sphere or dew drop' to describe the 'intense unity' of his preferred sonnet forms, arguing that in 'the better half' of Milton's sonnets 'the sense does not close with the rhyme at the eighth line, but overflows into the second portion of the meter' (*LY* II. 604–5). For commentary on the scientific, geometric, intertextual, and theological aspects of Wordsworth's fluvial poetics see Ralph Pite, 'Wordsworth, *The River Duddon*, and John Dalton's Ultimate Particles', *The Wordsworth Circle* 50.2 (Spring 2019), pp. 180–201; Bates, '*The River Duddon* Volume's Golden Ratio Wheel and Spiraling "Orbicular" Sonnets', and Raven, 'Now Expands Majestic Duddon'.
40 Daniel Robinson, '*The River Duddon* and Wordsworth, Sonneteer', in *The Oxford Handbook of William Wordsworth*, ed. Gravil and Robinson, pp. 289–308 (p. 295).
41 Fulford, *Wordsworth's Poetry, 1815–1845*, p. 224.
42 Ibid.
43 Giorgio Agamben, *Stasis: Civil War as a Political Paradigm*, trans. Nicholas Heron (Edinburgh: Edinburgh University Press, 2015), p. 41.

44 For further analysis of the politicisation of 'simple natural life' see Agamben, *Homo Sacer*, pp. 1–8.
45 *Sonnet Series and Itinerary Poems*, ed. Jackson, p. 56. In broader terms, Cox reads Wordsworth's focus on 'the native, homey Duddon' and his corresponding endorsement of poetry that is 'pure, vigorous, free, and bright' as an attack on the cosmopolitan pretensions and unbridled sensuality of the Cockney School. See *William Wordsworth, Second-Generation Romantic*, pp. 147–9.
46 Wordsworth's allusions to Ode 3.13 are numerous. See *The Dog: An Idyllium* (1786); *An Evening Walk*, ll. 72–85; his translation of 1794; 'To Liberty' (1820), ll. 91–110; 'Musings near Aquapendente' (1837), ll. 256–7. For discussion of Wordsworth's translation of Horace's ode see Bruce Edward Graver, *Wordsworth's Translations from Latin Poetry* (Chapel Hill, NC: University of North Carolina Press, 1983), pp. 53–4. See also Edward W. Clancey, *Wordsworth's Classical Undersong: Education, Rhetoric and Poetic Truth* (Houndmills: Macmillan, 2000), pp. 56–8.
47 Latin quotations taken from Horace, *The Odes*, ed. Kenneth Quinn (Houndmills: Macmillan, 1980), p. 75.
48 For an excellent reading of this poem see Dan Curley, 'The Alcaic Kid (Horace, "Carm." 3.13)', *The Classical World* 97.2 (Winter 2004), pp. 137–54.
49 Callimachus, *Hymn to Apollo*, l. 110, *The Hymns*, trans. Susan A. Stephens (Oxford: Oxford University Press, 2015), p. 81.
50 Quotations taken from Wordsworth, '[Ode] (from Horace)', *Early Poems and Fragments, 1785–1797*, ed. Carol Landon and Jared R. Curtis (Ithaca, NY: Cornell University Press, 1997), p. 769. In *An Evening Walk* (1793) Wordsworth makes clear his wish to supplant Horace's 'ruthless minister of death' (l. 74) with a 'more benignant sacrifice' (l. 78). *An Evening Walk*, ed. James Averill (Ithaca, NY: Cornell University Press, 1984), p. 41.
51 Erwin Panofsky, *Meaning in the Visual Arts* (New York: Doubleday, 1995), p. 300. The connections between war and pastoral are explored by Kate McLoughlin in *Authoring War: The Literary Representation of War from the Iliad to Iraq* (Cambridge: Cambridge University Press, 2011), pp. 97–106.
52 *The Iliads of Homer Prince of Poets· Neuer Before in Any Languag Truely Translated. With a Co[m]ment vppon Some of His Chiefe Places; Donne according to the Greeke by Geo: Chapman* (London, 1611), p. 287. Wordsworth's library held at least two early modern editions of Chapman's translation. See Chester L. Shaver and Alice C. Shaver, *Wordsworth's Library: A Catalogue* (New York and London: Garland, 1979), p. 126.
53 *The Iliads of Homer*, p. 291.
54 Agamben, *Homo Sacer*, p. 88.
55 Quotations taken from Wordsworth's translation in *Translations of Chaucer and Virgil*, ed. Bruce Graver (Ithaca, NY: Cornell University Press, 1998), p. 248. Wordsworth's account of the bleeding and speaking tree owes much to Dante, Tasso, and Spenser.

56 Virgil, *Eclogues, Georgics, Aeneid I–VI*, trans. H. Rushton Fairclough, Loeb Classical Library. Issue 194, vol. 1 of Horace (Cambridge, MA: Harvard University Press, 1960), p. 113.
57 Ibid., p. 115.
58 Ibid., p. 7.
59 On the accenting of '*now*' as an effort to overcome the vitiating effects of time, see Paul de Man, 'Time and History in Wordsworth', in *Romanticism and Contemporary Criticism: The Gauss Seminar and Other Papers*, ed. Kevin Newmark (Baltimore, MD, and London: Johns Hopkins University Press, 1993), pp. 74–94 (p. 91).
60 The octave of 31 and the sestet of 32 originally formed one sonnet. See *Sonnet Series and Itinerary Poems*, ed. Jackson, p. 109.
61 Along similar lines, Cox, citing Garrett (*Wordsworth and the Writing of the Nation*, pp. 145–8), reads the closing sonnets of the sequence as an attempt to free the Duddon from 'the increasingly imperial history of combat and commerce'. *William Wordsworth, Second-Generation Romantic*, p. 151.
62 Kim, 'Generating a National Sublime', pp. 65–7.
63 See also Kim's observations on the martial significance of flood imagery in *Regarding the Convention of Cintra* (1809) and the conclusion of the *Duddon* sonnets. Ibid., pp. 63–4.
64 'Character of the Happy Warrior', ll. 12–18. *'Poems, in Two Volumes', and Other Poems, 1800–1807*, ed. Curtis, pp. 84–6.
65 Steven Miller, *War after Death: On Violence and Its Limits* (New York: Fordham University Press, 2014), p. 4.
66 Ibid.
67 The copies of the three-volume *Poems* that I have examined in the Jerwood Centre attest to this eclectic response to the recommended order of binding.
68 James Chandler has suggested that the positioning of the 'Thanksgiving Ode' alludes deliberately to the placing of the 'Immortality' ode at the end of the 1807 *Poems, in Two Volumes* and the 1815 *Poems*. '"Wordsworth" after Waterloo', in *The Age of William Wordsworth*, ed. Kenneth R. Johnston and Gene Rouff (New Brunswick and London: Rutgers University Press, 1987), pp. 84–111 (p. 474).
69 Quotations from *Duddon* sonnet XXXII, line 9, and *Duddon* sonnet XXXI, line 4.
70 As noted by Cox, *William Wordsworth, Second-Generation Romantic*, pp. 166–7.
71 *Shorter Poems*, ed. Ketcham, pp. 201–6.
72 Ibid., p. 43.
73 Ibid. pp. 200–1.
74 Peter Manning, 'Wordsworth Reshapes Himself and Is Reshaped: *The River Duddon* and the 1820 *Miscellaneous Poems*', *The Wordsworth Circle* 50.1 (Winter 2020), pp. 35–53 (pp. 41–2).
75 Ibid., pp. 42–3. Quotation from 'Written in London, September, 1802', ll. 13–14. *'Poems, in Two Volumes', and Other Poems, 1800–1807*, ed. Curtis, p. 165.

76 Quotations taken from *The Miscellaneous Poems of William Wordsworth. In Four Volumes* (London: Longman, Hurst, Rees, Orme, and Brown, 1820).
77 Homer: *The Iliad*, trans. Robert Fagles (New York: Penguin, 1990). Book XXI, ll. 246–50, p. 527.
78 Fenwick note. *Sonnet Series and Itinerary Poems*, ed. Jackson, p. 235.
79 Joseph Phelan, *The Nineteenth-Century Sonnet* (New York: Palgrave, 2005), p. 14. In *Wordsworth's Poetry, 1815–1845*, Fulford argues that the 'sonnet sequence bespoke an exemplary program of almost daily literary self-discipline. Each was an exercise in movement from free thought to historical form, an act of self-definition by submission to rule, ranged against what Wordsworth saw as the disruptive forces of political and religious reform' (p. 225).
80 For commentary on the ideological purposes of *Ecclesiastical Sketches* see: Regina Hewitt, 'Church Building as Political Strategy in Wordsworth's "Ecclesiastical Sonnets"', *Mosaic* 25 (1992), pp. 31–46; Anne L. Rylestone, *Prophetic Memory in Wordsworth's 'Ecclesiastical Sonnets'* (Carbondale, IL: Southern Illinois University Press, 1991); Lori Branch, *Rituals of Spontaneity: Sentiment and Secularism from Free Prayer to Wordsworth* (Waco, TX: Baylor University Press, 2006); Michael Tomko, 'Superstition, the National Imaginary, and Religious Politics in Wordsworth's *Ecclesiastical Sketches*', *Wordsworth Circle* 39 (2008), pp. 16–19; Fulford, *Wordsworth's Poetry, 1815–1845*, pp. 214–39.
81 *Sonnet Series and Itinerary Poems*, ed. Jackson, pp. 241–2.

Chapter 6 Wordsworth after Byron: *Memorials of a Tour on the Continent, 1820*

1 Moorman, *William Wordsworth: A Biography. The Later Years, 1803–1850*, pp. 386–8. A full account of the Wordsworths' itinerary in Paris is given in Mary Wordsworth's travel journal, DCMS 92. A transcription of the journal is available at www.day-books.com/assets/daybooks_wordsworth_diary.pdf.
2 Helen Maria Williams, *Poems on Various Subjects: With Introductory Remarks on the Present State of Science and Literature in France* (London, 1823), p. 203.
3 Charles Lamb to William Wordsworth, 9 August 1814. *The Letters of Charles and Mary Anne Lamb*, ed. Marrs. III. 95–9.
4 Robert Southey to Henry Herbert Southey, 23 August 1815. *The Collected Letters of Robert Southey*. Part Four, ed. Lynda Pratt and Ian Packer, Romantic Circles: n.p. Web. Accessed 9 July 2021.
5 'Brighton Herald'. *Morning Chronicle* [London, England] (21 August 1815): n.p. *British Library Newspapers*. Web. Accessed 9 July 2021.
6 Jane Austen, *Lady Susan, The Watsons, and Sanditon*, ed. Kathryn Sutherland (Oxford: Oxford University Press, 2021), p. 118.
7 My thinking on the social significance of Romantic-era continental tour writing has been shaped by the following: James Buzzard, *The Beaten Track: European Tourism, Literature, and the Ways to Culture, 1800–1918* (Oxford: Oxford University Press, 1993); Dean MacCannell, *The Tourist: A New Theory*

of the Leisure Class (Berkeley, CA: University of California Press, 1999); Nigel Leask, *Curiosity and the Aesthetics of Travel Writing, 1770–1840* (Oxford: Oxford University Press, 2002); Carl Thompson, *The Suffering Traveller and the Romantic Imagination* (Oxford: Oxford University Press, 2007).

8 Austen, *Lady Susan, The Watsons, and Sanditon*, p. 111.
9 Critical studies of *Memorials* include: Donald E. Hayden, *Wordsworth's Travels in Europe I* (Tulsa: The University of Tulsa, 1988), pp. 41–109; John Wyatt, *Wordsworth's Poems of Travel, 1819–1842: 'Such Sweet Wayfaring'* (Houndmills: Macmillan, 1999), chapter 4: '*Memorials of a Tour, 1820*: The Lessons of Europe', pp. 55–79; Robin Jarvis, 'The Wages of Travel: Wordsworth and the Memorial Tour of 1820', *Studies in Romanticism* 40.3 (Fall, 2001), pp. 321–43; Pamela Woof, *William, Mary and Dorothy: The Wordsworths' Continental Tour of 1820* (Grasmere: Wordsworth's Trust, 2008); C. E. J. Simons, 'Itinerant Wordsworth', in *The Oxford Handbook of William Wordsworth*, ed. Gravil and Robinson, pp. 97–115 (pp. 107–11).
10 Austen, *Lady Susan, The Watsons, and Sanditon*, p. 130; p. 143.
11 Ibid., p. 132.
12 Simons, 'Itinerant Wordsworth', p. 108.
13 Dorothy Wordsworth, 'Journal of a Tour on the Continent', in *Journals of Dorothy Wordsworth*, ed. Ernest de Selincourt, 2 vols. (London: Macmillan, 1970), II. 297.
14 Peter Larkin, *Wordsworth and Coleridge: Promising Losses* (Houndmills: Palgrave Macmillan, 2012), p. 13.
15 Ibid., p. 12.
16 Jarvis, 'The Wages of Travel: Wordsworth and the Memorial Tour of 1820', p. 333.
17 Tim Fulford, *The Late Poetry of the Lake Poets: Romanticism Revisited* (Cambridge: Cambridge University Press, 2013), p. 202.
18 Peter J. Manning, 'The Other Scene of Travel: Wordsworth's 'Musings near Aquapendente', in *The Wordsworthian Enlightenment: Romantic Poetry and the Ecology of Reading*, ed. Helen Reguiro Elam and Frances Ferguson (Baltimore, MD: Johns Hopkins University Press, 2005), pp. 191–211 (p. 206). See also Jeffrey Cox's thoughtful and illuminating discussion of Wordsworth's reaction to 'the Byronic version of European travel' in *William Wordsworth, Second-Generation Romantic*, pp. 170–99 (p. 177).
19 Larkin, *Wordsworth and Coleridge: Promising Losses*, p. 13.
20 Francis Jeffrey, 'Review of *Memorials of a Tour on the Continent*', *The Edinburgh Review, or Critical Journal* 37 (June–November, 1822), pp. 449–56 (pp. 450–1).
21 *The Literary Chronicle and Weekly Review* 187 (14 December 1822), p. 791.
22 'Dedication'. Quotations from *Memorials* are from *Sonnet Series and Itinerary Poems, 1820–1845*, ed. Jackson, pp. 358–411.
23 Although plans for a publication combining Dorothy's prose account of the tour with William's poetry did not come to fruition, a fair copy manuscript circulated within the family for many years. See Michelle Levy, *Family*

Authorship and Romantic Print Culture (Houndmills: Palgrave Macmillan, 2008), chapter 4: 'The Shelleys, the Wordsworths, and the Family Tour', pp. 108–42.
24 'Preface' to *Lyrical Ballads*. *'Lyrical Ballads', and Other Poems, 1797–1800*, ed. Butler and Green, p. 743.
25 Jeffrey, 'Review of *Memorials of a Tour on the Continent*', p. 451.
26 Pliny, *Natural History, Volume III: Books 8–11*, trans. H. Rackham, Loeb Classical Library, vol. 353 (Cambridge, MA: Harvard University Press, 1940), pp. 164–5.
27 *Sonnet Series and Itinerary Poems, 1820–1845*, ed. Jackson, p. 412.
28 Ibid., p. 419.
29 Compare the poem, for example, with the account of the subterranean sea in *Endymion*, II. ll. 600–32.
30 Fulford, *Wordsworth's Poetry, 1815–1845*, pp. 181–2. Jeffrey Cox's reading of Keats's and Byron's attempts to radicalise the Ovidian leanings of the representation of myth in Book IV of *The Excursion* is especially pertinent here: *William Wordsworth, Second-Generation Romantic*, pp. 48–54.
31 'Calais, August 15th, 1802', l. 11. 'To a Friend, Composed near Calais, on the Road Leading to Andres, August 7th, 1802', l. 11. *'Poems, in Two Volumes', and Other Poems, 1800–1807*, ed. Curtis, pp. 158–9; pp. 156–7.
32 William Hogarth, *The Analysis of Beauty: With the Rejected Passages from the Manuscript Drafts, and Autobiographical Notes*, ed. Joseph Burke (Oxford: Clarendon Press, 1955), pp. 227–8.
33 See Jarvis's complementary account of this poem: 'The twilight beauty Wordsworth cherishes seems all too brief an interlude between the imperial "robe of power" constituted by full sunlight and the "gentle Power of Darkness" to come – suggesting that peace may be an uncertain intermission in the "desolating storms" of war'. 'The Wages of Travel: Wordsworth and the Memorial Tour of 1820', p. 334.
34 Kelley, *Wordsworth's Revisionary Aesthetics*, pp. 88–9.
35 *Don Juan*, 'Dedication', l. 5, l. 46. From volume 5 of *Lord Byron: The Complete Poetical Works*, ed. McGann and Weller.
36 *Memoirs, Journal, and Correspondence of Thomas Moore*, ed. Lord John Russell, 8 vols. (London, 1853), III. 161.
37 Added as a conclusion to the *Memorials* sequence in 1840, the sonnet 'At Dover' was initially sent to Dora as a 'peace offering' during a period of estrangement from her father in February 1838. *SNL*, p. 238. *Sonnet Series and Itinerary Poems, 1820–1845*, ed. Jackson, p. 411. For a reading of the biographical and literary significance of this poem see my 'Wordsworth's "Dread Voice": Ovid, Dora, and the Later Poetry', *Romanticism* 8.1 (2002), pp. 34–48.
38 Quotations from *Childe Harold's Pilgrimage* are from volume 2 of *Lord Byron: The Complete Poetical Works*, ed. McGann and Weller.
39 Thomas Medwin, *Conversations of Lord Byron with Thomas Medwin, ESQ* (London, 1832), pp. 24–5.
40 Ibid., p. 25.

41 Stanzas 71–5 were cited in early reviews of the poem as containing distinctive echoes of Wordsworth's poetry, with 'Tintern Abbey' being the most-cited touchstone. See, for example, 'Childe Harold's Pilgrimage: Canto the Third. By Lord Byron', *The Critical Review; or, Annals of Literature* 4 (1816), pp. 495–506 (p. 505).

42 Notable studies of Byron's imitations of Wordsworth in Canto III include: Robert R. Harson, 'Byron's "Tintern Abbey"', *Keats-Shelley Journal* 20 (1971), pp. 113–21; Michael G. Cooke, 'Byron and Wordsworth: The Complementarity of a Rock and the Sea', in *Lord Byron and His Contemporaries,* ed. Charles E. Robinson, (London and Toronto: Associated University Presses, 1982), pp. 19–42; James L. Hill, 'Experiments in the Narrative of Consciousness: Byron, Wordsworth, and *Childe Harold*, Cantos 3 and 4', *English Literary History* 53.1 (1986), pp. 121–40; Vincent Newey, 'Authoring the Self: *Childe Harold* III and IV', in *Byron and the Limits of Fiction*, ed. Bernard Beatty and Vincent Newey (Liverpool: Liverpool University Press, 1988), pp. 148–90; Drummond Bone, 'Shelley, Wordsworth, and Byron: The Detail of Nature', *The Wordsworth Circle* 20.1 (1992), pp. 43–50; Jerome McGann, 'Wordsworth and Byron', in *Byron and Romanticism*, ed. James Soderholm (Cambridge: University of Cambridge Press, 2002), pp. 173–202; Daniel Westwood, '"Living in Shattered Guise": Doubling in *Childe Harold's Pilgrimage* Canto III', *The Byron Journal* 44.2 (2016), pp. 125–37.

43 See, for example, Mark Kipperman's reading of the storm scene in *Beyond Enchantment: German Idealism and English Romantic Poetry* (Philadelphia, PA: University of Pennsylvania Press, 1986), pp. 187–9. See also Jerome McGann, 'Byron and the Anonymous Lyric', in *Byron and Romanticism*, pp. 93–112 (pp. 103–5).

44 Tuite, *Lord Byron and Scandalous Celebrity* (Cambridge: Cambridge University Press, 2015), p. 95.

45 *Sonnet Series and Itinerary Poems, 1820–1845*, ed. Jackson, p. 413.

46 Note to *Childe Harold's Pilgrimage*, Canto III, stanza 40. *Works of Lord Byron: With His Letters and Journals, and His Life by Thomas Moore, Esq*, 17 vols. (London, 1836), VIII. 159.

47 Jeffrey, 'Review of *Memorials of a Tour on the Continent*', p. 453.

48 *Sonnet Series and Itinerary Poems, 1820–1845*, ed. Jackson, p. 368.

49 *The Poems and Fables of John Dryden*, ed. Kinsley, p. 574.

50 Noting how a 'parallel vocabulary of flood and destruction characterises French discussions of the Revolution in the 1790s', Kelley asserts that the poem 'illustrates the two views of the sublime which [Wordsworth] had kept separate for so many years: the mind's capacity to resist revolutionary torrents and remain free; and its parallel capacity to participate in those torrents and in doing so also remain free'. *Wordsworth's Revisionary Aesthetics*, pp. 182–4. See also Jarvis's response to this reading: 'The Wages of Travel: Wordsworth and the Memorial Tour of 1820', pp. 334–5.

51 Larkin, *Wordsworth and Coleridge: Promising Losses*, p. 24. Jarvis, 'The Wages of Travel: Wordsworth and the Memorial Tour of 1820', pp. 335–6.

52 *Sonnet Series and Itinerary Poems, 1820–1845*, ed. Jackson, p. 414.
53 Ibid.
54 Wyatt, *Wordsworth's Poems of Travel*, p. 65.
55 Jarvis, 'The Wages of Travel: Wordsworth and the Memorial Tour of 1820', pp. 336–40. See also Alan Liu's influential discussion of this poem in *Wordsworth: The Sense of History*, pp. 540–1.
56 Peter J. Manning, 'Cleansing the Images: Wordsworth, Rome, and the Rise of Historicism', *Texas Studies in Literature and Language* 33.2 (Summer 1991), pp. 271–326 (p. 307).
57 *Lord Byron: The Complete Poetical Works*, ed. McGann and Weller, II. 311.
58 MS. 177; ll. 9–14. *Sonnet Series and Itinerary Poems, 1820–1845*, ed. Jackson, p. 395.
59 27 August 1820. *Diary, Reminiscences, and Correspondence of Henry Crabb Robinson*, ed. Sadler, I. 357.
60 Eric Walker points out that although Wordsworth was in London at this time, aside from the watercolour, the documentary status of which is itself weakened by the inclusion of a portrait of Byron, who remained in exile in Europe, no other evidence has been found to corroborate the poet's attendance at the trial. *Marriage, Writing and Romanticism*, p. 245.
61 *The Task*, Book VI. l. 325; l. 364. Cowper, *The Task and Selected Other Poems*, ed. Sambrook.
62 Ibid., l. 368.
63 *Sonnet Series and Itinerary Poems, 1820–1845*, ed. Jackson, p. 355.
64 See Ernest De Selincourt's account of the relationship in *Wordsworthian and Other Studies* (Oxford: Clarendon Press, 1947), pp. 34–56. Also Moorman, *William Wordsworth: A Biography. The Later Years, 1803–1850*, pp. 584–9.
65 For a related approach to the poem see Keith Hanley, *Wordsworth: A Poet's History* (Houndmills: Palgrave, 2001), pp. 65–6.
66 Comparison should be made with Keats's frank and unabashed treatment of the legend in *Endymion*, Book II, ll. 915–1009.
67 C-Stage Reading Text. Book X, ll. 1069–73. *The Thirteen-Book 'Prelude'*, ed. Reed. II. 201–02.

After Wordsworth

1 *The Peace Almanac and Diary, for 1846, under the Superintendence of the Manchester and Salford Peace Society* (Manchester and London, 1846), p. 5.
2 'On the Poetry of the Age', *The Grange Magazine. A Series of Papers in Prose and Verse* (Edinburgh, 1846), pp. 195–203.
3 The view of Wordsworth as the poet of 'peace – above all, peace' that prevailed in discussions of the poet in the 1840s was initiated in 'Wordsworth', an article for *Blackwood's Edinburgh Magazine* 49 (January–June 1841), pp. 359–71 (p. 367). Wordsworth's doctrine of 'peace and silence' was the subject of 'Mr George Dawson's Lectures on Wordsworth', as reported in the *Manchester Times*, 24 October 1846, *British Library Newspapers*, link-gale-com.ezproxy4.lib.le.ac.uk/apps/doc/BC3206363709/GDCS?u=leicester&sid=bookmark-GDCS&xid=d247cd1a.

Accessed 23 September 2021. See also 'Thoughts on the Poets', *The Literary Gazette and Journal of the Belles Lettres, Arts, Sciences &c.* 1598, 4 September 1847, pp. 637–40.
4 Robert Hopkins, 'De Quincey on War and the Pastoral Design of *The English Mail-Coach*', *Studies in Romanticism* 6.3 (1967), pp. 129–51 (pp. 130–3).
5 Anonymous, 'A Moral from Walmer', *Blackwood's Magazine* 72.445 (November 1852), pp. 630–3 (p. 631).
6 Ibid., p. 632; p. 630.
7 For discussion of Cobden and the Peace Societies see Ceadel, *The Origins of War Prevention*, pp. 414–69. See also Hopkins, 'De Quincey on War', pp. 130–1, and Daniel Pick, *War Machine: The Rationalisation of Slaughter in the Modern Age* (New Haven, CT, and London: Yale University Press, 1993), pp. 19–27.
8 See Timothy Ziegenhagen, 'War Addiction in Thomas De Quincey's *The English Mail-Coach*', *Wordsworth Circle* 35.2 (2004), pp. 93–8.
9 Shaw, *Waterloo and the Romantic Imagination*, pp. 203–9.
10 *The Poetical Works of Leigh Hunt*, ed. H. S. Milford (Oxford: Oxford University Press, 1923), pp. 687–8.
11 Ibid., p. 688.
12 Ibid., p. 697.
13 Ibid.
14 Christopher Wordsworth, *Memoirs of William Wordsworth*, I. 73.
15 *'Lyrical Ballads', and Other Poems, 1797–1800*, ed. Butler and Green, pp. 277–82.
16 Mark Offord, *Wordsworth and the Art of Philosophical Travel* (Cambridge: Cambridge University Press, 2016), p. 77.
17 Alan Bewell, *Romanticism and Colonial Disease* (Baltimore, MD: Johns Hopkins University Press, 1999), p. 117. In a carefully mounted rejoinder to new historicist takedowns of the poem's 'ideology of transcendence', Mark Offord argues that new historicism should recognise that 'it is history itself that has aestheticized or sacrificed – "discharged" – the man. A historical suffering, effected by causes of personal "importance" to its conscripts, has subsided into "weakness" and "indifference". This is what dissociates the figure from context. The lapse registers a historical *experience*'. *Wordsworth and the Art of Philosophical Travel*, p. 80. Offord is responding to readings of the poem by Mary Jacobus, *Romanticism, Writing, and Sexual Difference: Essays on 'The Prelude'* (Oxford: Oxford University Press, 1989), p. 73, and Celeste Langan, *Romantic Vagrancy: Wordsworth and the Simulation of Freedom* (Cambridge: Cambridge University Press, 1995), pp. 194–5.
18 Milton, *Paradise Lost*, ed. Fowler.
19 Offord, *Wordsworth and the Art of Philosophical Travel*, p. 83.
20 *The Fourteen-Book 'Prelude'*, ed. W. J. B. Owen (Ithaca, NY, and London: Cornell University Press, 1985).
21 Ll. 209–24, *passim*. Interestingly, the poem makes frequent allusion to the association of noise with violent conflict, noting the 'shrieks, that revel in abuse/ Of shivering flesh' (ll. 9–10), the 'martial *pageant*' that 'spreads/Incitements of battle-day' (ll. 73–4), and the revelatory 'Trumpet' that 'we, intoxicate with

pride,/Arm at its blast for deadly wars' (ll. 213–14). *Last Poems, 1821–1850*, ed. Curtis, pp. 116–24.
22 Walter Benjamin, *The Arcades Project*, trans. Howard Eiland and Kevin McLaughlin (Cambridge, MA: Harvard University Press, 1999), p. 400.
23 Theodor Adorno, *Minima Moralia: Reflections from Damaged Life*, trans. E. F. N. Jephcott (London and New York: Verso, 2020), p. 212.
24 *Last Poems, 1821–1850*, ed. Curtis, pp. 388–9.
25 C. M. Ingleby, 'Modern Metaphysicians. The Late Sir William Rowan Hamilton', *The British Controversialist and Literary Magazine* (London, 1869), pp. 161–77 (p. 167).

Select Bibliography

Adorno, Theodor. *Minima Moralia: Reflections from Damaged Life*. Trans. E. F. N. Jephcott. London and New York: Verso, 2020.
Agamben, Giorgio. *The Coming Community*. Trans. Michael Hardt. Minneapolis, MN: University of Minnesota Press, 1993.
Agamben, Giorgio. *Homo Sacer: Sovereign Power and Bare Life*. Trans. Daniel Heller Roazen. Stanford, CA: Stanford University Press, 1998.
Agamben, Giorgio. *Idea of Prose*. Trans. Michael Sullivan and Sam Whitsitt. Albany, NY: SUNY Press, 1995.
Agamben, Giorgio. *The Man without Content*. Trans. Georgia Albert. Stanford, CA: Stanford University Press, 1999.
Agamben, Giorgio. *Potentialities: Collected Essays in Philosophy*. Trans. Daniel Heller Roazen. Stanford, CA: Stanford University Press, 1999.
Agamben, Giorgio. *Stasis: Civil War as a Political Paradigm*. Trans. Nicholas Heron. Edinburgh: Edinburgh University Press, 2015.
Agamben, Giorgio. *The Time That Remains: A Commentary on the Letter to the Romans*. Trans. Patricia Dailey. Stanford, CA: Stanford University Press, 2005.
Austen, Jane. *Lady Susan, the Watsons, and Sanditon*. Ed. Kathryn Sutherland. Oxford: Oxford University Press, 2021.
Bainbridge, Simon. *British Poetry and the Revolutionary and Napoleonic Wars*. Oxford: Oxford University Press, 2003.
Bainbridge, Simon. *Napoleon and English Romanticism*. Cambridge: Cambridge University Press, 1995.
Bainbridge, Simon. 'Wordsworth, War and Waterloo'. In *Wordsworth, War and Waterloo*. Ed. Simon Bainbridge and Jeff Cowton, pp. 16–28. Grasmere: The Wordsworth Trust, 2015.
Bamford, Samuel. *Passages in the Life of a Radical*. Oxford: Oxford University Press, 1984.
Barrell, John. '"Laodamia" and the Moaning of Mary'. *Textual Practice* 10.3 (1996), pp. 449–77.
Bates, Brian R. *Wordsworth's Poetic Collections, Supplementary Writing and Parodic Reception*. Abingdon: Routledge, 2012.
Batho, Edith. *The Later Wordsworth*. Cambridge: Cambridge University Press, 1933.

Behrendt, Stephen C. 'Placing the Places in Wordsworth's 1802 Sonnets'. *Studies in English Literature, 1500–1900* 35.4 (1994), pp. 641–57.
Benjamin, Walter. *The Arcades Project*. Trans. Howard Eiland and Kevin McLaughlin. Cambridge, MA: Harvard University Press, 1999.
Benjamin, Walter. *One-Way Street and Other Writings*. Trans. Edmund Jephcott and Kingsley Shorter. London and New York: Verso, 1997.
Benjamin, Walter. *Toward the Critique of Violence: A Critical Edition*. Ed. Peter Fenves and Julia Ng. Stanford, CA: Stanford University Press, 2021.
Bennett, Jane. *Vibrant Matter: A Political Ecology of Things*. Durham and London: Duke University Press, 2010.
Bewell, Alan. *Romanticism and Colonial Disease*. Baltimore, MD: Johns Hopkins University Press, 1999.
Blanchot, Maurice. *The Writing of the Disaster*. Trans. Ann Smock. Lincoln: University of Nebraska Press, 1995.
Blunden, Edmund. *Undertones of War*. Harmondsworth: Penguin, 1982.
Boas, Frederick S. *Wordsworth's Patriotic Poems and Their Significance Today*. London: The English Association, Pamphlet 30, 1914.
Bogost, Ian. *Alien Phenomenology, or What It's Like to Be a Thing*. Minneapolis, MN and London: University of Minnesota Press, 2012.
Bone, Drummond. 'Shelley, Wordsworth, and Byron: The Detail of Nature'. *The Wordsworth Circle* 20.1 (1992), pp. 43–50.
Branch, Lori. *Rituals of Spontaneity: Sentiment and Secularism from Free Prayer to Wordsworth*. Waco, TX: Baylor University Press, 2006.
Bryant, Levi, Srnicek, Nick, and Harman, Graham (eds). *The Speculative Turn: Continental Materialism and Realism*. Melbourne: re-press, 2011.
Bugg, John. *British Romanticism and Peace*. Oxford: Oxford University Press, 2022.
Burke, Edmund. *A Philosophical Enquiry into the Origin of Our Ideas of the Sublime and Beautiful*. Ed. Adam Phillips. Oxford: Oxford University Press, 1990.
Burke, Edmund. *Revolutionary Writings*. Ed. Iain Hampshire-Monk. Cambridge: Cambridge University Press, 2014.
Bushell, Sally. *Re-Reading The Excursion: Narrative, Response and the Wordsworthian Dramatic Voice*. Aldershot: Ashgate, 2002.
Butler, James A. 'Wordsworth's "Tuft of Primroses": An "Unrelenting Doom"'. *Studies in Romanticism* 14.3 (Summer 1973), pp. 237–48.
Butler, Judith. *The Force of Non-violence: An Ethico-political Bind*. London and New York: Verso, 2020.
Butler, Samuel. *The Effects of Peace on the Religious Principle Considered. A Sermon, Preached in the Chapel of Berwick, on Tuesday, June 1, 1802, Being the Day Appointed by Proclamation for a General Thanksgiving*. Shrewsbury, 1802.
Buzzard, James. *The Beaten Track: European Tourism, Literature, and the Ways to Culture, 1800–1918*. Oxford: Oxford University Press, 1993.
Byron, George Gordon, Lord. *Lord Byron: The Complete Poetical Works*. Ed. Jerome J. McGann and Barry Weller. 7 vols. Oxford: Clarendon Press, 1980–93.

Callimachus. *The Hymns*. Trans. Susan A. Stephens. Oxford: Oxford University Press, 2015.
Cameron, William. *A Review of the French Revolution*. Edinburgh and London, 1802.
Carlson, Julia S. 'Charting the Stream of Time: William Wordsworth and Joseph Priestley'. Conference paper delivered at 'After Wordsworth: Water, Writing'. University of Leicester, 8 January 2021.
Ceadel, Martin. *The Origins of War Prevention: The British Peace Movement and International Relations, 1730–1854*. Oxford: Oxford University Press, 1996.
Chalmers, Thomas. *Thoughts on Universal Peace: A Sermon, Delivered on Thursday, January 18, 1816 [...]*. Glasgow, 1816.
Chandler, James. *England in 1819: The Politics of Literary Culture and the Case of Romantic Historicism*. Chicago and London: University of Chicago Press, 1999.
Chandler, James. '"Wordsworth" After Waterloo', *The Age of William Wordsworth*. Ed. Kenneth R. Johnston and Gene Ruoff, pp. 84–111. New Brunswick and London: Rutgers University Press, 1987.
Chandler, James. *Wordsworth's Second Nature: A Study of the Poetry and Politics*. Chicago: University of Chicago Press, 1984.
Christensen, Jerome C. *Romanticism: At the End of History*. Baltimore, MD: Johns Hopkins University Press, 2000.
Claeys, Gregory. '"The Only Man of Nature That Ever Appeared in the World": "Walking" John Stewart and the Trajectories of Social Radicalism, 1790–1822'. *Journal of British Studies* 53.3 (July 2014), pp. 636–59.
Clancey, Edward W. *Wordsworth's Classical Undersong: Education, Rhetoric and Poetic Truth*. Houndmills: Macmillan, 2000.
Class, Monika. *Coleridge and Kantian Ideas in England, 1796–1817: Coleridge's Responses to German Philosophy*. London: Bloomsbury, 2012.
Coleman, Deirdre. 'Re-living Jacobinism: Wordsworth and the Convention of Cintra'. *The Yearbook of English Studies* 19 (1989), pp. 144–61.
Coleridge, Samuel T. *The Collected Coleridge: Biographia Literaria*. Ed. James Engell and W. Jackson Bate. 2 vols. Princeton, NJ: Princeton University Press, 1983.
Coleridge, Samuel T. *Collected Letters of Samuel Taylor Coleridge*. Ed. Earl Leslie Griggs. 6 vols. Oxford: Oxford University Press, 1956–71.
Collings, David. 'Blank Oblivion, Condemned Life: John Clare's "Obscurity"'. In *Romanticism and Speculative Realism*. Ed. Chris Washington and Anne C. McCarthy, pp. 75–92. New York: Bloomsbury, 2019.
Cooke, Michael G. 'Byron and Wordsworth: The Complementarity of a Rock and the Sea'. In *Lord Byron and His Contemporaries*. Ed. Charles E. Robinson, pp. 19–42. London and Toronto: Associated University Presses, 1982.
Cookson, J. E. *The Friends of Peace: Anti-war Liberalism in England, 1793–1815*. Cambridge: Cambridge University Press, 1982.
Cotes, Henry. *Another Mite for Waterloo. A Sermon, Preached in the Parish Church of Bedlington, in the County of Durham, on Sunday, the Twentieth of August, 1815*. Newcastle, 1815.

Cowper, William. *The Task and Selected Other Poems*. Ed. James Sambrook. London and New York: Longman, 1994.
Cox, Jeffrey N. *Romanticism in the Shadow of War: Literary Culture in the Napoleonic War Years*. Cambridge: Cambridge University Press, 2014.
Cox, Jeffrey N. *William Wordsworth, Second-Generation Romantic: Contesting Poetry after Waterloo*. Cambridge: Cambridge University Press, 2021.
Curley, Dan. 'The Alcaic Kid Horace, "Carm." 3.13'. *The Classical World* 97.2 (Winter 2004), pp. 137–54.
de Man, Paul. 'Time and History in Wordsworth'. In *Romanticism and Contemporary Criticism: The Gauss Seminar and Other Papers*. Ed. Kevin Newmark, pp. 74–94. Baltimore, MD and London: Johns Hopkins University Press, 1993.
de Paolo, Charles. 'Kant, Coleridge and the Ethics of War'. *The Wordsworth Circle* 16.1 (1985), pp. 3–12.
de Selincourt, Ernest. *Wordsworthian and Other Studies*. Oxford: Clarendon Press, 1947.
Derrida, Jacques. *Adieu to Emmanuel Levinas*. Trans. Pascale-Anne Brault and Michael Naas. Stanford, CA: Stanford University Press, 1999.
Derrida, Jacques. *The Animal That Therefore I Am*. Ed. Marie-Louse Mallett. Trans. David Wills. New York: Fordham University Press, 2008.
Derrida, Jacques. *Cosmopolitanism and Forgiveness*. Trans. Mark Dooley and Michael Hughes. London and New York: Routledge, 2001.
Derrida, Jacques. 'Hostipitality'. *Angelaki* 5.3 (2000), pp. 3–18.
Derrida, Jacques. *Margins of Philosophy*. Trans. Alan Bass. Chicago: University of Chicago Press, 1982.
Derrida, Jacques. *Of Grammatology*. Trans. Gayatri Chakravorty Spivak. Baltimore, MD: Johns Hopkins University Press, 1967.
Derrida, Jacques. *Spectres of Marx: The State of the Debt, the Work of Mourning and the New International*. Trans. Peggy Kamuf. New York and London: Routledge, 1994.
Derrida, Jacques. *Writing and Difference*. Trans. Alan Bass. London: Routledge & Kegan Paul, 1978.
Dicey, Albert V. *The Statesmanship of Wordsworth: An Essay*. Oxford: Clarendon Press, 1917.
Dobie, Madelaine. 'The Enlightenment at War'. *PMLA* 124.5 (2009), pp. 1851–4.
Dryden, John. *The Poems and Fables of John Dryden*. Ed. James Kinsley. London: Oxford University Press, 1962.
Fairbanks, A. Harris. '"Dear Native Brook": Coleridge, Bowles, and Thomas Warton, the Younger'. *The Wordsworth Circle* 6.4 (Autumn 1975), pp. 313–15.
Fairclough, Mary. *The Romantic Crowd: Sympathy, Controversy and Print Culture*. Cambridge: Cambridge University Press, 2013.
Fairer, David. *Organising Poetry: The Coleridge Circle, 1790–1798*. Oxford: Oxford University Press, 2009.
Favret, Mary. *War at a Distance: Romanticism and the Making of Modern Wartime*. Princeton, NJ and Oxford: Princeton University Press, 2012.

Fay, Jessica. *Wordsworth's Monastic Inheritance: Poetry, Place, and the Sense of Community*. Oxford: Oxford University Press, 2018.
Ferguson, Adam. *An Essay On the History of Civil Society*. New Brunswick and London: Transaction Books, 1980.
Finch, John. 'Wordsworth, Coleridge, and "The Recluse," 1789–1814'. Doctoral thesis. Ithaca, NY: Cornell University, 1964.
Folker, Brian. 'Wordsworth's Visionary Imagination: Democracy and War'. *ELH* 69.1 (Spring 2002), pp. 167–97.
Forrest, Alan. 'Contrasting Memories: Remembering Waterloo in France and Britain'. In *War, Demobilization and Memory: The Legacy of War In the Era of Atlantic Revolutions*. Ed. Alan Forrest, Karen Hagemann and Michael Rowe, pp. 353–70. Houndmills: Palgrave Macmillan, 2016.
Foucault, Michel. *Society Must Be Defended: Lectures at the Collège de France, 1975–76*. Ed. Mauro Bertani and Alessandro Fontana. Trans. David Macey London: Penguin, 2003.
Friedman, Michael H. *The Making of a Tory Humanist: William Wordsworth and the Idea of Community*. New York: Columbia University Press, 1979.
Fry, Paul H. 'History, Existence, and "to Autumn"'. *Studies in Romanticism* 25.2 (Summer 1986), pp. 211–19.
Fulford, Tim. *Landscape, Liberty and Authority: Poetry, Criticism and Politics from Thomson to Wordsworth*. Cambridge: Cambridge University Press, 1996.
Fulford, Tim. *The Late Poetry of the Lake Poets: Romanticism Revisited*. Cambridge: Cambridge University Press, 2013.
Fulford, Tim. *Wordsworth's Poetry, 1815–1845*. Philadelphia, PA: University of Pennsylvania Press, 2019.
Fussell, Paul. *The Great War and Modern Memory*. Oxford: Oxford University Press, 1975/2000.
Galperin, William H. *Revision and Authority in Wordsworth: The Interpretation of a Career*. Philadelphia, PA: University of Pennsylvania Press, 1989.
Galtung, Johan. 'Violence, Peace, and Peace Research'. *Journal of Peace Research* 6.3 (1969), pp. 167–91.
Garrett, James M. *Wordsworth and the Writing of the Nation*. Aldershot: Ashgate, 2013.
Gates, Barbara. 'Wordsworth's Symbolic White Doe: "The Power of History in the Mind"'. *Criticism* 17.3 (1975), pp. 234–45.
Girard, René. *Violence and the Sacred*. Trans. Patrick Gregory. Baltimore, MD: Johns Hopkins University Press, 1977.
Goodman, Kevis. *Georgic Modernity and British Romanticism*. Cambridge: Cambridge University Press, 2004.
Goodman, Kevis. '"Uncertain Disease": Nostalgia, Pathologies of Motion, Practices of Reading'. *Studies in Romanticism* 49.2 (Summer 2010), pp. 197–227.
Graver, Bruce E. *Wordsworth's Translations from Latin Poetry*. Chapel Hill, NC: University of North Carolina Press, 1983.
Gravil, Richard. 'A "Hideous Rout": Wordsworth's "Thanksgiving Ode" in Context'. *The Coleridge Bulletin* 46 (Winter 2015), pp. 59–78.

Gravil, Richard. 'Wordsworth as Partisan'. In *Concerning the Convention of Cintra. A Critical Edition*. Ed. Richard Gravil and W. J. B. Owen, pp. 17–29. Tirril: Humanities-Ebooks, 2009.
Gravil, Richard. *Wordsworth's Bardic Vocation, 1787–1842*. Houndmills: Palgrave Macmillan, 2003.
Grovier, Kelly. '"Shades of the Prison House": "Walking" Stewart, Michel Foucault and the Making of Wordsworth's "Two Consciousnesses"'. *Studies in Romanticism* 44.3 (Fall 2005), pp. 341–66.
Hanley, Keith. *Wordsworth: A Poet's History*. Houndmills: Palgrave Macmillan, 2001.
Hardt, Michael and Negri, Antonio. *Multitude: War and Democracy in the Age of Empire*. New York: Penguin, 2004.
Harman, Graham. *Quentin Meillassoux: Philosophy in the Making*. Edinburgh: Edinburgh University Press, 2015.
Harson, Robert R. 'Byron's "Tintern Abbey"'. *Keats-Shelley Journal* 20 (1971), pp. 113–21.
Hartman, Geoffrey H. *The Unremarkable Wordsworth*. Minneapolis, MN: University of Minnesota Press, 1987.
Hartman, Geoffrey H. *Wordsworth's Poetry, 1787–1814*. New Haven, CT: Yale University Press, 1964.
Haydon, Benjamin Robert. *The Diary of Benjamin Robert Haydon*. Ed. Willard Bissell Pope. 3 vols. Cambridge, MA: Harvard University Press, 1963.
Hayden, Donald E. *Wordsworth's Travels in Europe I*. Tulsa: The University of Tulsa, 1988.
Hegel, Georg W. F. *The Philosophy of Fine Art*. Trans. F. P. Osmaston. London: G. Bell, 1920.
Hewitt, Regina. 'Church Building as Political Strategy in Wordsworth's *Ecclesiastical Sonnets*'. *Mosaic* 25 (1992), pp. 31–46.
Hill, James L. 'Experiments in the Narrative of Consciousness: Byron, Wordsworth, and Childe Harold, Cantos 3 and 4'. *English Literary History* 53.1 (1986), pp. 121–40.
Hogarth, William. *The Analysis of Beauty: With the Rejected Passages from the Manuscript Drafts, and Autobiographical Notes*. Ed. Joseph Burke. Oxford: Clarendon Press, 1955.
Homer. *Homer: The Iliad*. Trans. Robert Fagles. New York: Penguin, 1990.
Hoock, Holger. *Empires of the Imagination: Politics, War, and the Arts in the British World, 1750–1850*. London: Profile Books, 2010.
Hopkins, Robert. 'De Quincey on War and the Pastoral Design of *The English Mail-Coach*'. *Studies in Romanticism* 6.3 (1967), pp. 129–51.
Horace. *Epistles, Satires and Ars Poetica*. Trans. H. B. Fairclough. Loeb Classical Library. Issue 194, vol. 2 of Horace. Cambridge, MA: Harvard University Press, 1978.
Horace. *Horace: Satires*. Trans. Emily Gowers. Cambridge: Cambridge University Press, 2012.
Horace. *The Odes*. Ed. Kenneth Quinn. Houndmills: Macmillan, 1980.
Horace. *Odes and Epodes. Loeb Classical Library*. Ed. Niall Rudd, vol. 33. Cambridge, MA: Harvard University Press, 2015.

Howley, William. *A Sermon Preached on Thursday, January 18, 1816, Being the Day Appointed for a General Thanksgiving [...]*. London, 1816.
Hunt, Leigh. *The Poetical Works of Leigh Hunt*. Ed. H. S. Milford. Oxford: Oxford University Press, 1923.
Hutchinson, Ben. *Lateness and Modern European Literature*. Oxford: Oxford University Press, 2016.
Hutchinson, Sarah. *The Letters of Sara Hutchinson*. Ed. Kathleen Coburn. London: Routledge and Kegan Paul, 1954.
Hutton, R. H. 'The Earlier and Later Styles of Wordsworth'. In *Wordsworthiana: A Selection from Papers Read to the Wordsworth Society*. Ed. William Angus Knight and Wordsworth Society, pp. 61–78. London, 1889.
Illbruck, Helmut. *Nostalgia: Origins and Ends of an Unenlightened Disease*. Evanston, IL: Northwestern University Press, 2012.
Jacobus, Mary. *Romantic Things: A Tree, a Rock, a Cloud*. Chicago and London: Chicago University Press, 2012.
Jacobus, Mary. *Romanticism, Writing, and Sexual Difference: Essays on 'The Prelude'*. Oxford: Oxford University Press, 1989.
Janowitz, Anne. *England's Ruins: Poetic Purpose and the National Landscape*. Oxford: Wiley-Blackwell, 1990.
Jarrells, Anthony. *Britain's Bloodless Revolutions: 1688 and the Romantic Reform of Literature*. Basingstoke: Palgrave Macmillan, 2005.
Jarvis, Robin. 'The Wages of Travel: Wordsworth and the Memorial Tour of 1820'. *Studies in Romanticism* 40.3 (Fall, 2001), pp. 321–43.
Jarvis, Simon. *Wordsworth's Philosophic Song*. Cambridge: Cambridge University Press, 2002.
Jeffrey, Francis. 'Review of *The Excursion*'. *Edinburgh Review* 24.47 (November 1814), pp. 1–30.
Johnston, Kenneth R. *The Hidden Wordsworth: Poet, Lover, Rebel, Spy*. New York and London: W.W. Norton, 1998.
Johnston, Kenneth R. *Wordsworth and 'The Recluse'*. New Haven, CT, and London: Yale University Press, 1984.
Kant, Immanuel. *Critique of Judgement*. Ed. And Trans. Walter S. Pluhar. Indianapolis, IN: Hackett Publishing, 1987.
Kant, Immanuel. *Essays and Treatises on Moral, Political, and Various Philosophical Subjects*. Trans. J. Richardson. 2 vols. London, 1798–9.
Kant, Immanuel. 'Perpetual Peace, A Philosophical Sketch'. In *Political Writings*. 2nd edn. Ed. H. S. Reiss. Trans. H. B. Nisbet, pp. 93–130. Cambridge: Cambridge University Press, 1991.
Kant, Immanuel. *Religion and Rational Theology*. Ed. Allen Wood and George di Giovanni. Cambridge: Cambridge University Press, 2001.
Kelley, Theresa. *Wordsworth's Revisionary Aesthetics*. Cambridge: Cambridge University Press, 1988.
Kettler, David. 'Political Education for Empire and Revolution'. In *Adam Ferguson: History, Progress, and Human Nature*. Ed. Eugene Heath and Vincenzo Merolle, pp. 87–115. London: Routledge, 2008.

Khalip, Jacques. 'Dead Calm: The Melancholy of Peace'. *The New Centennial Review* 11.1 (Spring 2011), pp. 243–75.
Khan, Jalal U. 'The Allegories of "The Pilgrim's Dream; Or, the Star and the Glow-Worm"'. *Studies in Philology* 94.4 (Autumn 1997), pp. 508–22.
Khan, Jalal U. 'Publication and Reception of Wordsworth's "The River Duddon" Volume'. *Modern Language Studies* 32.2 (Autumn 2002), pp. 45–67.
Kim, Benjamin. 'Generating a National Sublime: Wordsworth's "The River Duddon" and "The Guide to the Lakes"'. *Studies in Romanticism* 45.1 (Spring 2006), pp. 49–75.
Kipperman, Mark. *Beyond Enchantment: German Idealism and English Romantic Poetry*. Philadelphia, PA: University of Pennsylvania Press, 1986.
Lamb, Charles, and Mary Lamb. *The Letters of Charles and Mary Anne Lamb*. Ed. Edwin W. Marrs Jnr. 3 vols. Ithaca, NY and London: Cornell University Press, 1978.
Langan, Celeste. *Romantic Vagrancy: Wordsworth and the Simulation of Freedom*. Cambridge: Cambridge University Press, 1995.
Larkin, Peter. *Wordsworth and Coleridge: Promising Losses*. Houndmills: Palgrave Macmillan, 2012.
Latour, Bruno. *Aramis, or the Love of Technology*. Trans. Catherine Porter. Cambridge, MA: Harvard University Press, 1996.
Leadbetter, Gregory. 'The Lyric Impulse of *Poems, in Two Volumes*'. In *The Oxford Handbook of William Wordsworth*. Ed. Richard Gravil and Daniel Robinson, pp. 221–36. Oxford: Oxford University Press, 2015.
Leask, Nigel. *Curiosity and the Aesthetics of Travel Writing, 1770–1840*. Oxford: Oxford University Press, 2002.
Levinas, Emmanuel. *Time and the Other and Additional Essays*. Trans. R. A. Cohen. Pittsburgh: Duquesne University Press, 1986.
Levinas, Emmanuel. *Totality and Infinity: An Essay on Exteriority*. Trans. Alphonso Lingis. Dordrecht: Kluwer Academic Publishers, 1991.
Levinson, Marjorie. 'A Motion and a Spirit: Romancing Spinoza'. *Studies in Romanticism* 46.4 (Winter 2007), pp. 367–408.
Levinson, Marjorie. *Wordsworth's Great Period Poems: Four Essays*. Cambridge: Cambridge University Press, 1986.
Levy, Michelle. *Family Authorship and Romantic Print Culture*. Houndmills: Palgrave Macmillan, 2008.
Liu, Alan. *Friending the Past: The Sense of History in the Digital Age*. Chicago and London: University of Chicago Press, 2018.
Liu, Alan. *Wordsworth: The Sense of History*. Stanford, CA: Stanford University Press, 1989.
MacCannell, Dean. *The Tourist: A New Theory of the Leisure Class*. Berkeley, CA: University of California Press, 1999.
Manning, Peter. 'Cleansing the Images: Wordsworth, Rome, and the Rise of Historicism'. *Texas Studies in Literature and Language* 33.2 (Summer 1991), pp. 271–326.
Manning, Peter. 'The Other Scene of Travel: Wordsworth's 'Musings near Aquapendente'. In *The Wordsworthian Enlightenment: Romantic Poetry and the*

Ecology of Reading. Ed. Helen Reguiro Elam and Frances Ferguson, pp. 191–211. Baltimore, MD: Johns Hopkins University Press, 2005.

Manning, Peter. *Reading Romantics: Text and Context*. Oxford: Oxford University Press, 1990.

Manning, Peter. 'Wordsworth Reshapes Himself and Is Reshaped: *The River Duddon* and the 1820 *Miscellaneous Poems*'. *The Wordsworth Circle* 50.1 (Winter 2020), pp. 35–53.

Martin, Philip. *Mad Women in Romantic Writing*. Brighton and New York: Harvester Press and St Martin's Press, 1987.

McGann, Jerome J. *The Beauty of Inflections: Literary Investigations in Historical Method and Theory*. Oxford: Clarendon Press, 1985.

McGann, Jerome J. *Byron and Romanticism*. Ed. James Soderholm. Cambridge: University of Cambridge Press, 2002.

McLoughlin, Kate. *Authoring War: The Literary Representation of War from the Iliad to Iraq*. Cambridge: Cambridge University Press, 2011.

Medwin, Thomas. *Conversations of Lord Byron with Thomas Medwin*. London: ESQ, 1832.

Melville, Peter. *Romantic Hospitality and the Resistance to Accommodation*. Waterloo: Wilfred Laurier University Press, 2007.

Miller, Steven. *War after Death: On Violence and Its Limits*. New York: Fordham University Press, 2014.

Milton, John. *Paradise Lost*. Ed. Alastair Fowler. London: Longman, 1971.

Moore, Thomas. *Memoirs, Journal, and Correspondence of Thomas Moore*. Ed. Lord John Russell. 8 vols. London, 1853.

Moorman, Mary. *William Wordsworth: A Biography. The Later Years, 1803–1850*. Oxford: Oxford University Press, 1968.

Morton, Timothy. *Hyperobjects: Philosophy and Ecology at the End of the World*. Minneapolis, MN and London: University of Minnesota Press, 2013.

Moutray, Tonya. 'Remodelling Catholic Ruins in William Wordsworth's Poetry'. *European Romantic Review* 22.6 (2011), pp. 819–31.

Muir, Rory. *Britain and the Defeat of Napoleon, 1807–1815*. New Haven, CT and London: Yale University Press, 1996.

Navickas, Katrina. *Protest and the Politics of Space and Place, 1789–1848*. Manchester: Manchester University Press, 2015.

Negri, Antonio. *Empire and Beyond*. Trans. Ed Emery. Cambridge: Polity, 2008.

Newey, Vincent. '*Authoring the Self: Childe Harold III and IV*'. Ed. Bernard Beatty and Vincent Newey, pp. 148–90.

Newey, Vincent. *Byron and the Limits of Fiction*. Liverpool: Liverpool University Press, 1988.

Offord, Mark. *Wordsworth and the Art of Philosophical Travel*. Cambridge: Cambridge University Press, 2016.

Ovid. *Metamorphoses*. Trans. A. D. Melville. Oxford: Oxford University Press, 1986.

Page, Judith W. *Wordsworth and the Cultivation of Women*. Berkeley, CA: University of California Press, 1994.

Panofsky, Erwin. *Meaning in the Visual Arts*. New York: Doubleday, 1995.

Patteson, Edward. *A Sermon Delivered in the Parish Church of Richmond in Surrey, On Sunday the 30th Day of July* 1815 [...]. London, 1815.

Phelan, Joseph. *The Nineteenth-Century Sonnet*. New York: Palgrave Macmillan, 2005.

Pick, Daniel. *War Machine: The Rationalisation of Slaughter in the Modern Age*. New Haven, CT, and London: Yale University Press, 1993.

Pite, Ralph. 'Wordsworth, *The River Duddon*, and John Dalton's Ultimate Particles'. *The Wordsworth Circle* 50.2 (Spring 2019), pp. 180–201.

Pliny, *Natural History, Volume III: Books 8–11*. Trans. H. Rackham. Loeb Classical Library 353. Cambridge, MA: Harvard University Press, 1940.

Ramsey, Neil. *The Military Memoir and Romantic Literary Culture, 1780–1835*. Farnham: Ashgate, 2011.

Ramsey, Neil. *Romanticism and the Biopolitics of Modern War Writing*. Cambridge: Cambridge University Press, 2022.

Raven, Andrew. '"Now Expands Majestic Duddon": Wordsworth's Textual Expansion of the "The River Duddon" and Its Theological Implications'. *The Wordsworth Circle* 51.1 (Winter 2020), pp. 20–34.

Read, Donald. *Peterloo: 'The Massacre' and Its Background*. Manchester: Manchester University Press, 1958.

Reed, Mark L. *Wordsworth: The Chronology of the Middle Years*. Cambridge, MA: Harvard University Press, 1975.

Rieder, John. *Wordsworth's Counterrevolutionary Turn: Community, Virtue, and Vision in the 1790s*. Newark: University of Delaware Press, 1997.

Robinson, Daniel. '*The River Duddon* and Wordsworth, Sonneteer'. In *The Oxford Handbook of William Wordsworth*. Ed. Richard Gravil and Daniel Robinson, pp. 289–308. Oxford: Oxford University Press, 2015.

Robinson, Henry C. *Correspondence of Henry Crabb Robinson with the Wordsworth Circle*. Ed. Edith J. Morley. 2 vols. Oxford: Oxford University Press, 1927.

Robinson, Henry C. *Diary, Reminiscences, and Correspondence of Henry Crabb Robinson*. Ed. Thomas Sadler. 3 vols. London, 1869.

Robinson, Jeffrey C. *Poetic Innovation in Wordsworth's Poetry, 1825–1833: Fibres of These Thoughts*. London: Anthem Press, 2019.

Robinson, Jeffrey C. *Unfettering Poetry: The Fancy in British Romanticism*. Basingstoke: Palgrave Macmillan, 2006.

Roe, Nicholas. 'Keats's Commonwealth'. In *Keats and History*. Ed. Nicholas Roe, pp. 194–211. Cambridge: Cambridge University Press, 1995.

Rosenberg, Daniel, and Grafton, Anthony. *Cartographies of Time: A History of the Timeline*. New York: Princeton Architectural Press, 2010.

Rousseau, Jean-Jacques. 'The Plan for Perpetual Peace, on the Government of Poland, and Other Writings on History and Politics'. In *The Collected Writings of Rousseau*. Ed. Roger D. Masters and Christopher Kelly. Trans. Christopher Kelly and Judith Bush, pp. 25–49. 14 vols. Hanover: University Press of New England at Dartmouth College, 2005.

Rousseau, Jean-Jacques. 'The State of War'. In *The Basic Political Writings*, 2nd edn. Trans. Donald A. Cress, pp. 253–65. New York: Hackett, 2011.

Ruskin, John. *The Literary Criticism of John Ruskin*. Ed. Harold Bloom. New York: De Capo Press, 1965.
Rylestone, Anne L. *Prophetic Memory in Wordsworth's Ecclesiastical Sonnets*. Carbondale, IL: Southern Illinois University Press, 1991.
Said, Edward W. *On Late Style*. London: Bloomsbury, 2006.
Scott, John. 'Mr. Wordsworth's Poems'. *Champion* 129 (25 June 1815), pp. 205–6.
Semmel, Stuart. *Napoleon and the British*. New Haven, CT and London: Yale University Press, 2004.
Shakespeare, William. *The Complete Sonnets and Poems*. Ed. Colin Burrow. Oxford: Oxford University Press, 2002.
Shapiro, Michael J. *Violent Cartographies: Mapping Cultures of War*. Minneapolis, MN: University of Minnesota Press, 1997.
Shaver, Chester L. and Shaver, Alice C. *Wordsworth's Library: A Catalogue*. New York and London: Garland, 1979.
Shaw, Philip. 'Longing for Home: Robert Hamilton, Nostalgia and the Emotional Life of the Eighteenth-Century Soldier'. *Journal for Eighteenth-Century Studies* 39.1 (2016), pp. 25–40.
Shaw, Philip. 'On War: De Quincey's Martial Sublime'. *Romanticism* 19.1 (2013), pp. 19–30.
Shaw, Philip. *Waterloo and the Romantic Imagination*. Houndmills: Palgave Macmillian, 2002.
Shaw, Philip. 'Wordsworth after Peterloo: The Persistence of War in *The River Duddon ... and Other Poems*'. In *Commemorating Peterloo: Violence, Resilience and Claim-Making during the Romantic Era*. Ed. Michael Demson and Regina Hewitt, pp. 250–70. Edinburgh: Edinburgh University Press, 2019.
Shaw, Philip. 'Wordsworth, Waterloo, and Sacrifice'. In *Sacrifice and Modern War Literature*. Ed. Alex Houen and Jan-Melissa Schramm, pp. 20–48. Oxford: Oxford University Press, 2018.
Shaw, Philip. 'Wordsworth's "Dread Voice": Ovid, Dora, and the Later Poetry'. *Romanticism* 8.1 (2002), pp. 34–48.
Shelley, P. B. *Selected Poems and Prose*. Ed. Jack Donovan and Cian Duffy. London: Penguin, 2016.
Simons, C. E. J. 'Itinerant Wordsworth'. In *The Oxford Handbook of William Wordsworth*. Ed. Richard Gravil and Daniel Robinson, pp. 97–115. Oxford: Oxford University Press, 2015.
Smith, Stevie. *The Holiday*. London: Virago, 1981.
Southey, Robert. The Collected Letters of Robert Southey. Part Four. Ed. Lynda Pratt and Ian Packer. Romantic Circles: n.p. Web. Accessed 9 July 2021.
Spinoza, Benedict de. *Ethics*. Ed. and Trans. Edwin Curley. London: Penguin, 1996.
Spinoza, Benedict de. *Political Treatise*. Trans. Samuel Shirley. Indianapolis, IN, and Cambridge: Hackett, 2000.
Stansfield, Dorothy A. 'A Note on the Genesis of Coleridge's Thinking on War and Peace'. *The Wordsworth Circle* 17.3 (Summer 1986), pp. 130–4.

Stauffer, Andrew. *Book Traces: Nineteenth-century Readers and the Future of the Library*. Philadelphia, PA: University of Pennsylvania Press, 2021.

Stewart, John. *The Apocalypse of Human Perfectuability [sic.], to Consummate the Great Science of Man and Nature, as Revealed in the Opus Maximum*. London, 1808.

Tennant, Bob. 'On the Good Name of the Dead: Peace, Liberty, and Empire in Robert Morehead's Waterloo Sermon'. *Religion in the Age of Enlightenment* 1 (2009), pp. 251–77.

Thomas, Gordon K. *Wordsworth's Dirge and Promise: Napoleon, Wellington and the Convention of Cintra*. Lincoln, NE: University of Nebraska Press, 1971.

Thompson, Carl. *The Suffering Traveller and the Romantic Imagination*. Oxford: Oxford University Press, 2007.

Thompson, E. P. *The Making of the English Working Class*. Harmondsworth: Penguin, 1968.

Tilly, Charles. *Popular Contention in Great Britain, 1758–1834*. Cambridge, MA: Harvard University Press, 1995.

Tomko, Michael. *British Romanticism and the Catholic Question: Religion, History and National Identity, 1778–1829*. Basingstoke: Palgrave Macmillan, 2011.

Tomko, Michael. 'Superstition, the National Imaginary, and Religious Politics in Wordsworth's *Ecclesiastical Sketches*'. *Wordsworth Circle* 39 (2008), pp. 16–19.

Tuite, Clara. *Lord Byron and Scandalous Celebrity*. Cambridge: Cambridge University Press, 2015.

Tuite, Clara. *Virgil, Eclogues, Georgics, Aeneid I–VI*. Trans. H. Rushton Fairclough. Loeb Classical Library. Issue 194, vol. 1 of Horace. Cambridge, MA: Harvard University Press, 1960.

Voltaire. *Candide and Other Stories*. Trans. Roger Pearson. Oxford: Oxford University Press, 2006.

Walker, Eric C. *Marriage, Writing and Romanticism: Wordsworth and Austen after War*. Stanford, CA: Stanford University Press, 2009.

Walker, Eric C. 'Wordsworth's "Third Volume" and the Collected Editions, 1815–20'. *Papers of the Bibliographical Society of America* 80 (1986), pp. 437–53.

Walmsley, Robert. *Peterloo: The Case Reopened*. Manchester: Manchester University Press, 1969.

Washington, Chris. 'Romantic Postapocalyptic Politics: Reveries of Rousseau, Derrida, and Meillassoux in a World without Us'. In *Romanticism and Speculative Realism*. Ed. Chris Washington and Anne C. McCarthy, pp. 133–56. New York and London: Bloomsbury, 2019.

Watson, J. R. *Romanticism and War: A Study of British Romantic Period Writers and the Napoleonic Wars*. Houndmills: Palgrave Macmillan, 2003.

Westwood, Daniel. '"Living in Shattered Guise": Doubling in *Childe Harold's Pilgrimage* Canto III'. *The Byron Journal* 44.2 (2016), pp. 125–37.

White, R. S. *Pacifism and English Literature: Minstrels of Peace*. Basingstoke: Palgrave Macmillan, 2008.

Wilson, John. 'Essays on the Lake School of Poetry. No. 1. Wordsworth's *White Doe of Rylstone*'. *Blackwood's Edinburgh Magazine* 3.16 (July 1818), pp. 369–81.

Wittman, Laura. *The Tomb of the Unknown Soldier, Modern Mourning, and the Reinvention of the Mystical Body*. Toronto: University of Toronto Press, 2011.
Woof, Pamela. *William, Mary and Dorothy: The Wordsworths' Continental Tour of 1820*. Grasmere: Wordsworth's Trust, 2008.
Wordsworth, Christopher. *Memoirs of William Wordsworth*. 2 vols. London, 1851.
Wordsworth, Dorothy. *Journals of Dorothy Wordsworth*. Ed. Ernest de Selincourt. 2 vols. London: Macmillan, 1970.
Wordsworth, John. *The Letters of John Wordsworth*. Ed. Carl H. Ketcham. Ithaca, NY: Cornell University Press, 1969.
Wordsworth, Mary. *The Letters of Mary Wordsworth, 1800–1855*. Ed. Mary E. Burton. Oxford: Clarendon Press, 1955.
Wordsworth, William. *The Fenwick Notes of William Wordsworth*. Ed. Jared Curtis. Tirril: Humanities-Ebooks, 2007.
Wordsworth, William. *The Miscellaneous Poems of William Wordsworth*. 4 vols. London: Longman, Hurst, Rees, Orme, and Brown, 1820.
Wordsworth, William. *Our English Lakes, Mountains, and Waterfalls, as Seen by William Wordsworth. Photographically Illustrated*. London, 1864.
Wordsworth, William. *The Poetical Works of William Wordsworth*. Ed. Ernest de Selincourt and Helen Darbishire. 5 vols. Oxford: Clarendon Press, 1940–49.
Wordsworth, William. *The River Duddon, a Series of Sonnets: Vaudracour and Julia and Other Poems. To Which Is Annexed, a Topographical Description of the Country of the Lakes, in the North of England*. London, 1820.
Wu, Duncan. 'Wordsworthian Carnage'. *Essays in Criticism* 66.3 (July 2016), pp. 341–59.
Wu, Duncan. *Wordsworth's Reading, 1800–1815*. Cambridge: Cambridge University Press, 1995.
Wyatt, John. *Wordsworth's Poems of Travel, 1819–1842: 'Such Sweet Wayfaring'*. Houndmills: Macmillan, 1999.
Yen, Brandon C. *'The Excursion' and Wordsworth's Iconography*. Liverpool: Liverpool University Press, 2018.
Ziegenhagen, Timothy. 'War Addiction in Thomas De Quincey's *The English Mail-Coach*'. *Wordsworth Circle* 35.2 (2004), pp. 93–8.

Index

Adorno, Theodor, 148, 218–19
Agamben, Giorgio, 18, 100, 158, 231, 235
Alcaeus of Mytilene, 155
Arnold, Matthew, 211
Austen, Jane (*Sanditon*), 175–6

Bainbridge, Simon, 221, 228–9, 240
Beaumont, Sir George, 76, 85, 105, 181, 237
Beddoes, Thomas ('Kant: Zum Ewigen Frieden'), 8, 223
Bell, William (*Descriptive Guide to the Stream of Time*), 151
Benjamin, Walter, 218–19, 228, 231, 239
  'Toward the Critique of Violence', 17–18
Bethune, John, 110
Betz, Paul, 132
Blanchot, Maurice, 227
Blunden, Edmund ('A House in Festubert'), 19
Bogost, Ian, 129, 232
Bowles, John (*Reflections at the Conclusion of the War*), 225
Brougham, Henry, Lord, 121, 124, 153, 205, 212
Bugg, John, 225
Burns, Robert, 15, 94, 135–6
  'Tam O'Shanter', 135–6
Butler, James A., 233
Butler, Samuel (*The Effects of Peace on the Religious Principle Considered. A Sermon*), 226
Byron, George Gordon, Lord, 12, 68, 71, 73, 95, 174–206
  Childe Harold's Pilgrimage, 33, 158, 177, 185–206
  Don Juan, 33, 109, 131, 155, 186, 187, 249
  and Dryden, 197–8
  English Bards and Scotch Reviewers, 131
  and Napoleon, 190, 193, 199
  and Waterloo, 186–8, 209
  and Wordsworth, 32, 94, 109, 113, 130–1, 154–5, 158, 169, 174–206, 249

Callimachus (*Hymn to Apollo*), 159
Carlson, Julia S., 148
Castlereagh, Lord (Robert Stewart, 2nd Marquess of Londonderry), 105, 106
Chalmers, Thomas (*Thoughts on Universal Peace*), 103, 110
Chapman, George (translation of *Iliad*), 159
Chaucer, Geoffrey ('The Knights Tale'), 197–8
Christensen, Jerome C., 10, 224, 225
Clare, John, 40, 232
Clarkson, Catherine, 34, 68, 70, 94
Clarkson, Thomas, 9
Cobden, Richard, 211
Cockney School, 95, 122–5, 156, 176, 182, 201–2, 250
Coleridge, Samuel Taylor, 58, 77, 123, 132, 142–3, 200, 204, 213, 224
  'The Brook', 148, 156
  'The Rime of the Ancient Mariner', 98, 126–8
  and Wordsworth, 5, 8, 35–6, 70, 80, 143, 156, 208
Cox, Jeffrey N., 74, 122–4, 182, 249, 251, 253
Crimean War, 33, 209–12

Daniel, Samuel, 27, 172
  Civil Wars, 27
  The Collection of the History of England, 171
De Quincey, Thomas, 33, 209–14, 219, 226
  'On War', 33, 209–12
  and Wordsworth, 209–14, 219, 226
Derrida, Jacques, 44, 93, 226, 232, 239
Dryden, John, 82, 197
Dugas, Kristin, 77

Favret, Mary A., 234
Fay, Jessica, 49, 237
Ferguson, Adam, 61–2
Fry, Paul, H., 126
Fulford, Tim, 122, 157, 182, 223, 252

Galperin, William, 223
Girard, René, 100, 241

Goodman, Kevis, 39, 221
Gravil, Richard, 53, 238
Gray, Thomas ('Elegy Written in a Country Churchyard'), 133

Hartman, Geoffrey, 46–7, 77, 81, 86, 203, 223, 224, 237
Haydon, Benjmin Robert, 115
Hazlitt, William, 34, 36
  'On the Late War', 60–1, 231
  review of *Coriolanus*, 108, 130
  review of *Excursion*, 9, 37, 60, 68, 224, 235
  and Wordsworth, 9, 29, 37, 61, 64, 95, 108–9, 130, 185, 188, 235
Hegel, G. W. F. 16, 92, 222, 239
  Philosophy of Fine Art, 239
Hogarth, William (*The Gate of Calias, or the Roast Beef of Old England*), 180–3, **181**
Homer, 133–5, 137, 141, 146
  Iliad, 159
Horace, 57, 111, 155
  Ode 3.13, 111, 158–9, 250
  Ode 3.29, 148–51
  Satire 1, 15
Howley, William (*A Sermon Preached on Thursday, January 18, 1816*), 102
Humfrays, Samuel (*The Sword is the Lord's*), 110
Hunt, Leigh, 8, 36, 95, 97, 124, 155, 182, 201, 219
  Captain Sword and Captain Pen, 33, 212–13
  The Descent of Liberty, 74, 95, 124
  and Wordsworth, 212–14
Hutchinson, Sarah, 123

Jarvis, Robin, 177, 198, 200, 254
Jeffrey, Francis
  review of *Excursion*, 69
  review of *Memorials of a Tour on the Continent, 1820*, 178–83, 196
  review of *The White Doe of Rylstone*, 93
Johnston, Kenneth, 38, 98, 113, 233

Kant, Immanuel, 12, 14, 18
  Critique of Judgement, 7, 130, 139, 210
  'End of All Things', 12
  'Perpetual Peace', 7, 210, 222
Keats, John, 12, 36, 117, 122, 124, 152–5, 160, 201
  Endymion, 124, 182, 230, 256
  'To Autumn', 152–3
Kelley, Theresa, 60, 138, 139, 185, 198, 232, 237, 238, 255
Khalip, Jacques, 11, 224

Lamb, Charles, 4, 143, 175, 239
  and *Excursion*, 69
  and *The Waggoner*, 135, 139
  and *The White Doe of Rylstone*, 70
  and Wordsworth, 69, 132–3
Landor, Walter Savage, 34, 81
Larkin, Peter, 177, 198, 219
Latour, Bruno, 89
Leadbetter, Gregory, 12
Levinas, Emmanuel, 90–1, 152, 223, 226, 232, 239
Levinson, Marjorie, 24, 152
Lowther, William (Earl of Lonsdale), 35, 121, 145, 204–5, 231

Manning, Peter, 73, 167, 177, 201, 236
Martin, Philip, 228–9
Mathias, Daniell (*Waterloo Subscription. A Sermon, to Recommend the Same*), 101, 103, 107
McGann, Jerome J., 152–3, 248
Meillassoux, Quentin, 64, 235
Milton, John, 16, 27, 35, 43–4, 52, 57, 60, 66, 79, 94, 95, 113, 118, 123, 131–5, 169
  Elegia Sexta, 135
  Lycidas, 208
  Paradise Lost, 41, 88, 131, 134, 138, 190, 216, 237
Moore, Thomas, 186

Napoleon, 5, 46, 53, 56, 59–60, 95, 103, 107, 119, 146, 185, 189–90, 193, 195, 199, 203
  abdication (1814), 13, 29, 34, 59, 69, 76, 231
  and Waterloo, 22, 71, 119, 155, 236
Negri, Antonio, 228, 245, 246
Nelson, Admiral Lord (Horatio), 43, 105, 137–40

Offord, Mark, 215, 217, 257
Ovid, 8, 73, 201, 202

Page, Judith, 74, 90–1, 230
Pasley, General Sir Charles William, 9, 29, 37, 58, 60, 65, 95, 97
Patteson, Edward (*A Sermon Delivered in the Parish Church of Richmond in Surrey*), 242
Peninsular War, 53–60, 151
Peterloo, 4, 6, 24, 32, 75, 118, 145–57, 174, 185–6, 246
Pliny, 116
Prentice, Archibald, 146
Priestley, Joseph (*A New Chart of History*), 148, **149**, 151

Quillinan, Edward, 134, 207

Raven, Andrew, 248
Reynolds, John Hamilton, 95, 123

Robinson, Henry Crabb, 4–5, 135, 136, 174, 204–5, 207
Robinson, Jeffrey C., 223
Roe, Nicholas, 152, 153
Roe, Peter (*A Sermon Preached in the Episcopal Chapel of Harrogate*), 102–3
Rousseau, Jean-Jacques, 8, 18, 89, 191–2
  'The State of War', 6–7, 222
Ruskin, John, 109

Said, Edward, 148
Scott, John
  and Wordsworth, 70, 104, 111–12, 236
Scott, Walter, 30, 68, 71–3, 75, 95, 106, 176, 178, 187, 209
  The Field of Waterloo, 104
Shakespeare, William, 5
  Coriolanus, 108
Shelley, Percy Bysshe, 36, 96, 122, 153, 176, 182, 189, 201
  Peter Bell the Third, 109
  'Verses Written on Receiving a Celandine in a Letter from England', 30
Smith, Stevie, 3
Southey, Robert, 61, 73, 95, 104, 106, 123, 135, 185–7, 224
  and Byron, 185–6
  and Hunt, 213–14
  'To Horror', 213
  'The Sailor's Mother', 228–9
  and Wordsworth, 112, 175, 185–6, 201
Spenser, Edmund, 79, 94–6, 104, 200, 237, 240, 250
  Epithalamion, 31, 96, 112, 114
  The Faerie Queene, 77
Spinoza, Baruch, 14, 30, 64, 142, 226–8, 230, 245
Stauffer, Andrew, 221
Stewart, John 'Walking', 14, 226, 227
Strass, Friedrich (*Der Strom der Zeiten* (*The Stream of Time*)), 148, **150**, 151

Tomko, Michael, 238
Treaty of Amiens, 10, 22–4, 28, 34, 37, 54, 225
Treaty of Paris, 12

Virgil, 8, 23, 57, 73, 158
  Aeniad, 160–2
  Eclogues, 25, 51, 161
Voltaire, 63

Walker, Eric C., 114, 116, 256
Waterloo, 70, 73, 75, 92, 95–115, 145–6, 151, 174–5, 185–9, 195, 200, 209–13, 236, 239–41, 246

Watson, Richard (Bishop of Llandaff), 97
Wellington, Duke of (Arthur Wellesley), 53, 95, 99, 105, 210–11
Williams, Helen Maria, 174
Wilson, John
  review of *The White Doe of Rylstone*, 71–2, 90, 93
Wordsworth, Christopher, Jr, 73, 214
Wordsworth, Dora, 206–8
Wordsworth, Dorothy, 27, 35, 100, 153, 176, 179–80, 184, 198, 199, 203
  and Catherine Clarkson, 70, 94
  and 1820 continental tour, 175–80, 184, 187–8, 191, 194, 198, 199, 202, 206, 253
  and Napoleon, 34, 203
  and Peterloo, 145
  and Waterloo, 100–1, 145, 187–9
Wordsworth, John, 17, 76, 80, 132
Wordsworth, Mary, 115–16, 145–6, 156
Wordsworth, William
  A Letter to a Friend of Robert Burns, 135
  'Aerial Rock—whose solitary brow', 122
  'After Landing—The Valley of Dover', 204–6
  'After Visiting the Field of Waterloo', 114, 145, 187–8
  'Anticipation. October, 1803', 26–8
  'At Dover', 206–8
  'Author's Voyage down the Rhine (Thirty Years Ago)', 194
  and Beaumont, 76, 105, 181, 237
  and beauty, the beautiful, 139, 185
  'Bruges I saw attired with golden light', 183–4
  and Burke, 54, 55, 108
  and Burns, 135–6
  and Byron, 33, 95, 121–2, 131, 155, 158, 169, 174–206
  and Catholicism, 77, 79, 81–2, 84–6, 170–3, 202
  and Cave, William, 49–50
  'Character of the Happy Warrior', 43, 73, 138, 164
  and Clarkson, Catherine, 68
  and the Cockney School, 176, 182, 201–2
  and Coleridge, 5, 8, 35–6, 70, 80, 143, 156, 208
  'Composed in the Valley, *near* Dover, on the Day of landing', 26, 207
  Convention of Cintra, 53–60
  Descriptive Sketches, 51–2
  'Desultory Stanzas upon Receiving the Preceding Stanzas from the Press', 203
  'Dion', 116–17
  and Dryden, 82
  Ecclesiastical Sketches, 32, 152, 168–202
  'Elegiac Verses', 110–11, 119

'Elegiac Verses, *February* 1816', 166–7
'Essay upon Epitaphs', 81
'Eve's lingering clouds extend in solid bars', 141, 166
Excursion, 8–9, 35–7, 60–9, 96, 117–18, 131, 182
and Fancy, 13–14, 22–3, 29, 36, 45, 95, 97, 140, 166, 178, 182, 195
'Fish-Women.—On Landing at Calais', 178–84
'Fort Fuentes—At the Head of the Lake of Como', 199–200
and Gray, 133
'Hart-leap Well', 42, 77–8
'Home at Grasmere', 29, 37–44, 50, 194
and Homer, 133, 135, 141
'How sweet it is when mother Fancy rocks', 22–3
'Hymn, For the Boatmen, as They Approach the Rapids, under the Castle of Heidelberg', 195
'I griev'd for Buonaparte', 27
'I would not strike a flower', 19–21
and Imagination, 13–14, 36, 46–7, 59, 80, 93, 96, 97, 107, 113
'In a carriage, upon the Banks of the Rhine', 193–4
'In trellis'd shed with clustering roses gay', 77
'Inscriptions to Be Found in, and near, a Hermits Cell', 120
'Intrepid sons of Albion!—not by you', 104–5
'It is not to be thought of that the flood', 27
'Laodamia', 73–4, 115–16
Letter to the Bishop of Llandaff, 7–8, 51, 97–8
'Lines Written in Early Spring', 15, 219–20
and Lloyd, Charles, 185
'Local Recollections on the Heights near Hockheim', 195
and Lowther, 35, 121, 145, 204–5
Lyrical Ballads, 40, 129
 preface to, 40
'Malham Cove', 122
'Memorial. Near the Outlet of the Lake of Thun', 199
Memorials of a Tour of the Continent, 1820, 32, 152, 176, 204–8
and Milton, 35, 79, 96, 133, 208
Miscellaneous Poems (1820), 112, 152, 167–8
and Moore, 186
and Napoleon, 199, 203
'Near the Spring of the Hermitage', 121
and Nelson, 138–40
'Not Love, nor War', 5
'Nuns fret not at their Convent's narrow room', 169–70

'October, 1803', 26
'Ode. Composed in January 1816', 111, 166
'Ode. 1815', 113
'Ode. Intimations of Immortality from Recollections of Early Childhood', 23–5, 165, 195, 218
'Ode to Enterprize', 203
'On Approaching the Staub-Bach, Lauterbrunnen', 198
'On Being Stranded near the Harbour of Boulogne', 203–4
Our English Lakes, Mountains, and Waterfalls. as Seen By William Wordsworth (1864), 1–3, **2**, 10–11
and Ovid, 141, 201, 202
and Pasley, 58, 95
Peter Bell, 31, 75–6, 123–9, 135, 147, 165
Poems (1815), 4, 140
 'Essay, Supplementary to the Preface', 74, 80
 preface to, 59, 79, 140
Poems, in Two Volumes (1807), 13, 23
Poems (1820; 3 volume edition), 152, 165, 166
Prelude, 36–7, 98, 107, 113–15, 128, 132–3, 136–7, 143, 208, 214–19
'Processions. Suggested on a Sabbath Morning in the Vale of Chamouny', 200–2
and Queen Caroline affair, 204–6
'The Recluse', 29, 34–7, 43–8, 53, 110, 133–4, 144, 148, 156–7, 214–15
'Resolution and Independence', 133
'Retirement', 5
and Reynolds, 95
River Duddon, 32, 145–69, 176, 186, 194, 197, 248–51
'Scenery between Namur and Liege', 195
and Scott, John, 70, 104, 111–112, 236
and Scott, Walter, 71–3
'September, 1802', 207
'September 1815', 155
'September, 1819', 152–6
'Simon Lee', 129
'Sky-Prospect—From the Plains of France', 203
'Song, at the Feast of Brougham Castle', 238
'Sonnet. On Seeing a Tuft of Snowdrops in a Storm', 121–2
and Southey, 185
and Spenser, 77, 79, 95, 104, 112–13, 200
and Spinoza, 68
'the Spirit of Antiquity, enshrined', 185
'St Paul's', 46–7

Wordsworth, William (cont.)
  and sublime, 31, 44, 47, 54–5, 57, 59–60, 139–40, 146, 162, 177–8, 183, 190, 198, 201–2, 210, 238, 255
  'Suggested upon Loughrigg Fell', 219–20
  'Thanksgiving Ode', 30–1, 94–119, 130, 135, 147, 165–6, 209, 212–14
  Thanksgiving volume, 9, 24, 30–1, 94–119, 123, 152, 166–7, 187
  'The Barberry-Tree', 22
  'The Bard, whose soul is meek as dawning day', 104
  'The Brownie's Cell', 161
  'The Column Intended by Buonaparte for a Triumphal Edifice in Milan, Now Lying by the Way-Side on the Semplon Pass', 199–200
  'The Discharged Soldier', 215–19
  'The Fall of the Aar—Handec', 198
  'The Female Vagrant', 136
  'The Haunted Tree', 122
  'The Jung-frau—And the Rhine at Shauffhausen', 197–8
  'The Pilgrim's Dream', 134
  'The Power of Sound', 218
  'The Ruined Cottage', 47–8, 64, 133
  'The Sailor's Mother', 21
  'The Small Celandine', 28
  'the Spirit of Antiquity, enshrined', 185
  'The Thorn', 14, 39
  The White Doe of Rylstone, 30, 47, 70–93, 110, 170, 171
  'There is an active principle alive in all things', 66
  'Tintern Abbey', 19, 39, 152, 188, 191–3
  'To a Friend, Composed near Calais, on the Road Leading to Andres, August 7th, 1802', 26, 182
  'To a Snow-drop, Appearing Very Early in the Season', 121
  'To the Clouds', 45–7
  'To the Daisy' ('In youth from rock to rock I went'), 10–15
  'To the Daisy' ('Sweet Flower! belike one day to have'), 17
  'To the Daisy' ('With little here to do or see'), 15–16
  'To the Men of Kent. October, 1803', 26, 27
  'To the River Duddon', 148
  'To the Same Flower' ('Bright Flower!'), 10, 15–16, 19
  'Topographical Description of the Country of the Lakes', 154
  'The Tuft of Primroses', 37, 47–53, 86
  Two Addresses to the Freeholders of Westmorland, 120
  'Upon the Same Occasion', 153–6
  and Vallon, Annette, 21, 97, 98, 113–15, 207
  and Vallon, Caroline, 21, 25, 31, 95, 97, 114, 174, 207
  and Voltaire, 63
  The Waggoner, 31, 75–6, 124, 129–44, 147, 165
  and Waterloo, 73, 94–119, 145–6, 154–5, 174–5, 183–9, 195, 200, 213, 221, 239
  and Wellington, 95
  and West, Thomas, 49
  'Who rises on the banks of Seine', 118–19
  'The world is too much with us', 27
  and Wrangham, 29, 35, 81
  'Written in London. September, 1802', 27
Wither, George (*The Shepherd's Hunting*), 11
Wrangham, Francis, 29, 35, 81
Wu, Duncan, 96, 240

CAMBRIDGE STUDIES IN ROMANTICISM

General Editor
JAMES CHANDLER, University of Chicago

1. *Romantic Correspondence: Women, Politics and the Fiction of Letters*
   MARY A. FAVRET
2. *British Romantic Writers and the East: Anxieties of Empire*
   NIGEL LEASK
3. *Poetry as an Occupation and an Art in Britain, 1760–1830*
   PETER MURPHY
4. *Edmund Burke's Aesthetic Ideology: Language, Gender and Political Economy in Revolution*
   TOM FURNISS
5. *In the Theatre of Romanticism: Coleridge, Nationalism, Women*
   JULIE A. CARLSON
6. *Keats, Narrative and Audience*
   ANDREW BENNETT
7. *Romance and Revolution: Shelley and the Politics of a Genre*
   DAVID DUFF
8. *Literature, Education, and Romanticism: Reading as Social Practice, 1780–1832*
   ALAN RICHARDSON
9. *Women Writing about Money: Women's Fiction in England, 1790–1820*
   EDWARD COPELAND
10. *Shelley and the Revolution in Taste: The Body and the Natural World*
    TIMOTHY MORTON
11. *William Cobbett: The Politics of Style*
    LEONORA NATTRASS
12. *The Rise of Supernatural Fiction, 1762–1800*
    E. J. CLERY
13. *Women Travel Writers and the Language of Aesthetics, 1716–1818*
    ELIZABETH A. BOHLS
14. *Napoleon and English Romanticism*
    SIMON BAINBRIDGE
15. *Romantic Vagrancy: Wordsworth and the Simulation of Freedom*
    CELESTE LANGAN

16. *Wordsworth and the Geologists*
    JOHN WYATT

17. *Wordsworth's Pope: A Study in Literary Historiography*
    ROBERT J. GRIFFIN

18. *The Politics of Sensibility: Race, Gender and Commerce in the Sentimental Novel*
    MARKMAN ELLIS

19. *Reading Daughters' Fictions, 1709–1834: Novels and Society from Manley to Edgeworth*
    CAROLINE GONDA

20. *Romantic Identities: Varieties of Subjectivity, 1774–1830*
    ANDREA K. HENDERSON

21. *Print Politics: The Press and Radical Opposition in Early Nineteenth-Century England*
    KEVIN GILMARTIN

22. *Reinventing Allegory*
    THERESA M. KELLEY

23. *British Satire and the Politics of Style, 1789–1832*
    GARY DYER

24. *The Romantic Reformation: Religious Politics in English Literature, 1789–1824*
    ROBERT M. RYAN

25. *De Quincey's Romanticism: Canonical Minority and the Forms of Transmission*
    MARGARET RUSSETT

26. *Coleridge on Dreaming: Romanticism, Dreams and the Medical Imagination*
    JENNIFER FORD

27. *Romantic Imperialism: Universal Empire and the Culture of Modernity*
    SAREE MAKDISI

28. *Ideology and Utopia in the Poetry of William Blake*
    NICHOLAS M. WILLIAMS

29. *Sexual Politics and the Romantic Author*
    SONIA HOFKOSH

30. *Lyric and Labour in the Romantic Tradition*
    ANNE JANOWITZ

31. *Poetry and Politics in the Cockney School: Keats, Shelley, Hunt and their Circle*
    JEFFREY N. COX

32. *Rousseau, Robespierre and English Romanticism*
    GREGORY DART

33. *Contesting the Gothic: Fiction, Genre and Cultural Conflict, 1764–1832*
    JAMES WATT

34. *Romanticism, Aesthetics, and Nationalism*
    DAVID ARAM KAISER

35. *Romantic Poets and the Culture of Posterity*
    ANDREW BENNETT

36. *The Crisis of Literature in the 1790s: Print Culture and the Public Sphere*
    PAUL KEEN

37. *Romantic Atheism: Poetry and Freethought, 1780–1830*
    MARTIN PRIESTMAN

38. *Romanticism and Slave Narratives: Transatlantic Testimonies*
    HELEN THOMAS

39. *Imagination under Pressure, 1789–1832: Aesthetics, Politics, and Utility*
    JOHN WHALE

40. *Romanticism and the Gothic: Genre, Reception, and Canon Formation, 1790–1820*
    MICHAEL GAMER

41. *Romanticism and the Human Sciences: Poetry, Population, and the Discourse of the Species*
    MAUREEN N. MCLANE

42. *The Poetics of Spice: Romantic Consumerism and the Exotic*
    TIMOTHY MORTON

43. *British Fiction and the Production of Social Order, 1740–1830*
    MIRANDA J. BURGESS

44. *Women Writers and the English Nation in the 1790s*
    ANGELA KEANE

45. *Literary Magazines and British Romanticism*
    MARK PARKER

46. *Women, Nationalism and the Romantic Stage: Theatre and Politics in Britain, 1780–1800*
    BETSY BOLTON

47. *British Romanticism and the Science of the Mind*
    ALAN RICHARDSON

48. *The Anti-Jacobin Novel: British Conservatism and the French Revolution*
    M. O. GRENBY

49. *Romantic Austen: Sexual Politics and the Literary Canon*
   CLARA TUITE

50. *Byron and Romanticism*
   JEROME MCGANN AND JAMES SODERHOLM

51. *The Romantic National Tale and the Question of Ireland*
   INA FERRIS

52. *Byron, Poetics and History*
   JANE STABLER

53. *Religion, Toleration, and British Writing, 1790–1830*
   MARK CANUEL

54. *Fatal Women of Romanticism*
   ADRIANA CRACIUN

55. *Knowledge and Indifference in English Romantic Prose*
   TIM MILNES

56. *Mary Wollstonecraft and the Feminist Imagination*
   BARBARA TAYLOR

57. *Romanticism, Maternity and the Body Politic*
   JULIE KIPP

58. *Romanticism and Animal Rights*
   DAVID PERKINS

59. *Georgic Modernity and British Romanticism: Poetry and the Mediation of History*
   KEVIS GOODMAN

60. *Literature, Science and Exploration in the Romantic Era: Bodies of Knowledge*
   TIMOTHY FULFORD, DEBBIE LEE, AND PETER J. KITSON

61. *Romantic Colonization and British Anti-Slavery*
   DEIRDRE COLEMAN

62. *Anger, Revolution, and Romanticism*
   ANDREW M. STAUFFER

63. *Shelley and the Revolutionary Sublime*
   CIAN DUFFY

64. *Fictions and Fakes: Forging Romantic Authenticity, 1760–1845*
   MARGARET RUSSETT

65. *Early Romanticism and Religious Dissent*
   DANIEL E. WHITE

66. *The Invention of Evening: Perception and Time in Romantic Poetry*
   CHRISTOPHER R. MILLER

67. *Wordsworth's Philosophic Song*
   SIMON JARVIS

68. *Romanticism and the Rise of the Mass Public*
   ANDREW FRANTA

69. *Writing against Revolution: Literary Conservatism in Britain, 1790–1832*
   KEVIN GILMARTIN

70. *Women, Sociability and Theatre in Georgian London*
   GILLIAN RUSSELL

71. *The Lake Poets and Professional Identity*
   BRIAN GOLDBERG

72. *Wordsworth Writing*
   ANDREW BENNETT

73. *Science and Sensation in Romantic Poetry*
   NOEL JACKSON

74. *Advertising and Satirical Culture in the Romantic Period*
   JOHN STRACHAN

75. *Romanticism and the Painful Pleasures of Modern Life*
   ANDREA K. HENDERSON

76. *Balladeering, Minstrelsy, and the Making of British Romantic Poetry*
   MAUREEN N. MCLANE

77. *Romanticism and Improvisation, 1750–1850*
   ANGELA ESTERHAMMER

78. *Scotland and the Fictions of Geography: North Britain, 1760–1830*
   PENNY FIELDING

79. *Wordsworth, Commodification and Social Concern: The Poetics of Modernity*
   DAVID SIMPSON

80. *Sentimental Masculinity and the Rise of History, 1790–1890*
   MIKE GOODE

81. *Fracture and Fragmentation in British Romanticism*
   ALEXANDER REGIER

82. *Romanticism and Music Culture in Britain, 1770–1840: Virtue and Virtuosity*
   GILLEN D'ARCY WOOD

83. *The Truth about Romanticism: Pragmatism and Idealism in Keats, Shelley, Coleridge*
   TIM MILNES

84. *Blake's Gifts: Poetry and the Politics of Exchange*
   SARAH HAGGARTY

85. *Real Money and Romanticism*
    MATTHEW ROWLINSON

86. *Sentimental Literature and Anglo-Scottish Identity, 1745–1820*
    JULIET SHIELDS

87. *Romantic Tragedies: The Dark Employments of Wordsworth, Coleridge, and Shelley*
    REEVE PARKER

88. *Blake, Sexuality and Bourgeois Politeness*
    SUSAN MATTHEWS

89. *Idleness, Contemplation and the Aesthetic*
    RICHARD ADELMAN

90. *Shelley's Visual Imagination*
    NANCY MOORE GOSLEE

91. *A Cultural History of the Irish Novel, 1790–1829*
    CLAIRE CONNOLLY

92. *Literature, Commerce, and the Spectacle of Modernity, 1750–1800*
    PAUL KEEN

93. *Romanticism and Childhood: The Infantilization of British Literary Culture*
    ANN WEIRDA ROWLAND

94. *Metropolitan Art and Literature, 1810–1840: Cockney Adventures*
    GREGORY DART

95. *Wordsworth and the Enlightenment Idea of Pleasure*
    ROWAN BOYSON

96. *John Clare and Community*
    JOHN GOODRIDGE

97. *The Romantic Crowd*
    MARY FAIRCLOUGH

98. *Romantic Women Writers, Revolution and Prophecy*
    ORIANNE SMITH

99. *Britain, France and the Gothic, 1764–1820*
    ANGELA WRIGHT

100. *Transfiguring the Arts and Sciences*
     JON KLANCHER

101. *Shelley and the Apprehension of Life*
     ROSS WILSON

102. *Poetics of Character: Transatlantic Encounters 1700–1900*
     SUSAN MANNING

103. *Romanticism and Caricature*
    IAN HAYWOOD

104. *The Late Poetry of the Lake Poets: Romanticism Revised*
    TIM FULFORD

105. *Forging Romantic China: Sino-British Cultural Exchange 1760–1840*
    PETER J. KITSON

106. *Coleridge and the Philosophy of Poetic Form*
    EWAN JAMES JONES

107. *Romanticism in the Shadow of War: Literary Culture in the Napoleonic War Years*
    JEFFREY N. COX

108. *Slavery and the Politics of Place: Representing the Colonial Caribbean, 1770–1833*
    ELIZABETH A. BOHLS

109. *The Orient and the Young Romantics*
    ANDREW WARREN

110. *Lord Byron and Scandalous Celebrity*
    CLARA TUITE

111. *Radical Orientalism: Rights, Reform, and Romanticism*
    GERARD COHEN-VRIGNAUD

112. *Print, Publicity, and Popular Radicalism in the 1790s*
    JON MEE

113. *Wordsworth and the Art of Philosophical Travel*
    MARK OFFORD

114. *Romanticism, Self-Canonization, and the Business of Poetry*
    MICHAEL GAMER

115. *Women Wanderers and the Writing of Mobility, 1784–1814*
    INGRID HORROCKS

116. *Eighteen Hundred and Eleven: Poetry, Protest and Economic Crisis*
    E. J. CLERY

117. *Urbanization and English Romantic Poetry*
    STEPHEN TEDESCHI

118. *The Poetics of Decline in British Romanticism*
    JONATHAN SACHS

119. *The Caribbean and the Medical Imagination, 1764–1834: Slavery, Disease and Colonial Modernity*
    EMILY SENIOR

120. *Science, Form, and the Problem of Induction in British Romanticism*
    DAHLIA PORTER

121. *Wordsworth and the Poetics of Air*
    THOMAS H. FORD

122. *Romantic Art in Practice: Cultural Work and the Sister Arts, 1760–1820*
    THORA BRYLOWE

123. *European Literatures in Britain, 1815–1832: Romantic Translations*
    DIEGO SIGALIA

124. *Romanticism and Theatrical Experience: Kean, Hazlitt and Keats in the the Age of Theatrical News*
    JONATHAN MULROONEY

125. *The Romantic Tavern: Literature and Conviviality in the Age of Revolution*
    IAN NEWMAN

126. *British Orientalisms, 1759–1835*
    JAMES WATT

127. *Print and Performance in the 1820s: Improvisation, Speculation, Identity*
    ANGELA ESTERHAMMER

128. *The Italian Idea: Anglo-Italian Radical Literary Culture, 1815–1823*
    WILL BOWERS

129. *The Ephemeral Eighteenth Century: Print, Sociability, and the Cultures of Collecting*
    GILLIAN RUSSELL

130. *Physical Disability in British Romantic Literature*
    ESSAKA JOSHUA

131. *William Wordsworth, Second-Generation Romantic: Contesting Poetry after Waterloo*
    JEFFREY COX

132. *Walter Scott and the Greening of Scotland: The Emergent Ecologies of a Nation*
    SUSAN OLIVER

133. *Art, Science and the Body in Early Romanticism*
    STEPHANIE O'ROURKE

134. *Honor, Romanticism, and the Hidden Value of Modernity*
    JAMISON KANTOR

135. *Romanticism and the Biopolitics of Modern War Writing*
    NEIL RAMSEY

136. *Jane Austen and Other Minds: Ordinary Language Philosophy in Literary Fiction*
    ERIC REID LINDSTROM

137. *Orientation in European Romanticism: The Art of Falling Upwards*
    PAUL HAMILTON

138. *Romanticism, Republicanism, and the Swiss Myth*
    PATRICK VINCENT

139. *Coleridge and the Geometric Idiom: Walking with Euclid*
    ANN C. COLLEY

140. *Late Romanticism and the End of Politics: Byron, Mary Shelley and the Last Men*
    JOHN HAVARD

141. *Experimentalism in Wordsworth's Later Poetry: Dialogues with the Dead*
    TIM FULFORD

142. *Romantic Fiction and Literary Excess in the Minerva Press Era*
    HANNAH DOHERTY HUDSON

143. *Byron's Don Juan*
    RICHARD CRONIN

144. *Sound and Sense in British Romanticism*
    JAMES GRANDE AND CARMEL RA

For EU product safety concerns, contact us at Calle de José Abascal, 56–1°,
28003 Madrid, Spain or eugpsr@cambridge.org.

www.ingramcontent.com/pod-product-compliance
Lightning Source LLC
LaVergne TN
LVHW020341260326
834688LV00045B/1479